To access the quizzes and additional learning materials your instructor has provided in **CourseCompass to accompany this text**, you must first register online.

Before you begin, you will need:

- a computer running Windows® or Mac OS® with an internet connection and web browser
- a valid email address that you check regularly
- the course ID **from your instructor**
- your access code (below)

BSISP-CHUBB-SHALE-SALON-DOLBY-GIBES

D1529885

You may redeem your student access code only once!
Write your instructor's course ID in the space provided:

_____

To register and enroll:
Go to **http://www.coursecompass.com**
Click **Register** beneath **Students**.
Follow the on screen instructions and enter your student access code (above), your instructor's course ID, and your registration information.

To log in:
Go to **http://www.coursecompass.com**
Click **Log In** beneath **Students**.
Enter your login name and password created during registration. From your **My CourseCompass** page, simply select your instructor's course to explore CourseCompass!

For additional help, visit: http://247.pearsoned.com/ or
http://info.coursecompass.com/website/students.html

To take advantage of all the available resources in this course you may also need to install some browser plug-ins, such as the Macromedia® Flash™ player.

Frank Taylor

Lawrence Mencotti

Ivan Chompalov

Read this Book!

Sociology

Not for Dummies

Edinboro University

PEARSON

Custom
Publishing

Contents

iv

Contents

Contents

Contents

Figures

Tables

Preface: Why another Sociology Textbook?
by Lawrence J. Mencotti

Why another sociology textbook? Combined, the authors have decades of experience at teaching sociology at the college level and we have used a wide variety of texts. In our estimation too often introductory sociology textbooks seem to be written for two audiences: other sociologists and photographers. Most texts today, while competent, seem to worry about what other sociologists will think by either being too comprehensive or obsessed with citations or both. At the same time most contemporary texts have way too many pictures. With movies, the 'Net,' and just life all around us, why do we need superfluous and costly pictures?

Consequently, we think that we can offer an affordable alternative to the standard fare. This is NOT a comprehensive introduction to the field. It is a series of essays introducing the beginning student to the discipline of sociology: its concepts, methods, perspectives, and major subfields. We have tried not to write in a one-size fits all style; rather the reader will have to adjust to a variety of styles as befitting multiple authors. Further, there is no artificial agreement or consensus that binds the chapters together save one: an abiding interest in social life and the systematic and disciplined investigation of it: _sociology_.

1 | Culture and Instinct: Why We Are What We Are.
by Lawrence J. Mencotti, Ph.D

Is our destiny as humans a story already written by our biology [both as individuals and as a species] or is it a story yet to be completed? Sometimes this issue is stated as nature v. nurture. For our purposes, we will contrast instinct with culture.

Instinct. This is a term freely and frequently used by many of us. However, everyday usage of this term, while seemingly useful, does not really pass muster when held up to the critical gaze of social science. Let us begin with a definition: "Instinct is the inherent disposition of a living organism toward a particular action. Instincts are generally inherited patterns of responses or reactions to certain kinds of stimuli." [Wikepedia—The Free Encyclopedia] Put another way, instincts are genetically encoded instructions found in all members of a particular species to respond to particular situations. In a phrase, instinct means to be preprogrammed. Choice is not a choice. If your behavior is instinctively determined, you *will* respond to a specific stimulus in a specific way. Therefore, if confronted with a particular stimulus, a member of a species governed by instinct will react in a particular stimulus-specific way. However, will humans?

Do humans have instincts that are determinative of important behaviors? Let us look at a few popular uses of instinct when applied to ourselves. First, every day, several times a day, we humans get hungry. Does this mean that there is a food/nutrition instinct? That is, when the hunger pangs start do we automatically look for and take in food? Not necessarily. We may delay or forego eating for a variety of reasons of which dieting and fasting are only two. Further, even if we do eat, is there some instinctual imperative that dictates that we will only ingest that which is healthy for us? Trans-fats anyone? The important point to remember is that leaving aside compulsive eating disorders that afflict relatively few of us, we can choose when and what to eat; and how much. Our choices may not just override what we eat but even, at times, if we eat.

Are there other examples of human non-instincts? Let us look at two closely related phenomena that are supposed by many to be instinctual. Any numbers of people believe that there is a human maternal instinct. This has at least two variants: a biological drive to have children and a biological drive to care for children. The former is easily refuted as countless women choose not to have any children while countless more choose to limit and space whatever children they do have.

1

by Lawrence J. Mencotti, Ph.D.

When pregnant, many women choose to abort. Still other women choose to have the children and then give them up for adoption or even abandon the infants. Obviously, the operative term is *choice*. The other variant is, sadly, too often trumped by child abuse and child neglect on the part of the mother. Now, it can be argued that many women who do abuse and/or neglect their children do so because of tremendous stresses in their lives. One may or may not grant legitimacy to that interpretation of a very sad reality but nevertheless women do not have an instinct to have children or if they do give birth, to instinctively care for them adequately. Indeed, untold children throughout history would have been better off if women did in fact have an instinct for caring for their offspring.

If the evidence for a **maternal instinct** is flimsy, then is there any hope for evidence of a paternal instinct in humans? If there were some instinctual drive for men to sire children then no male would ever ask of his girlfriend, "You are what???" If there was some instinctual drive for men to adequately care for their children, then why do so many men "miss" their child support obligations? If there was some instinctual drive for men to nurture their children, then how to explain so many gross examples of men doing violence to their own offspring? The answer to all of these rhetorical questions is the same: there is no paternal instinct.

A great many people believe in a **survival instinct**. This belief is used to rationalize all sorts of less than saintly behavior. However, there is a frequent occurrence that undercuts the idea of a human survival instinct: suicide. Suicide is the conscious choice of ending one's own life. Every suicide is an example of how humans have no such instinct which given any situation, forces us to act in such a way as to ensure our physical survival.

Cultures vary as to the circumstances if any in which suicide is tolerated or even expected. The traditional Japanese rite of suicide, *hara-kiri*, was the expectation for those in public service who had acted disgracefully. Another example: "In Highland New Guinea a Bena Bena woman whose husband has just died may decide to kill herself rather than be inherited by another man. If this is her decision, she will call upon her brother for assistance [in hanging herself]." Among the Dobuan, there is revenge suicide in which an aggrieved husband kills himself, pressuring his kin into avenging him by killing his wife. Still other societies such as the traditional Native American Mohave dreaded suicide. [Edgerton 1976]

2

The tragic events of September 11, 2001 provide a dramatic refutation to a survival instinct. Consider all of the New York City police and firefighters who ran into the World Trade Center as it was being destroyed. If there was some overriding survival instinct, it surely was not turned on in all of those public servants. We can assume that all had an urge to live. All had a longing to see their families at the end of that day. However, their training and their commitment to duty overrode those urges and sent them into the chaos and a great many of them to their deaths. Survival instinct? That would be a very hard sell to their families and friends.

No discussion of human instincts would be complete without mentioning the possibility of a sex instinct. Obviously, we do have sexual urges, longings, and the like and they most definitely have a biological basis, but our sex lives are dictated more by choices than by genes. A cursory comparison of adult human sex with that of a dog or cat will leave one much more impressed with the differences than with the similarities. To put it as succinctly as possible, we choose whether or not to have sex; with whom to have sex; when to have sex; how to have sex; where to have sex; and whether to have unprotected sex. Animals are far less discriminating.

The careful reader might balk and protest that one's sexual orientation is biologically determined. Indeed, there is much evidence for a heavy genetic component to one's sexual orientation. However, we should distinguish between sexual preference and sexual choice. One may prefer to have sex with a member of one gender while still having sex with a member of the other. Please note that the wording of this previous sentence allows for both "situational homosexual behavior" engaged in by straights in a prison setting for example as well as "situational heterosexual behavior" engaged in by a married person with a secret gay life. In any case, a heavy biological component to one's sexual orientation does not mean that there is a single sexual instinct that governs the whole of human sexual activity.

Furthermore, sex practices and frequencies vary widely across cultures. For example, in Africa the Pokot "expect and demand that sexual relations culminate in orgasm for man and woman alike." Should the wife go unsatisfied she may engage with her female friends in a *kilapat* [shaming party] that publicly degrades her husband for neglecting her. A few hundred miles away, the other extreme is encountered with the Gusii who have "developed extraordinary sexual antagonism between men and women. This hostility is expressed in various ways, not the least of which is a wedding night performance in which the wife attempts to delay consummation by act or artifice (including tying her pubic hair across her vagina), and the husband takes pride in his ability to inflict the maximal degree of pain by his sexual assault." [Edgerton 1976] Certainly one could argue that with these examples, one is subjected to the pressures of conformity to cultural expectations but the point still holds: it is not biology that rules humans' sex lives. At most, our biology predisposes us while culture, social situations, peer pressure, and choice are the proximate causes of how and why we act sexually the way we do.

At this point, it should be clear that, as defined, it is extremely difficult to build a case that humans have instincts. Whether you invoke cultural conformity or individual choice, variation in human action is so widespread that the idea of humans possessing instincts [as opposed to reflexes such as flinching or sneezing] that are powerful enough to drive our behavior is really a non-starter. Or is it? There might be one human phenomenon that qualifies and that is so defining of us as humans that it is too often overlooked. I am using this phenomenon as I type these words and you use this phenomenon as you read these words and we both use this very same phenomenon if we happen to discuss these thoughts. It is language: written, read, or spoken.

Language. Have you ever heard of a law regulating children and language acquisition? I know of no such law. It is so natural and universally accomplished that we should immediately sense that something akin to a hard-wired program is at work in humans. It is the considered opinion of most, if not all, linguists that humans are born with an innate capacity to acquire and use a language. If given rather minimal conditions we will all acquire at least one language. Does that mean its acquisition is instinctually based? To put it another way, if you take a human infant and expose him/her to people on a regular basis then that infant cannot help but to acquire the language to which s/he has been exposed. Once a language is grasped, barring some neurological/anatomical disorder, it is almost impossible NOT to use it. One way of seeing how pervasive language becomes in our lives is to practice meditation. It is not easy to blot out thoughts as the natural state of the awakened brain is to think. What else is thinking but sub-vocal talking to oneself?

There are several case studies of children who were raised in social isolation that examine the impact such an upbringing had on their development. Interestingly, all three of the "classic cases" involve girls and the most recent and infamous of these is the instance of Genie. Here was a young female who [from about 1.5 years old until after the onset of puberty, when she was discovered by the outside world] was confined to a back bedroom of her parents' house. The

4

obvious dysfunctionality of her family life should not detain us. Though after her liberation she was given intensive work to try and catch-up, she had passed the critical period [pre-school age] of acquiring a first language without actually acquiring facility in one. Consequently, her social, emotional, and mental development were severely stunted. This case sensitizes us not only to the very early window of opportunity for the acquiring of a language but also why, in the absence of language acquisition, so much else crucial to development is compromised.

The Need for Culture. Absent instincts, humans need culture to be human. Think of the problem this way: if an important behavior in question were truly instinctually governed then it would be automatically triggered when and as needed. If that is so, then why do we have norms, customs, taboos, and laws governing our most important behaviors? If certain behaviors were truly instinctual, then laws, customs, norms, and taboos would be superfluous. It is because these behaviors are social phenomena, socially constructed, and varying greatly by historical age, culture, and group, that these social constraints are put in place. They may and will vary and that is the point. Sex, parenting, aggression, and other important social stuff are **variable** and not unitary. They are socially made, unmade, and remade because of the plasticity of individuals.

Elements of Culture. As sociologists we put a great deal of emphasis on culture as it is all pervasive to our lives. A quick examination of the elements of culture will bring some of this together for you. Perhaps you are the kind of reader that makes notes as you read. By doing so you have literally grasped the essence of culture—especially literate culture. All cultures have three dimensions: artifacts [and the technology that produces artifacts], behavior, and symbols. In our culture, examples of artifacts include books, paper, pens, laptops, etc. Behavior includes writing and typing. Symbols are illustrated by words [and their meanings]. There you have it: note taking is a distilled example of the idea of culture. Of course, many, many societies have existed [and still do exist] which have been non-literate and so their cultural repertoire would be obviously different from ours. The point is however, all cultures are composed of variations on those three elements. As we have seen, the most important of all is language—a complex symbol system that when spoken or written allow humans to be human.

Culture and Our Potential. Excepting language, in place of instinct humans have culture. Without culture we cannot fulfill any of our human potential and without language culture is impossible. Just as individuals have personal habits, cultures can be seen as collections of people who share group habits: distinctive ways of living life, doing the world, solving problems. Language allows humans to do is to adapt to varying conditions and create new ways of organizing their lives. It is the original human tool. Language frees us from the need to have instincts—save one: the only instinct we humans require is that innate drive and capacity to learn a human language. Limited language acquisition by apes notwithstanding it is our ability to fully embrace language in whatever guise it appears that makes us humans unique [to this earth] with our dreams, ideals, myths, institutions, and technologies. Language is also our tragic flaw in that our ability to make promises, dreams, ideals, and desires outstrips our powers to deliver on them. However our lives may turn out it is language that is central to them.

Here is a common example: an infant from Latin America, China, sub-Saharan Africa, or Eastern Europe is adopted by an American couple and raised in the United States. That child brings with it no biological differences due to its land of birth that will effectively prevent it from becoming a fully acculturated American citizen. This is because wherever we are born we are born of the same species. That adopted infant will lead a very different life in America than if it had remained in its country of origin. It has the "natural equipment" to adapt readily to conditions no matter where it is raised. To a very real extent, at birth we are interchangeable beings. We are as easily brought up Estonian as American; lower class as upper class; Muslim as Baptist. We have the natural equipment to be successfully raised anywhere.

That does not mean that there are no biological inputs worth noting. There are, for example, genetic predispositions to many diseases. There will be biological factors in the child's intelligence, temperament, and other important dimensions. Nothing of what has been discussed to this point denies that there are biological inputs into whatever constitutes human beings. I have been arguing that except for a language acquisition instinct, it is very difficult to posit that instincts, in any appreciable way, govern human life. To the contrary, once we have language we are off and running, so to speak.

Human Nature allows us to be greatly but not infinitely plastic beings. Put another way, we do not possess a "**blank slate**" in the sense that environment is *all* determinative of our behavior. Minimally, our genetic makeup [both species-wide as well as the unique genetic codes that each of us possesses] and our "experiences" in utero undoubtedly have significant, but still to be precisely determined effects on our future lives. With that said, it is language which makes us social

6

creatures allowing for human interaction at a very early age and this language based interaction is what enables us to participate, more or less fully, in our culture.

Choice. The strong biological argument can be stated that there are forces inside each of us that impel us to act in ways that we cannot control. The equally strong cultural argument is that there are forces whose origins are outside of us compelling us to act in ways over which we have no effective control. Both arguments are deterministic and both arguments "over-do" it.

While we are not enslaved by biology, neither are we wholly oppressed by the culture in which we are reared. A third factor is choice: to choose is to make decisions based upon what are seen to be available options, possible costs, potential benefits, and the like. In contemporary America, the options for purchasing things are limited mostly by available money. While the overall culture seems to stress the maxim, "buy 'till you die," what you buy, when, from whom, and for how much is pretty much up to you [and your credit line]. Choice is a consideration that we will return to frequently so we will not spend much time with it here except to say that the idea of choice in social science assumes the philosophical position of **free will**.

Contingency. There is one more idea that we need to examine. This idea addresses unpredictable things, events, and so forth that "just happen." No one leads such a tightly structured life that the unexpected never happens. Sometimes this is referred to as change. We prefer to use the more value-neutral term of contingency. Examples include finding the proverbial $20 bill on the sidewalk or being caught in an elevator when the power goes off. The characteristics of contingency are: you did not consciously choose what happened to you; it was not caused by your biology; and cultural inputs were irrelevant. It is a notion that neither biology nor culture deals with effectively and in addition, it is not really found to be that well developed from the perspective of choice.

With that in mind, let us look at an illustration of how biology, culture, choice, and contingency can contribute to a common situation: an unplanned pregnancy. A young [18-year-old] woman has a family history of a serious malady, which she has inherited. To treat her condition she takes a powerful medicine on a daily basis. She is attending college and after a particularly great party in which she becomes somewhat inebriated, she has unprotected sex with her boyfriend and subsequently discovers that she is pregnant. She consults a physician who warns her that continuing to take her medicine would probably result in a serious birth defect to the fetus. Alternatively, her physician warns her that prolonged refraining from taking the drug will likely result in a rapid and significant deterioration of her personal health. She does not feel that she can discuss the matter with her family, as they are devout members of a religion that forbids abortion under any circumstance. After finding out that she is pregnant, her boyfriend stops seeing her, saying that he is too young to be married and raise a family. She spends a miserable month and a half trying to decide on a course of action that would not likely bring disaster. Despairing of her plight, she contemplates suicide. Her worries and the attendant stress prove to be of such intensity that she becomes totally preoccupied with her situation. One day while crossing the street absentmindedly, she is hit by a slow moving vehicle. Though her injuries are relatively minor, she nevertheless miscarries. During and after her several weeks of personal hell she has mulled over all of the forces that have contributed to the situation:

> biology—chronic disease, drug regimen, pregnancy;

> culture—family, religion that condemns abortion;

> choices—terminate pregnancy, discontinue drugs, do neither and have and keep child, do neither and have child and give it up for adoption, etc. and

> contingency—auto accident and miscarriage.

We do not believe that the above example is altogether far-fetched and it does have the virtue of bringing together the four important factors addressed in this discussion.

Fate. In addition to these forces, there are the factors that influence our lives over which we have little or no control. Certainly our lives will be significantly different if we are born an illegitimate child into an impoverished community in a developing nation but in turn are adopted by a Western middle-aged affluent couple. We have no effective control over whether we stay within that dead-end life or are transported as an infant and raised in affluence going on to college and a successful professional career. From this perspective, our fate is due to others' choices and thus our lives are highly contingent. For example, in the illustration above the fetus has no life since its eventual fate, as a confluence of factors, resulted in a miscarriage.

One other point should be noted. Biologically speaking we are culturally interchangeable: given a normal birth, there is no reason why we cannot grow up in any of a thousand different ways. This, however, points to another way that fate can interpose itself in our lives: fate not as the choice of others but rather that of biological contingency. For most of us, biology is not really destiny. Try telling that to someone with spina bifida, Lou Gehrig's disease, cerebral palsy, or childhood leukemia. Those are cruel cards to be dealt people and they in turn must play those cards to the best of their abilities. As you can see, our lives are governed by choice, contingency, and occasionally, by fate. The particular ingredients and their proportions make for very important constraints and, in some cases, opportunities for us all.

Not to be detained by the controversy swirling around Intelligent Design it is our position that humans are the product of a very long evolutionary process. Once reaching our distinctly human state we did not cease being animals. There **are** biological inputs: both species-wide and those idiosyncratic to every individual. Given that as our baseline we are arguing that in addition to our starting point—culture—choice, contingency, and fate work with our biological heritage to shape and give direction to the lives we eventually lead.

೫ ೧೩ ೫ ೧೩

DEFINITIONS

Blank Slate. aka *Tabula rasa* (Latin: "scraped tablet," though often translated "blank slate") is the notion that individual human beings are born "blank" (with no built-in mental content), and that their identity is defined entirely by their experiences and sensory perceptions of the outside world.

Choice. Also known as free will.

Contingency. A possible event or occurrence or result.

Culture. A learned set of practices, beliefs, values, rules for proper conduct, and material objects shared by members of a society.

Fate. The ultimate agency that predetermines the course of events.

Free Will. The power of making free choices unconstrained by external agencies.

Hara-kiri. Also known as Seppuku (Japanese "stomach-cutting" or "belly slicing") is a form of Japanese ritual suicide by disembowelment. It was used by warriors to avoid falling into enemy hands, and to attenuate shame.

Instinct. The inherent disposition of a living organism toward a particular action. Instincts are generally inherited patterns of responses or reactions to certain kinds of stimuli.

Language Acquisition. Possibly the only human instinct.

Language. Refers to a system of symbols that allows communication between people to take place. Language is the medium through which culture is transmitted from one generation to the next.

Maternal Instinct. The belief that there is an unconscious drive to give birth to and nurture children.

Paternal Instinct. The belief that there is an unconscious drive to sire and care for children.

Sex Instinct. The belief that we are predisposed to mate, but our sex lives are dictated more by choices than by genes.

Sexual Orientation. Sexual orientation is the sexual preference for members of the same sex or opposite sex. If one likes members of the same sex one would be classified as having a homosexual orientation. If one likes members of the opposite sex, one would be classified as having a heterosexual orientation.

Suicide. The conscious choice of ending one's own life.

Survival Instinct. The belief that we are predisposed to stay alive under any circumstance.

REFERENCES

Edgerton, Robert B. 1976. *Deviance: A Cross-Cultural Perspective.* Menlo Park, CA: Cummings Publishing Company.
Linton, Ralph. 1936. *The Study of Man: An Introduction.* New York: D. Appleton-Century.
Pinker, Steven. 2002. *The Blank Slate: The Modern Denial of Human Nature.* New York: Penguin Books.
Rymer, Russ. 1994. *Genie: A Scientific Tragedy.* New York: Harper Perennial.

2 | Socialization: Why We Are Who We Are.
by Lawrence J. Mencotti, Ph.D. with Alexander F. Rice

When born infants are helpless little barbarians. They communicate rather poorly and are not yet capable of being anything that resembles an acceptably functional human being. They will become human however. Not because of their instincts, we have already disposed of that. Rather, because of the language they are exposed to they will learn to become human. They will acquire the "stuff" of their culture and will learn appropriate and inappropriate behavior. How they eventually behave is another matter and the fodder for other essays in this collection. It is the learning that shall concern us here and this learning is what we call **socialization**. Further, given the enormity of human learning we will concentrate on one of the most important aspects of learning to be human: gender socialization.

Children are taught at an early age what it means to be a boy or a girl in our society. They are socialized into society by parents, teachers, peers, and the media.

Symbolic Interaction (SI) Theory. Let us begin by examining three of the most important theories of socialization: symbolic interactionism, learning theory, and gender schema theory. Since symbolic interactionism has wide applicability beyond that of helping to explain gender socialization let us look at SI theory as a whole and then apply it.

The sociologist Cooley was one of the first social scientists to investigate how thoroughly social one's self is. He saw **self-concept** as a continuing process which can be analyzed as a sequence of three phases. At any moment in time, we imagine how we appear to others. Then we imagine how others are judging that appearance. Finally, these imaginings result in a self-feeling or emotion. This has been termed the "**looking glass**" approach to self-concept: how we see ourselves is in large part how others see us, especially others that are important to us whom we often term "**significant others**." While this might seem somewhat obvious, Cooley's approach has some radical implications. For example, Cooley sees the idea of society as not something that is "out there" existing independently but rather the idea of society is just that: an idea that people have of other people in the abstract. Society is ultimately a product of the imagination. Another implication of Cooley's approach is that rather than seeing one's self-concept as fixed it is actually rather fluid depending a great deal on, once again, people's imaginations.

11

Is there any evidence for this? In an excellent, study Dornbusch and Miyamoto tested Cooley's approach by [A] having students rate themselves on such factors as intelligence, physical attractiveness, likeability, and self-confidence (Note that all of these cited factors tend to be very important for most people's self-concept.); [B] students rated the others on these same traits; and, finally, [C] each student was asked how he/she thought they had been rated. Well, students with a strong overall positive self-concept were, in fact, more highly rated on the tested dimensions than those with negative overall self-concepts. Overall, self-concepts were closely related to the way others actually saw them. Thus, there was a correspondence between A and B above. However, the self-concepts were more closely related to the way students thought others rated them [C] than the way others actually did rate them [B].

A counterpart of Cooley, sympathetic to his approach, was George Herbert Mead. Mead saw the self as alternating but interrelated processes, which he termed the "I" and the "**me**." The "I" is the knower principle of the person while the "me" is what the person [and others] knows about the person. Mead's "I" would be the process that Cooley would say imagines what others are thinking of you. Mead's "me" would be akin to what Cooley would emphasize as the imaginations that you have of how others see you.

Contrasting Views of Human Nature: Motive and Motivation. With our discussion of gender socialization now considered let us move on to more selected and more generalized issues of self, personality, and socialization by beginning with this persistently interesting question: Why do people do what they do? This is the issue of motivation that refers to all of those forces, drives, impulses, and urges that push our behavior. It refers to the source, intensity, and perhaps direction of our energies. Usually one thinks of motivation as coming from within the person. The idea of motivation attempts to answer the question WHY [do we act as we do] with a BECAUSE. In general, sociologists are quite wary of this approach to explaining human behavior. They feel that too often motivational schemes fail to take the influence of others into account and in turn tend toward **reductionism**: reducing motivation to biological urges or will-o-the-wisp notions of personality traits. Rather than looking for motivations sociologists emphasize **motives**—the reasons people give for why they do what they do. Note how the notion of motive highlights the importance of others in explaining why you do what you do. If motivation points to reasons within you then motives redirect attention toward focusing on the importance of how others affect your behavior especially the expectations that others have of your behavior.

For those of you who are familiar with Freud, the contrast with Mead over the notion of mind, self, and society is both stark and instructive. For Freud mind is more of a thing, a noun whereas Mead would see mind as a process, more of a verb. To Freud, one's self is something to be discovered especially the unconscious motivational structure of the mind that allegedly underlies our behavior. For Mead, the self is more an invention. One is more explicitly self-conscious and the important issue would be not so much to discover some deep seated motivation but rather to concentrate on the reasons ["motives"] people give for why they act as they do. Looked at another way, Freud would see surface motives as symptomatic of deeper realities while Mead would emphasize why the motives people give would be an important resource for interaction. Finally, Freud would see society as existing over and above individuals; something that imposes itself on people, while Mead would see society as fundamentally people interacting with one another; more precisely, those with whom I am not interacting at present.

Let us look at the idea of motive a bit more closely. Remember that motives refer to the reasons people give [to themselves as well as to others] for why they act as they do. Thus, motives can be seen as markers of group membership. For example, while a group of fundamentalist Christians would think it entirely appropriate to say, "I didn't do that since I want to avoid sin and God's displeasure." a group of atheists would see that comment as an object for derision. Suppose that during your day you encounter several groups with whom you must interact. Is it so unreasonable to assume that each group you encounter will have expectations as to what are acceptable motives for explaining behavior and what are not? Not at all. As a matter of fact, it is part of group life to accept certain explanations [motives] while rejecting others in no small part as a test for the worthiness of participation in that group. Back to the fundamentalist example. Just how long would you last as a member in good standing if periodically you did not cite avoiding sin or following God's will as motives for your behavior?

Mead and Freud: Open v. Closed Systems of Personality Development. Mead felt that the essential characteristic of human nature was plasticity: a cluster of unformed impulses possessing neither organization nor goal that are shaped only through socialization. In short, the biological inputs to human behavior are significant but not determinative for social behavior.

13

Freud's multiplicity of thoughts on drives from cathexis to libido to thantos focused on discharge so that tension may be released and the human organism gratified. Motives, personality, and social structures were derivatives of the inner dynamics of the organism. In short, they were made dependent variables.

The Meadian pragmatic idea of man as an active agent in shaping his destiny is a far cry from Freud's actor governed by a "script" of unconscious, irrational, ascoial demands resulting necessarily in frustration. Their differing views of human nature also reflect differences in methodological positions in explaining behavior. For Mead, the inner state of people was to be explained by analyzing what was observable: behavior. This is a corollary of his concept of a rational human conscious of his/her self and place in the world. Alternatively, Freud's ideas on the genesis of personality meant that unconscious motives had no necessary direct correspondence to behavior and so interpretation via therapy, secondary analysis, and the case study became paramount. Further, Freud would judge certain Meadian ideas as to the staging of social behavior, as unnecessary. Freud's backdrop was his metaphorical concepts [id, Oedipus complex] that strained toward reification in the form of structures. Mead's discussion of "**reflexiveness**" as an essential condition for the development of the Mind, the symbolic nature of the social setting, the sharing of socially learned meanings necessary for behavior and the evaluation of mind and language from conversation of significant gestures—in short, the crux of Mead's explanation of social behavior—emphasizing the ongoing social process, stems from an opposed perspective [to Freud's] of what humans were about.

Mead's Perspective on Socialization. Mead suggested that socialization occurs through a maturational process. Through interaction with others, children go through four stages of social and personality development. As children move through these stages, they go from being the center of the universe, toward understanding others' rights and expectations. The four stages that Mead refers to are:

Preparatory Stage (birth to 2 years): The child is unaware of any other personality and behaves as though he or she is the center of the universe.

Play Stage (2 to 7 years): The child moves through rapid emulation of roles he or she perceives. Through the practice of pretending to be others, for example, a doctor, teacher, or rock star, the child begins to understand the concept of "others."

Game Stage (7 years and up):   The maturing child perceives others' expectations, and self's rights, gradually acquiring the ability to take the role of the generalized other, which is a mixture of all the socially approved values and behaviors necessary for social adaptation and interaction.

Reference Stage (15 to adult):   The person uses knowledge he has acquired from family, school, church, etc. as reference on how to act in certain social settings.

When children interact with a parent, friend, or teacher, they use imagination to put themselves in the other's role. When doing this, children primarily learn to view themselves from the point of view of a particular person. Eventually, as children come to understand how social relationships work, they begin to see themselves from the point of view of the **generalized other**, and understand the expectations that society has of them. Through role-playing, children learn the give and take, compromise, adjustment, and reciprocity that help lead to a sense of self. As children move through the stages that Mead describes, they come to understand that symbols have specific functions for the individual (Charon 2001). Children then develop a sense of self, including gender identity, and participate in their socialization.

In general, symbolic interactionism has operated as a unisex theory of development emphasizing those processes that are common to boys and girls. As such, while it is very insightful, it is incomplete. Let us now turn to other theoretical perspectives that deal directly with gender differences.

Social Learning Theory. As a starting point, when we look at the toys children play with, it is easy to see that the gender roles are instilled at an early age. Boys are taught to play with trucks and girls are given dolls to play with. Several theorists have explained this predisposition of social roles specifically to males or females as the result of classic social learning.

According to social learning theory, the child learns appropriate behavior through **reinforcement** and **modeling**. Initially it is the parent who teaches the dos and do nots by way of reinforcement and modeling. The family is the child's first reference group. In addition, friends, teachers, and the media also play a part in acting as role models and reinforcing acceptable behavior (Beal 1994). Parents begin this process by encouraging sons to be more independent, competitive, and achieving than daughters. Parents encourage daughters to be more passive and to seek protection. Parents also tend to dress their daughters more decoratively and their sons in more practical styles. Parents also provide children with sex-typed toys and encourage sex-appropriate play activities while discouraging play activities that are deemed more appropriate for the opposite sex, such as boys playing with dolls. [Technically, boys are given dolls too—but they tend to be of the action, athletic, blood and guts variety.]

One area in which there was marked difference was the encouragement of sex-typed activities (Lytton and Romney 1991). When sex-specific toys are provided to children, the result is different play and problem-solving experiences for children. Because boys are given more opportunities to explore their world and engage in more physical activities than girls, girls usually experience a more restricted world.

The key components of social learning theory are reinforcement and modeling. Children receive social rewards for engaging in the activities and behaviors that society deems appropriate for their gender. While role models are important for children to imitate, the absence of role models also has an effect on children. When girls see few other girls enrolled in higher math classes or boys see few boys enrolled in home economics or nursing classes, for example, they may be less likely to pursue those activities themselves (Beal 1994). The nature of children within the social learning framework is as imitators of behavior. This puts children in the role of waiting for reinforcement of a behavior and learning by engaging in behaviors that are observed or reinforced. Research conducted by Bandura (1977) on the relationship between children and aggression has shown that children will engage in aggressive behaviors after observing those behaviors—even without direct reinforcement.

There are differences in the reinforcement fathers and mothers give to sons and daughters. A study of parent-toddler interaction found that mothers responded more to daughters and fathers to sons. Fathers gave more emotional responses and mothers gave more instructions (Fagot, Leinbach, and O'Boyle 1992). Another study found that mothers give more verbal stimulation to sons than to daughters. Even parents who claim to be egalitarian in their dealings with their children have been found to discourage certain nontraditional play behaviors more in one gender than the other. Again, the example of parents discouraging their sons from playing with dolls, or their daughters from playing with trucks comes into effect (Weisner and Wilson-Mitchell 1990). This behavior on the part of parents serves to model and reinforce stereotyped behaviors in children. Children learn through observation of their culture and society how to fit in and manage their environment. According to social learning theory, children are motivated by their strong desire to be like those whom they are with (Beal 1994). Children want to identify with their same sex parent; when they imitate role models, it is because they have admiration for those role models (Beal 1994). When children imitate what they see, they are either reinforced positively for behaving as society dictates, or negatively if they stray from the norm. For example, a boy who takes a home economics course may feel uncomfortable if he is the only male in the class, whereas, when a young woman tries to go to an all male school, she may be disliked and considered an outsider because she is doing something that society considers inappropriate. Because children are conditioned through social learning to behave in socially approved ways if they want to get along in society, it is easier and more comfortable to simply accept those behaviors which society deems appropriate. The desired outcome for children is that they imitate appropriate behaviors and become suitable members of society. These behaviors are rewarded with praise and encouragement. Behaviors, which are deemed to be inappropriate or unacceptable, are discouraged by society. This support for certain behaviors and lack of support for others comes from those in society whom the child looks up to and admires such as parents, peers, teachers, siblings, and the mass media.

Gender Schema Theory. This perspective offers an information processing approach to socialization in that the theory describes and explains the child's developing content and organization of gender knowledge (Bem 1981). A basic assumption of gender schema theory is that gender knowledge is multidimensional, with children believing that there are behaviors, attitudes, characteristics, and occupations that are gender related (Huston 1983). These beliefs are internalized by children and become a part of their socialization into adult roles. Within gender schema theory, children are seen as active participants in the socialization process. As children move through childhood, they increase their knowledge about gender and as early as two years of age begin to understand about gender and recognize that the world is divided into male and female categories (Fagot, Leinbach, and O'Boyle 1992). Preschool children in particular, have been shown to rely heavily on gender labeling (Martin, Wood, and Little 1990). As children grow older, they have more knowledge about gender roles and are more likely to make inferences about gender behavior and attitudes based on little information (Golombok and Fivush 1994). Some studies have shown that children become more flexible in their gender differentiations as they get older (Signorella, Bigler, and Liben 1993). For most children gender is an important way of organizing their environment and thinking about the world. These children are very concerned with what behaviors are appropriate or inappropriate based on gender (Levy and Carter 1989). Gender schema theory also views gender typed behavior as being guided by the child's anticipation of the responses of others (Bussey and Bandura 1992). Thus, motivation for the child comes through the desire to do what is culturally and socially correct.

Gender schema theory also has elements of social learning because children are observing gender related behaviors and imitating them. Symbolic interaction theory focuses on the learning of language and other symbols commonly used in society and developing a sense of self and a sense of how to get along in society based on these symbols. Children determine their self-concept by accepting the view of others, or looking glass self, and also by taking the role of others, or generalized other. Socially approved behaviors come from family, friends, the media, and school. Whether or not those socially approved behaviors and attitudes are acceptable for both males and females throughout life is sometimes raised as a question of concern, and leads to the question of whether a neutral gender role orientation might be more salient for individuals in today's society. Whether that is possible, or desirable, is of course another question.

Gender role socialization, which usually includes some degree of gender role stereotyping, begins at birth. As children grow and develop, the gender stereotypes they are exposed to at home are reinforced by other experiences in their environment and are thus perpetuated throughout childhood (Martin, Wood, and Little 1990). As children move into the larger world of friends and school, those around them reinforce many of their ideas and beliefs. A further reinforcement of acceptable and appropriate behavior is shown to children through the media. Through all these socialization agents, children learn gender-stereotyped behavior. As children develop, these gender stereotypes become firmly fixed beliefs. It has been suggested that children develop gender stereotypes in three stages:

1. Learning what types of things are associated with each sex (i.e., boys play with cars, girls play with dolls),

2. Learning associations for what is relevant to their own sex but not the opposite sex, and

3. Learning the associations relevant to the opposite sex (Martin, Wood, and Little).

Parental Influence. A child's earliest exposure to what it means to be male or female comes from parents. From the time their children are babies, parents treat sons and daughters differently, dressing infants in gender specific colors, giving gender-differentiated toys and expecting different behavior from boys and girls (Thorne 1993). Parents have different expectations of sons and daughters as early as 24 hours after birth. Children internalize parental messages regarding gender at an early age, with awareness of adult sex role differences being found in two-year-old children (Weinraub et al. 1984). One study found that children at two and a half years of age use gender stereotypes in negotiating their world and are likely to generalize gender stereotypes to a variety of activities, objects, and occupations (Fagot, Leinbach, and O'Boyle 1992). Parents encourage their sons and daughters to participate in sex-typed activities, including doll playing and engaging in housekeeping activities for girls and playing with trucks and engaging in sports activities for boys (Eccles, Jacobs, and Harold 1990). Children's toy preferences have been related to parental sex typing (Etaugh and Liss 1992). Parents provide gender-differentiated toys and reward the child for behavior that is gender stereotyped. While both mothers and fathers contribute to the gender stereotyping of their children, fathers have been found to reinforce gender stereotypes more often than mothers do. Even children's rooms are gender stereotyped. Girls' rooms have more pink, dolls, and manipulative toys, and boys' rooms have more blue, sports equipment, tools and toy trucks. Boys are more likely to have maintenance chores around the house, such as taking out the trash and mowing the lawn, while girls are more likely to have domestic chores such as washing the dishes and doing the laundry. This assignment of household tasks by gender leads children to link certain types of work with gender. Some studies have suggested that parent shaping as a socializing factor has little impact on a child's sex role development (Lytton and Romney 1991). Other research suggests that parents are the primary influence on gender role development during the early years of life (Kaplan 1991).

by Lawrence J. Mencotti, Ph.D. with Alexander F. Rice

Parental attitudes towards their children have a strong impact on the child's developing sense of self and self-esteem, with parental warmth and support being key factors for the child. Often, parents give subtle messages regarding what is acceptable behavior for each gender. Sex role stereotypes are well established in early childhood. Messages about what is appropriate based on gender are so strong that even when children are exposed to different attitudes and experiences, they will revert to stereotyped choices. Children who have parents with strong egalitarian values tend to be more informed about non sex-typed objects and occupations than do other children (Weisner and Wilson-Mitchell 1990). Children whose mothers work outside the home are not as traditional in sex role orientation as children whose mothers stay home (Weinraub, Jaeger, and Hoffman 1988). In fact, preschool children whose mothers work outside the home experience the world with a sense that everyone in the family gets to become a member of the outside world, and their sense of self includes the knowledge that they have the ability to make choices that are not hindered by gender (Davies and Banks 1992).

Boys and girls also have different styles of play and interaction from one another. Boys choose more rough and tumble play and competitive activities than girls. Often, girls and their activities are seen as inferior to boys and their activities. The skills and abilities children learn from friends are different for boys and girls. In peer interactions, boys learn to negotiate conflict and be one of the guys. Girls are more likely to communicate one-on-one and learn the skill of listening. Boys and girls also use language in different ways, with boys using language to maintain independence and girls using language to establish a relationship with their friends. Boys initiate more conflicts than girls initiate and are more likely to solve those conflicts with physical aggression. Children tend not to like aggressive girls, and girls are likely to be shunned when acting aggressively (Fagot, Leinbach, and O'Boyle 1992). Feedback from friends on gender appropriate behaviors and attitudes is important to children, and children seek out same sex friends because of their need to establish gender identity (Beal 1994). There also appears to be differences in the ways that boys and girls approach friendships. Boys seem to need to establish status with a group of friends; girls are more likely to create intimate friendships with one or two close friends (Beal 1994).

Boys also appear to be more sensitive than females to peer feedback on what constitutes appropriate gender activities (Fagot, Leinbach, and O'Brien 1992). Within their same sex playgroups, children punish those who deviate from gender appropriate activities, by making critical remarks or ignoring the friend (Beal 1994). It is more acceptable among children's peer groups for girls to be "tomboys" than it is for boys to be "sissies" (Kaplan 1991). This seems to indicate that masculine behaviors are valued more highly by children; i.e. boys have more to "lose" by not meeting gender expectations than do girls who do not. According to this reasoning, because masculine behaviors are indicators of higher self-esteem in children than are feminine behaviors, this may indicate that the cultivation of an androgynous orientation may be particularly beneficial for girls (Bem 1981). Because peer groups have a strong influence on the gender role socialization of children, and because gender stereotypes are reinforced by parents, schools, and the media, children often grow up with a sense of self that is based on outdated or unrealistic ideas of what it is to be male or female. Parents who wish to raise their children in a non-gender stereotyped way face several difficulties because so many aspects of society are gender stereotyped with behaviors and attitudes differentiated by sex (Bem 1981). Non-gender stereotyped behavior takes longer to develop in children than stereotypic behavior because the child has to learn, and then unlearn, traditional behaviors (Sedney 1987). Stereotypic behavior leads to gender inequality throughout the life process.

Annette Lareau, in her multi-award wining ethnography: *Unequal Childhood*, considers the relationship between gender socialization and social class. In this study, Lareau analyzes twelve families who are raising third grade children. The socioeconomic backgrounds of the families are middle class, working class, and poor. Not surprisingly, but with great subtlety and compassion, Lareau finds that different social classes have different styles of child rearing that ultimately contribute to the reproduction of social inequalities.

A Short Digression on a Neo-Freudian Approach. One of the most important truisms [and thus an assumption] of Freudians is that one's life is, essentially, a mess of inner conflicts hidden from one's consciousness. The psychoanalytic sociologist Nancy Chodorow has argued, subtly and persuasively, that learning to be and feel female and male incepts as a very early experience with the infant's attachments to its parents. In so doing, Chodorow emphasizes the mother much more than did Freud as children tend to become emotionally involved with the mother since she is generally by far the dominant influence in a child's early life.

To create a separate sense of self for the child the mother ultimately needs to become less important so to break the mother-child attachment and allow an autonomous self to emerge. Now

21

this breaking process occurs differently for boys than for girls. Girls remain closer to mom and are able to continue to show physical affection longer without the suspicion of sexuality. As such, females learn early on to emphasize continuity in relationships. Of course, since every plus seems to have a minus one can also say that just as females develop traits of sensitivity and compassion it will be difficult when necessary to break off relationships as an adult and, in keeping with the emphasis on continuity, it is too easy for women to become extensions of others rather than their own person.

For boys, their sense of self comes from an earlier and more thorough separation from mother. Boys come early to understand that being masculine is in large part: not being feminine. There is a principle of discontinuity at work here. In this sense, Chodorow reverses Freud: boys lose their mothers not to dad but to separating from mom herself and later feel threatened or feel vulnerable if they develop relationships that are too close or too complex. For girls it is the absence of relationships, especially close relationships, which will be damaging to their self-concept. In this vein, regarding adult relationships, we can say that males are threatened when they get too close and females feel threatened when they are not close enough.

Gender Inequality. Gender inequality continues through adolescence and into adult work roles. In spite of the massive entry of women in the workplace and the increasing numbers of women in mid-level managerial positions, gender equality at the workplace remains elusive to women today. Working in a world dominated by male decision-makers and their established practices, women encounter a variety of barriers hindering their advancement to the top of their careers. One of the most significant factors is cultural stereotype. To many CEOs, women cannot compete against their male counterparts because they may become pregnant, have families, and are thus responsible for domestic tasks. Given this environment, it is little wonder that women earn 74 percent of men's wages and have only 11.2 percent of the executive positions in Fortune 500 companies.

Types of Gender Inequality. There are many different types of inequality facing women in today's society. Some of the issues associated with gender and power in the workplace include gender relations in division of labor, the "glass ceiling," sexual harassment, and gender inequality.

Gender Relations in the Division of Labor. The gendered division of workplace labor is embedded in the ideology of innate sex differences in traits and abilities, and operates through various control mechanisms. These control mechanisms are primarily exercised by men over women and serve to exaggerate the differences between the sexes, especially surrounding women's presumed incapability for doing "man's work." However, if one were to look at the "hunting and gathering" societies in history, they would realize that it was actually the women who provided most of the food. Women were responsible for picking berries, digging roots, and hunting small game such as rabbits and rodents, which made up a large part of the society's diet. The men mainly hunted large game, which was not as productive. Although gender inequality was less extreme in hunting and gathering societies, men did assume control over trade and conflict with other tribes (Hodson and Sullivan 1995). However, as society changed, male dominance and control advanced, as did the positioning of women in subordinate roles.

Most forms of workplace control take the form of harassment and gender based jokes and comments, which make gender differences a salient aspect of work relations. Jan Grant and Paige Porter emphasize, "the gendered logic of accumulation" in the discussion of gender in the workplace, which states that men in Western societies have traditionally acquired and maintained the bulk of wealth in society.

These "traditional roles" and thus, women's identities, have been formed and maintained by relations in the workplace. Therefore, understanding any gendered differences in labor requires further examination. The reality of being male and female is not independent of the workplace but is strongly influenced and determined by the relationships of men and women in society.

The gendered division of labor has maintained its origins in the home, where gender role socialization takes place, while reproducing its structure in the workplace. This can be seen inside families through the sharp distinctions between paid and unpaid work, paid and unpaid productivity, and even the separation of the private and public spheres where women are perceived as attached to the private and men to the public domains (Grant and Porter 1994). This is an important issue because while home and work may be physically separated for working men and women, home is often not a haven for women but rather just another place of work. The gendered division of labor then, is not limited to the paid work force, but continues into the realm of unpaid work at home.

Socialist feminism has explored issues surrounding power inequalities in the workforce. This ideology argues that since the control of material resources necessary for survival was largely outside the home historically, the location of women in the home became their source of dependence on men and their subordination to men (Boyd 1997). This argument appears to be more gender specific than other socialist theories such as Marxism, as it emphasizes that gender inequality reflects not only the type of economic system in place, but also the power that men have within the household and the economy.

The Glass Ceiling and Walls (Power Inequality). For a long time, invisible barriers called "**glass ceilings**" were viewed as the big obstacle facing women trying to climb the corporate ladder. Today, women also face "**glass walls**," which keep women from moving laterally. Lack of lateral movement deprives women of the experience, especially in supervision, that they need to move vertically. In other words, women tend to be placed in staff or support positions, in areas such as public relations and human resources and are often steered away from jobs in core areas such as marketing, production, and sales. Women are trapped in these positions because of stereotyping that labels them as people who can provide support. Support functions such as human resources usually do not offer the critical experience expected of those advancing to senior levels. Although women account for as many as half of the professional employees in the largest industrial and service companies, they hold fewer than five percent of the senior executive positions. This is a definite sign of power inequality. In her study, Monica Boyd proposes that power inequality in the workplace between genders has been maintained through occupational segregation, because it is the occupations themselves that differ in the capacity that current workers have to impose their will upon others. This statement implies that in any workplace, there not only exists a technical division of labor, but also a gender based social division ensuring that there is an imbalance in power in favor of men. Boyd is able to back her claims by noting that Canadian women are employed in positions with fewer decision-making powers; women are more likely to supervise other women only; and although women have increased their presence in the workforce, this presence is mostly in the service industry only, and that this increase in presence has not converted into a presence of power (Boyd 1997). Grant and Porter also support this view by stating that most female workers find themselves in female dominated industries, and trapped at the lower levels of power. These findings are particularly disturbing as they seem to be supported by the patriarchal ideology of women being subordinate to men, and that men are seldom, if ever subordinate to women. This gender typing of jobs leads to poverty among the female workforce because many of these jobs are

24

at low-income levels. These occupations also include sexist qualifications such as attractiveness and pleasantness.

Meika Loe's work adds to the debate of gender based power differences in the workplace by noting the presence of formal and informal power. Informal power acts as a passive aggressive force employed through "interactional techniques," often used by men to sustain dominance and maintain the inferior status of women. Loe notes that common methods of exercising informal power include derogatory terms of address, disciplinary actions, direct orders, threats, general avoidance of concerns, cynicism, and even humiliation. These formal powers refer to the traditional concepts of the ability to exercise control over a subordinate worker. She also comments on the interesting addition to her theory of power in the workplace by suggesting that informal power is capable of undermining the formal power structure in the workplace. Although this seems problematic, perhaps a strategy for the exploited female subordinate class could be to develop an autonomous informal power structure to balance against the patriarchal dominance of their supervisors.

Sexual Harassment. Another source of conflict between genders is a very specific issue of power and control, namely the existence of sexual harassment in the workplace. This gendered behavior varies in its definition due to its subjective nature, however it can generally be described as unwanted sexual advances, requests for sexual favors, creating a hostile, intimidating, or offensive work environment, or more simply, an unwelcome verbal or physical conduct of a sexual or gender related nature (Smith 1995).

Kathleen Rospenda wrote that various models exist to explain sexual harassment such as the organizational model, the socio-cultural model, and the model of contrapower sexual harassment. The organizational model suggests that the structural aspects of organizations promote power inequalities between individuals and set the stage for sexual harassment, while socio-cultural models reflect a feminist perspective, concentrating on sexual harassment as an outcome of patriarchal systems that enable men to exercise sexual power to assert and maintain male dominance (Rospenda, Richman, and Nawyn 1998).

The contrapower model is a unique combination of these previous models in that it focuses on the organizational positions of the individuals involved. However, it assumes that gendered

25

socio-cultural power is at the basis of sexual harassment. This model argues that originating sexual harassment in the organization structure is flawed, because this would require embracing the structure as gender neutral. To understand sexual harassment then, the researcher must consider the social and cultural facilitators of men's achievements to high-level positions and likewise the barriers facing women; rather than blindly attributing the harassment to men because they occupy these high-level positions (Rospenda, Richman, and Nawyn 1998).

Gender Inequalities. In addition to gendered issues in the workplace surrounding the division of labor, power differentials, and sexual harassment, there also exists an embedded structure of gendered inequalities. Perhaps the most common and widely accepted form of inequality in the workplace is the hiring and treatment of part-time workers. Boyd argues that part-time work is more than a strategy used by women; it also functions as a mechanism for continued gender inequality in that it leaves intact the organization of domestic labor, existing power structures, and relations of male control and dominance. From a feminist perspective, the concentration of women in part-time employment highlights concerns that the constraints of domestic labor are left intact, and that the marginalization of women and their subordination to men continues (Boyd 1997). Even the part-time work itself is humbling due to its diminished access to wages, benefits and other economic resources and rewards.

Boyd also points out gendered inequalities in part-time work when employers have devised gender-specific ways of attaining flexibility in their employees. For example, in establishments where full-time employees are primarily women, employers may use part-time work as a way of attaining flexibility. When men constitute the majority of the full-time employees, flexibility is more often attained by overtime work and temporary workers (Boyd 1997). So, as can be seen from this analysis, the movement of women into the workplace has been accompanied by the continued feminization of domestic work, part-time work, and by sex typing occupations through power differentials and workplace harassment. As long as our patriarchical society keeps women in subordinate roles, gender equality in the workplace will be practically impossible to attain. Until society learns to teach their children that gender roles are not innate, inequality will always be present, and our children deprived of knowledge.

൭ infinity ൭ infinity

DEFINITIONS

Game Stage. (7 years and up) The stage in which the maturing child perceives others' expectations, and self's rights, gradually acquiring the ability to take the role of the generalized other, which is a mixture of all the socially approved values and behaviors necessary for social adaptation and interaction.

Gender Inequality. Inequality based on gender.

Gender Schema Theory. The idea that children are encouraged by parents and other social agents to internalize gender scripts.

Generalized Other. The self's organization of the roles of others. It means the self is taking the related roles of all others in a social situation rather than the role of just one other person. The term generalized other does not refer to an actual group of people, but rather to an idea or conception a person derives from his or her experiences. The person then regulates behavior in terms of the supposed opinions and attitudes of others.

Glass Ceiling. A barrier that tends to keep women in the bottom rungs of the corporate ladder.

Glass Walls. A barrier that tends to keep women from moving laterally. Lack of lateral movement deprives women of the experience, especially in supervision, that they need to move vertically. In other words, women tend to be placed in staff or support positions, in areas such as public relations and human resources and are often steered away from jobs in core areas such as marketing, production, and sales.

I. According to George Herbert Mead, a process of interaction between two components characterize the self: "I" and the "me." The "I" is the unsocialized and free part of the self. The "I" is often creative and spontaneous, and sometimes impulsive. Unexpected and novel responses to situations reflect the presence of the "I." The "I" is the subject part of the self.

Internalization. The processes through which children learn to identify and use the appropriate set of norms in different social settings.

Looking Glass Self. Cooley's concept that individuals use others like mirrors and base their conceptions of self on what is reflected to them during social interaction.

Me. The "me" is the part of the self that is almost entirely social and responds to social norms concerning behavior. The "me" is a reflection of social expectations within the self. The "me" refers to that part of the self that is socially shaped and created. The "me" is the objective part of the self.

Modeling. The acquisition of a new skill by observing and imitating that behavior being performed by another individual.

Motives. The reasons people give for why they behave as they do. Motives answer a "why" with a "because."

Play Stage. (2 to 7 years) The stage in which the child moves through rapid emulation of roles he or she perceives. Through the practice of pretending to be others, for example, a doctor, teacher, or rock star, the child begins to understand the concept of "others."

Preparatory Stage. (birth to 2 years) The stage in which the child is unaware of any other personality and behaves as though he or she is the center of the universe.

Reductionism. Reducing motivation to biological urges or will-o-the-wisp notions of personality traits.

Reference Stage. (15 to adult) The stage in which the person uses knowledge he or she has acquired from family, school, church, etc. as reference on how to act in certain social settings.

Reflexiveness. Of, relating to, characterized by, or being a relation that exists between an entity and itself.

Reinforcement. A stimulus that strengthens or weakens the behavior that produced it.

Self-Concept. How we think and feel about ourselves. Our sense of self comes from our communication and interaction with others.

Sexual Harassment. Refers to unwanted sexual attention in the workplace or school.

Significant Others. Parents, siblings, close friends, teachers, bosses, lovers, spouses, and our own children from whom we seek reflected appraisal. Because most of us choose friends and social locations staffed with similar others, and because significant others tend to be in our lives for a long time, continuity in these "reflected appraisals" contributes to a feeling of self-stability.

Social Learning Theory. The idea that children learn from positively rewarded behavior molded by role models.

Socialization. The lifelong process of learning culture. During the process of socialization individuals learn and internalize the norms of our culture, attitudes, values, beliefs, ways of thinking and learning, social expectations of society, and develop a sense of self.

Symbolic Interaction. Focuses on the social construction of reality in face-to-face interaction through language and symbols.

REFERENCES
_____

Albelda, Randy and Chris Tilly. 1997. *Glass Ceilings and Bottomless Pits: Women's Work, Women's Poverty.* Cambridge, MA: South End Press.

Apter, Terri. 1993. *Working Women Don't Have Wives: Professional Success in the 1990s.* New York: St. Martin's Press.

Bailyn, L. 1993. *Breaking the Mold: Women, Men, and Time in the New Corporate World.* New York: Free Press.

Beal, Carol R. 1994. *Boys and Girls: The Development of Gender Roles.* New York: McGraw-Hill.

Beer, C. A. 1990. *Gender Roles: A Handbook of Tests and Measures.* New York: Greenwood.

Bem, Sandra L. 1981. "Gender Schema Theory: A Cognitive Account of Sex Typing." *Psychological Review* 88(4):354-364.

Boyd, Monica. 1997. "Feminizing Paid Work." *Current Sociology* 45(2):49-73.

Bussey, Kay and Albert Bandura. 1992. "Self-Regulatory Mechanisms Governing Gender Development." *Child Development* 63(5):1236.

Charon, Joel M. 2001. *Symbolic Interactionism.* Upper Saddle River, NJ: Prentice Hall.

Chodorow, Nancy. 1994. *Femininities, Masculinities, Sexualities: Freud and Beyond.* Lexington, KY: University Press of Kentucky and London, UK: Free Association Books.

Cooley, Charles Horton, 1964. *Human Nature and the Social Order.* New York: Schoecken.

Davies, B. and C. Banks. 1992. "The Gender Trap: A Feminist Poststructuralist Analysis of Primary School Children's Talk About Gender." *Journal of Curriculum Studies* 24:1-25.

Eccles, J. S., J. E. Jacobs, and R. D. Harold. 1990. "Gender Role Stereotypes, Expectancy Effects, and Parents' Socialization of Gender Differences." *Journal of Social Issues* 46:186-201.

Etaugh, C. and M. B. Liss. 1992. "Home, School, and Playroom: Training Grounds for Adult Gender Roles." *Sex Roles* 26:129-147.

Fagot, B. I., M. D. Leinbach, and C. O'Boyle. 1992. "Gender Labeling, Gender Stereotyping, and Parenting Behaviors." *Developmental Psychology* 28:225-230.

Golombok, Susan and Robyn Fivush. 1994. *GenderDevelopment.* New York: Cambridge University Press.

Grant, Jan and Paige Porter. 1994. "Women Managers: The Construction of Gender in the Workplace." *Australian and New Zealand Journal of Sociology* 30(2):149-164.

Hodson, Randy and Theresa A. Sullivan. 1995. *The Social Organization of Work.* Belmont, CA: Wadsworth Publishing Company.

Huston, Aletha C., Marion O'Brien, and Todd R. Risley. 1983. "Sex-Typed Play of Toddlers in a Day Care Center." *Journal of Applied Developmental Psychology* 4(1):1-9.

Kaplan, P. 1991. *A Child's Odyssey.* St. Paul, MN: West Publishing Company.

Lareau, Annette. 2003. *Unequal Childhoods: Class, Race, and Family Life.* Berkeley, CA: University of California Press.

Levy, Gary D. and Bruce D. Carter. 1989. "Gender Schema, Gender Constancy, and Gender-Role Knowledge: The Roles of Cognitive Factors in Preschoolers' Gender-Role Stereotype Attributions." *Developmental Psychology* 25:444-449.

Loe, Meika. 1996. "Working for Men - At the Intersection of Power, Gender and Sexuality." *Sociological Inquiry* 66(4):399-421.

Lytton, H. and D. M. Romney. 1991. "Parents' Differential Socialization of Boys and Girls: A Meta-Analysis." *Psychological Bulletin* 109:267-296.

Martin, C. L., C. H. Wood, and J. K. Little. 1990. "The Development of Gender Stereotype Components." *Child Development* 61:1891-1904.

Mead, George Herbert. 1934. *Mind, Self, and Society.* Chicago, IL: The University of Chicago Press.

Rospenda, Kathleen M., Judith A. Richman, and Stephanie J. Nawyn. 1998. "Doing Power: The Confluence of Gender, Race, and Class in Contrapower Sexual Harassment." *Gender and Society* 12(1):40-60.

Sedney, M. A. 1987. "Development of Androgyny Parental Influences." *Psychology of Women Quarterly* 11:311-326.

Signorella, Margaret L., Rebecca S. Bigler, and Lynn S. Liben. 1993. "Early Gender-Role Development." *Developmental Review* 3:147-183.

Smith, Deborah. 1995. "Sexual Harassment in the Workplace: The Silent Oppression." *The Social Worker* 63(2):85-88.

Thorne, B. 1993. *Gender Play: Girls and Boys in School.* New Brunswick, NJ: Rutgers University Press.

Valian, Virginia. 1999. *Why So Slow?: The Advancement of Women.* Cambridge, MA: MIT Press.

Weinraub, M., E. Jaeger, and L. W. Hoffman. 1988. "Predicting Infant Outcomes in Families of Employed and Nonemployed Mothers." *Early Childhood Research Quarterly* 3:361-378.

Weinraub, M., L. P. Clemens, A. Sachloff, T. Ethridge, E. Gracely, and B. Myers. 1984. "The Development of Sex Role Stereotypes in the Third Year: Relationships To Gender Labeling, Gender Identity, Sex-Typed Toy Preferences, and Family Characteristics." *Child Development* 55:1493-1504.

Weisner, T. S. and Jane E. Wilson-Mitchell. 1990. "Nonconventional Family Life-Styles and Sex Typing in Six-Year-Olds." *Child Development* 61(6):1915.

3 | The Sociology of Everyday Life: What Happens When We Meet Up?
by Lawrence J. Mencotti, Ph.D.

Exchange Theory. One of the most systematic attempts in sociology to deal with rationality, sacrifice, and value is exchange theory. In the broadest sense exchange theory asserts that we will voluntarily gravitate to those people with whom we will derive the greatest satisfaction. Underlying all social exchanges is the obvious fact that for A to get something B must give something and exchange theory reminds us what life teaches us: nothing is for nothing. So, if B is to give then B must receive something from A if only A's gratitude.

The exchange may be crass as in a prostitute-trick relationship or it may be loving and long lasting as with partners in a committed relationship or close friends of longstanding. What is exchanged can vary widely but both people must feel that they derive something in roughly equal value to what they give to the other. In other words, each must feel that the relationship is approximately *equitable*. If it becomes too imbalanced, then work must be done to rebalance it; or the relationship will die; or the relationship will be transformed into something else from which one or both partners cannot escape [e.g., "shell marriages"].

We realize that a one-way derivation of happiness has exploitation as its other face. In that circumstance, the exploited one stays only if they literally or figuratively cannot escape. No, if we do have a say-so in our interactions it is because each brings/gives something to the other. Friendship building requires many exchanges not exclusively of a material sort. As a variety of equitable exchanges accumulate, and trust develops, then friendship may blossom. After being established stable ongoing relationships do not require daily exchange. Knowing that the interactants have built up a store of shared goodwill and that each can count on the other if something important came up is enough to keep the relationship going.

Self-Interest and Altruism: Some Qualifications of Exchange Theory. If it is reasonable to assume, as does exchange theory, that humans act out of self-interest then how can we account for altruism? Acts of altruism [in which one gives some time, energy, money, or any other valued resource] can be seen as instances in which a person extends their "circle of concern" to include others. This can be as mundane as holding a door open for a stranger to donating a kidney to a relative. What is important to remember is that these acts of inclusion also are simultaneously acts of exclusion. Put another way, every act of love is also a sign of a special relationship from which non-participants are excluded. As Weitman points out, in a very real way, by making private our acts of intimacies we decrease potential ill feelings on the part of outsiders. Here we can see how actions are linked with emotions. Jealousy is what you feel in an inclusionary relationship which you think might be in jeopardy. Every time a person fears losing his/her significant other to a rival [real or imagined] the resulting emotion is jealousy. Alternatively, to see two people madly in love when you do not have a partner yourself is likely to arouse the emotion of envy in you. More generally, ***jealousy*** *is what you feel when you fear losing what you currently possess while **envy** is what you feel toward another when you want but do not have what they do.* You feel jealous of a rival but you feel envy toward someone who has what you want but do not. It is important to see that these emotions [as with all emotions] are as social as they are personal. This brings us to an important point: **emotions** are thoroughly social phenomena. While they certainly have psychological and biochemical components, and are experienced by individuals, first and foremost emotions are social in that they are socially constructed and maintained.

It is probably this emotional [the fancier term would be affective] dimension to our lives that can help explain why so much of our behavior [and so many of our commitments] seemingly defies rational explanation. It seems likely that it is precisely because we are emotional beings we are not rational automatons. From this perspective, it is not our rationality that makes us thoroughly human [and social] but our irrationality expressed by the emotional side of our lives.

We are such emotionally laden creatures that much effort is invested in making sure that we feel what we are supposed to feel: a kind of ongoing [triangular] dialectic between situational expectations, inner states, and one's self-concept. Arlie Hochschild has referred to this as **emotion work**. There are innumerable instances of this; here are a few:

- Getting yourself psyched for a party

- Trying to remain calm during a stressful situation

- Showing some enthusiasm for a parental visit.

Far from being strictly internal and purely personal, emotions are thoroughly social and as such are not innate but learned. We need to learn what to feel, when to feel, how to feel, and why to feel and all of this comes from socialization starting early on and continuing for the rest of our lives.

Some of the most intensely felt emotional experiences of our lives have been in close friendship groups. For many, such groups have long substituted for bad family relations. Witness the important role peer groups play in moving adolescents away from the status of children on the road to adulthood. The all-important approval of one's friends can be as bewildering [and frightening] to parents as is it is necessary for the adolescent. In fact, one could see the early stages of converting to a religion as a kind of adolescent period for the newly saved in which he/she rigorously devotes him/herself to the demands of God while putting all else on the back burner. The early stages of falling in love serve as an interesting parallel in this regard as well. Whereas the convert to God might emphasize the divine glow of being in communication with the Almighty, the couple in love would bask in the warmth of love knowing their love is unlike any other that the world has ever known. Eventually however, the relationship with the Divine becomes more settled though not necessarily any less rewarding and the early romantic phases of love become settled as well while not necessarily becoming any less fulfilling.

In fact, pursuing this just a bit we can arrive at a very important insight into relationships. Anticipating a limitation to exchange theory the sociologist Willard Waller saw very clearly that many intensely emotional bondings were not equitable and certainly were imbalanced as to who wielded power and influence in the relationship. Waller termed this phenomenon the ***principle of least interest***: "that a person is able to dictate the conditions of association whose interest in the continuation of the relationship is least." Put somewhat differently, with all else equal the person with the least interest *in* the relationship has the most power *over* it. Looking at this a bit more closely we can realize the inequity of such an arrangement as well as the potential for exploitation. An equitable relationship exists where one derives satisfaction commensurate with the degree of one's investment [sacrifice to it]. This, of course, relies upon an economic conception of a relationship that might make sense in the work world but has some application problems in the world of love. For here, Waller is reminding us, a love relationship can be quite lopsided [more technically, asymmetrical]. People do not usually love equally; or, equally well. Here the one who needs the relationship the most [is the most dependent upon its continuance—for psychological, or economic, or status needs] is in the lesser bargaining position. This person is obviously very vulnerable to exploitation as the other has the potential to be exploitative. To not exploit in such instances means that the more powerful person must *not* exercise the full potential of his/her position. This can be done via self-control, adherence to a wedding vow, and/or devotion to a higher principle [often religious]. In analogues fashion true friendship is not based on economic advantage but a mutuality of non-economic interests.

Parent-child relationships are also interesting to examine in this regard. On one level, the child is in an economically dependent relationship at least through adolescence. On another level, the child [too often for some observers] is in the emotionally dominant position as is so often the case when the parents are overly needy to demonstrate how competent they are as parents or how grateful they are for someone to love [and to love them back]? In this instance, it is the parent who may need the child more [emotionally] and much parent-child conflict during adolescence derives from losing parental control [and meaning] as the child steadily though haltingly becomes more adult-like.

One more application will suffice. In the religious sphere, it is common in organized religion to see God as omnipotent, all just, all merciful, and all loving. Leaving aside the issue that some of these traits may be contradictory, it is the consensus that the modern Western idea of God carries with it a strong element of mercy and love. Be that as it may, who here is more dependent? We miserable sinners who need God's mercy and grace without which we cannot meaningfully cope with the world or God who needs the sinners to repent for fulfillment of a divine plan? Put another way, do we have less interest than God in things divine? Perhaps to some, this is an inappropriate application of Waller's principle. Still, the principle is suggestive of new ways of seeing familiar phenomena.

To sum up this section, Waller's principle of least interest can show how people can remain in groups that from an outsider's perspective seem to be irrational behavior. In a very important way, it is not just that people derive great benefits from certain group memberships [though that is frequently true]. Rather, it is often the case that many people need to derive *some* rather important benefits from certain memberships regardless of the cost to themselves. Thus, it is not that our group participation is strictly rational or utterly irrational so much as for most of us most of the time our important group memberships are characterized by both rational and irrational elements.

Rationality, Value, and Sacrifice: Social Life as Rational Investment? To be **rational** is to select from available options that option which will maximize benefits and minimize costs. You go shopping and among available items that are comparable in value, you pick the one with the lowest price. That seems reasonable until we examine our lives a bit more closely and find that while we do try to increase benefits this does not always involve minimizing costs. To illustrate, here is a brief exercise to help set the stage for the following discussion. Very quickly, who or what do you value? Write down the first thing[s] that pops into your consciousness. Okay, now what have you or what will you sacrifice to attain what you value? Upon reflection, notice how what we value highly generally seems to be associated with great sacrifices: the more we value someone or something, the more we are willing to sacrifice to have that object of our desire. Seen another way, just how much do you value someone or something for which you have sacrificed little to attain? Small sacrifices yield little of value from this perspective.

Notice that it works another way as well: the more we have sacrificed for some person/object/relationship the more we come to value it. Why? Think of this in terms of investments. The more we have invested our time, money, energy, self-concept, and reputation the more we come to value that in which we have invested so much of ourselves. *The more we have invested [broadly speaking] the more we "need" to believe in the value of what we have invested in.* This is why so many cling to toxic relationships, delusional policies, bankrupting lifestyles, absurd ideologies, and the like. It is because we have put so much of ourselves [invested so much of our lives] in something that to walk away from it would involve too much loss: time, money, reputation, self-esteem. Here fear of loss of irretrievable inputs drive us to stay with a loser, relationship, policy, or belief system. This is why heavy investments are so often associated with delusions: both personal and collective. While this hardly seems rational, we muddle onward hoping that things will somehow miraculously get better or at the very least prove in the future not to be as damaging as it has in the past. Put another way, we can invest so much of ourselves that a rational course will not be pursued because of the enormity of our investments.

For some however, there comes a point where we confront reality in all of its brutality and find that this string of investments have added up to a huge loss that can no longer be denied. Indeed, some of the most traumatic events of our lives come from the realization that our investments have proven to be in someone or something that is unworthy, empty, meaningless, etc.

35

To summarize, the more we value something the more we will sacrifice [invest] to *attain* it. Once attained, the more we have sacrificed to attain it the more we will value it and thus the more likely we will make further sacrifices to *maintain* what we have valued so highly. Is this rationality? In a strict sense, it would seem that rationality has its limits as an explanatory perspective.

Role-Complements: The Sociological Alternative to Personality. While the reader might concede that emotions do have a social dimension you might nevertheless argue that your personality is unique and is something independent of social setting. In a wonderful article Schmidt and Davis show that what are commonly seen as personality types are actually **role-complements.** A role-complement consists of two [or more] roles that people play that reinforce one another. More than that, role-complements enact each other. Common examples include teacher-student, parent-child, and husband-wife. In the Schmidt and Davis piece, they concentrate on the obnoxious and the nice.   When assessing others people usually say things like "he's obnoxious" or "she's nice." Schmidt and Davis argue that not only cannot you understand the obnoxious without the nice but also that people who are so tagged actually "use" one another in a very basic way. To illustrate, how is it possible to see someone as obnoxious in a nonsocial situation? It is not. One is not obnoxious to oneself in the mirror alone in a shabby little room. No, one can only be obnoxious to others in a social situation. Well, obnoxious to whom then? To others who will put up with an obnoxious person. Consider a party where there are too many social "performers" who insist upon imposing their charms, witticisms, and cosmic insights onto any and all available hapless bystanders. The obnoxious drive out the graceful [those who make others feel comfortable and accepted] by monopolizing the social spotlight until all who are left are those who cannot or will not escape. Among them are people that we would consider to be truly nice people who will put up with the most boorish behavior of others. While most of us will escape at the first opportunity, some will stay to absorb the social abuse. Why? Well, perhaps it is in the person's self-interest to do so. Perhaps, the person who puts up with the boor needs to see himself/herself as a really nice person and what better way to demonstrate to oneself that one is actually nice than to test oneself with a truly obnoxious partner: "Gee, she's so nice. Why does she put up with him?" Here psychological need meets sociological enactment.

In a similar fashion, Mencotti has explored the role-complement of the shy and the socially graceful in which one becomes the audience for the other. Each is a role-complement of the other.

Just as the obnoxious cannot be obnoxious except in the presence of others so too the social adept/graceful cannot shine except in the presence of others. In many ways, the graceful person is the mirror opposite of the obnoxious. Where the obnoxious is self-centered, the graceful is, well, gracious. The obnoxious person demands to monopolize attention while the graceful person will steer the conversation to elicit contributions from others. The obnoxious person does not know when to quit. The conversational partners of the graceful person do not want them to leave. Who makes the best partners [or in sociological jargon: role-complements] for the graceful? Well, the obnoxious certainly would not but the shy might just fill the bill. We have all been in situations when we have been strangers and reticent to just barge in and announce ourselves. Have not we all been truly appreciative of the gracious host who steers us to people who might just make us feel more comfortable in this new setting full of strangers? Further, have not we all felt some gratitude in being in the presence of a truly gifted storyteller who can make faraway places and events come alive for us? We contribute to such an encounter by putting our shyness to work by being an attentive audience. Therefore, in a way parallel to the obnoxious and the nice the socially graceful and the shy enact role-complements as well.

Three additional items to note. First, one can be shy-nice in one situation while being very graceful in another depending on our comfort zone in the two situations. We have not changed but the social circumstances have, thus allowing different aspects of our personalities to emerge while other aspects are submerged, if only temporarily. Second, social emotions may occur simultaneously: one may be socially nice while inwardly envious of that person who is so perfectly gracious—something we secretly long to be but think we cannot. While we do not express our envy openly we feel it and the context in which we are feeling it is, well, social. Third, these role-complement examples: obnoxious-nice and graceful-shy may also be seen as extensions of exchange theory but in the realm of personality typing.

So as "nice" people, we hide our inner feelings while enacting a role that externally is very different and this brings us to the ideas of Erving Goffman and his dramaturgical view of social life.

Another Take on Social Life: Goffman's Dramaturgy. One of the most original of modern sociologists, Erving Goffman was the epitome of the detached, wry observer of the social scene. It is little wonder that his most famous and enduring contribution to sociological theorizing was his "dramaturgical" model of social interaction.

Let us approach Goffman in the following way. Many will argue that what really counts in life are not intentions but consequences. I am sure we are all familiar with the phenomenon [as perpetrator, victim, or bystander] illustrated by the famous adage—"the road to hell is paved with good intentions." While one might mean well in performing such-and-such an act nevertheless the actual payoff sometimes brings disaster. So, are we agreed that good intentions are nice but that consequences are what really matter?

Good, because as any sociologist worth his/her salt Goffman would caution us: not so fast. Goffman would ask us to distinguish between two people each performing the same act. Both people write identical checks [let us be generous here] for $1,000 to a charity's annual gala event. When thanked each person utters similar clichés about how important the charity is in helping the unfortunate of the community. Now while person A is utterly devoid of scheming [she truly believes in the cause] person B writes that check for the same amount to the same charity knowing deep down that a) there is a tax credit for such an act and b) more importantly, this act of generosity will be seen by certain board members of the charity very favorably [as wise board members they have learned not to question the motives of donors]. Now is not $1,000 a somewhat expensive way of impressing these folk? Well, if several of the board members are "well connected" then person B might see his check as an investment that could eventually be parlayed into a lucrative business deal.

Thus, A is a genuinely good person and B is manipulative. Assuming we were the board members most of us would see A as the "better" person [here motives/intentions count for something] but we would be foolish to refuse the check from B. However, what would our assessments [and actions] be if the issue was love? There are areas of social life where intention is minor and there are other areas where it is of paramount importance and we expect motives in the realm of love to be genuine, authentic if you will.

Goffman's theory of dramaturgy in essence claims that society is really comprised of many different and, at times, overlapping smaller social worlds. In turn, each of the mini-worlds have **encounters** that make up the fundamental interactions that make up our social lives. These encounters have frames that define the reality, expectations, and norms that govern the behavior of the participants. Now each of the important encounters is structured along the lines of a play.

There are appropriate ways of dressing, acting, and talking in a given encounter and there are inappropriate ways as well. Goffman is talking about how, when, and why we "perform" in social situations. The classroom setting is clearly different in a myriad of ways from a wedding. A wedding is different from a funeral and both are radically different from a fraternity party. Note that a college student might attend all four events in a short period of time and know how to act appropriately in each thus performing in such a way that they are four different people. Think of it this way: if you act *that* differently are you, in effect, four different people? You may retort that you are the same person acting four different ways but that brings up the issue of self-consciousness. Are you aware that you are acting when you are in one of these situations? If so, then there is a distance between your outward performance and your inner state. You search for just the right things to say [and what not to say]. You agonize about how to approach the bereaved or that "hottie." You rehearse what you are going to say to the bride or what kind of excuse will work with the professor, etc. If there is this distance involving this mental rehearsal then, to Goffman, as you are acting in that particular way, you are acting *cynically:* you are consciously constructing what you are going to say and do next. You are aware of yourself performing in a social setting. You are, in this way, like person B who rather cynically gave his check to charity: aware of what the situation demands and how you can get through it and maximize benefits [or at least minimize costs] to yourself in the process.

Well, are you always cynical or are there any instances in which you are like person A? I am sure there are plenty of instances in which you are as person A. You are whenever your behavior and intent fuse: become as one. When you are, as it were, acting in the moment: when you act so well you become the part you are playing. It is in these moments, where behavior and consciousness come together, that Goffman would call ***sincerity***. You do not think about what you are doing; you just do it. You do not fret over who you are; you just are who you are. Another example of sincerity would be when you become so overjoyed at reuniting with a loved one that you unselfconsciously gush and let fly with all kinds of wonderful sentiments not caring who else might hear or see you. Consequences be damned! You are ecstatic to see this person! Another instance would be to engage in a terrible argument. Flush with anger you lose control and say the most god-awful things not screening/censoring your language at all. Perhaps being caught up in the emotional moment is one way in which we act sincerely. Another might be when you are so comfortable in a particular social situation or around a group of close associates that you again are not aware of what you "have to say" [or do]—you just are.

Here is a somewhat crude way of distinguishing a good deal of **cynical behavior** from a good deal of **sincere behavior**. You are acting cynically when you know you are B.S.-ing someone. You are sincere when you are taken in by your own B.S. Please note that during any given encounter you might alternate between cynicism and sincerity depending on how the interaction evolves. Thus, though encounters are framed and function as social containers wherein interactions take place the nature of the interaction is more liquid than solid. That is, interactions typically involve a lot of give-and-take and also have a certain minimal degree of unpredictability so that often they swirl rather than just sit there at the bottom of the bowl.

Though Goffman's career produced a great many insights into everyday interactions there is one implication of his thought that should not go unmentioned. Goffman's emphasis on the "play-acting" dimension to our lives should not prevent us from seeing the upside of pretense. A simple illustration should suffice. To always speak one's mind would play havoc with the stability of social relations. Few of us indeed would tolerate unrelenting candor. Our self-concepts would take a terrific beating and we would retreat into ourselves or, more likely, gravitate to those others who would pull their punches when speaking to us or of us. We, in turn, would be expected to be less harsh and more praiseworthy with our interaction partners. Thus, a good deal of work relations, friendships, marriages, and family life all have a quality of exchange built into them: an exchange of pretense that functions as a social glue: I will be less than forthright and candid about your faults if you are less than candid and forthcoming about mine. As Goffman might say, the bald truth may be needed in close relationships but not too often and, if applied, not too candidly.

Groups and Everyday Life. Not only is culture created, transmitted, and changed by group activity everyday life takes place primarily in group settings. In every group of any duration whether it is a pure friendship group or a pure work group or an amalgam of several types there seems to be one or [several] members whose major function is to make the other group members look good—by looking bad themselves. While many observers would interpret this from a psychological model emphasizing the dysfunctionalities of these arrangements, as sociologists we can approach it differently and more pragmatically. Assuming the membership in such groups is more or less voluntary then the higher status members obviously derive some of their higher status by including some of the "dopeys" of the world with which to compare them. As long as these dopeys are not too embarrassing or too detrimental to the team effort then they are functional for the overall group. In addition, the low status members also fulfill many of the tasks that the higher status members would find too demeaning.

Alternatively, what is in it for the dopeys? Certainly, reflecting in the glow of higher status group members might be one such benefit. How else to explain the composition of some high school cliques wherein the higher status and more popular kids allow somewhat "less worthy" peers to hang around and in turn "pay for the privilege" by being around as handy scapegoats, doing servile errands, etc. In a parallel manner, many voluntary organizations in need of fresh infusions of cash will allow membership to folks who might otherwise be turned away.

One can readily see why low-status types would put up with being at the bottom of a particular heap if there was no ready alternative: the work setting supplies many such examples of office denizens who stick around and bear with the discomfort of bad working conditions because they need the money, health benefits, etc. In anything approaching a voluntary setting however, why stick around? One reason would be that many people prefer to be low status in a high prestige group rather than high status in a lower prestige group. This is somewhat like living in the cheapest house in a "good" neighborhood as opposed to living in the best house in a marginal neighborhood. As long as they keep up their house and do not drag down the surrounding property values then they can be solid neighbors. In similar fashion as long as the lower status members of a group are "good members," which usually involves not making trouble for others as well as proving themselves worthy by conforming to all of the important group norms, then their membership may not be just tolerated but actually welcomed.

So far, we have just considered this from a vertical/hierarchical perspective. That is, we have seen this as groups ranking their members from high to low internally and also groups ranked as groups, against each other, from high to low. However, we can branch out a bit, remember that rare is the person who belongs to only one group. For example, if the work group really is nightmarish then family life might partially compensate for that. If both prove to be inadequate in providing meaningful experiences then identification with a successful sports team might bring temporary psychic relief and regular dramatic catharsis to one's otherwise drab life. In this way, tailgating is a communal ritual among like-minded clansmen [and women] all paying homage to the flesh and blood representatives of their chosen totem. That the tailgaters dress in similar colors with identical emblems and occasionally paint their bodies in the sacred colors of the team they are worshipping only adds to the Discovery Channel flavor of the spectacle.

Lacking that opportunity people have been known to turn to God for respite to a seemingly banal meaningless existence. Certainly, religion is a well-known compensator for many in which much of the solace comes from knowing that all are equal in the sight of God. We will return to this topic in the essay on the sociology of religion.

Reference Groups and Relative Deprivation. Finally, we should look at a way in which individuals link their beliefs and behavior with others: **reference groups**. The idea behind reference group theory is that people not only do not act in a social vacuum but they must take other peoples' views of themselves into account when they do act. [We discussed this idea earlier in our treatment of Cooley and Mead in the essay on socialization.] More than that however, reference group theory asserts that people have social "points of comparison" with which they actively, though not necessarily consciously, use to guide their behavior. These social points of comparison are termed reference groups and function as standards by which one evaluates oneself. What can be a reference group? Any group with which you compare yourself, your life, or your position in society can be a reference group. An obvious reference group is a group of friends. Another would be your family. A third might be a work group, a sports team, or a fraternity/sorority. Reference group theory assumes that groups exist and that they have relatively coherent standards by which people govern, guide, and evaluate their behavior. So, if your closest pals are a church group your behavior and beliefs are likely to be different than if you rode with the Hell's Angels.

So far, this is pretty obvious stuff. We do need to introduce a second, related concept to make things a bit more interesting. This term is **relative deprivation**. What this allows us to do is to emphasize the consequences of using reference groups as social points of comparison. For example, if you are solidly middle class your reference groups will communicate certain acceptable levels of consumer behavior. A certain kind of house in an acceptable neighborhood decorated in a tasteful style. While there are choices, here the message is clear: to be middle class you must not just act with middle class manners but you must do so while exhibiting middle class standards. If you do not and you do not often enough then those reference groups might begin to marginalize you so that you are no longer invited to certain parties, weddings, etc. In a phrase, you are not living up to certain standards, the group's standards. This perspective can also be applied to having your children go to an acceptable college with a respectable reputation.

If that is all true, then you may ask where the deprivation comes in. Well, if you feel deprived/inadequate you do so in relation to a reference group. To take another kind of example, if your family is your reference group then you could feel deprived compared to the attention and resources a favored sibling might receive and that can hurt; and hurt sharply. Even though compared with your friends you might receive more attention and resources within your own family than they do with theirs, still you feel deprived and no doubt envious of the favored sib. That is the point. One is not absolutely deprived but relatively so, in relation to some discernible reference. So, to take a concrete example, if your friends drive nice, new, Euro sport sedans and you are still driving that 5-year-old perfectly serviceable domestic station wagon, then if that reference group puts a premium on spending big bucks on upscale cars then you either sink dollars into one [maybe leasing a BMW] so as to keep up with them or stick to your budget and continue to drive that Ford wagon. However, if you fall behind enough times then perhaps the marginalization process takes effect and perhaps you will find yourself gravitating toward a new group of friends; one whose standards are less exacting and easier to meet.

At this point, we are back to the discussion above where we wondered if it was better to be at the top of group A or at the bottom of group B when group B is clearly the more socially desirable group to be in. It is not that you will sit down with pen and paper, tote up all of the pluses and minuses, and then plan your strategy. No, it is usually more subtle less consciously calculating than that and further it is not as if all of your social fate is in your own hands anyway [note the ways in which one can be marginalized/frozen out of certain groups no matter how desperately one wants to belong].

To sum up this section, in a hyper-competitive society such as ours with constantly changing demands for consumption, the incessant ranking of members is inevitable. What we consume [homes, autos, vacations, clothes, education] become markers of our status and thus our "worthwhileness." From there it is but a small step to linking our worthwhileness to our worthiness and, in a perverse way, somehow think that our ability to consume somehow reflects on our moral worth. Too easily we become what we consume and we consume in the hopes of becoming who we think we want to be. At the core of this analysis is the assertion that guiding and governing our beliefs and behavior are our reference groups and that when we do not feel we measure up or when we are told [subtly or bluntly] that we do not measure up we become deprived: relative to that reference group. It does little good for well-meaning family and friends to tell us that compared to the poor and the starving we have all that is necessary to have a contented life. Well, reference group theory tells us, NO! It is NOT enough. It is not enough because your reference group is not the poor and/or the starving and/or the afflicted. Your reference group is that group that you oh-so-badly want to be part of but cannot [for whatever reasons]. You are deprived and it hurts relative to THAT group and that, in turn, is what counts and thus will motivate much of your compensatory behavior.

Microsociology, Reductionism Higher Levels of Social Reality. This somewhat formidable section heading is really just another way of stating an important problem: What is the most appropriate level at which to study social life?

Let us try to figure this out without too much discomfort for the reader. If you step back and look at how we experience our lives we do so from the inside out. That is, we look out and act upon the social world as individuals who nevertheless are connected with other individuals. Our actions seem to be acts of individuals and it is quite difficult to see how they may add up to anything but just the actions of individuals.

If this is indeed the case then perhaps nothing adds up to anything more than just individuals and their acts and in fact maybe that is an illusion as well since we could go in the other direction and say there is nothing of integrity about our individual consciousness since it is all ultimately reducible to the study of neurophysiology anyway.

Well, before we take that particular step lets step back and catch our breath. What disciplines such as neurophysiology and cognitive psychology are up to is a reductionism when we look at ourselves as social creatures. If push came to shove, the more enthusiastic of these good folk would argue that whatever we are as social beings ultimately prove explainable by rather detailed studies of the brain and its non-material cousin: the mind. Social life will be the ultimate dependent variable from this perspective.

Alternatively, the rest of this collection of essays will emphasize something radically different: that there are independently existing social entities such as culture and society and social structures that are comprised of various institutions such as government, family, economy, military, education, etc. It is these social phenomena that are the ultimate independent variables and we as individuals are the dependent variables.

So, who is right? Well, let us try this. Yes, it is true that without our minds [and more basically our brains] we could not exist as individuals and we certainly could not act as social beings. However, it is equally true that without the social "stuff" provided by culture, society, institutions and the like there would be no content with which the brain could work. Thus, the brain is the machinery of individuals; without our brains [and bodies] we could not act. However, it is the social entities that give direction to our life's journey. Think, for example, of yourself as a citizen of India and being raised as an observant Hindu rather than as an observant Christian, Jew, or Muslim. The payoff is that *what* you fervently believe is a product of your *social* environment and not your neurophysiology. If we as humans all have about the same biological equipment then it cannot be the equipment that can explain these important variations in what we believe and how we act. Ultimately, we must rely upon social explanations.

To close this essay with a rough analogy, as the recurring functioning of our brains allow us to act as individuals with self-consciousness and personal memory, so our recurring individual actions allow social structures to flourish and without these social structures we cannot be fully human.

છ ભ છ ભ

DEFINITIONS

Cynical Behavior. Acting in a way that is detrimental to another, often through deception. Note that during any given encounter you might alternate between cynicism and sincerity depending on how the interaction evolves.

Dramaturgy. Goffman's study of social interaction as theater in which actors play roles before audiences.

Emotion Work. Generating prescribed emotions that override automatic reactions. This has become a key concept for understanding how people respond in social arrangements where prescribed emotion norms conflict with emotional reactions (Thoits 1990).

Emotions. Any strong feelings. The affective aspect of consciousness. Emotions such as anger or fear involve physiological changes in the body.

Encounters. A casual or unexpected convergence.

Envy What you feel toward another when you want but do not have what they do.

Exchange Theory. The idea that social rewards can be traded and spent like money.

Groups. A number of people who regularly interact with each other and share similar values, norms, and expectations.

Jealousy. What you feel in an inclusionary relationship which you think might be in jeopardy. Every time a person fears losing his/her significant other to a rival (real or imagined) the resulting emotion is jealousy.

Microsociology. The focus on face-to-face interaction.

Principle of Least Interest. The concept that the person with the least interest in the relationship has the most power over it.

Rational. To be able to select from available options that which will maximize benefits and minimize costs.

Rationality. A reliance on reason and the scientific method as the basis of decision making.

Reference Groups. Any group with which you compare yourself, your life, or your position in society. An obvious reference group is a group of friends. Another would be your family. A third might be a work group or a sports team or a fraternity/sorority.

Relative Deprivation. Occurs where individuals or groups subjectively perceive themselves as unfairly disadvantaged over others perceived as having similar attributes and deserving similar rewards (their reference groups).

Role-Complements. Two (or more) roles that people play that reinforce one another, such as student/teacher or parent/child. More than that, role-complements enact each other. Common examples include teacher-student, parent-child, and husband-wife.

Sincere Behavior. Acting in a trusting way. Note that during any given encounter you might alternate between cynicism and sincerity depending on how the interaction evolves.

REFERENCES

Blau, Peter Michael. 1964. *Exchange and Power in Social Life*. New York: J. Wiley.

Collins, Randall. 1988. "The Micro Contribution to Macro Sociology." *Sociological Theory* 6:242-53.

Davis, Murray S. and Catherine J. Schmidt. 1977. "The Obnoxious and the Nice." *Sociometry*.

Goffman, Erving. 1959. *The Presentation of Self in Everyday Life*. New York: Doubleday.

Goffman, Erving. 1974. *Frame Analysis*. New York: Harper and Row.

Hochschild, Arlie. 1983. *The Managed Heart*. Berkeley, CA: University of California Press.

Mencotti, Lawrence. 1986. "A Common Malady." *Contemporary Psychiatry*.

Simmel, Georg. 1971. *On Individuality and Social Forms*. Chicago, IL: University of Chicago Press.

Waller, Willard. 1938. *The Family* The Cordon Company.

Weitman, Sasha R. 1970. "Intimacies: Notes Toward a Theory of Social Inclusion and Exclusion." *European Journal of Sociology* 11:348-67.

4 | Deviance and Social Control: Behaving Well and Not So Well.
by Theodore R. Curry, Ph.D.

All societies will have examples of behaviors that are considered "wrong," "bad," or "immoral." Criminologists refer to such actions as *deviance* and, in general, deviance is thought of as having negative impacts on society, such as creating chaos and instability for the larger society as well as harms for individuals who may be victimized by deviant behavior. In an attempt to limit the corrosive effects of deviance, societies employ what is called *social control*, which consists of negative **sanctions** or punishments as well as positive sanctions or **rewards**. The basic idea is that punishments in response to deviance will curb such behavior while rewards for conforming behavior will encourage people to obey the rules—leading to a more stable, safe, and orderly society as well as enabling the larger society and its leaders to focus their attention on other concerns.[1]

By way of example, when people commit a crime in American society, the police may arrest them, and the courts may bring them to trial and, if they are convicted, decide upon a punishment. The correctional system will often implement the punishment in the form of probation, imprisonment, boot camps, etc. Here, criminal behavior (a subset of deviant behavior) prompts social control, which, in this case, is a punishment implemented by the criminal justice system. When deviance of a non-criminal nature occurs (such as talking back to parents, lying to a spouse, excessive tattooing or body piercing), and social control is the response, this response may come from virtually anybody—which, in these cases may consist of expressions of disapproval, avoidance, etc. A few things to remember at this point are that both deviance and social control are behaviors, and that any and all individuals may perform social control as well as engage in deviance (in fact, all of us engage in deviance as well as perform social control on a fairly regular basis).

Fascinating though this discussion has already become, you may begin to wonder what importance deviance and social control may have for society as a whole. Among the many potential answers to this question, two of the most important will suffice for now. First, when deviance is performed and detected in a society, and social control responds to this behavior, then the rule

---

1 The vast majority of sociological research on social control focuses on punishment. While this undoubtedly represents a shortcoming in knowledge, for the remainder of this chapter the term social control will mainly refer to punitive sanctions.

that prohibits the deviant act in question is upheld, or receives validation. Depending on the severity of the social control reaction, the degree of importance of the violated rule can be known. Thus, deviance and social control function to identify behaviors that are "bad" and denote the relative degree of wrongfulness of a given deviant act. This process therefore communicates to the larger society what the rules are and how important they are. As a result, deviance and social control are one way that the rules espoused by the larger culture are created and maintained. In addition, according to Emile Durkheim (1858-1917), a towering figure in sociology, deviance and social control also serve to create "**social solidarity**," or a sense of togetherness or "we-ness" among members of society. Solidarity is a necessary prerequisite for society to exist in the first place. Therefore, for Durkheim, deviance and social control are essential building blocks of society, without which society would be impossible.

A second important feature of deviance and social control concerns something more insidious: the potential for the misuse of social control. History is replete with examples where societies used social control against certain groups as a way to oppress them. Lynchings of African-Americans in the post-bellum South and elsewhere in the United States, the attempted extermination of Jews in Europe by German Nazis in World War II, and the sudden and large increase in the numbers of African-Americans and Hispanics in prison and jail as part of modern America's "War on Drugs" may all be used as examples of **discrimination** or unfairness in social control (as well as in definitions of what constitutes deviance). Although the latter example may be controversial (and will be revisited later in this chapter), these examples of social control may be seen as unfair or discriminatory in that they specifically target members of certain groups to receive social control.

In sum, bad behavior (deviance) and punitive responses (social control) may be important for creating and maintaining society, but they may also raise the specter of oppression and discrimination if used unfairly. Now that you have a taste of the importance that deviance and social control have for society, let us next explore these concepts in greater detail before returning to a more thorough exploration of their social implications.

WHAT IS DEVIANCE?

At the most basic level, deviance can be thought of as behavior that violates any social norm. **Norms** refer to rules about what is appropriate and inappropriate behavior in a given situation. A key feature of norms is that they can change considerably across different situations and over time. Such differences in *context* mean that rules about deviance are fluid, rather than fixed. For example, shouting hello to one of your friends is acceptable in many public places, but is considered inappropriate (or deviant) during one of your classes or in the library. As a result, *definitions of deviance may vary across space* in that different social situations contain different rules about right or wrong. This same principle holds when comparing norms from different societies to one another or comparing different **subcultures** within a given society. Take the case of how people greet one another, as another example. When people in the United States meet for the first time or when they get together for social activities, males in particular often greet one another by shaking hands. Members of Hispanic cultures often greet one another with an embrace and perhaps a single kiss on the cheek—except for male-male greetings, which tend to consist of handshakes or a firm one-handed hug and several strong pats on the back. Same sex greetings among members of many Arab cultures, however, usually include an embrace and several cheek kisses, even for male-to-male greetings. Members of many Asian cultures bow to one another as a greeting. Yet, even within these cultures, there may be considerable variation as to how greetings are performed, depending on the age, gender, and degree of familiarity among those involved. If you feel that the type of greeting seems to be an unimportant or esoteric topic, consider the consequences of using deviant greetings such as when you meet the parents of your "significant other" for the first time and decide to slug the father on the arm and say "what's up dude!?" or if you embraced and kissed on the cheek several times a stranger who was interviewing you for a job. *Definitions of deviance may also show a great deal of variation over time.* For example, both social and legal norms regarding tobacco have become stricter in the United States since the late 1980s, while norms about gender roles loosened considerably in the latter half of the twentieth century.

The importance of context to understanding and identifying what is or is not deviant cannot be over-emphasized. Thus, what may be considered by mainstream American society as deviant, such as recreational drug use, may not be considered deviant in certain times and places. For example, marijuana use was not considered deviant among the "hippie" subculture of the 1960s—in fact, it was considered "normative," meaning that the hippies considered people who did *not* smoke the drug to be deviant. For Jamaica's Rastafarian subculture, marijuana use is also normative. Heavy alcohol consumption, viewed as deviant by American society as a whole, may not be considered deviant at certain times, such as New Year's eve, or certain places, such as college fraternity parties, and bachelor and bachelorette parties. Some groups, such as outlaw biker gangs, may not see even violent acts such as rape, fighting, and even murder, as deviant, especially under certain circumstances.

In addition to showing variation over time and space, the relative importance of norms is another essential consideration. Violating certain norms is seen as more wrong or deviant than other violations. At the least severe end are *folkways*, which largely consist of social customs and manners, such as how greetings are performed, table manners, toilet habits, general cleanliness and grooming, courtesies performed while driving a car, and many other aspects of day to day social interactions. Violating a folkway is not generally considered particularly wrong or serious, and indeed many times is inadvertent. Sanctions, therefore, are usually mild for this type of deviance. *Mores* (pronounced "more-ays") represent more important norms and thus receive more severe sanctions when they are violated. Mores typically pertain to maintaining social members' wellbeing, such as their physical safety and freedom, as well as their property, and to appropriate economic behavior. Thus, if a person is victimized in any way, such as being sexually or physically assaulted or having their money or property taken through force or fraud, this type of deviance violates mos.[2]

While violations of mores such as theft, physical assaults, selling unsafe consumer goods, and convincing investors to buy worthless stock or other property are considered very wrong and serious deviant acts, they do not represent the most serious type of deviance. For that distinction, we turn to the idea of *taboos*, which pertain to the behaviors that a society or culture considers most sacred or profane. Performing a profanity, or failing to perform a sacred act, is often considered more wrong and more serious than many mores, and can sometimes result in more severe sanctions. In the United States, for example, it is taboo to murder a young child, or for a child to kill a parent, because such acts are almost beyond the idea of "wrong"—they are profanities, as they profane some of our most cherished norms about family and the vulnerability of children. Yet, many other types of homicide are probably not considered taboo, such as arguments among friends

---

2 Mos is the singular of mores. Typically, though, scholars refer to the plural mores.

that escalate into murder, or even the murder of a convenience store clerk during a robbery (as awful as these acts are). Oddly, many taboos concern food and sex. In most cultures, it is taboo to commit cannibalism and for Jews and Moslems eating pork violates a taboo. In the United States, it is taboo to eat insects, yet some Asian and African cultures regularly eat certain insects. Most cultures also have an incest taboo, a bestiality taboo, and a taboo against having sexual relations with children. For some cultures, homosexuality is taboo, although it is no longer considered taboo in the United States and most of Europe (and in many major metropolitan areas is no longer even considered deviant). Conversely, consciously not marrying and having children may be taboo in certain times and places. Interestingly, unlike the less serious mores, many taboos do not involve victims. Most if not all religions will identify certain actions as taboo and, again, many of these pertain to food and sex, but some will also pertain to proper worship and prayer. Not every act identified as wrong by a religion, however, will be considered taboo among the adherents of that religion—some acts, such as missing worship services or dressing casually at services, may be seen a violating folkways (or perhaps mores).

A final type of norm consists of legal definitions. Laws are norms that have been codified or written into law. Such laws may come from folkways (such as parking violations), mores (many acts of force and fraud), or taboos (such as incest). Scholars frequently distinguish between two different types of laws. *Mala en se* laws refer to behaviors that "are wrong in and of themselves." Typically, these criminal acts involve a victim and some type of force or fraud. *Mala prohibita* laws pertain to acts that "are wrong because society defines them as wrong." Such crimes do not include direct victims, such as prostitution and drug possession. Mala prohibita laws are also called "victimless crimes" because their violation usually does not directly harm people other than those engaging in the crime itself.

Obviously, even though they are deviant, most folkways and even some mores are not written into law and, therefore, are not considered **crimes**. Many taboos are also not legal violations, such as those that involve food consumption. Conversely, some law violations are not considered deviant (such as speeding). Yet, many "wrong" acts are considered both deviant and criminal. It is important to remember the distinctions between crime and deviance, as well as their similarity. Figure 1 is a Venn diagram that portrays these three different combinations of deviant and criminal acts. The area in the left hand oval labeled "A" represents all behaviors that are against the law (criminal) but typically not seen as deviant by the larger society, such as walking a dog without a leash or being in a public park after closing. Area "B," in the right hand oval, corresponds to actions that are widely seen as deviant but are not criminal, such as loudly passing gas in a crowded movie theater. Area "C," where the two ovals overlap, stands for the collection of behaviors that are considered both deviant and criminal, such as stealing a car or using heroin.

Figure 4.1   Comparison of Criminal and Deviant Behavior

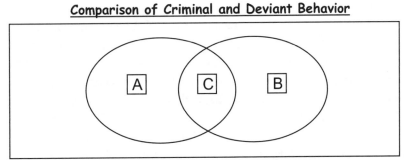

A = Criminal but not Deviant; B = Deviant but not Criminal;
C = Both Deviant and Criminal

Given the extreme contextual relativism of what is or is not deviant, it has proven especially difficult to give a succinct definition of what "deviance" really is. Indeed scholars to this day disagree on how to define deviance. Several different perspectives or definitions have been offered: statistical, absolutist, normative, **labeling**, **conflict**, and the new "synthetic approach." The statistical approach to deviance is perhaps the most limited and at times most misleading. It defines deviance as any behavior or status that is statistically rare. This emphasizes the "different-ness" of deviance and how people who occupy unusual statuses, such as having physical disabilities or deformities, or who perform unusual behavior, such as homosexuality or religious snake handling, might be reacted to with disgust or avoidance. However, some usual statuses and behaviors might be seen as desirable (rather than as deviant). Being unusually rich or beautiful seems to fit the statistical definition of deviance, as might the performance of exceptional athletic feats, such as winning an Olympic gold medal, yet we do not typically think of these statuses and behaviors as "deviant." Thus, the statistical definition has fallen out of favor and offers scholars of deviance little utility.

The *absolutist* perspective defines as deviant only those behaviors that are thought to be deviant at all times and all places—hence the idea that such acts are "absolutely" deviant. Few, if any, acts could fit this definition, however. Incest is often pointed to as being absolutely deviant. But the precise definition of incest varies considerably over time and space. Even siblings could sometimes marry and not be considered deviant—as in the case of ancient Egyptian pharaohs, such as King Tutankhamen marrying his sister. Homicide may be another example, but in times of war homicide is actually normative, rather than deviant. Even if a few behaviors could be identified as absolutely deviant, no matter the time or place, they would likely be so few in number as to be of little use to scholars. The relativist nature of deviance, pointed to above, renders the absolutist perspective on deviance little more than a chimera. Yet, the innovative and popular "self-control" theory of crime (Gottfredson and Hirschi 1990:15) utilizes a rather expansive and potentially useful absolutist definition: "acts of force and fraud undertaken in pursuit of self-interest." I personally find the idea of "force and fraud" to be quite interesting and have used it numerous times throughout this chapter. But this definition leaves out a lot of what scholars and laypersons alike might consider to be deviant, such as recreational drug use, strange sexual practices like bestiality and "swinging" (also known as partner swapping). In essence, all types of victimless deviance are ignored in this particular absolutist definition, which, again, points to a major flaw of this type of perspective.

The *normative* approach defines deviance as behavior that violates a social rule or norm held by people in a given time and place. This type of definition is the one most commonly used by scholars today, and has much to recommend it. Different from the absolutist approach, the normative definition is fluid rather than rigid, and so can cope with contextual differences in what is or is not deviant. However, how do we resolve the question of inter-group differences when, for example, one group argues that **affirmative action** policies should be banned, while another group argues for their continuation? On one hand, we could say that these groups have different norms, and call the case closed. But what happens when both groups belong to the same society and each is vying to have its views be seen as acceptable by the larger society? Because it sees all individuals' and all groups' opinions as equal in importance, the normative perspective cannot deal with the issues of competing claims regarding deviance. Thus, while it is quite useful for many purposes, there are some problems with the normative approach to deviance.

What are variously called reactivist, labeling, conflict, or radical approaches to deviance are all expressly directed toward contending with the issue of **"power"**—namely the power to create or impose definitions of deviance, the implications of these definitions, and the power of individuals and groups to avoid being labeled deviant and receiving punishment. For the labeling or reactivist approach Howard S. Becker (1963:9) famously stated:

> "Social groups create deviance by making rules whose infraction constitutes deviance, and by applying those rules to particular people and labeling them as outsiders. From this point of view, deviance is not a quality of the act a person commits, but rather a consequence of the application by others of rules or sanctions to an 'offender.' The deviant is one to whom that label has been successfully applied; deviant behavior is behavior that people so label."

This statement has several important features. First, building on the normative approach, no behavior is inherently deviant; rather, social processes must define what is or is not deviant. However, according to the labeling perspective, deviance cannot exist, until deviant labels have been successfully applied to behaviors and perpetrators. Thus, the key to labeling is social control, which, thorough its mobilization, creates deviance. Second, the conflict and radical traditions emphasized the differential power of social groups to create social norms in the first place. Groups with more economic or political power are better able to have their views of wrong or deviant behavior become accepted by the larger society—whether it concerns a social norm or a criminal law. Weaker groups, on the other hand, are not only less likely to have their views manifested in social norms or laws, but may even have deviant labels applied to the norms and behaviors that they advocate or perform. A brief example concerns the use of intoxicating substances. The drug of choice of Whites and the middle and upper economic classes is alcohol, which is legal for those over age 21. Drugs such as marijuana and cocaine are associated with "outsider" groups and are criminal. A final feature of the labeling approach also concerns power, but at the individual level. Here, the differential power of individuals to resist the application of the deviant label is highlighted— powerful people will be better to avoid labeling. As an example, guilty or not, O. J. Simpson was able to avoid the official "murderer" label mainly because of the vast financial resources he possessed, which he mobilized to present a successful defense in court. Average United States citizens, not possessing such resources, would likely have been unable to avoid the murderer label in such a case.

However, a major problem with the labeling approach is that, even if they commit what might be seen by the larger society as a deviant or wrong act, people are not actually "deviant" until they are caught and successfully labeled as such. "Secret deviants," who may perform acts widely viewed as wrong, such as heroin use, are not actually performing deviance unless they are caught and labeled. This seems to violate one of the major tenets behind the idea of deviance—that wrong or bad behavior constitutes deviance.

A new "synthetic approach" (Tittle 1995:124) defines deviance as "any behavior that a majority of a given group regards as unacceptable *or* that typically evokes a collective response of a negative type" (emphasis added). This definition combines or synthesizes the normative and labeling approaches but, in doing so, attempts to avoid the major shortcomings of each. From the labeling view comes the idea that social control mobilization is itself sufficient to identify deviance; but, because it is not required, the "secret deviance" of the heroin user mentioned above would now be seen as actual deviance. Additionally, the relative, contextual features of deviance, emphasized by the normative approach, are also considered. However, the relative power of actors to impose or avoid the deviant label is largely neglected, as is the issue of identifying deviance when separate groups define deviance differently. Thus, while perhaps an advance, the synthetic approach to defining deviance does not resolve all issues.

WHAT IS SOCIAL CONTROL?

Social control is behavior, performed by various *agents* of social control (i.e., people, groups, or organizations), who attempt to label or define specific behaviors, persons, or groups as wrong, bad, evil, or unacceptable—in essence to apply the deviant label. When applied to specific individuals, social control takes the form of a **sanction** or punishment. In this case, social control can be thought of as actions that punish those who perform deviance (or, in the view of labeling theory, social control consists of actions that create deviance through labeling). Although social control also refers to the process of defining behaviors as deviant or criminal, and can seek to label entire groups as deviant, for the time being, we will focus on the dynamic between individual deviants and social control agents.

Agents of social control are of two types. ***Formal social control agents*** are representatives of the state or government, such as police, prosecutors, judges, and members of the correctional system, such as probation officers, prison wardens, and correctional officers. Such formal social control is ***coercive*** in that it focuses on punitive sanctions. A less recognized type of formal social control is termed *beneficent*, because it is intended to appease certain groups as a way to discourage their deviance. Beneficent formal social control emanates from "benefits" to marginalized groups, such as the poor, in the form of public education, health care, job training, affirmative actions policies, etc. Such social control is intended to placate certain groups (and, perhaps, society as a whole) as a way to control or reduce possible deviance. Benefits may also be offered to powerful groups such as wealthy individuals and large corporations, mainly in the form of tax reductions, as a way to reduce white-collar crimes such as tax evasion. Whether coercive or beneficent, formal social control is rigid, operating according to an elaborate system of rules and procedures. Although specific individuals are involved, formal social control is best viewed as performed by a group or organization, which in this case is the government.

In contrast, ***informal social control agents*** can be (and are) anybody and everybody, and such behavior may be performed singly or in groups. Indeed, we all act as informal social control agents in many ways. Our body language and facial expressions can indicate subtle disapproval. More obviously, verbal comments we might make, like "that wasn't cool," "what a jerk," "she is such a slut," and "I think he's becoming an alcoholic," also constitute social control. Another key difference is that **informal social control** is fluid, meaning that it operates in many different ways at different times and places, and not according to specific procedures. Yet, like beneficent **formal social control**, informal social control can also be viewed as consisting of rewards or inducements toward conformity, such as expressions of affection by parents toward children when they succeed at school and saying "thank-you" to a spouse for doing housework. However, social control in the form of rewards is much less commonly examined than coercive types, which will be the focus of the rest of our discussion.

Whether performed by formal or informal agents, social control can take on many different forms; some of the major types are: avoidance or banishment, physical pain (such as spankings, beatings, executions, or any type corporal punishment), detention (in a prison or being "grounded" to one's home), financial sanctions (such as fines or loss of job or allowance), and emotional sanctions (like gossip, ridicule, humiliation, intimidation, and withdrawal of affection). Some of these sanctions, like executions, are obviously severe, while others might seem relatively innocuous or mild, perhaps to the point where you may wonder how they could really be effective punishments. Avoidance, for example, may not seem like a big deal. However, consider how you might feel if your family and closest friends simply refused to speak with you or be in your presence. The loneliness, isolation, and sense of rejection you would experience would most likely feel oppressive, even unbearable, in a very short time. Alternatively, consider banishment from society. How might you feel if you were permanently banished from society? Loneliness might be the least of your worries. Poverty and mere survival might quickly head to the top of the list. Similarly, consider the withdrawal of affection from friends and family. Suppose that your repeated bad behavior has so upset your mother (or your spouse, best friend, etc.) that they no longer seek out your company, no longer share with you in any of the emotional experiences that make you enjoy life, such as friendship, camaraderie, being loved or cared for. If you have a young child, think about how you might feel if he or she no longer smiled at you or came to you when they were scared or upset, or no longer wanted to hug or be held by you. While these informal sanctions do not involve physical or financial dimensions, they can be quite severe nonetheless. Yet an important feature of these punishments is that they rely on close personal bonds to be effective. If you are not close to your mother, or if a friend does not have your respect, then avoidance or withdrawal of affection in these cases might not bother you in the least. Figure 2 lists a number of formal and informal social control agents and some of the specific sanctions they might administer.

Figure 4.2   Agents of Social Control and Examples of Their Controlling Behavior

Agents of Social Control and Examples of their Controlling Behavior:

I.   Formal Social Control Agents
1. Police
    - Detain
    - Arrest
2. Prosecutors
    - Prosecution
    - Plea Bargain
3. Judges and Juries; Prison Wardens and Correctional Officers
    - Jail or Prison Time
    - Execution
    - Monetary Fine
    - Community Service
    - Solitary Confinement

II.   Informal Social Control Agents
1. Family Members
    - Avoidance
    - Weakened Attachment
    - Loss of Financial Support
    - Physical Punishment
    - "Grounding"
2. Spouse or "Significant Other"
    - Avoidance
    - Weakened Attachment
    - Withhold Affection (sexual or emotional)
    - Spend or Withhold Money
3. Friends and Acquaintances
    - Avoidance
    - Disrespect
    - Weakened Attachment
    - Gossip
4. Bosses and Co-workers
    - Avoidance
    - Loss of Job
    - Demotion
    - Loss of Pay

While the immediate goal of coercive types of social control is undoubtedly to sanction or punish, there is a great deal of debate as to what the larger implications of social control are—whether for groups as large as society as a whole, or as small as a husband and wife dyad. For scholars, the question becomes "What does social control intend to accomplish for society?"

One widely agreed-upon purpose of social control is that it is intended to create and maintain the **social order** (or social stability and cohesion) by minimizing behavior that is socially disruptive or otherwise defined as bad or wrong—in essence, to reduce or control the level of deviance. For one group of scholars, the **functionalists**, controlling deviance is unquestionably good and beneficial for society, because it identifies norms and their relative importance, thereby creating and maintaining cultural norms or rules, as well as the larger social order. However, for **conflict** scholars, social control is inherently unfair, as it will tend to reflect the norms of powerful groups and may actively criminalize (or "deviantize") the norms of weaker groups, and, is most likely to be directed toward weaker groups. In such a portrayal, formal social control becomes a tool that elites manipulate to protect their interests and to oppress threatening groups and their members. Social control may thus serve to maintain the status quo (i.e., the way things are). These two positions are explored below.

The functionalist position on social control is closely tied to the writing of French sociologist Emile Durkheim (1982) who famously wrote, "Crime is normal, because a society without it is utterly impossible." Thus, Durkheim was arguing that crime actually produces benefits for society—that is, it is "functional." For Durkheim, certain acts are defined as crimes because they offend the "collective conscience" of a society and, therefore are condemned. Norms deemed important by a society are cherished because they define the content of the society's culture: what the society stands for, what it means to be a social member, what members can expect from each other in social interactions, and what responses they can expect from society as a whole. Violations of these norms (crimes) and society's response in the form of social control serve as a reminder of the content of specific norms and their importance. Thus, deviance and social control identify cultural content in particular, which also functions to create and maintain social boundaries and social identity—crucial aspects of the social order.

For functionalists, deviance and social control operate in two important ways on the social order. First, by classifying behaviors as deviant and setting boundaries on behavior, society fosters solidarity (a sense of "we-ness" or togetherness) among its members by communicating notions of right and wrong and establishing social expectations and obligations. Second, identifying individuals who have violated society's standards of right and wrong and labeling them as deviant strengthens the social solidarity among non-deviant members of society by validating the will of the collective conscience. Such understandings disintegrate when people who violate standards of right and wrong are not punished because this throws the collective conscience into disarray, weakens social solidarity, and attenuates social boundaries. Steven Pfohl (1994) identifies four main "functions" of crime, according to Durkheim (Figure 3). However, while Durkheim and other functionalists seem to argue that it is deviance per se that has functional qualities, the social control response that is prompted by deviance is in many cases that behavior that actually serves to produce beneficial outcome for society. Yet, Durkheim also argued that too much crime could be pathological for society, as it could overwhelm social control resources and produce social chaos and anomie. Finally, while this discussion has been directed at society as a whole, these same processes should hold (with perhaps some variation) for smaller groups, such as subcultures within a society, workgroups, friendship groups, even families and dyads.

Figure 4.3   The Functions of Deviance and Social Control

The Functions of Deviance and Social Control

Boundary-Setting Function: the performance of deviance and the social control response identify limits of right and wrong, or the moral boundaries of culture.

Group Solidarity Function: social control indicates the moral revulsion felt by society in response to deviance and may actually draw the society closer together by reinforcing cultural norms and beliefs.

Innovation Function: societies can stagnate if deviance is absent or too rare because deviance spurs social change in the form of new ideas, technologies, and other "innovations."

Tension-Reduction Function: the social control of deviants may be one way that society reduces social tension; as may certain events, such as festivals and holidays, such as Mardi Gras, Oktoberfest, and Homecoming where social members are permitted to engage in certain acts, such as heavy drinking, that are normally considered deviant.

An interesting application of some of Durkheim's ideas about deviance and social control comes from Kai Erikson's (1966) *Wayward Puritans*, a historical analysis of puritan colonial society in the 1600s. In this analysis, Erikson not only asserts that examples of deviance and social control help establish normative boundaries, but that each society will, of necessity, produce a certain *volume* of deviance and social control. Societies will ensure a certain volume of deviance not only through the making of norms and laws, but also through fluctuation in their enforcement. Because such enforcement is dependent on social control resources, the goal of social control, for Erikson, is to stabilize deviance, so that its functions can be manifested. Thus, if deviance increases in a society, social control will focus its effort on the most serious violations and ignore some of the less serious ones. Likewise, if deviance decreases, social control will, of necessity, begin to rigorously enforce all norms—and may even create new norms to create sufficient levels of deviance. To demonstrate his ideas, Erikson wrote that Puritan society, being small and homogeneous with low levels of deviance, developed a need to increase deviance so that the functions of deviance and social control could be performed. Puritan society accomplished this by either narrowing the definitions of deviance or by labeling more people as deviant. Specifically, during the "antinomian controversy," Puritan society defined certain topics of religious discourse as seditious or deviant; during the "Quaker persecutions," members of the Quaker religion came to be defined as an invading army and were harassed and imprisoned; while at the infamous Salem Witch Trials, the testimony of a clique of teenage girls was sufficient to label dozens of innocents as "witches." In all these cases, increases in social control served Puritan society by drawing it more tightly together and highlighting social boundaries.

While Durkheim, Erikson and other functionalists look for social meaning and purpose in deviance and social control, this perspective is lacking in several respects. First, functionalism assumes a common set of norms or "consensus" in a society—failing to consider the possibility of competing norms and the process by which some group norms (and not others) become applicable to the larger society. Second, functionalism is not concerned with potential differences in enforcement of norms (social control) across different groups, or with the implications that the successful application of the deviant label might have on individuals or groups. Yet perhaps the most blatant shortcoming of functionalists is the failure to examine which groups benefit and which suffer from the creation of particular norms. To say that the deviantization of Jews in Nazi Germany was functional for that society ignores the horrors the Jews suffered in the Holocaust (Pfohl 1994). Thus, the repercussions of creating populations of "outsiders" and scapegoats through deviance definitions and enforcement are ignored in the functionalist tradition (Becker 1966; Szasz 1985).

The reactivist or conflict perspective picks up these threads of thought, and indeed is unique in the study of deviance and social control for viewing the creation of norms and laws as problems or issues to be studied. Like Durkheim, the conflict perspective reaffirms the position that deviance is not an inherent characteristic of certain behaviors, individuals, or groups. Instead of arising from a society wide "collective conscience," however, definitions of deviance are viewed by conflict scholars as being socially constructed through the collective action of individuals and groups (with potentially competing interests) who lobby for public attention and legislative access. To the extent that an attempt to create a new definition of deviance is successful, then the norms espoused by the prevailing group are more likely to be accepted by the larger society and even become written into law.

The key determinant of success of these efforts is the relative amounts of "power" those involved can mobilize. Power may come from many sources, including personal charisma, connections or relationships with important others, as well as religion and ascribed characteristics such as race/ethnicity, gender, and sexual orientation. However, for the conflict tradition, the most important source of power is economic—specifically income, wealth, and occupation. Notably, in the United States these sources of power intersect with race/ethnicity and gender such that those with the most economic power tend to be White males. Thus, as a group, rich White males have the most power and, as a result, are the most successful at having their norms become part of law and culture.

This is not to say that relatively powerless groups can never achieve successes in the effort to influence definitions of deviance. Prominent examples come from the women's and civil rights movements that expanded legal rights for women and racial/ethnic minorities, as well as altering cultural norms surrounding these groups. The more modern "gay rights" movement is a similar effort. In addition, the prohibition of alcohol during the first half of the twentieth century resulted largely from the efforts of relatively powerless groups—namely the rurally based Women's Christian Temperance Movement. Furthermore, the mere existence of laws against white-collar crimes, presumably more likely to be directed against those with more economic power, attests that the power of rich White males is not absolute. Yet, according to the conflict perspective, such examples are uncommon when compared to social norms and laws as a whole.

The conflict tradition derives its name from the view it holds regarding the creation and enforcement of norms and laws. In large, heterogeneous societies such as the United States and many other industrial nations, normative consensus may be rare. Instead, **conflict** among groups regarding norms will be common. While society can accommodate some normative variation across different groups and subcultures, the law cannot accommodate competing norms. Therefore, a society that contains cultural variation will necessarily codify some norms that run against the norms and beliefs of some groups. Different groups advocating different norms will thus compete within a society for the right to have their views reflected in laws. These assertions suggest a process of normative conflict among social groups in the process of creating laws. The logical outcome of such conflict is that norms reflecting the morals and interests of the most powerful groups are most likely to receive the protection of law—and, again, rich White males are predicted to benefit most from the outcomes of these conflict processes.

The implications of normative conflict for deviance and social control are many. First, by definition, new norms and laws create new deviants and criminals. People not otherwise involved in crime or deviance may have their status altered by these new definitions. In becoming deviants and criminals, these individuals are marginalized and placed in jeopardy by the threat of social control. If many of these newly created deviants belong to specific groups, then these groups become marginalized, and such group membership may even become a deviant status in itself. Perhaps the best examples of this process concern the Jim Crow south and Nazi Germany. As the Nazis rose to power in pre-World War II Germany, the already marginalized Jews became an even more deviant status. By law, Jews now had to wear symbols on their clothing indicating their Jewish status, could only live in certain places, hold certain jobs, and eventually were subjected to Hitler's attempted "final solution:" **genocide**. Here, the politically powerful Nazis socially constructed "Jew" as a deviant status, and subjected them to the most awful manifestation of social control imaginable. A similar process occurred in the United States south following the Civil War and reconstruction. The freed slaves, viewed by Southern Whites as highly threatening to their power and status, became the focus of Jim Crow laws, which placed severe restrictions on the most basic civil rights of African-Americans, including the right to vote and have a fair and impartial trial. Social norms associated with this era led to thousands of lynchings of Blacks by White mobs for infractions as minor as not stepping off the sidewalk when a White person passed by or, in the well documented case of Emmitt Till, for whistling at a White woman.

Such ugliness is in the past you might think, or at least things like these could not happen in the modern United States. Well, sociologist Michael Tonry would disagree with you. Writing about the "War on Drugs," Tonry (1994) notes that African-Americans increasingly comprised the rapidly growing population of incarcerated drug offenders in spite of voluminous research, which shows that Black-White differences in drug offending, are negligible. Furthermore, drugs associated with Whites, such as powdered cocaine, receive much less severe sanctions than drugs associated with African-Americans, such as crack cocaine. In fact, according to federal law, the penalty for possessing 100 grams of powdered cocaine is equal to the penalty for 1 gram of crack cocaine. The so-called "100:1 rule" and the other findings Tonry presents are strong evidence that certain drug laws, and even the "War on Drugs" as a whole, targets certain racial groups, much as the conflict perspective on deviance and social control suggests.

According to the conflict approach, if threats to dominant groups' interests arise (as in the 1960s counterculture movements), or when certain segments of the populace become problematic for the larger society, as when poverty increases, social control will mobilize to quash these threats by defining behaviors specific to these problematic groups as criminal (Spitzer 1975). The segments of the population that disrupt the forces of production or which question the ideology, arrangements, and operations of capitalist economies are most likely to be seen as problematic in nations like the United States. (Quinney 1970).

While provocative and thought-provoking, the conflict tradition views all laws as evolving from conflict processes, and fails to consider that certain laws (i.e., mala in se offenses) may result from a real (not false) consensus across groups. Conflict scholars also fail to consider that all groups may benefit from the creation and enforcement of certain laws. Additionally, conflict theory cannot account for why certain behaviors more specific to the wealthier and more powerful classes (e.g., corporate crime) have become criminalized, though it can provide an explanation for its level of enforcement and why its penalties are relatively weak.

What can we make of the functionalist and conflict perspectives? In spite of their contradictions and shortcomings, both views make some sense and have contributed to our understandings of the relationships between deviance and social control, as well as between culture, social structure, and social order. It is to these issues that we next turn.

CONNECTING DEVIANCE AND SOCIAL CONTROL TO CULTURE, SOCIAL STRUCTURE, AND SOCIAL ORDER

After having explored the ideas of deviance and social control in some depth, you might reconsider the opening statement of this chapter—that all societies will have examples of deviant behavior and that they will respond to deviance with social control. According to functionalism, the social processes surrounding deviance and social control are beneficial to society. Deviance and social control serve to define the content of culture through their "boundary-setting" function. Setting boundaries and fostering social solidarity, in combination, are fundamental for the maintenance of the social order. Thus, deviance and social control are necessary for society to exist and endure.

However, functionalists also maintain that, depending on the characteristics of a given society, definitions of deviance will take on different dimensions. For very large, diverse, modern societies such as the United States, deviance definitions are much more permissive than in small homogeneous groups like the Puritans discussed by Kai Erikson. In fact, according to Durkheim's "community of saints" parable, deviance will be present even within a small group of very honest, gentle, caring persons, such as a society of saints, because such a society could not exist without the social functions performed by deviance and social control. Granted, acts of force and fraud might be almost entirely absent in such a society. Therefore, other norms, perhaps pertaining to food, sex, and religious worship, will have to emerge that will produce a requisite amount of deviance so that social control can be mobilized often enough to create the social solidarity this (or any other) society will need to exist. Again, in this portrayal, deviance and social control serve to help define culture and are seen as beneficial to the social order.

In contrast, the conflict tradition views the relationship between the social order and deviance and social control as problematic and rife with unfairness. For conflict thinkers, the labeling of behavior, individuals, and groups as deviant serves a beneficial function—but only for certain social groups, namely rich White males. Cultural content including laws, therefore, primarily represent the views of groups that are at the top of structural hierarchies. By having *their* norms written into law, such powerful groups benefit from conflict processes in that they result in a social order that suits their ideas and interests. More insidiously, since the outcome of conflict processes also produces a caste of "outsiders" whose behavior has become deviant or criminal,

66

dominant classes also ensure the production of deviance—necessary fodder for the maintenance of this social order. Thus, while the social order may be maintained through deviance and social control, as functionalists argue, for conflict thinkers this situation is inherently unfair as powerful groups benefit, and weaker groups suffer, such as women, the poor and racial/ethnic minorities.

Yet, a number of problems have been identified with both the functionalist and conflict approaches. A middle ground position is suggested by the *pluralistic-conflict* approach (Akers 1994). This position argues that both the functionalist and conflict perspectives, while making some valid points, are overstated. Especially for large, heterogeneous societies like the United States, with its many racial/ethnic groups (many of which are growing in size and influence) and large immigrant population, the kind of **"collective conscience"** discussed by Durkheim, where all norms are largely agreed upon, is unrealistic. Similarly, to portray society as fractured and ridden with a vast array of competing views over all norms is also untenable. One way to resolve the tension between conflict and functionalist theories, and to contend with their respective problems, is to consider where and when each point of view is strong or weak. In support of functionalism, much public opinion research shows that mala en se crimes, such as murder, theft, assault, embezzlement, and insider stock trading are almost unanimously seen as very wrong or deviant by members of society. Such laws may, therefore, reflect a core collective conscience in United States society. Yet, this collective conscience may dissolve when mala prohibita laws are considered. It may be here that norms no longer reflect social interests as a whole, but rather the interests of certain groups, that the conflict perspective becomes more useful.

The pluralistic-conflict approach argues that a so-called power elite, if it exists, is not able to enforce its will at all times and in all places. Rather, in United States society, multiple power centers exist—some based on economics, others based on morality, religion, politics, and still others based on ad-hoc social movements, such as **"Megan's Law"** which requires that neighbors be made aware of sex offenders living in their midst. Pluralistic-conflict approaches assert that groups with the most power and resources are most likely to emerge as victorious whenever their norms conflict with those of other groups. While common sense would argue that economic power, being most relevant in the United States, might win most social battles, according to the pluralistic-conflict perspective, it will not win them all.

4 | Deviance and Social Control: Behaving Well and Not So Well.
by Theodore R. Curry, Ph.D.

ဢ ဢ ဢ ဢ

DEFINITIONS

Anomie.   A condition characterized by the absence or confusion of social norms or values in a society or group. According to Martindale, anomie is the "strict counterpart of the idea of social solidarity. Just as social solidarity is a state of collective ideological integration, anomie is a state of confusion, insecurity, 'normlessness'. The collective representations are in a state of decay." – From Don Martindale, *The Nature and Types of Sociological Theory* (Boston, MA: Houghton Mifflin Co., 1960).

Collective Conscience.   Durkheim's term for the moral consensus of the community that is violated by deviant acts.

Conflict Theory.   A theoretical perspective that focuses on the struggle among different social groups over scarce rewards.

Conflict.   Usually refers to the state of tension that exists between the powerful and powerless.

Criminal Behavior. Behavior which violates the law.

Deviance.   Behavior that violates any social norm.

Deviant Behavior. Behavior that violates any social norm.

Deviants. Those who violate social mores.

Folkways.   The set of manners and customary acts that characterize everyday life in a social system.

Formal Social Control Agents. Representatives of the state or government, such as police, prosecutors, judges, and members of the correctional system, such as probation officers, prison wardens and correctional officers.

Formal Social Control. Includes things such as laws and codes that a society abides by. It includes efforts by the police, courts, and correctional institutions to produce social conformity of the law.

Functionalism. Approach or orientation of studying social and cultural phenomena. It holds that society is essentially a set of interrelated parts, e.g., institutions, beliefs, values, customs, norms, etc., and that each of these parts has a particular purpose, i.e., that each of these parts functions in a particular way. It is held that no part, its existence, or operation, can be understood in isolation from the whole. Society is seen, from this position, as analogous to the human body or any other living organism. Each of the "parts" of society are seen as operating much like organs of the body. As in the body, it is held that if one part of society changes it affects the other parts and how they operate or function, and it also affects how the total system performs as it may also affect the continued existence of the total society (organism).

Genocide. The systematic attempt to kill all occupants of a particular status, especially ethnic, religious, racial, or national.

Informal Social Control Agents. Can be (and are) anybody and everybody, and such behavior may be performed singly or in groups.

Informal Social Control. Is achieved through social sanctions rather than laws. This implied social control usually has more control over individual minds because they become ingrained in their personality.

Labeling. The process by which powerful actors apply positive or negative labels to others.

Mores. The set of deeply held cultural ideas about how people ought to appear or behave.

Norms. A rule that attaches sanctions to the behavior or appearance of status occupants.

Pluralistic-Conflict. Conflict between a number of relatively equal groups.

Social Control. The manner in which behavior is regulated in society. The means and processes by which a group secures its members' conformity to its expectations—to its values, its ideology, its norms, and to the appropriate roles that are attached to the various status positions in the group.

Social Order. Refers to social mechanisms that regulate individual and group behavior, in terms of greater sanctions and rewards. It may also designate the processes of informal social control such as custom and formal social control such as law of deviant behavior which falls beyond the bounds set by social norms.

Taboos. A strong social prohibition (or ban) relating to any area of human activity or social custom declared as sacred and forbidden; breaking of the taboo is usually considered objectionable or abhorrent by society.

REFERENCES

Akers, Ronald L. 1994. *Criminological Theories: Introduction and Evaluation.* Los Angeles, CA: Roxbury.

Becker, Howard S. 1963. *Outsiders.* New York: Glencoe.

Durkheim, Emile. 1951. *Suicide.* New York: Free Press.

Durkheim, Emile. 1982. *Rules of the Sociological Method.* New York: Free Press.

Durkheim, Emile. 1984. *Division of Labor in Society.* New York: Free Press.

Erikson, Kai T. 1966. *Wayward Puritans.* New York: John Wiley and Sons.

Gottfredson, Michael R. and Travis Hirschi. 1990. *A General Theory of Crime.* Stanford, CA: Stanford.

Pfohl, Stephen. 1994. *Images of Deviance and Social Control.* 2nd ed. New York: McGraw-Hill.

Quinney, Richard. 1970. *The Social Reality of Crime.* Boston, MA: Little, Brown.

Spitzer, Steven. 1975. "Toward A Marxian Theory of Deviance." *Social Problems* 22:638-651.

Szasz, Thomas. 1985. *Ceremonial Chemistry: The Ritual Persecution of Drugs, Addicts, and Pushers.* Rev. ed. Holmes Beach, FL: Learning Publications, Inc.

Tittle, Charles R. 1995. *Control Balance: Toward A General Theory of Deviance.* Boulder, CO: Westview.

Tonry, Michael. 1994. "Racial Politics, Racial Disparities, and the War on Crime." *Crime and Delinquency* 40:363-385.

5 | Basic Concepts of Sociology: What and How We Think.
by Lawrence J. Mencotti, Ph.D.

Two of the most basic sociological concepts, ones that you will run across time and again, are status and role. Both are designations of social position and both have been used in a variety of ways.

Status refers to your position within a group/society. Examples of status include parent or child in a family setting; student or professor in a college setting; or more fundamentally: male or female [this last example indicates that gender is a status]. Therefore, a status is a social designation of people. Many people can and do occupy the same status: all of us at one time were children and the rule is for people to have many statuses [the man who is a husband, father, brother, police officer, catholic, Big Brother volunteer, Democrat, etc.]. Each of the statuses is sufficiently important and different to merit its own label. Note that sociologists did not make up these status labels; society did.

A status may be either **ascribed** or **achieved**. The former means you are slotted into a status and you have no control over the assignment whereas the latter refers to your position that is due to your own efforts. One prime example of an ascribed position is your sex: male or female. An example of an achieved position is that of college graduate. An example that could be both would be member of the middle class. What? Well, yes under many circumstances that is a true statement. One could be born middle class [ascribed] and be raised middle class and graduate from college and eventually pursue a middle class career [these latter two are illustrative of achieved status.] As we will see later in the text, social mobility is intimately connected with status.

Upon reflection we realize that at birth we are assigned [ascribed] all sorts of statuses: gender, race, ethnicity, religion, nationality, and the social class of our parents. Hardly any of us try to change/pass as anther gender or race. Few of us contemplate changing nationality. Many will change religions or try to minimize their ethnicity. A great many of us try and "better" ourselves by moving up the social class ladder. If we can change our status and do so then the new status is an achieved one; if not, then it remains an ascribed status. One of the hallmarks of open mobile societies is that there is relatively speaking a good deal of potential to change our ascribed statuses into achieved ones. However, with most societies throughout the history of the world the operative acronym is WYAIWYS [what you're assigned is what you stay].

Now, it takes no great deal of imagination to realize that your particular cluster of statuses goes a long way in describing your public identity to people and thus your own self-concept as well. As obvious as that may be it carries with it an important implication. Statuses are ranked and the ranking process occurs in two ways. First, depending on who is doing the ranking some statuses are more valued/seen to be more important than are others. While nearly everyone ranks surgeons higher than assembly-line workers we might get a lot more heat generated if our concern was ranking one gender over another or ranking some religions as better than others.

The other ranking that occurs is how well [or how poorly] a person is in meeting the standards associated with a particular status. It is this second that we will take up with the concept of to role.

The Power of Status. Several years ago, Karen Dion conducted an ingenious experiment. She decided to test empirically how we evaluate behavior: by the content of the act or by the traits of the person. Note that in a somewhat simplistic fashion we could say that the content of the act roughly equates into role while the traits of the person is just as roughly a proxy for status. This is what she did. Her population was 243 female undergraduate, senior year, education majors. So right away, she is controlling for three variables of her subjects: gender, major field, and year in college. She also, and this is very important, controlled for behavior by having each of her subjects evaluate children for what the kids allegedly did: detailed accounts of misbehavior by seven-year-olds. Attached to half the reports was a picture of a very pretty/handsome child while the other half came with pictures of children who were....well, without putting too fine a point on it: homely. In all of the instances, the judgments were considerably less severe for the good-looking kids. The misbehavior that Dion alleged was throwing sharp rocks at a sleeping dog until the dog's leg bled. The dog yelped in pain and limped away. The comments of one very sweet little girl was typical: "She appears to be a perfectly charming little girl, well mannered and basically unselfish. She plays well with everyone, but, like everyone, a bad day may occur....Her cruelty need not be taken too seriously." Note all of that character assessment from the picture of a pretty little child who supposed was bouncing rocks off of a poor canine! Here is a typical comment when the "perpetrator" was not so good looking, "I think this child would be quite bratty and would be a problem to teachers. She would probably try to pick a fight with other children...She would be a brat at home. All in all, she would be a real problem." Again, note the character assessment from a simple statement of behavior and a picture! Would you want to be a not so attractive student in that future teacher's classroom? In any case, score one for the power of status. Dion's finding showed pretty conclusively that this population of subjects did not evaluate people based upon the objective content of their actions but by their appearance.

Now you may dissent by saying that beauty is not a status trait as such but something that we can alter if we choose. However, that begs the question of one's position in an "attractiveness hierarchy;" i.e. one's status. Whether we are ranked high or low we *are* ranked and we are ranked in no small part by others' evaluations of us. Conventional ideas of beauty are not so much from within as much as they are evaluations of us by others.

Another instance of classic research showing the power of status in our lives is the one by David Rosenhan.   In this study, Rosenhan convinced seven people in addition to himself to participate in an experiment.   The subjects included one housewife and all of the rest were professional types. There were three women and five men. They all presented themselves for admission to a mental health facility. They all gave phony names, occupations, and symptoms. Each of these "pseudo patients" reported hearing voices that were the same gender as the patient. The voices were sometimes unclear but often enough the patients "heard" the voices say single words such as "empty," "hollow," and "thud."   Supposedly, these words referred to painful concerns regarding the meaninglessness of the pseudopatients' lives. They were all diagnosed as psychotic [severe mental disorder] with seven of them defined as schizophrenic and the remaining one depressive.

Now here is where it gets really interesting. Once admitted to the mental facility each of the patients acted normally at all times. Normal, that is, in terms of the real outside world. They were always friendly and cooperative. The length of the stay varied from 7 to 52 days with an average stay of 19 days. All were discharged as psychotics in remission. No staff member, that is, no psychiatrist, no nurse, and no ward attendant ever caught on in any of the 8 instances. However, about 30 percent of all of the fellow patients did realize that the pseudopatients were, in fact, fake patients. The analogy that springs to mind here is that it takes a thief to spot a thief.

In any case, some psychiatric professionals at a famous west coast research and training hospital heard of Rosenhan's experiment and challenged him to try to pull a fast one on them. So Rosenhan devised a bet with them. He told them over the three months one or more pseudopatients would gain admittance to their hospital and they had to find out how many and who. Over the next 90 days, 193 patients were admitted. Of those, 23 were suspected by at least one psychiatrist as being fake. In reality, there were no fake patients!

Let us take a breath here and try to analyze what happened. In the main experiment, the professionals were gullible—they knew no reason why anyone "in their right mind" would fake their way into a mental facility so they were susceptible to a misdiagnosis: seeing illness when there "really" was none [or what statisticians would call a Type II error—a false positive. In this case, the psychiatrists saw sickness when the pseudopatients were really normal.]. In the subexperiment, all of the patients admitted were legitimate though the suggestible staff, on the alert for fake patients, saw illegitimacy [in a little more than 10 percent of the cases] when there really was none. This was another kind of misdiagnosis by the experts [what is known as a Type I error: in this case, seeing a sick person as healthy; a.k.a. a false negative].

At this point, you may be amazed but you might also be thinking: is this not more about role than status? Well, in Rosenhan's interpretation once the pseudopatients were assigned a status: psychotic, then all subsequent behavior was interpreted in terms of that status. For example, "a nurse unbuttoned her blouse and adjusted her brassiere in the presence of an entire ward of viewing men." Was this a sexual act? No, it was not sexual at all because the ward full of men were seen as non-sexualized patients; such was their status that sex was not even to be considered.

The Rosenhan research has been studied, argued, and debated ever since it was published. One thing to remember though is that it is an excellent case study as to how behavior [describing one's false symptoms] indicates faulty role performance [normal people do not act this way] and that in turn leads to being assigned a status [psychotic]. Once labeled with that status then subsequent behavior is in turn defined in terms of that status: when the patients were discharged, they were discharged as psychotics "in remission."

Role. As important and [at times] as fascinating as it is status is basically a static concept. The behavioral dimension to it is usually implied. Role can be and has been defined in many ways but for our purposes let us just simply say that role is the dynamic, behavioral dimension to a status. Refer back to the paired statuses on an earlier page: parent-child, student-professor, and female-male. Each one has a role attached to it: an expectation by the status holder and by others as to how the status should be enacted. What is appropriate behavior for the student is not so for the professor; the same with the parent and the child and, also for that of male and female though in this latter pairing there is much more overlap than there was 50 years ago when being a male and being a female were much more distinctly separate.

In an important sense, we can say that given one's status the crucial question is how is the status played out? In other words, you can play the role associated with a status either well or poorly.   If the status-role is important enough then society ensures compliance with its expectations by attempting to guide your behavior or what we call social control.

Informal v. Formal Social Control. Looked at somewhat differently, social control refers to how a group maintains discipline and focus among its members. If the group is small and attachments to other group members are important [as they usually are] then deviance from norms [group rules that prescribe or proscribe behavior] will be infrequent and not very serious. If deviance does occur that is serious enough and/or sufficiently chronic then informal techniques of social control including gossip, criticism, ridicule, and ostracism will be invoked to deal with the offender. So called primitive societies are analogous to neighborhood communities which are not unlike friendship groups since all three invoke informal techniques of social control to deal with deviance: real, potential, or imagined.

However, as the scale of association increases then things get more complex. When groupings become large and less personal deviance begins to evolve into many forms and the techniques to deal with deviance evolve commensurately. For example, with the emergence of separate institution of religion sin makes its appearance. Sin is a moral transgression against God's will and as such, it is the major task of religion to regulate sin. Of course, different religions can have different notions of what constitutes sin which should tip us that sin has a healthy dollop of human creation to it.

In a sense crimes are secular sins: transgressions against the law which represents the civil dimension of society. If a religion can threaten sinners with the potential of eternal damnation fittingly, the law threatens criminals with physical punishments in this world including imprisonment or even execution.

If both sin and crime are serious offenses that merit severe punishment then illness and error represent "softer," more "enlightened" alternatives. Both illness and error represent those acts or states of being where the offender has neither broken a law nor committed a sin but nevertheless is found to be "lacking." The deviant either is not operating at full capacity [illness] or violates everyday normative expectations by making a mistake [error]. An illustration of how both can occur together is the student who does poorly on an assignment and then gives as an excuse that the sub par performance was due to being sick. The remedy [assuming there is one] for this student is that next time, when presumably the illness has passed, the assignment will be of a much higher quality. Note that the student can only invoke the illness excuse so many times before they are told to either "get better or get out." Error works in much the same way: there is some initial leeway allowed in getting the student up to speed but if after reasonable instruction, the errors continue the student will not be allowed to continue. Likewise, both illness and error in the workplace follow similar patterns. Note: whether it is school or career, illness and error do not elicit direct punishment. Rather, they bring about indirect punishment: failure to measure up and contribute satisfactorily brings about exclusion via dismissal from either the school or the workplace.

What about failing to fulfill normative expectations in non-formal groupings such as family and friendship circles? Well, certainly in our society parental abuse and neglect are often seen in terms of crime and sin. However, there are other, much more frequent, examples of missing the mark. Parents who have good intentions but still elicit more estrangement than love from their children, for example. Or people who try as they may to have friendships still ending up as social loners. Often what these hapless parents and unrequited friends turn to are variations on the self-help theme: they resort to books, tapes, courses, workshops, group therapy sessions and the like to improve their interpersonal skills and minimize the error of their ways. It is as if with enough persistence and the right self-help technique you too can attain, if not eternal happiness, then at least temporal satisfaction. Similar concerns hold true for the chronically ill.

It is no great secret that our society spends billions on preventatives and remedies for everything from the most serious diseases and afflictions to those of the most mundane. From surgery and prescription drugs to herbal supplements and aerobics; from anti-depressants to meditation to psychiatric ministrations our society is one seemingly devoted to "getting better" as well as getting ahead. However, what if all else fails and the errors continue and illness does not dissipate? Well, there is always shopping: consumption as solace; buying stuff from bric-a-brac to trans-fats as temporary diversions from aimless, empty, unproductive and dispirited lives.

One hugely popular approach to error and illness [and often crime and sin as well] not to mention just general malaise is therapy. This rests on the assumption that personal problems if not caused by psychic disorder are experienced as psychic distress. From this approach what is begged is: what constitutes mental illness?

Strictly speaking, there is no such thing as either mental illness or mental health as the mind is not an organ to be diseased as a brain can be. Leaving aside the issue that much of what is called "mental" illness can be located as neurological pathology, we can say that mental illness is more a metaphor than a medical condition. Be that as it may, it is still a big business so let us at least attempt a sociological definition of it.

1. Mental illness is behavior that is problematic. That is, **behavior** that violates normative expectations and is unsettling to self and/or others. It may also violate legal codes—the search for psychopathology of murderers [especially multiple murderers excepting wartime excepting if the victims are innocent civilians. Note all of the exceptions.]. The search for pathology has also joined in earnest looking for psychiatric reasons as to why men rape, parents abuse their kids, and why people abuse their domestic partners. One function of interpreting these behaviors as due to psychological problems is to deflect attention away from the rest of us as potential perpetrators. If we can isolate psychological reasons why some "other" people do these horrible acts then we do not have to worry that we "regular, normal" folk would ever do such nasty things. Another major function of psychologizing these phenomena is that it helps keep psychiatrists, clinical psychologists, and counselors employed.

2. The person in question can give no adequate account for his/her **action.** That is, the person can give no adequate excuse or justification for why they did what they did.

3. The person is unable or perhaps even unwilling to **neutralize** a diagnosis of mental illness and what therapy is to occur. Note that the more serious the behavior the greater the interpretation of "negative essence" of the person by people in authority. This idea of negative essence is important because to the social control agents the interpretation is that the person is deeply flawed and something must be done, preferably with the person's cooperation: giving oneself up [and over] to therapy.

Please note the boldfaced terms in the above definition—behavior, action, neutralize. They all convey a dynamic, behavioral element. More than this, the role-playing is highly questionable and the role-player's status is tainted and possibly stigmatized. So, the behavior has been questioned; it is troublesome; and it calls for correction [through therapy]. This is an excellent example of how status and role merge: the behavior leads to the label [mental] patient and the label/status then becomes a consideration for interpreting future behavior.

The psychotherapeutic ethos certainly is a popular one. However, troubling questions aside as to why it can persist, grow, and mutate into a myriad of diagnostic categories and therapies *du jour* while still being empirically questionable in its effectiveness we must look elsewhere for a further clue to its ongoing popularity. It is arguable that the psychotherapeutic ethos [and industry] is as popular as it is because it fits so well with American traditions and values as can be seen by viewing it as a secular re-statement of the myth of original sin. Traditional Christianity teaches that we are born with sin but through grace and faith we can attain salvation. With the therapeutic perspective one is born into pathology [according to Freud] or one can acquire it later [e.g., posttraumatic stress disorder] or perhaps one is simply biologically predisposed toward it [schizophrenia or bi-polar disorder]. Through therapeutic insight [and increasingly a drug regimen] insight can be gained into one's problems and recovery is possible. Psychological rehabilitation is a secular form of rebirth, a diluted version of salvation. Put into a rough analogy: from the Christian standpoint: sin [ascribed or achieved] → penance/faith → grace → salvation and in parallel fashion: psychiatric condition → therapy → insight → secular rebirth with a new and improved self/self-concept/whatever. Just as Christians can be saved a comparable secular vision compatible with American optimism is detectable in the therapeutic perspective: have hope, seek help, work hard, become rehabbed, and get back in the American game of life. Do not wallow in your depression; DO something about it.

The Power of the Situation. During a period of over a decade Stanley Milgram researched the issue: Would Americans make good Nazis? In a more formal phrasing, Milgram investigated the issue of obedience to authority.

Milgram investigated subjects in a pseudo-laboratory setting. Each of the subjects [in the role of a teacher] sat at an imposing console filled with switches and labels signifying different levels of voltage. Each switch, when engaged, supposedly would send an electric shock to a "learner" [really an actor] who was strapped into a chair in another room. When the learner made "mistakes" the teacher/subjects were supposed to punish them into learning by shocking them. Not only that, but also as more mistakes were made the shocks were to increase. The learners were also to communicate that they were in severe pain. [In fact, some of them ahead of time had communicated to the teacher that they suffered from a heart condition.] If the teachers were reluctant to continue, one of the experimenters in charge would advise the teacher "you must go on." In sum, though a great many subjects [males and females] clearly were troubled by what they were doing they nevertheless continued to follow orders and deliver what could have been in real life lethal punishments.

One very interesting fact about the Milgram experiment is that the proportion of everyday Americans that delivered the maximum punishment [giving a whole new meaning to "going all the way"] was far in excess of the estimates given before the experiment by psychiatrists. Another consideration is that when Milgram varied the experimental conditions the closer the learner sat to teacher the lesser the punishments administered. Evidently impersonal, especially long-distance, death is easier to administer than face-to-face murder.

One moral that many have drawn from the Milgram experiments is not to be caught in the wrong situation. Obviously, in the revelations about American guards' behavior at Iraq's Abu Ghraib prison Milgram's lessons are as relevant as ever: That perhaps you cannot rely on your good character to prevent you from doing nasty things to other human beings.

The Power of Roles. It is one thing to experimentally simulate a situation that produces pseudo-violence but it is another to structure an experiment in which college students performed roles that overwhelmed [temporarily] their entire character. Zimbardo did exactly that with his [in-] famous prison experiment. The subjects were all Stanford University undergraduate males who volunteered [for money] to participate. The experiment was scheduled to last for two weeks. Importantly, all of the volunteers were prescreened by taking personality tests and all of the volunteers who did participate scored in the "normal" range. Even more importantly, all of the participants were randomly assigned the role of either guard or prisoner. The students designated as prisoners were "arrested," taken to the Palo Alto police station, and from there transported to the basement of a college building that had been outfitted to function as a jail. They were issued prison garb complete with ID numbers and had already been apprised that certain of their 'civilian' civil liberties had been suspended. The guards were also issued uniforms, nightsticks, and so on and they were instructed to maintain order. The guards worked eight hour shifts while the prisoners were imprisoned around the clock.

Zimbardo suspended the experiment after only six days since he feared severe psychological trauma would ensue if he allowed the experiment to continue. Some of the guards became nasty [corrupted by their power and position] and enjoyed degrading the prisoners for the sheer fun of it. However, none of the "good" guards attempted to have the "bad" guards ease off. Similarly, by the second day several of the prisoners had rebelled but were greeted with fire extinguisher blasts and then put in closets [solitary confinement]. Some of the prisoners petitioned to be "paroled" but when Zimbardo turned down their request they docilely went back to their cells. If they had been thinking of themselves as students caught in a nightmarish experiment that they wanted to be rid of they would have told Zimbardo what to do with his money and experiment and demanded to be let go. They did not because after only a few days they saw themselves as prisoners.

When we review the extended examples we have introduced in this essay we do not gaze upon a nice, reassuring picture. We saw with Dion that rather than evaluating others on merit we too often let superficialities such as physical attractiveness taint our judgment. Rosenhan's research cautions us that being saddled with the "wrong" status can prove to be quite dehumanizing. Milgram asks us to reflect upon how certain situations can lead good people to do bad things.

Finally, Zimbardo asks us to consider how normal people playing difficult roles can act less than admirably.

Reflecting on the research of Dion, Rosenhan, Milgram, and Zimbardo we do not see confirmation of the American myths of the power of individual effort, the primacy of individual character, and that the good and meritorious eventually triumph. Rather we see the power that situations and roles have over normal everyday citizens. We also see the power of groups in shaping individuals, beliefs, and behaviors.

Groups. If culture is the "social stuff" which makes us human, then group membership in large part determines what particular stuff we will believe. Culture cannot exist without human beings to create it, destroy it, recreate it, neglect it, borrow it, transform it, and discard it. However, it is ultimately people acting in group settings that are these agents of culture. Take away our group affiliations and the human enterprise is impossible. Groups teach their members [the sociological term is socialization] how to behave, what to believe, and with whom to interact. Groups are identifiable as clusters of people that are as small as two and, practically speaking, can go well into the thousands. Examples include a family, a best friend, a sports team, a social organization, a work team, a local church, a combat unit, and so forth. Thus, groups are stable clusters of roles and statuses that persist over time even though all original members may have left or died. A really good example of a group in this regard would be a sports team. You can follow a college team for five years and while the uniforms, fieldhouse, and offensive and defense schemes have remained the same all of the original players have left to be replaced by new ones. So to follow a team is to follow a TEAM over time while favored players come and go. Therefore, it is with any stable group: the group persists while the members turn over.

If this is at all true then there should be certain identifiable elements held in common; and there are. At its most basic, a group is a collection of people who are united by social relations. When people are members of a group they share a **common fate**—a "we-feeling" where what happens to one member has a felt impact on other members. This basic distinction between us and them is often termed in-group v. out-group. Further, to use a common college example, a group of people may join a fraternity or sorority and the pledging and hazing to which they are subjected is a trial period or what is often called a **rite de passage** which is necessary to pass successfully for full acceptance as a member. Groups often but not always sport some **emblem**—an article of clothing [a jacket with Greek letters] or a uniform and sometimes a special insignia [armed services], and perhaps a distinctive name [family/secret society], etc.

What follows from this is what we can call a **double standard of morality.** Members of the in-group become the preferred members of interaction. More is expected from them and more is given to them. When in the presence of special in-group activities a heightened sense of emotional wellbeing—**esprit d'corps**—is expected and enhanced. An exaggerated and selective perspective of the superiority of the in-group is cultivated and manifested whenever appropriate [and often when not appropriate]. Out-group members are, in extreme cases, to be shunned and exploited.

An excellent example of this would be fans at a football game. They often sit together in a special student section, dress in school colors, chant encouragement to the team, collectively feel that their team is "special" and thus so are they and regrettably sometimes engage in less than the friendliest behavior with the opposite team's fans. [Comparatively speaking however, in contrast to Europe's soccer hooligans American fans are generally tame.]

Now let us look at the notion of group in a somewhat different way. Imagine a group to which you belong. With you as a member then everything that goes on in that group is from your viewpoint point *intra*-group [intra means among or within]. Ok, now think of another group to which you are not a member but with which members of your group interact act. In this case, the interaction of members of these different groups is termed *inter*-group.

With this basic terminology out of the way we can note that there is a considerable body of empirical evidence pointing to the conclusion that if different groups approximately equal in status interact in cooperative [or at least non-competitive] ways then prejudice by group members will decrease. An example of this would be two college student organizations getting together to cooperate in doing community service projects such as collecting and distributing clothes and toys for poor kids in their college town.

Alternatively, groups of unequal status competing with one another will probably intensify their inter-group hatreds. An example of this might be two groups of workers competing for the same jobs: one group comprised of persons who share the same ethnicity of the dominant culture and the other composed of workers who are recent immigrants who are willing to do the same work for less pay. Labor history gives us innumerable instances of this occurring.

THOUGHT EXPERIMENT

Now let us push our thinking a little bit. We know from examining societies from around the world and in all different time periods that people overwhelmingly prefer to live large portions of their lives in groups from which they derive much satisfaction. You can demonstrate this to yourself as follows: would you prefer to work in a group in which people are hyper-competitive, back-stabbing, boorish selfish creatures or would you prefer to work in a group in which cooperation between members is emphasized; where members "cover" for one another as needed; and where the members are friendly, sincere, and work toward a common and worthy goal? Let us just assume that most of you would prefer the latter work setting. The same preference would hold true for families, neighborhood communities, church-groups and so on.

Keeping this in mind let us put forth some statements [hopefully reasonable ones] and see where they take us.

1. Group members prefer to associate with their "own kind"—those people with whom they feel comfortable because of shared interests, shared background, etc. They **identify with** each other. Sociologists refer to this as an in-group. The world is made up of innumerable examples of in-groups.

2. Whenever possible group members prefer to engage in everyday interactions [including just hanging out] with one another. If you need a concrete example think of high school cliques.

3. One important result of points 1 and 2 is a rather intense "we-feeling" or what sociologists call group solidarity.

4. Out-groups, especially perceived competitors, are seen by in-group members as "others," strangers, even, at times, the enemy. Consequently, the in-group tends

to avoid or at least minimize contact with members of out-groups. If it is necessary to have contact with them then the interaction is limited, superficial, and sometimes even marked by elaborate social rituals.

5. Notice that one important result of the above steps is the reinforcement of stereotypes: our group is good and it pleases me to associate with its members while other groups are bad and I want to avoid them.

6. Another important result of all of this is **ethnocentrism** or what group members believe when they see the world through their in-group eyes. Ethnocentrism also results in disliking those who are different and because they are different they are seen as inferior, less morally worthy, and so to be...guess what? Avoided!

7. Thus, contact between an in-group and an out-group often leads to conflict. So while most of us would see intra-group solidarity to be a worthwhile goal and a good many of us would like to see a significant decline in conflict between groups it is **very likely the case that the pursuit of intra-group solidarity will quite often lead to inter-group conflict** [and the necessity of somehow managing that conflict].

8. On the other hand, conflict with others may drive some people to shelter of other groups for protection. That can be seen in stark terms with inmates who would prefer to "just do their time" and avoid all entanglements but because of racial animosity in our prisons typically gravitate to the group of prisoners that most closely matches their own race. So conversely, **inter-group conflict is quite capable of increasing intra-group solidarity.**

Group Life and Moral Standards. One of the things about group life that sociologists find so fascinating is that morality and moral standards are completely bound up with groups and group life. Sociologists [and their more exotic academic cousins: anthropologists] start from the point of **cultural relativism.** We do not mean by cultural relativism that every belief system and moral standard is as good as any other. Rather, we mean that to truly understand another group's/culture' belief system you must suspend judgment of those beliefs until you understand it from the group's point of view and not yours. Put another way, the ethnocentrism of your background must be put aside so it does not interfere with the understanding of another group's ethnocentric worldview and customs.

With that said it is obvious but sometimes still necessary to point out to students that the morals you were taught growing up have a profound influence on you right as you are reading these words. Even if your college experiences have "liberated" you from what you consider to be the stultifying and stuffy religion of your childhood you are not really free from that religion. After all, to be liberated is to react against the old chains that bound you and so those old chains still serve as something to react against.

Be that as it may, let us look at that stuffy old religion. Let us say that you are reacting against it in no small measure because of its moral absolutism in which it seems that every nook and cranny of your conscience is crammed full of do's and don'ts governing every possible situation. Well, you have perhaps taken an introductory philosophy course and perhaps have also made some new friends from very different backgrounds and in any case you have come to realize that there are many different ways of living life.

So at one end of the spectrum is moral absolutism with its tendency to measure [and judge] everyone and everything in harsh terms with an unbending yardstick. At the opposite end is moral chaos, which is the logical conclusion of cultural relativism [if pushed to extremes], where nothing is any better or worse than anything else is. The former position is inhumane while the latter position is unworkable and leads to chaos.

With that said it may dawn on you that while it is very true that your college experience is a golden opportunity to explore alternative views of the world that nevertheless while exploring the idea of cultural relativism you run a risk. The risk is by trading in your ethnocentrism you face a dilemma of trying to find a more humane less judgmental alternative. Just what is this alternative? We, the authors of these essays, refuse to suggest one to you. Rather we are trying to offer in sociology an alternative way of seeing the world but we are not offering sociology as some substitute morality since sociology is not a system of morals. It is a disciplined way of studying the social world. What you come up with in terms of your moral quest is your business. Good luck with it.

Of course, social life is rarely so simple. There is another aspect of group membership to consider. In-group members are not necessarily pre-ordained from all time to remain in their original in-groups. Some may break with the group for various reasons. They may be discontented with being a group member because of unfair treatment of friends or even themselves. They may resent the stigma attached to them because they could not live up to the group's ideals and think: what is the point of being the resident deviant/scapegoat—and thus they might strike out on their own. Others may leave not because of "wrongdoing" by the group but because of their own discontent with what the group can offer [or not offer] them. Many marriages breakup because of this situation. What about those instances in which the member of an in-group [for whatever reason] becomes unduly fascinated with an out-group. This can lead to an intense ambivalence in which both positive and negative feelings toward the out-group have to be somehow reconciled. One possibility is to attempt to deny the fascination. Another is to engage in efforts to keep the out-group under control [for example, doing missionary work with members of the out-group to get them to convert to the "correct" way of seeing and doing the world]. Still another reconciliation is explore the out-group, tentatively at first, and then more vigorously and then finally perhaps joining it [sometimes only for a while; sometimes permanently]. An example of this would be young people exploring the dimensions of their sexuality experimenting with homosexual behavior with some of them returning to exclusive heterosexuality; some eventually being mostly straight with the occasional gay sex encounter; and still others forging a new homosexual identity and lifestyle.

Functional Analysis. The idea of function in sociology assumes that there exists some social arrangement [a family or a society to take two examples] that exhibits some continuity over time. To analyze the system a functional approach breaks down the arrangement into its identifiable elements: e.g. statuses, processes, etc. The elements are examined to see how they contribute to the system's continuity. To illustrate, in a family one might examine the status of parents and the accompanying parental duties. Fulfilling these expectations of what parents are supposed to do illustrates how there are functions [consequences] for the arrangement that we call a family. To act as a responsible parent helps to ensure the continuation of the family. To act badly [e.g., child abuse or child neglect or other irresponsible personal behavior] then would demonstrate what are called dysfunctions: acts/processes which disrupt rather than maintain.

Therefore, there may exist functions and dysfunctions. However, the matter is a bit more complicated: functions may be either manifest or latent. A function is manifest if the consequences are intended and recognized by the participants involved and it follows that a pure latent function would be a consequence that would be neither recognized nor intended from the viewpoint of the participants. For example, if we look at the functions of formal education we can see that both students and professors want knowledge to be effectively imparted from the latter to the former [though not necessarily for identical reasons]. If such a joyous exchange occurs then the manifest function of the college course experience is evident.

What about some latent functions of higher education, though? Well, one latent function of the ever increasing demands for professional training would be to delay the entrance of practitioners of a particular field from joining the ranks of the employed. That would not be the upfront reason why training seems to last so long but it does operate that way. Thus, a latent function of delaying your employment via additional education would be to maintain the bargaining position [and short-term employability] of those who are already working in your field.

However, once you do actually get a real job—one you have been trained for—you increase the supply of available and willing applicants who are able to do that work. In addition, because you have next to no experience in the particular field you are willing to work for less [often far less] than more established members of your profession. So while possessing the latest training is functional for the newly employed [and for the field as a whole] it also could be argued that it is dysfunctional for the already established who must either rely on their experience and contacts or be willing to subject themselves to periodic retraining.

The upshot of this is that functional analysis is useful but arbitrary and ultimately dependent upon consciousness: awareness of what is going on and for whom. What might be a manifest function of a particular structure from the perspective of a participant could easily also contain a latent dysfunction from the viewpoint of a sociologist studying the situation. In fact, much of the appeal of sociology is making latent functions manifest—a kind of debunking function of practicing sociology itself.

The Leavitt Thesis. For a very recent example of a perceptive and acute analysis of latent functions, we can do no better than to alert the reader to Steven Leavitt's "Freakonomics." Among many challenging essays, one stands out: "Where have all the criminals gone?" To summarize his argument [much too briefly] Leavitt states that in 1989 violent crime was up 80 percent from 1974. By the end of the 1990s, the violent crime rate was back to where it was in the early 1960s. What had happened? Leavitt rounds up the usual suspects of social analysts who have tried to explain this very unexpected [but welcome] phenomenon:

- innovative policing strategies

- increased incarceration [imprisonment]

- changes in the crack and other drug markets

- aging of the population

- tougher gun control laws

- strong economy

- increased number of police

He then proceeds to either dismiss or minimize the impact of each of them [at least to his satisfaction but there are critics who think he is too dismissive]. He then proposes an incredibly controversial alternative: the plummeting violent crime rate was due to the legalization of abortion because of the Supreme Court's decision in 1973 of Roe v. Wade.

Before Roe v. Wade, it was middle class women/daughters who had the illegal abortions since they were the ones who could afford it. After Roe v. Wade legal abortion became much more common among disproportionately young and/or unmarried and/or poor; very often all three. The relevance of this demographic profile is that research has pretty much conclusively demonstrated that growing up in a single parent home doubles the chances that a child will get into legal trouble. The same is true with having a teenaged mom. In fact, the single most powerful predictor is low maternal education. One study concluded that the hypothetical typical child who went unborn in the earliest years of legalized abortion would have been 50 percent more likely than average to live in poverty and would have also been 60 percent more likely than average to grow up with one parent. These two factors are among the very strongest predictors of criminality.

Leavitt's thesis is that "the very factors that drove millions of American women to have an abortion also seemed to predict that their kids, had they been born, [disproportionately] would have led unhappy and possibly criminal lives."

That is a breathtaking example of teasing out latent functions [decreasing crime] from manifest actions [abortions] and thus contributing to the overall balance of the social system. Though the cynic would say that if Leavitt's analysis is correct then abortion is a very cost-effective crime fighting policy few others seem to be pleased with his conclusions. For example those who are pro-choice are very [shall we say] "uncomfortable" with touting abortion as a crime-fighting policy as there are, from their perspective, much more acceptable policies to be championed: anti-poverty programs, educational opportunities, anti-discrimination policies, etc. Many [possibly most] who are pro-life are absolutely apoplectic over Leavitt's analysis for a variety of reasons—several of them based on grave moral concerns.

Leavitt himself states, "One need not oppose abortion on moral or religious grounds to feel shaken by the notion of a private sadness being converted into a public good." In any case, should Roe v. Wade be overturned and if socio-economic conditions remain the same [or worsen] then in about a decade and a half we can expect a sharp spike in crime in general and violent crime in particular. Well, no one ever said that social science was always going to be the most popular kid on the academic block.

ഈ ൦ഃ ഈ ൦ഃ

Achieved Status. A status entered after birth and usually due at least in part to individual behavior.

Ascribed Status. A status assigned at birth.

Common Fate. A "we-feeling" where what happens to one member has a felt impact on other members.

Cultural Relativism. A concept that refers to the fact that the importance of a particular cultural idea varies from one society or subgroup to another.

Double Standard of Morality. Members of the in-group become the preferred members of interaction. More is expected from them and more is given to them. When in the presence of special in-group activities a heightened sense of emotional well-being—**esprit d'corps**—is expected and enhanced.

Ethnocentrism.   Refers to the fact that the dominant group tends to record history from their point of view, paying little attention to the point of view of other groups or their accomplishments. Judging other cultures by your own cultural standards and since, of course, other cultures are different, they are therefore inferior. Ethnocentrism means an inability to appreciate others whose culture may include a different racial group, ethnic group, religion, morality, language, political system, economic system, etc. It also means an inability to see a common humanity and human condition facing all women and men in all cultures and societies beneath the surface variations in social and cultural traditions.

Formal Social Control. Includes things such as laws and codes that a society abides by. It includes efforts by the police, courts, and correctional institutions to produce social conformity of the law.

Functional Analysis. A functional analysis focuses on the positive benefits to society which accrue from the normal operation of social institutions.

Groups. A number of people who regularly interact with each other and share similar values, norms, and expectations.

Informal Social Control. Is achieved through social sanctions rather than laws. This implied social control usually has more control over individual minds because they become ingrained in their personality.

Inter-Group Conflict. An overt expression of tensions between the goals or concerns of one party and those of another.

Intra-Group Solidarity. Members of groups tend to share the same values and beliefs.

Role. A role is the expected behavior associated with a particular status position—What the individual or group occupying a particular status position is supposed to do.

Status. Status is a socially defined position in a social structure. It is a position that an individual occupies in a group, such as leader or follower; doctor or nurse; mother or son; student or professor, etc. A status can also be a specific position of one group in relation to another group, such as executives and secretaries in a large office.

References

Coser, Lewis. 1956. *The Functions of Social Conflict*. New York: Free Press.

Davis, Kingsley. 1949. *Human Society*. New York: MacMillan.

Dion, Karen, Ellen Berscheid, and Elaine Walster. 1972. "What is Beautiful is Good." *Journal of Personality and Social Psychology* 24:285-90.

Leavitt, Steven and Stephen Dubner. 2005. *Freakonomics: A Rogue Economist Explores the Hidden Side of Everything*. New York: William Morrow.

Milgram, Stanley. 1974. *Obedience to Authority*. New York: Harper and Row.

Rosenhan, David. 1973. "On Being Sane in Insane Places." *Science*.

Simmel, Georg. 1971. *On Individuality and Social Forms*. Chicago, IL: University of Chicago Press.

Zimbardo, P. G., C. Haney, W. C. Banks, and D. Jaffe. 1974. "The Psychology of Imprisonment: Privation, Power and Pathology." Pp. 61-73 in *Doing Unto Others: Explorations in Social Behavior*, edited by Z. Rubin. Englewood Cliffs, NJ: Prentice-Hall.

6 | Social Structure: The Heart of the Matter.
by Frank O. Taylor, IV, Ph.D.

What is **social structure**? This is perhaps the most difficult concept to understand for students studying sociology. You do not have to study society for very long before you discover that your reality is highly structured. In other words, you tend to see the same people on a daily basis. Your relationship to those people rarely changes. You tend to follow a recurrent pattern in your daily activities. These recurrent patterns of relationships are the basis of social structure. For example, you have a social relationship with the instructor of your sociology course. You see this person at least a couple of times each week throughout the semester. This interaction always takes place the same days of the week, at the same time of the day, in the same location. There is a pattern. The relationship between you and your professors is almost completely scripted. There are certain norms you are expected to follow, regardless of the particular professor. Additionally, your interactions with the professor occur within certain social boundaries. Whenever you interact with a professor, you probably follow the norms of the situation. In part, following the norms of the student/professor script is what allows you to be perceived as a good student.

STATUS AND ROLE

To understand social structure you must understand four other related concepts: role, status, institution, and social control. Continuing with the education setting, when you interact with a professor there are two statuses that structure the interaction—the status of professor and the status of student. A **status** is the name of a position in the social structure, or a position within a group of positions. Each status has certain rights, duties, and obligations, known as **roles**. Think of it like this—when you interact with a professor, there is a social script that each of you follows, in general. Professors lecture, write tests, grade tests, prepare for lectures by reading and studying, publish research, attend conferences, hold office hours, and so on. The status of professor implies certain roles. Students, on the other hand, play their role by attending lectures, taking notes, listening attentively, taking tests, and socializing with other students. Thus, we say that there is a structural relationship between the statuses of professor and student and the interactions between the two are based, in large degree, on a pattern of relationships or roles.

92

by Frank O. Taylor, IV, Ph.D.

Think about your most favorite and least favorite professors for a moment. Although both professors occupy the same status, and have similar roles, obviously there are differences between them or you would not have a favorite. This is an important point: no two professors and no two students behave in identical ways. To help us understand the relationship between statuses and roles it is useful to use the metaphor of the theatre: the statuses within a group are like a cast of characters in a play, while the roles are like a script that defines how characters are related to each other. Perhaps the play has a scene in which the actor is supposed to show disappointment. Let me assure you that professors disappoint their students and students their professors, on a regular basis. However, as on the stage, no two students or professors enact disappointment in an identical fashion. **Role performance** refers to the fact that there is room for a lot of variation in the way roles are enacted. Everyone plays his or her roles slightly differently. You *occupy* a status, but you *play* a role. One reason you may have a favorite and least favorite professor is that your favorite professor plays the role in a pleasing manner and your least favorite professor plays the role in a poor fashion.

We can differentiate between two types of statuses, achieved and ascribed. An **achieved status** is a status that is attained in one's lifetime. Many achieved statues, while optional, are normative. In other words, we are encouraged to want to attain some statuses, such as high school graduate, parent, or retiree. Becoming a father or a mother, being elected to public office, or being promoted at work are examples of achievements. There are some statuses, on the other hand, which we are born with and cannot escape. An **ascribed status** is fixed by birth. Sex and race are two statuses that a person can neither escape nor change. The expense of a sex-change operation is beyond the means or desire of most people. Ascribed characteristics greatly influence achieved statuses.

Ascribed statuses are an important component of social structure because they influence our outcomes in life and color every interaction. When we meet someone for the very first time, we tend to notice that person's ascribed and achieved characteristics. Gender and race are probably the first to be noticed, followed by other social characteristics such as age, attractiveness, or how the person is dressed. It is a lot like walking into a play in the middle of a scene without knowing what character you are playing or what your role is. You are forced to look for clues. The most obvious clues are those related to ascribed statuses. Once you have a general sense of statuses the other actors occupy, you have a better sense of what your relationship to each actor is, and you can use that knowledge to help you interact with them. You are able to function in some social settings, such as when you attend a class for the first time, due to understanding, in a broad sense, what your role is in relationship to the professor and the other students. Sociologists refer to this situation as the **negotiated order**. We use statues, both ascribed and achieved, to help us decide the nature of the ongoing interaction and how to proceed. Still, each actor plays their role in different ways and gives somewhat different performances, depending upon their personality and experiences.

Sociologists can use statuses to study a broad range of social relationships. For any society, you might try to identify the status structure by listing the existing statuses. Another way to study society is to look at the distribution of people among the statuses. The numbers of people who are mothers or fathers, in the United States, for example, are far greater than the number of people who are doctors. Every society has a status structure and a distribution of people among the statuses. You might discover that certain combinations of statuses seem to go together. Race, age, and unemployment are statuses in our society. Black teens between 16 and 19 years of age have a 36 percent rate of unemployment. White teens of similar age have an unemployment rate of only 14 percent. Another example of certain statues being correlated is the fact that 99 percent of nurses are women. Lastly, you might discover that statuses are also correlated with social rewards. In fact, on almost any measure you care to use, you will find an inequality in social rewards for women and minorities compared to males and whites in the United States.

During every minute of every day, you occupy one status or another. You are always someone's child. If you are reading this essay, you are probably a student. You may also be an employee. I hope that you are someone's friend. Perhaps you are a brother or a sister. Being an eldest child entails different roles than being the youngest child. For each one of your statuses there is a set of roles. Language is certainly important but this social structure of statuses and roles provides the foundation for interaction. Statuses and roles provide a framework for us to be able to relate to each other. By the time you are a young adult you have internalized a fairly accurate picture of the status structure and have a general idea of what the roles are for most any status. Sociologists call this mental image of the status structure the **generalized other**.

Human beings rely on social structure so as to make sense of their social world, and, in turn, statuses and roles order and structure our social lives. For example, you probably behave differently when you interact with your grandparents than you do with your friends. When you are with your friends you probably use different language, dress differently, and act differently. You may dress differently when you are with your friends than you do when you go to church. If you think about it, you may realize that as the social setting changes, your body language, demeanor, dress, and vocabulary may change quite substantially. For example, I use a lot of sociological jargon around sociology majors and professors. When I am visiting my friends, I change almost everything about myself. Human beings rely on social structure in order to make sense of their social world.

INSTITUTIONS

Statuses, and their attendant roles, are always located within **institutions**. Institutions are complex social structures that meet basic human needs.   Through a process of social evolution, institutions provide ready-made patterns that people rely on in their daily lives to survive. It is because of these social patterns that much of our life seems orderly and predictable. There are five basic institutions found in every society. These institutions include the family, the economy, the government, education, and religion. Remember, institutions meet basic human needs and normally provide positive consequences for society. The family provides replacement members for society and helps care for and socialize children. The primary function of the economy is the production and distribution of goods and services. The government regulates and protects society. Education provides training to the children of each generation. Religion supplies a value and belief system to help people deal with the unknown.

Let us look at the institution of health care. We can think about institutions on three levels, the micro, macro, and meso levels of interaction. A **micro-level** analysis refers to face-to-face interactions in small groups of people. When you visit the doctor's office, you are in a face-to-face social setting. Recall that social structure refers to recurrent patterns of social relationships. When you go to the doctor's office you know that you will encounter people of certain statuses and that your interactions with the people who occupy those statuses are highly structured and governed by norms. The person in the clinic with the greatest amount of power is the doctor, followed by the nurses. The person with the least amount of power is usually the patient. You will be expected to wait quietly in the waiting room until the nurse calls for you. Then you cooperate with the nurse while vital statistics, such as your blood pressure and temperature are taken.

Usually, you will wait in a private room to see the physician. Finally, you will get to see the physician, who will attempt to diagnose your illness and prescribe either a drug or some regimen to help you recover your health. You will be expected to follow the physician's advice. The point is the pattern of social norms and behaviors are nearly the same no matter when you visit the clinic, where you visit a clinic, or what illness you have.

A **meso-level** of analysis would refer to all the clinics in your community. For the sake of example, let us say that you work for a consulting agency that has been retained to study protocols for treating the victims of an anthrax terrorist attack in your city. This will necessarily involve every aspect of health care in the city, including clinics, hospitals, and first responders, such as ambulance, emergency, police, and firefighter services. The analysis here is beyond the simple face-to-face norms of a particular clinic. The focus is on policies and treatments that will ensure that large numbers of patients will be able to have access to health care in an emergency. You will be interested in such things as whether or not there is enough medicine on hand, the availability of hospital beds, and the level of training and readiness for the first responders. If shortcomings are discovered, your agency will work with physicians, police, firefighters, and other emergency responders in order to develop efficient policies. Once these policies are in place, a social structure for dealing with a civil emergency exists. While a microanalysis focuses on the face-to-face level of interaction, a meso-level analysis is focuses at the institutional level.

A **macro-level** institutional analysis refers to national, and sometimes even global, social structures. The American Medical Association and other national bodies of accreditation govern the operation of medical schools, to ensure that certain standards of instruction and achievement are observed by all. At the national level, there is a great degree of continuity in the training of physicians of every specialty. There are also standards of achievement related to the internships physicians must complete and board examinations to pass before physicians can begin to practice medicine. The same is true for nursing. A macro-level analysis of health care institutions would address issues on a national level and include technology, insurance companies, the drug industry, and the federal agencies that regulate the health care industry. The point of this brief discussion is to point out that social structures exist at three levels of reality, the face-to-face level, the institutional level, and the national level.

Table 6.1   **Levels of Analysis**

MICRO	MESO	MACRO
Classes	College/University	Department of Education
• Face-to-face interactions in the particular classes you are enrolled in. • Norms and rules are in the Course Syllabus	• The college or university you attend and the policies and bureaucratic structures that govern it. • Norms and rules are in the Student Handbook	• Federal regulations and laws associated with education in the United States • Federal Loans and Grants • Title IV

RATIONALITY AND SOCIOCULTURAL EVOLUTION

Hunting and gathering, horticultural, and other simple societies are based on traditional sentiments passed from generation to generation. Modern societies are more likely to be based on **rationality**, a reliance on reason, and the scientific method as the basis of decision making. The sociologist Max Weber referred to the rationalization of society to illustrate the change from traditional modes of thought to rationality as the dominant form of human thinking. For example, people in traditional societies may believe in evil spirits and other supernatural beings. People in modern societies are not very inclined to believe that their automobile has been invaded by an evil spirit when it breaks down. Usually, modern people believe that a mechanical breakdown has occurred. Weber believed that in societies based on rationality people are more likely to adopt technology. In Western society the industrial revolution occurred, in part, because the spirit of rationality predisposed people to accept and exploit scientific discoveries.

by Frank O. Taylor, IV, Ph.D.

To a very large degree rationality orders our lives through its impact on social institutions. In hunting and gathering societies, the family is the basic institution and the center of all social life. Modern societies, however, have separated religious, political, governmental, and educational functions from the family and have evolved distinctive social institutions to deal with those aspects of life on a rational basis. Bureaucracies, which evolved along with modern institutions, are quite large and impersonal. In bureaucratic settings, technical competence replaces personal relationships and people interact more on the basis of their areas of expertise than as individuals concerned about each other's welfare. Modern rational institutions emphasize personal discipline, achievement, time management, and efficiency. The modern emphasis on rationality has created a fundamentally different social world than that of hunters and gatherers.

For much of each day you are under the sway of one institution or another. In the morning, children leave the family for the school and return to the family in the evening. Parents leave the family to go to work, where they are under the supervision of employers for most of the day, and return to the family in the evening, where society expects them to uphold the norms of family life. On Sunday, millions of people shuffle between family and church. On weekdays, we move between family, school or work, and sometimes both, and back to the family. When you are on the road driving to work, you follow the rules, laws, and norms of driving. When you are at work or school, there are rules, regulations, and norms to abide by. Of course, there may be a great degree of variability in how each individual fulfills his or her work obligations. In other words, institutions constrain our behavior and suppress change. Institutions support the status quo and promote stability and order.

As well as necessary and while often enriching, institutions can be stifling, oppressing, and alienating as well. Institutions are associated with various types of inequality. In educational institutions, for example, tracking children into college, general education, or vocation education, promotes inequality. Economic institutions adhere to the profit motive and practice outsourcing, downsizing, and globalization as means to reduce work force and increase profit. While it is true that many people find work rewarding and form warm friendships with co-workers, in other respects, rationalization at work often turns people into cogs in the machine. Work can be tedious, routine, and boring. I once worked at a factory that assembled diesel engines. As the engines went by on the assembly line, I mounted fuel ejectors. It was the same series of steps, repeatedly, all day long, every day. You were not allowed to talk to the person on the other side of the engine (even if you wanted to because it was very loud in the plant). Once I had mastered the series of movements required to perform my job, it became second nature to me. In order to survive the day I had to retreat into my mind, where I relived my fondest memories, planned out how to build a sailboat, and other such fantasies. **Alienation** is the feeling that you are not in control of your life. Worse, you have no other recourse, if you want to earn a living and build that sailboat, than to submit to that which is alienating you in the first place.

In capitalist economic institutions, workers are usually denied a say in what they make or how it is produced. That can also be alienating. Other people decide what to produce, how much to produce, how it will be produced, and so on. In fact, workers are often turned into another part of the machine, especially in factory work. Work should be an activity that is personally fulfilling while meeting the needs of the community. All too often, however, it is miserable, low-paid, and so repetitive that it actually harms your body and mind. Moreover, we have no choice: we must sell our labor for a wage or a salary, or someone else in the household must do it, in order to survive. To make matters worse, employers are always contemplating ways in which to pay workers less or replace us entirely with computers and machines. Rationality and alienation are two important components of social structure in capitalist societies. No employee, even up to middle level management, is safe from the forces of rationality and alienation. White-collar workers are now being replaced by computer software, just as blue-collar workers lost jobs to robots a decade ago.

SOCIAL CONTROL

Any consideration of the ways in which social life is structured must include a discussion of social control. **Social control** refers to the manner in which behavior is regulated in society. If society is to function, people must work, follow the rules and norms of behavior, interact with relatives, friends, and peers, and carry out innumerable other social acts in any given day. The more complex and specialized the society and the division of labor, the more complex, and specialized are the rules of behavior in a variety of settings. Give a thought to just how dependent you are upon everyone else in your community following the rules and getting things done. As a teacher, I produce absolutely nothing! One may argue that I at least produce knowledge, and occasionally tell a funny story, but you cannot subsist on lectures. In order for me to use technology, eat, drive to work, write this essay, lecture and teach, dress myself, raise my children, and so forth, thousands, and perhaps millions of others, must also be doing their jobs and taking care of their responsibilities. Sociologists call this **interdependence**. A high degree of interdependence is characteristic of complex societies. Imagine how quickly society would breakdown if massive numbers of people failed to meet their social obligations. There are two additional ways to think about social control beyond the processes that structure our social experiences:

1) the processes that lead us to internalize the norms of society, and

2) the employment of formal and informal sanctions.

Ultimately, social control rests upon the threat of force, which we will discuss when we turn to sanctions. However, society is likely to function much more efficiently if people simply prefer to engage in normative behavior. **Socialization** refers to the lifelong process of learning your culture. During the process of socialization, individuals learn the norms, values, beliefs, ways of thinking and feeling, and social expectations of society. Children learn the norms of a variety of social settings, including the family, school, church, and peer group. One of the first words parents try to get children to learn, after their name, is the word "no." Imagine where society would be if no one understood the word no. Children initially respond to external controls, but the goal is for children to eventually monitor their own behavior.

Internalization is the process through which children learn to identify and use the appropriate set of norms in different social settings. When children use the norms, values, and beliefs of their culture to solve problems, sociologists say that they have internalized culture. You may recall asking your parents to buy you something when you were a teenager and hearing a parent ask you when you plan to get a job. When a young adult finds employment and begins to make his or her own purchases, he or she is using the norms of culture to solve the problem of acquiring what they want. Often children are faced with the choice of doing what is socially acceptable, or normative, or engaging in deviant behavior. Children not only have to learn what the norms are they must also believe that the norms are legitimate. Internalization means that social norms have become part of the child's personality. How often have you seen young men and women getting ready for a date? Most women are concerned with their appearance, and may spend a considerable amount of time getting dressed and putting on makeup. Men, while not necessarily unconcerned with their appearance, may spend more time washing and cleaning their car then they spend on themselves. How does society encourage children to internalize norms?

Fear of punishment probably goes a long way toward explaining why we conform. Society has a range of positive and negative sanctions, both formal and informal, that encourage us to conform. **Informal sanctions** usually occur in response to norm violations in small groups or face-to-face social settings. When you forget a friend's birthday, that person may express disappointment in a number of ways. However, such sanctions are usually mild. When you are married and you forget to pick your spouse up after work you might experience an informal sanction slightly more severe. Possibly the most severe type of informal sanction is the cold shoulder. When your friends do not want to interact with you it usually means that you have violated an important norm of friendship. We like people who like us. We like to be recognized and rewarded with respect and appreciation. It does not take children long to realize that the best way to have friends is to be a friend. Giving a friend a card on their birthday, going out to the movies or restaurant, disclosing confidences, and the like, are all types of informal positive sanctions. Getting the "look" of disapproval or the cold shoulder are types of informal negative sanctions. Of course, we give birthday cards and other forms of emotional support because we like to receive birthday cards and emotional support. We learn at a very early age that if we want to receive social rewards we must play the game! That means following the norms of the situation.

Formal sanctions refer to sanctions associated with the official agents of social control. If you have ever received a traffic citation for speeding or some other violation of traffic laws, you have received a mildly negative formal sanction. If you earn a superior grade for this course, you will receive a mildly positive formal sanction. It is better, in general, to receive passing grades rather than failing grades because failing grades may entail a range of formal and informal negative sanctions. Parents, for example, may disapprove of a failing grade. If you receive failing grades often, eventually you will face the formal negative sanctions of probation and suspension. Probation and suspension are pretty severe formal sanctions. I know that a good number of students reading this book will eventually end up in divorce court. A divorce from your spouse is a formal sanction. I once received a medal, when I was in the Navy, for good conduct. Military medals are formal sanctions awarded for various acts that usually uphold military values and norms. Of the two types of sanctions, informal sanctions are usually the most effective because they are usually received in primary groups to which we are highly attached, such as the family and peer groups.

Social control is largely a matter of people internalizing norms during the process of socialization and behaving as they are expected to in a variety of situations. We simply take for granted that our way of doing things is natural. People conform because they like social rewards and dislike negative informal and formal sanctions. Three interesting experiments in social psychology demonstrate how powerful the influence of others can be in getting us to conform, the Sherif, Asch, and Milgram experiments.

Muzafer Sherif was interested in how the behavior of individuals could be influenced by a group. He believed that even our most basic perceptions were susceptible to prevailing frames of reference. Sherif built his experiment around the autokinetic illusion, in which a stationary point of light projected on a screen appears to move in a completely darkened room. In a completely darkened environment, there is no frame of reference that would allow the subject to assess his or her perception of the light's movement. Sherif hypothesized that if other people were put into the room they would serve as each other's frame of reference. First, he put the subjects in the room individually, noting that some people felt the light moved only a little, while others thought it moved quite a bit, as much as five inches. In the second part of the experiment, he put all the subjects in the room together and had them call out their estimates of the light's movements. Sherif discovered that over time the subjects' estimates about how much the light moved tended to converge. Subjects who thought the light moved very little increased their estimates. Subjects who thought the light had moved greater distances decreased their estimates. Very quickly, everyone began to agree upon how much the light moved and this agreement influenced everyone's perception, in spite of the fact that the movement of the point of light was an illusion. The results of this experiment indicate that in ambiguous situations people look to others for guidance and that guidance alters their perception of reality.

Solomon Asch was interested in situations in which there is a clear conflict between the subject's perception and a judgment advanced by the group. Asch felt that the Sherif experiment was too ambiguous. In such situations, it is not surprising that subjects would rely on each other. Consequently, Asch designed an experiment in which the subjects knew perfectly well that the feedback from the group was erroneous. Asch hypothesized that when there was a clear conflict between the subject's assessment and the group's assessment, and the subject knew the group was wrong, the influence of the group would be reduced and there would be far less conformity. He was correct but nonetheless surprised by just how often the subjects did conform even when they knew the group was in error. Asch asked the experimental subjects to perform a simple perceptual task, to determine which one of the three lines on a card was the same length as a target line on a separate card. Everyone in the group, except the one research subject, was instructed to respond incorrectly when calling out their answer. In this manner Asch's confederates in the group would exert group influence and try to get the subject to change his mind. The difference between Asch's experiment and Sherif's was that with Asch the research subjects knew the correct answer, since all they had to do was compare the length of the target line on one card to the lengths of three lines on the other card, selecting the line of corresponding length. The lengths of the lines were sufficiently different as to make the answer clear. Three-quarters of the participants eventually succumbed to the pressure of the group. This experiment indicates that even when people know they are in the right they will often conform to the will of the group.

Stanley Milgram was interested to see just how far people could be pushed when caving in to authority. Incorrectly reporting the length of a line seemed trivial. Milgram wondered if research subjects would still conform if asked to deliver an electric shock to a confederate (a helper in the experiment). Milgram placed an ad in the newspaper asking for participants in a learning experiment. Of course, he rigged the assignment to the teacher and learner roles, making sure that a confederate always became the learner while others who answered the newspaper ad were assigned the teacher role. Milgram had an elaborate prop that looked like a real shock generator but in reality no one was actually shocked during the experiment. The teachers were shown that the learners were strapped into a chair and attached to the shock delivery apparatus. The teachers were then led to another room where they would manipulate the bogus shock generator. Whenever the learner missed a question on the learning exercise, the teachers were asked to administer a 15-volt shock, with a 15-volt increase for each subsequent mistake. As the experiment went on the teachers thought they were delivering electric shocks of up to 450 volts. Some of the teachers could hear the learners pounding on the wall, presumably desperate to get the teacher to stop. Nevertheless, 66 percent of the teachers continued to shock the learner all the way up to 450 volts of electricity, the maximum amount. Other teachers could hear the learner desperately plead that they had a bad heart and to stop. However, with very little encouragement, such as hearing "please continue," or "the experiment must go on," from the researcher, 62.5 percent of the teachers continued to deliver shocks up to the maximum amount. Some of the teachers stopped when it became clear that they were causing another human being to suffer.

Milgram hypothesized that those who continued did so for a number of reasons that amount to social pressure, including the fact that they had accepted payment to participate, they believed in the advancement of scientific understanding of human behavior, or they simply desired to avoid the disapproval of the experimenter. The results of this experiment suggest that the norms of social situations become a powerful influence over human behavior. Once you accept payment to do a job the norms of the situation require you to carry out your obligations, for example. Because of ethical concerns for the psychological welfare of the subjects, the Milgram experiment could never be repeated today. However, there is clear evidence from these three experiments that it does not take much to get people to conform to group pressure or authority.

THE STRUCTURE OF SOCIAL EXPERIENCE

Your particular social experience is highly structured by your culture. This is true for every human being in every time and place. **Culture** is like a toolbox of ready-made solutions to the problems of survival. Culture tells us what to eat, when and how often to eat, what to wear, how to reproduce, what to think about, and even whom to like. Culture is always present. Even when you are completely alone, if you are thinking, culture is still there. The process of thinking is to a large degree simply an internal conversation. To think, you speak to yourself. Thus, implicitly, since the language you speak is a product of your culture, you are never free of culture. Human beings are fundamentally creatures that interpret, categorize, and evaluate. In order for meaning to exist at all, language and symbols must also exist. Culture influences every aspect of your life.

When I drive my car to work I sometimes see an automobile with the symbol of the fish attached to the back. The fish is widely used to symbolize the Christian religion, since Jesus was a fisher of men. I think to myself, there goes another Christian. **Symbols** structure reality because they carry a particular meaning widely recognized by the members of a culture. After 911, it was popular to attach a United States flag to your automobile. For many people, the flag inspires feelings of unity and patriotism. Since I am older, I remember the coffins of soldiers who died in Vietnam, draped with the flag, as they returned home for burial. When I see the flag, I think of dead young men, not patriotism. This brings up an interesting point. We often disagree about the meaning of symbols. Symbols can structure reality in fundamental ways. The Bush administration does not want people to see the war dead. President Bush claims that it is disrespectful to families for the media to publish images of flag-draped coffins coming home from Iraq. Sociologists, on the other hand, understand that symbols can help support a war or create anti-war sentiments. Flag-draped coffins, especially in great numbers, have historically led to anti-war sentiment. This is probably why the Bush administration is limiting our access to such symbols. I often wonder how many people connect the flags on their cars to the dead soldiers in coffins. When a President encourages people to put flags on their cars but discourages media coverage of causalities of war, he is attempting to structure your reality through symbols, specifically encouraging the use of some symbols and discouraging the use of other symbols.

When people drive expensive sport utility vehicles, that use large amounts of gasoline, wear expensive clothing and jewelry, and purchase homes big enough to function as apartment buildings, they are sending the rest of us a symbolic message: I have enough money for **conspicuous consumption**. The act of consuming, let alone what is actually consumed, can be symbolic of affluence and power. Why do people wear a Rolex when a Timex is just as accurate, and much less expensive? Why do people drive Jaguars when they could drive Honda Civics and spend a lot less on insurance and other expenses? The answer is obvious. They want to be seen as someone who is well off and has money to burn, although it is often not the case that they have a lot of money. Conspicuous consumption is a form of symbolic communication. The need to keep up with your neighbor's level of consumption is very powerful in our society.

Language refers to a system of symbols that allows communication between people to take place. Language is the medium through which culture is transmitted from one generation to the next. It is hard to see how culture could exist without language, because language allows us to transcend our immediate experience. Language is also the key to the cultural stock of knowledge. In this respect, language allows human knowledge to be cumulative. Language links us to history, giving those in the present access to a shared past. Conversely, language also grants us access to a shared future. Language allows us to plan, to dream about and envision a different future, make appointments, communicate goals, and coordinate activities. Most importantly, language allows us to reflect, to create, and to become self-conscious. The ability to think about the processes through which we become human is what distinguishes us from the animals.

Thus, language greatly influences, shapes, and structures reality. Research indicates that people who speak different languages experience, to varying degrees, the world differently. Different language systems have at least a few words and symbols that are unique to that society and culture. People perceive the world through the language and symbol system they use. I once saw a commercial on television that suggested that if you drank a bottle of a certain soft drink you would feel refreshed. The same commercial, translated into Japanese, suggested that consuming the soft drink would bring your ancestors back from the dead. A few decades ago, I remember remarking to my father, "man, that's heavy!" He looked around to see what object I was referring to. Sometimes, when someone says you are bad, they really mean you are good. Such nuances of language often grant children access to a reality their parent's cannot share. The idea that language is comprised merely of words people attach labels to is misleading. Language does much more than that, since the words we use convey certain ways of looking at the world.

Recently I applied for a home loan. I talked to an agent, who seemed very enthusiastic when she discovered that I was a college professor, which implies a certain amount of income and job security. The last step in the process was the submission of my credit application and obtaining a credit report. Several days went by and after waiting patiently to hear from her, I decided to drop into the office to speak to her and check on the status of my application. I was waiting in the lounge when I overheard her complain to another agent that she was tired of being bothered by "roaches." I mistook her meaning entirely, thinking she was talking about a home infested with cockroaches. However, after learning that I had been turned down for the home loan due to something on my credit report, which later turned out to be a mistake, I understood that she was referring to me as being like a roach.

Even if you do not qualify for a loan, it is hardly likely that you will see yourself as a bad person, and certainly not someone with the qualities of a cockroach. The agent's whole demeanor toward me, after discovering that she would not make a commission, was that of someone dealing with a nasty little insect. A friend of mine, who happens to sell cars for a living, told me that his dealership even has a "roach-list," a list of people who, because of poor credit, cannot get a regular loan but qualify for high interest "special" financing. The word "roach," when used to refer to someone not eligible for a loan has a *particular* meaning embedded in it. Referring to good people, who happen not to qualify for a loan, as roaches, is demeaning and dehumanizing. When people are portrayed as roaches, it becomes easier to marginalize them and view them as unworthy of your help, or anyone's help. When you equate human beings with roaches, you are one step away from condoning extermination. I wonder how the real estate agent would feel if we referred to people who make a living from sales commissions as vampires? Language influences the way that we perceive people and social settings. Language structures reality.

Material culture refers to the tangible things we create as a culture. Material culture can refer to homes, automobiles, highways, roads, and interstates, buildings, boats, books, computers, or anything else that society produces. Our reality is highly structured by material culture. When I get up in the morning, I like to take a shower, shave my face, and brush my teeth. To do any of these things requires material culture. I sleep in a bed, of a certain type of construction, rather than in a tent or some other shelter. I drive an automobile to work, instead of a bicycle. I do not ride to work on an animal. When I want to communicate with a friend, I used to write letters or use the telephone. Now I use email. Material culture structures everyday life in innumerable ways. To get from point A to point B involves material culture. Work involves material culture. Even marriage and family requires material culture. Think about where you live and what type of home you will need. Then think about all the Christmas, birthday, and anniversary presents you will have to purchase. Presents are part of material culture too. Guys, here is some good advice: do not give your third wife a card on the anniversary of your first marriage! She probably will not appreciate it. Material culture and norms often interact in strange ways.

Values and beliefs also structure our social experience. **Values** are the standards by which our culture defines what is good or bad, desirable or undesirable, beautiful or ugly. Values serve as broad guidelines that define how things ought to be. **Beliefs** refer to specific ideas people hold to be true. As a culture, for example, we tend to value hard work. We believe hard work will get us ahead in life, in spite of the fact that many people work hard their entire lives and never get ahead. The values and beliefs of our culture structure how we perceive others, our friends, our surroundings, and ourselves. It would not be possible to have a personality without values and beliefs. Many Christians, and members of other religions for that matter, identify their belief in God as the major belief that defines who they are as people. Other people identify their occupation as the major component of their identity. During the process of socialization, we learn our culture's values, beliefs, principles, and goals, and are taught by family and school to pursue them.

by Frank O. Taylor, IV, Ph.D.

It is unrealistic to think that everyone in our culture shares the exact same values and goals because there are so many different parts of cultures to be found in the United States. Nevertheless, researchers have discovered that there are some core values in our society to which a majority of people adheres. We believe that society should provide everyone with equal opportunity to succeed and experience upward social mobility. We also believe that social rewards should be commensurate with the level of effort people put forth. We do not believe that people should be allowed to enjoy great success in life if they are not willing to work for it. Although it is often said that money cannot buy happiness, it can buy the necessities of life, such as a home, material comforts, health care, transportation, vacations, clothing, and the like. We do not fault people for striving for material wealth. We are an active culture that favors doing over thinking and practicality over dreaming. We like the latest inventions and best technology. One only has to notice the number of people driving while talking on their cell phones to realize that we are fascinated with progress. In spite of the fact that we are polluting our environment, we believe that science will solve all of our problems. We also value democracy, even if we do not vote in very great numbers. We believe that we have certain human rights that the government should not, under any circumstances, violate. Free enterprise and private property are also highly valued in our society. Perhaps our most central value is that of freedom. We believe that as long as we do not harm anyone else we should be free to pursue whatever makes us happy.

Group superiority and **ethnocentrism** are also attitudes our culture values highly, although they may contradict our values of freedom, democracy, and equality. Ethnocentrism refers to the fact that the dominant group tends to record history from their point of view, paying little attention to the point of view of other groups or their accomplishments. Group superiority refers to the tendency to see one's own group and culture as superior to others. In discussions about how to deal with poverty and famine in the Third World, students often suggest that modern medicine, modern farming techniques and technology, modern science and technology, and family planning and contraceptives, are the answer. In short, students often suggest that Third World nations need to adopt our way of life and all their problems will be solved. Students do not realize that many of the problems, such as famine and starvation, facing the Third World are often the result of severe droughts, not their culture. More than a few Third World nations can lay their problems directly at the door of modernization. Many developing nations are former colonies of First World nations and are experiencing problems today because the colonizers shattered their indigenous economies.

Nevertheless, we have a tendency to see our family, our way of life, and our culture as the only correct way.

In our own nation, we only have to look at incomes and rates of poverty for different groups to see that our culture values affluent people over the poor, men over women, and whites over people of color. Less than 10 percent of white people are poor, compared to more than 25 percent of people of color. Black and Hispanic children under the age of 18 have a poverty rate of nearly 50 percent. Almost 30 percent of female-headed households are poor, compared to 10 percent of married households. Overall, women earn 77 cents for every dollar men earn. That amounts to a loss of $2,300 for women for every $10,000 earned by men. White persons with a high school degree earn an average income of $28,145 per year, compared to $22,823 for Blacks and $24,163 for Hispanics. White college graduates earn an average income of $52,479 per year, compared to $42,285 for Black college graduates and $40,949 for Hispanic college graduates. Low-income children have higher rates of infant mortality and are more likely to have lower birth weight than children of affluent parents. Poor children are also more likely to lack health care and experience hunger and malnutrition than affluent children are. We may, as a culture, value equal opportunity but it is clear that we do not value outright equality.

Ideologies structure our social experiences. **Ideologies** refer to clusters of values that tend to hang together to form a cohesive belief system. Ideologies are often used to justify inequalities. Three major ideologies help structure our experiences in United States culture: individualism, the Protestant Ethic, and meritocracy. Our culture nearly worships the individual. In the Bill of Rights, the framers of the Constitution went to great lengths to lay out the rights of the individual. **Individualism** is an ideology that stresses the economic and political independence of the individual and individual action, initiative, and interests. We tend to believe that successful people achieve their successes in life based on individual characteristics, such as skill, talent, ability, or hard work and effort. We do not like to see success as a matter of family advantage, even though there is much research that suggests that the best predictor of academic success, for example, is your parent's social class background. The ideology of individualism suggests that each person is unique, somewhat different from everyone else in terms of talents, proclivities, temperament, and personality. We do not like to see ourselves as similar to everyone else. Success and failure in our culture is measured in terms of personal attributes. We judge each other in individualistic terms.

One of the lenses we look through when we interpret others and ourselves is the lens of individualism.

The **Protestant Ethic** is another major ideology through which our social experiences are structured. Industrial capitalism in the United States was founded on the principles of Calvinism, a Christian religious doctrine and movement that emerged during the Protestant Reformation. Calvinists believed in the doctrine of predestination, which stressed that some people were destined for salvation while others were destined for damnation. In other words, predestination held that people's fate was set prior to their birth. In their desire to know whether or not they were among the saved, many Calvinists looked for signs of God's grace, because they felt that God would surely favor, in their Earthly lives, those bound for heaven, and disfavor those destined for hell. Consequently, Calvinists thought the poor to be sinners and affluent people, while they could not be certain, to be favored by the God. Calvinists believed in success, discipline, hard work, reason, and the reinvestment of profits toward greater success. This was, of course, beneficial for a fledgling capitalist society, as these values also tend to support capitalism. The religious underpinnings of the Protestant Ethic have long since weakened, and wealth and material success are now valued for their own sake. The Protestant Ethic has become secularized into a Work Ethic. This work ethic is another major lens we look through when we evaluate others and ourselves. There is a great deal of overlap and congruity between individualism and the Work Ethic.

The third major ideology through which our social experiences are structured is that of **meritocracy**. In theory, a meritocracy is a system in which the talented are chosen and moved ahead solely because of their achievements. Clearly, there is a great affinity between the ideologies of individualism, the Protestant Ethic, and meritocracy. Each tends to support the other. In our culture, we are socialized to believe that the social promotion and advancement of some individuals over others are based on their achievements. Affluent people do not like to see their advantages in life as the basis of their success; they are more likely to refer to their personal qualities than their family background. A good example of how meritocracy structures social experience is the number of people who truly seem to believe that Bill Gates started out poor and became the richest man in the world. Bill Gates dropped out of one of the most exclusive, expensive, and elite universities in the nation and came from an affluent background. His corporation has been found guilty of violating federal laws on a number of occasions, which might explain how he became so wealthy. Nevertheless, many people believe he succeeded based on his intelligence and hard work alone.

Here is how the ideology of meritocracy works: we tend to view our successes and other people's failures as a matter of individual merit. When we fail, however, we tend to blame others, not ourselves. The myths about poverty arise from these ideologies: poor people are viewed not as victims of a capitalist economic system but as individuals who have failed, or people of bad characteristics who are to blame for their poverty. The myths of poverty overlook the fact that the majority of the poor are children, the elderly, and the infirm. The ideology of individualism focuses our attention on individuals, rather than the cultural, economic, and political systems that create inequality. The Protestant Ethic encourages us to see success as a matter of hard work alone, not systematic advantages. The ideology of meritocracy allows us to feel that the poor deserve their poverty. The other side of that belief is the belief that we deserve our advantages. Ideologies are powerful cultural lenses that shape our perceptions of reality.

During the process of socialization we internalize social structure to such a degree that we take it almost entirely for granted. We refer to this internal picture of the status and social structure of society as the **generalized other**. At an early age social structure is firmly embedded in our minds and becomes part of our personality. Rather than instincts, human beings rely on social structure and culture to solve the problems of survival. Because human beings possess mind, we never simply see and react to stimuli in the world. We see the world *through* the lens of culture. We rely upon language, symbols, norms, values and beliefs, and ideology to interpret the world and make meaningful the actions of others. Our reality is highly structured by norms, statuses, ascribed statuses such as gender and race, formal and informal sanctions, and material culture. We live in a negotiated order, rather than the natural environment. How we interact, with ourselves and with others, is not a matter of instincts and biology, rather it is a matter of language and symbols. The very language and symbols we use to communicate with ourselves and others create certain ways of thinking and perceiving, while closing off other possible ways of thinking and perceiving. We use a cultural script in which the characters and roles are broadly laid out for us in advance. Sometimes we encounter situations that the script does not cover and we have to rely on previous experience to get us through, which may lead to new roles. Even when we are completely alone, culture is part of our mind and thinking process.

111

PERSONALITY AND SOCIAL STRUCTURE

When we think about the ways in which social structure influences our personality we run into a very old debate. In the 1920s and 1930s, **biological determinism** asserted that almost all of human behavior could be explained by instincts, rather than culture. Modern versions of biological determinism have focused on hormones, chromosomes, and genetics. The general idea of biological determinism is that human behavior can be understood by understanding human biology. Anthropologists and sociologists responded with an equally erroneous argument, known as **cultural determinism**. The cultural determinists held that individual personality was totally determined by culture through the process of early childhood socialization. The general idea of cultural determinism was that the ways people think and act are a result of a specific type of socialization. Neither position alone is correct. It takes biology and culture to produce a human being. Human biological prerequisites include a central nervous system, a brain, and a tongue and larynx, at the least. The biological prerequisites are necessary, but not sufficient in and of themselves to create a human being. Language, symbols, and interaction with other humans are the basic cultural components.

When we interact with a stranger for the first time, we try to anticipate how they will respond to us. Usually, we can rely to some extent on the norms of the situation, which help make behavior predictable. Personality refers to a stable pattern of thoughts, feelings, behaviors, and emotional characteristics of an individual. There are some universal components of human personalities. For example, all humans, normally, go through a process of socialization in which we learn the language, symbols, and norms of our culture. Therefore, in some respects, all humans are alike. However, socialization is differential. Some children are identified for different roles in society, and therefore receive a different kind of socialization from other children. An example of differential socialization is gender. Males and females are raised differently and prepared to lead different types of lives. Due to differential socialization, some people have personalities that are similar to one group yet quite different from other groups. Because of the effects of socialization and group similarity we might reasonable expect individuals to demonstrate a large degree of similarity in personality. On the other hand, everyone's personality is different because no two individuals have the exact same biography. To some extent, each of us is unique because our patterns of interaction with our family, friends, peers, and others are uniquely ours.

In relation to differential socialization, researchers have discovered that blue-collar parents place greater stress on values such as cleanliness, obedience, and neatness than middle class parents. Middle class parents are more interested in values like curiosity, happiness, consideration for others, and in particular, self-control. Middle class parents seem to be more concerned with self-expression and independence than working class parents are. Working class parents are more interested in conformity and good behavior. Thus, one aspect of personality and differential socialization appears to be what kind of work our parents do. If parents experience more autonomy at work, that is they are more in control of their time and work without supervision, they tend to stress self-discipline and initiative in the socialization of their children. On the other hand, if parental work experience stresses order-taking, punctuality, observance of the rules and the like, they are more likely to stress those values when raising their children. There is a loose association between social class and working conditions. Usually, middle class work involves more autonomy and blue-collar work requires more conformity and obedience. However, social class appears to be secondary to actual working conditions. Parents generally have the expectation that their children will grow up and obtain jobs similar to theirs. Therefore, children tend to be socialized differently depending upon parental expectations about the type of work children will find as adults.

Sociologists have discovered that there is an interaction between personality and type of work. In other words, people with flexible, self-directed personalities are more likely to look for work that allows a large degree of autonomy, where individual initiative and the ability to achieve goals without close supervision are required. On the other hand, people who are less self-directed and need a lot of structure and supervision are more likely to look for work suitable to their personality. In spite of what type of work individuals end up in, other research suggests that, as time goes by, your personality changes somewhat to accommodate your occupation. This means that people who prefer more structure and supervision, but who are in jobs that require self-direction and personal initiative, tend to acquire personality characteristics required by the job. The same is true for people who prefer autonomous working conditions; their personalities tend to change to become more accepting of closely supervised work if they are in that type of occupation.

Self-concept is closely associated with personality. Sociologists view the self as a collection of beliefs you hold about yourself. This set of beliefs might include your hobbies, your likes and dislikes, things you are good at, and other stable personality characteristics. It is not possible to have a self or personality without social structure. Think about all of the things you know about yourself. Where does this **self-knowledge** come from? Largely it comes from feedback from parents, teachers, friends, and peers, all of whom treat you in slightly different ways, depending on the social setting in which you interact. Race, social class, and gender are basic social categories that help you construct a personality. Your ethnic background, for instance, depends on ancestry, food, clothes, norms, traditions, holidays, and values associated with your ethnic group. As discussed above, your social class background influences your likes and dislikes, political attitudes, values, and beliefs. You cannot think of yourself as working class or middle class unless both social classes exist and there are differences between them. Gender is also a basic component of your personality. Boys and girls are treated differently from birth. When you see your self as a woman, you enact a feminine presentation-of-self, rather than a masculine self-presentation.

To have hobbies and leisure-time activities also requires social structure. Perhaps your self-concept is based on the following answers to the question "who am I?" I am a woman. I am a daughter. I am a sister. I am a good friend. I am a college student. I am an athlete. I am a good listener. I am an artist. I am a good chess player. I am a sociology major. Clearly, in order to have such conceptions of your self and descriptions of your personality, social structure, in which you interact with others, is necessary. Moreover, how can you be sure you are a good listener, for example? In order to maintain that part of your self-concept you need to receive positive feedback from others, such as your boyfriend, brothers and sisters, or other friends. We receive **reflected appraisals** from others that help us maintain our self-concept and personality. We learn about ourselves through the reactions of other people toward us. It would be difficult to maintain the idea that you are a good listener if you constantly get negative feedback concerning your listening and empathetic qualities. If you think you are a good student you probably get good grades, another form of reflected appraisal. If you think you are a good chess player you probably play chess a lot and win frequently.

Reflected appraisals are an important part of the process of acquiring self, identity, and personality. **Significant others**, such as parents and teachers, often give us explicit feedback. They tell us what our qualities are. If we hear that we have a certain personal characteristic enough times, and from different people, we begin to think we must have that quality. We think of ourselves what others think of us. Parental feedback is particularly important in early childhood. If you want your child to have certain personal qualities as an adult it is a good idea to treat them as if they already have that quality, and tell them they do often. In adolescence, feedback from peers becomes important. Once you go to school, join peer groups, and get involved in various activities and organizations, you have innumerable opportunities for direct feedback. For example, you may think you are an awesome guitar player. However, if your friends cover their ears when you play and you fail to make the cut for jazz band, you may alter your perception of your ability. People tend to prefer objective feedback concerning their personal attributes.

A uniquely human attribute is the ability to **take the self as other**—to infer your personal characteristics from observing and evaluating your own behavior. Observing regularities in your behavior may lead you to infer certain characteristics about yourself and your personality. Self-perception applies to such things as beliefs, attitudes, and preferences, and even less important aspects of the self. For example, you may be assigned to the anti-death penalty side of a debate in one of your classes. If during debate you find yourself strenuously debating against the death penalty, you may eventually infer that you really are anti-death penalty. Further, if in similar situations you find yourself arguing for affirmative action and gay rights, you may begin to realize that you are a liberal. The point is, without the social setting in which to observe your behavior it is impossible to learn anything about yourself and your personality.

Sociologists refer to the **looking glass self** as the component of self that evaluates how others view us and think about us. The looking glass self refers to our perceptions of how others evaluate us. How do you signal your personality to others? In no small measure it is by looking at yourself in the mirror in order to judge whether others will perceive you as you perceive yourself. We use the looking glass to regulate our self-concept and manage our **presentation of self**. Self-presentation is the process through which we try to convince others that we have the personal qualities and characteristics we believe we do. Why do you dress the way you do? Why do you wear your hair in a particular style? Why do you drive the car you do? Why do you spend so much time in the gym? Do you spend your spare time at the bar? The answers to these questions involve your self-concept and personality. You want others to see you as you see yourself. You use the looking glass self and self-presentation to manage their impression of you. Of course, not all public behavior is driven by processes of self-presentation. Sometimes you are in social settings that are more restrictive and call for a higher degree of conformity.

It is hard to see how we could have the qualities we recognize as uniquely human without social structure. At the moment of birth we arrive into an ongoing social enterprise. Culture, its history, norms, ideologies, values, and beliefs, are already in play. We are born into one of the major institutions in any culture, the family. Although there are many numbers of family types, depending upon the culture in question, such as the nuclear family or the extended family, every family in every culture is characterized by a status structure. Statuses are differentiated by the roles attached to them. The role of the parent is significantly different from the role of the child, for example. During the process of socialization, we begin to learn the status and role structure of our culture. Language and symbols allow us to communicate with each other and with ourselves. Language becomes a lens through which we perceive the world. In other words, the words that we use are more than just words; they imply attitudes, beliefs, and values. The nature of self and personality in a rational society is radically different from the type of self people develop in a traditional society. Through the process of socialization, we begin to internalize our culture's language and symbols, norms, statues, roles, values, ideologies, and beliefs. We use them to negotiate reality, to create meaning, to understand ourselves and others, to communicate, and to survive and prosper. Can you imagine trying to negotiate social reality without the recurring patterns of social structure? It would be difficult indeed.

இ ௦౩ ௦ ௦౩

DEFINITIONS

Achieved Status. A status entered after birth and usually due at least in part to individual behavior.

Alienation. A feeling that develops when workers have no control over the process of work or their labor and the work seems particularly meaningless. The feeling that you are not in control of your life. It is a feeling of powerlessness, normlessness, and of being cut off from the product of one's labor, from other people, and from oneself.

Ascribed Status. A status assigned at birth.

Beliefs.   Statements about what is real.

Biological Determinism. Based on the belief that genetic factors explain differences in human behavior.

Conspicuous Consumption. The open display of wastefulness. The purchasing of products intended to affirm or enhance an individual's prestige, and designed to impress others.

Cultural Determinism. The belief that individual differences are caused by socialization and are, therefore, changeable.

Culture. A learned set of practices, beliefs, values, rules for proper conduct, and material objects shared by members of a society.

Ethnocentrism. Refers to the fact that the dominant group tends to record history from their point of view, paying little attention to the point of view of other groups or their accomplishments. Judging other cultures by your own cultural standards and since, of course, other cultures are different, they are therefore inferior. Ethnocentrism means an inability to appreciate others whose culture may include a different racial group, ethnic group, religion, morality, language, political system, economic system, etc. It also means an inability to see a common humanity and human condition facing all women and men in all cultures and societies beneath the surface variations in social and cultural traditions.

Formal Sanctions. Refers to sanctions associated with the official agents of social control. A clearly defined reward or punishment with specific people authorized to deliver it.

Generalized Other. The self's organization of the roles of others. It means the self is taking the related roles of all others in a social situation rather than the role of just on other person. The term generalized other does not refer to an actual group of people, but rather to an idea or conception a person derives from his or her experiences. The person then regulates behavior in terms of the supposed opinions and attitudes of others.

Group Superiority. Refers to the tendency to see one's own group and culture as superior to others.

Ideologies. Refers to clusters of values that tend to hang together to form a cohesive belief system.

Individualism. An ideology that stresses the economic and political independence of the individual and individual action, initiative, and interests.

Informal Sanction. A loosely defined reward or punishment with no specific people authorized to impose it.

Institutions. Complex social structures that meet basic human needs. "Sets of roles graded in authority that have been embodied in consistent patterns of actions that have been legitimated and sanctioned by society or segments of that society; whose purpose is to carry out certain activities or prescribed needs of that society or segments of that society." - C. Wright Mills, *The Sociological Imagination* (New York: Oxford University Press, 1959), p. 30.

Interdependence. A reciprocal relation between interdependent entities (objects or individuals or groups).

Internalization. The processes through which children learn to identify and use the appropriate set of norms in different social settings.

Language. Refers to a system of symbols that allows communication between people to take place. Language is the medium through which culture is transmitted from one generation to the next.

Looking Glass Self. Cooley's concept that individuals use others like mirrors and base their conceptions of self on what is reflected to them during social interaction.

Macro-Level. Institutional analysis that refers to national, and sometimes even global, social structures.

Material Culture. Refers to the tangible things we create as a culture. Material culture can refer to homes, automobiles, highways, roads, and interstates, buildings, boats, books, computers, or anything else that society produces.

Meritocracy. A system in which the talented are chosen and moved ahead on the basis of their achievements. Can also be described as a society where status is achieved on the basis of merit; this might involve the possession of attributes, which are valued in a society.

Meso-Level. Analysis that is focused at the institutional level such as local governments and universities.

Micro-Level. Analysis that refers to face-to-face interactions in small groups of people.

Negotiated Order. You are able to function due to understanding in a broad sense what your role is in relationship to your superiors and other peers.

Presentation of Self. The process through which we try to convince others that we have the personal qualities and characteristics we believe we do.

Protestant Ethic. An ascetic orientation that encourages hard work, thrift, and righteous forms of godliness.

Rationality. A reliance on reason and the scientific method as the basis of decision making.

Reflected Appraisals. Messages we get about ourselves from others, often in terms of scripts.

Role Performance. The actual behavior of people who occupy a status.

Role. A role is the expected behavior associated with a particular status position—What the individual or group occupying a particular status position is supposed to do.

Self-Concept. How we think and feel about ourselves. Our sense of self comes from our communication and interaction with others.

Self-Knowledge. The understanding of one's self, or of one's own character, powers, limitations, etc.

Significant Others. Parents, siblings, close friends, teachers, bosses, lovers, spouses, and our own children from whom we seek reflected appraisal. Because most of us choose friends and social locations staffed with similar others, and because significant others tend to be in our lives for a long time, continuity in these "reflected appraisals" contributes to a feeling of self-stability.

Social Control. The manner in which behavior is regulated in society. The means and processes by which a group secures its members' conformity to its expectations—to its values, its ideology, its norms, and to the appropriate roles that are attached to the various status positions in the group.

Social Structure. Societies are "divided" generally into two components—social structure and social processes—that interpenetrate each other; i.e., are dialectically interrelated. The key to understanding social structure in a society is understanding its social institutions and their intertwining combinations. Social structure is the institutional framework that makes for order in daily, weekly, and yearly interaction between people. It is social institutions that promote the necessary order to make social structure possible.

Socialization. The lifelong process of learning culture. During the process of socialization individuals learn and internalize the norms of our culture, attitudes, values, beliefs, ways of thinking and learning, social expectations of society, and develop a sense of self.

Status. Status is a socially defined position in a social structure. It is a position that an individual occupies in a group, such as leader or follower; doctor or nurse; mother or son; student or professor, etc. A status can also be a specific position of one group in relation to another group, such as executives and secretaries in a large office.

Symbols. An object, sound, name, or event given meaning by a group that stands for something else, especially a material thing that stands for something that is not material. The bald eagle is a symbol of the United States of America.

Take the Self as Other. To infer your personal characteristics from observing and evaluating your own behavior.

Values. The standards by which our culture defines what is good or bad, desirable or undesirable, beautiful or ugly. Values serve as broad guidelines that define how things ought to be.

REFERENCES

The ideas expressed in my essay on social structure and the information presented are based on the following works:

Asch, Solomon E. 1951. "Effects of Group Pressure Upon the Modification and Distortion of Judgments." Pp. 177-190 in *Groups, Leadership, and Men,* edited by G. Guetzkow. Pittsburgh, PA: Carnegie Press.

Asch, Solomon E. 1956. "Studies of Independence and Conformity: A Minority of One Against a Unanimous Majority." *Psychological Monographs* 70: (Whole, No. 416).

Baumeister, R. F. and M. R. Leary. 1995. "The Need to Belong: Desire for Interpersonal Attachments as a Fundamental Human Motivation." *Psychological Bulletin* 117:479-529.

Benedict, Ruth. 1934. *Patterns of Culture.* New York: Houghton Mifflin.

Blau, Peter (ed.). 1975. *Approaches to the Study of Social Structure.* New York: Free Press.

Blau, Peter M. and Joseph E. Schwartz. 1984. *Cross-Cutting Social Circles.* Orlando, FL: Academic Press.

Blau, Peter M. and Marshall W. Meyer. 1971. *Bureaucracy in Modern Society.* 2nd ed. New York: Random House.

Blumer, Herbert. 1969. *Symbolic Interactionism: Perspective and Method.* Englewood Cliffs, NJ: Prentice-Hall.

Bourdieu, P. 1973. "Cultural Reproduction and Social Reproduction." In *Knowledge, Education, and Cultural Change,* edited by R. Brown. London, UK: Tavistock.

Children's Defense Fund. *The State of America's Children 2004.* Washington, DC: Children's Defense Fund.

Cooley, Charles Horton. 1902. *Human Nature and the Social Order.* New York: Scribner's.

Cooley, Charles Horton. 1967. "Primary Groups." In *Small Groups: Studies in Social Interaction,* edited by A. Paul Hare, Edgar F. Borgotta, and Robert F. Bales. New York: Knopf.

Eisenstadt, S. N. 1985. "Macrosocietal Analysis – Background, Development, and Indications." In *Macrosociological Theory: Perspectives on Sociological Theory,* edited by S. N. Eisenstadt and H. J. Helle. Newbury Park, CA: Sage.

Gibbs, Jack P. *Control: Sociology's Central Notion.* Urbana, IL: University of Illinois Press.

Giddens, Anthony. 1984. *The Constitution of Society.* Cambridge, England: Polity Press.

Goffman, Erving. 1959. *The Presentation of Self in Everyday Life.* Garden City, NY: Anchor Books.

Goffman, Erving. 1961. *Encounters: Two Studies in the Sociology of Interaction.* Indianapolis, IN: Bobbs-Merril.

Goffman, Erving. 1963. *Behavior in Pubic Places: Notes on the Social Organization of Gatherings.* New York: Free Press.

Gollwitzer, P. M. 1986. "Striving for Specific Identities: The Social Reality of Self-Symbolizing." Pp. 143-160 in *Public Self and Private Self,* edited by R. F. Baumeister. New York: Springer-Verlag.

Hogan, R. and J. Hogan. 1991. "Personality and Status." Pp. 137-154 in *Personality, Social Skills, and Psychopathology: An Individual Differences Approach,* edited by D. Gilbert and J. J. Connolly. New York: Plenum Press.

Jones, E. E. 1990. *Interpersonal Perception*. New York: Freeman.

Jones, E. E. and F. F. Baumeister. 1976. "The Self-Monitor Looks at the Ingratiator." *Journal of Personality* 44:654-674.

Jones, E. E. and T. S. Pittman. 1982. "Toward a General Theory of Strategic Self-Presentation." Pp. 231-262 in *Psychological Perspectives on the Self*, Vol. 1, edited by J. Suls. Hillsdale, NJ: Erlbaum.

Kluckhohn, Clyde and Henry A. Murray. 1956. *Personality: In Nature, Society, and Culture*. New York: Knopf.

Kohn, Melvin L. 1959. "Social Class and Parental Values." *American Journal of Sociology* 64:337-351.

Kohn, Melvin L. and Carmi Schooler. 1969. "Class, Occupation, and Orientation." *American Sociological Review* 34:659-678.

Kohn, Melvin L. and Carmi Schooler. 1982. "Job Conditions and Personality: A Longitudinal Assessment of Their Reciprocal Effects." *American Journal of Sociology* 87:1257-1286.

Kohn, Melvin L. and Carmi Schooler. 1983. *Work and Personality*. Norwood, NJ: Ablex.

Leary, M. R. 1995. *Self-Presentation: Impression Management and Interpersonal Behavior*. Madison, WI: Brown and Benchmark.

Leary, M. R. and R. M. Kowalski. 1990. "Impression Management: A Literature Review and Two-Component Model." *Psychological Bulletin* 107:34-47.

Mead, George Herbert. 1934. *Mind, Self, and Society: From the Standpoint of a Social Behaviorist*. (Charles W. Morris, ed.) Chicago, IL: University of Chicago Press.

Mead, Margaret. 1950. *Sex and Temperament in Three Primitive Societies*. 2nd ed. New York: Dell.

Milgram, Stanley. 1963. "Behavior Study of Obedience." *Journal of Abnormal Psychology and Social Psychology* 67(4):371-78.

Milgram, Stanley. 1964. "Group Pressure and Action Against a Person." *Journal of Abnormal and Social Psychology* 69(2):137-143.

Milgram, Stanley. 1965. "Some Conditions of Obedience and Disobedience to Authority." *Human Relations* 18:57-75.

Milgram, Stanley. 1974. *Obedience to Authority: An Experimental View*. New York: Harper and Row.

Milgram, Stanley. 1977. *The Individual in a Social World*. Reading, MA: Addison-Wesley.

Perlin, L. I. and Melvin L. Kohn. 1966. "Social Class, Occupation, and Parental Values: A Cross-National Study." *American Sociological Review* 31:466-479.

Rhodewalt, F. and S. Agustsdottir. 1986. "Effects of Self-Presentation on the Phenomenal Self." *Journal of Personality and Social Psychology* 50:47-55.

Sagarin, Edward. 1975. *Deviants and Deviance*. New York: Praeger.

Sapir, Edward. 1949. *Selected Writings of Edward Sapir in Language, Culture, and Personality*. David G. Mendelbaum, ed. Berkeley, CA: University of California Press.

Schlenker, B. R. 1980. *Impression Management: The Self-Concept, Social Identity, and Interpersonal Relationships*. Monterey, CA: Brooks/Cole.

Sherif, M. 1936. *The Psychology of Social Norms*. New York: Harper.

Sorokin, Pitrim A. 1937-1941. *Social and Cultural Dynamics*. 4 vols. New York: American Book Company.

Sumner, William Graham. 1906. *Folkways: A Study in the Sociological Importance of Usages, Manners, Customs, Mores, and Morals*. New York: Ginn.

Tucker, Robert C. (ed.). 1978. *The Marx-Engel's Reader*. 2nd ed. New York: Norton.

Turner, Jonathan H. 1990. "Emile Durkheim's Theory of Social Organization." *Social Forces* 68:1089-103.

Turner, Ralph H. 1964. "Collective Behavior." In *Handbook of Modern Sociology*, edited by R. E. L. Faris. Chicago, IL: Rand McNally.

Turner, Ralph H. 1968. "The Self-Conception in Social Interaction." In *The Self in Social Interaction*, edited by C. Gordon and K. J. Gergen. New York: John Wiley.

Turner, Ralph H. 1985. "Unanswered Questions in the Convergence Between Structuralist and Interactionist Role Theories." In *Microsociological Theory: Perspectives on Sociological Theory*. Vol. 2, edited by S. N. Eisenstadt and H. J. Helle. Newbury Park, CA.

Tyler, Tom R. 1990. *Why People Obey the Law*. New Haven, CT: Yale University Press.

United States Bureau of the Census. 2004. "Income, Poverty, and Health Insurance Coverage in the United States: 2004." Current Population Reports. Series P60-226 (September).

United States Bureau of the Census. 2004. Current Population Survey 2003-2004. "Annual Social and Economic Supplement." Table 3. Online. Accessed December 29, 2005. http://www.bls.census.gov/cps/asec/adsmain.htm.

Weber, Max. 1958. *The Protestant Ethic and the Spirit of Capitalism*. (Talcott Parsons, trans.) New York: Scribner's.

Weber, Max. 1970. "Bureaucracy." In H. H. Gerth and C. Wright Mills (trans.), *From Max Weber: Essays in Sociology*. New York: Oxford University Press.

7 | Society: Thinking Large.
by Frank O. Taylor, IV, Ph.D. and Ivan M. Chompalov, Ph.D.

FOUNDATIONS OF SOCIETY

Since sociology studies human societies, it behooves us to examine how society has changed historically and what underpins these changes. A popular saying holds that "as goes the economy, so goes the society." What this means, essentially, is that all societies are built upon economic foundations. Before we explore the relationship between society and economics, we should understand what is meant by the word society. Sociologists and anthropologists have long been interested in societies, including their history, diversity, how they change, and how they remain stable. In this chapter, we will look at some of the theories of social organization and development.

Society refers to a group of people who share a common culture and geographical territory. Culture refers to the shared language, symbols, values, norms, and beliefs of the society. Some societies are more complex than others. Societies can differ widely in their medium of exchange, their social organization, their economies, their religious practices and beliefs, their family systems, and so on. Gerhard Lenski and Jean Lenski describe social development as changes that take place in society due to technological advances. New technologies can dramatically revolutionize society, as can be seen in the transformation of European societies from an agricultural base to an industrial base. For the Lenskis, human history is a complex process of social change in which improvements in productive technology cause changes in the type of society and social organization.

Karl Marx understood social change and development in terms of social conflict. According to Marx, the social relations between classes of people are dependent upon the manner in which a society produces material goods. Max Weber made distinctions between types of societies based upon the ideas common to specific societies. Weber contrasted the ideas of traditional societies with the rational thinking common in modern societies. Another sociologist, Emile Durkheim explained societies in terms of their division of labor and level of interdependency between different groups.

123

SOCIAL ECONOMIC TRANSFORMATION

Gerhard and Jean Lenski (Lenski, Nolan, and Lenski 1995) have studied what they term sociocultural evolution, changes in society which are related to new technology. The Lenskis note how societies have changed over the centuries as they gain control over their physical environments.

Societies with simple technology have a simple division of labor. The members of such societies display great similarity of beliefs and behaviors. In contrast, societies that have technologies that are more complex also have larger populations and people pursue a wider range of livelihoods. Social change occurs very slowly in technologically simple societies. Men and women in these societies engage in much the same behaviors and pursuits as did their ancestors. However, dramatic transformations can occur very quickly in technologically advanced societies.

Imagine for a moment the changes that your grandparents must have witnessed. In the United States, people born just before or after World War II would have seen the first color television broadcasts, watched as astronauts walked on the moon, received transmissions from satellites orbiting the planet, and perhaps marveled at the advent of microwaves, cell phones, computers and the host of other inventions and discoveries which we now take for granted. It is no surprise that new technologies can fundamentally alter a society's way of life. Technological changes can affect every institution within society. Now, we will look at the five general types of societies described by the Lenskis. These societies are distinguished by technology: they are hunting and gathering societies, horticultural and pastoral societies, agrarian societies, industrial societies, and postindustrial societies.

Hunting and Gathering Societies. **Hunters and gatherers** are the most basic of human societies and are based on simple technology for hunting animals and gathering vegetation. Until about 10,000 years ago, all humans lived in hunting and gathering societies. Few of these societies remain today. Among the remaining hunters and gatherers are the Aka and Pygmies of central Africa, in southwestern Africa the Bushmen, the Aborigines of Australia, the Kaska Indians of Northwest Canada, and the Batek and Semai of Malaysia (Endicott 1992; Hewlett 1992). The land which hunters and gatherers live on has been severely encroached upon by technologically complex societies, depleting the game and vegetation necessary to their way of life. The Lenskis feared that by the year 2000, or shortly after, hunting and gathering societies might disappear from the Earth.

Hunters and gatherers have little control over their environment and must continually search for game and edible plants. Where hunters and gatherers live in areas of lush vegetation and plentiful game, they enjoy a good life. However, as noted, these conditions are rapidly disappearing. The risk of destruction of their food supply, however, increases the chance of early death from disease, drought, famine, and pestilence. Members of these societies have only a fifty-fifty chance of surviving childhood (Lenski and Lenski 1987).

Hunters and gatherers are typically small bands of just a few dozen people because they require a lot of land to support themselves. As they consume vegetation in one area, they must move to another and so they are nomadic. Frequently they follow migratory animals, as was the case with the plains Indians in America. Hunters and gathers rarely build permanent settlements.

Hunters and gatherers have few social divisions. Usually, the groups have a shaman, or priest. Due to their small size, kinship is the key organizing principle of hunters and gatherers. The family is the major institution, if not the only institution. The family obtains and distributes food, protects its members, and socializes children. Gender is also an important organizing principle. Women and children gather vegetation, men hunt the larger animals, and both women and men hunt small animals. While healthy adults obtain most of the food, older people contribute what they can. Everyone leads similar lives.

Of all societies, hunters and gatherers are the most egalitarian. Women's status may be equal to that of men because vegetation is a reliable food source. Indeed, women may contribute as much as four-fifths of the total food supply (Bernard 1992). Because of the perishable nature of what is hunted and gathered, accumulation of property is out of the question. Therefore, people remain equal. Simple needs preclude the accumulation of additional material possessions. Because there are no rulers and decisions are arrived at by discussion, the status differences that mark more complex societies are absent. The groups may have a part-time shaman, or priest, but they are also responsible for helping to obtain food. Hunters and gatherers have the most leisure of all human groups (Sahlins 1972; Lorber 1994; Volti 1995). Very few hunting and gathering societies remain and those may not survive much longer (Lenski and Lenski 1987).

by Frank O. Taylor, IV, Ph.D. and Ivan M. Chompalov, Ph.D.

Pastoral and Horticultural Societies. Around ten thousand years ago, people discovered a new technology, horticulture. This technology is based on using hand tools to cultivate plants. People used a hoe to work the soil and a digging stick to push holes in the ground to plant seeds. This allowed groups to give up gathering in favor of planting their own vegetation. Horticultural societies no longer had to abandon an area when the food supply gave out. They developed permanent settlements, moving only when the soil became depleted. Gardens first appeared in the fertile regions of the Middle East, followed by Latin America and Asia. Within 5,000 years, cultural diffusion had spread horticulture throughout the world.

In addition to horticulture people found that they could domesticate and breed some of the animals they had hunted, such as goats, sheep, cattle, and camels. This gave rise to pastoral societies, which are based on the pasturing of animals. Pastoral societies tended to develop in arid regions where cultivation of plants was impractical. These groups remained nomadic and followed their animals from fresh pasture to pasture. Not all hunting and gathering societies abandoned their way of life. Where vegetation and game was plentiful, the new technologies may have been ignored. The new horticultural technology was likely incorporated into traditional hunting and gathering (Chagnon 1992).

Domestication of plants and animals led to a material surplus: more resources than needed to support the minimum needs of the members of society. This in turn led to a more differentiated division of labor. In other words, compared to hunters and gatherers, horticultural societies display greater social complexity. Not everyone had to be engaged in the search for food. Now it was possible for some people to pursue craft making, others to be involved in trade, and still others to become priests. Other specializations developed—some people made weapons, others tools, or jewelry, etc.

The domestication of plants and animals thus led to the first social revolution. The creation of a food surplus brought about a series of interrelated changes that fundamentally altered every aspect of human life. As people became more specialized in the production of goods, they become interested in trading with each other. They began to accumulate possessions of value, such as gold, jewelry, and utensils.

by Frank O. Taylor, IV, Ph.D. and Ivan M. Chompalov, Ph.D.

The creation of a material surplus and an increasingly complex **division of labor** set the stage for increased social inequality. Families that produce more food than others can assume positions of greater power and privilege relative to others. These elite families tend to forge social bonds, usually through marriage, which ensures that their social advantages last over generations. A formal system of social inequality emerged and wealth became more concentrated. Moreover, groups now possessed the material goods, such as pastures, croplands, and jewelry, to fight over.

Feuds and wars soon erupted. Wars, in turn, lead to **slavery**, which added another dimension to the status hierarchy. These conflicts changed the forms of leadership, as chiefs and military leaders emerged. The emerging military institution supported the dominance of the elites granting them extensive control over society.

Agrarian Societies. In the Middle East about 5,000 years ago, another technological revolution was underway which would eventually impact the entire world. The agricultural revolution, like the technological revolutions before it, brought about a new type of society. Hoes and digging sticks are extremely inefficient compared to animal drawn plows and irrigation. Using the new plowing technology farmers were able to cultivate greater areas of land than the horticulturists. An additional advantage was that the turning action of the plow aerated the soil, allowing more nutrients to be returned to the earth, which, in turn, increased production.

This new technology allowed farmers to work the same land for generations and encouraged permanent settlements. The resulting food surplus was unlike anything that had preceded it. Once again, the division of labor increased in complexity. Agrarian societies expanded their land areas and populations due to large increases of food transported on animal-powered wagons. This era is known as the "dawn of civilization" (Lenski, Nolan, and Lenski 1995:177). As people built cities, advances were made in writing, mathematics, metallurgy, literature, art, philosophy, in short, what we think of as "culture." A good example of an agrarian civilization was the Roman Empire, which controlled over 2 million square miles of territory populated by some 70 million individuals (Stavrianos 1983; Lenski, Nolan and Lenski 1995).

Increased production means increased specialization and an increasingly complex division of labor. Daily activities once performed by nearly everyone became distinct occupations. Specialization had many important effects upon society. First, it increased social inequalities.

by Frank O. Taylor, IV, Ph.D. and Ivan M. Chompalov, Ph.D.

Some societies, such as the United States, had extremes of social inequality ranging from slavery to the subordination of women. A second effect of specialization was that it freed elites from manual work. Thus, they were able to study philosophy, art, religion, literature, etc., creating what came to be called "high culture." Lastly, specialization ended the old barter system and established money as the medium of exchange. This made trade easier and cities became economic centers with ever expanding populations.

Among hunters and gatherers, women were the primary providers of food. Marx and Engels suggested that with the advent of private property and an elite ruling class men wanted to ensure that their wealth was passed on to their descendants. Women lost their status and **patriarchy**—the subordination of women to men—was born. Agriculture propelled men into positions of social dominance. The sociologist Elise Boulding theorizes that a fundamental shift in women's responsibilities occurred because men were in charge of the cattle and plowing (Fisher 1979). The new technology of attaching metal to the tip of plows led to the farming of larger fields by the men. Thus, women were left with the secondary tasks, such as weeding and carrying water to the fields.

The power of the ruling class of elites was reinforced by organized religion. Elites were able to use religious doctrine to turn unpaid servitude into a moral obligation. In other words, the large mass of ordinary citizens owed the elites their labor. Many of the wonders of the Ancient World, such as the Great Pyramids of Egypt or the Great Wall of China, were possible only because rulers used their absolute power to compel their subjects to a lifetime of work. In the case of the pharaoh of Egypt, religious doctrine held that he was a god on earth. The feudal kings of European societies similarly held that they had a Divine right to rule.

Agrarian societies were vastly different from those that preceded them. Elites gained unparalleled power and established political systems through which to rule. Agrarian societies had the greatest level of specialization and social inequality of the societies discussed so far. In order to maintain control over the large empires, rulers needed a wide range of institutions, including religious, economic, military, and political. Some people gained control of the surpluses and used them to establish themselves as the ruling elite. They protected their advantage by establishing a military. Soon, they levied taxes on their "subjects." This concentration of resources and power, along with the oppression of the masses, was the beginning of the state. It must also be said that the technology of **agrarian society** afforded people a wider range of choices in how to live and make a livelihood.

Industrial Societies. In the 1700s, new technologies again made fundamental changes in society. The steam engine, first used in Britain in 1765, ushered in the industrial revolution. Industrialism is technology that uses sophisticated machinery with advanced sources of power. Although wind and water mills had been used prior to the steam engine, until the industrial revolution societies depended upon human and animal power. This new technology led to the development of what the sociologist Herbert Blumer termed **industrial society**. Goods are produced by machines powered by fuels and individuals are extremely interdependent upon each other for survival.

Social change began to occur very rapidly. Industrial societies changed more in a mere century than they had for thousands of years before. The nineteenth century saw the advent of technologies such as railroads and steamships, and steel-framed skyscrapers. The twentieth century saw the advent of electric light, the automobile, and many additional conveniences that we take for granted today. Electricity alone made possible many of the inventions used in households today: sewing machines, refrigerators, washing machines, etc. Advances in electronic communication soon followed, including the telephone, radio, and television. Recently, computers have ushered in an information revolution, which has increased our ability to analyze massive amounts of data quickly. These changes in computer technology have led to the Information Age.

Production could now be achieved quite efficiently and surpluses were substantially greater. Just as before, new surpluses increased the complexity and differentiation of society and its groups. Social inequality increased, particularly during the early stages of industrialization. Individuals who were first able to take advantage of the new technology accumulated vast wealth.

Karl Marx was very interested in what he termed the means of production and the social relations of production. The means of production refers to factories, machinery, tools, resources, and land. Societies with different productive technologies have different social relations among their members, or the social relations of production. In agrarian societies people worked in the home, developing close working relationships, strong kinship ties, customs and beliefs. Industrialization created factories with centralized machinery and resources. This called for leaving the home. Occupational specialization became more pronounced than ever. The ability to move from place to place also creates a good deal of anonymity and cultural diversity, which adds to the number of subcultures and countercultures. The family is no longer the center of life. In agrarian societies, the family served as the primary economic unit, and was the place for learning and religious worship. As society moves away from traditional families more single people, divorced people, single-parent families, and stepfamilies are created. Not only did social relations inside the family change but also new social relations came into being which were related to selling one's labor for a wage.

The early industrialists were able to dictate the terms under which people had to work. Much of the work of Marx and Engels is a reaction against the hideous conditions under which people had to labor. With the breakdown of feudal society, agrarian peoples were thrown off the lands they and their ancestors had farmed for centuries. They migrated to the new industrial cities where they had none of the rights that they had enjoyed under feudal society, such as they were. Under the new laws, employment was considered a private contract between the employer and the worker. Workers had no right to unionize, no rights to a safe working environment, and no rights to unemployment compensation if injured on the job. Workers who dared to band together and strike for higher wages and improved working conditions were fired. Some were arrested. In the United States, strikes were illegal and the relations between striking workers and the authorities often turned violent.

The Lenskis note that early industrialization benefited only a small segment of the population, those who were able to implement the new technology. In time however, workers won the right to unionize. The Great General Motors sit down strike during the mid-1930s ushered in a host of concessions from business and many new laws meant to protect workers. Most of the benefits workers enjoy today, although eroding quickly, such as the five-day work week, the eight hour working day, vacations, insurance, pensions, unemployment compensation, laws which secure the safety of the workplace, etc., were won during the labor union movement. These successes lead to the standard of living enjoyed by the middle class today. Home ownership became common and other advantages soon followed, such as owning an automobile and other consumer goods.

Today, the typical worker in the United States enjoys a comparatively high standard of living (although, as later chapters will note, this standard of living is declining). People are living longer, have greater access to health care and education than agrarian people ever dreamed of. Even though many are underemployed, uninsured, and poverty is still a major concern, the standard of living has risen dramatically, and economic, political, and social inequalities have declined.

Thus, the pattern of increased inequality accompanying increased complexity of social organization and the division of labor has been reversed in industrial society. Where most non-industrial societies are illiterate, industrial societies provide state-funded schooling. Citizens of industrial societies enjoy a vast array of consumer goods (some of which are frivolous indeed), better housing, heat, sanitary water, electricity, and so on. Additionally, industrial societies confer many political rights upon their citizens, including the right to vote, the right to run for office, the right to trial by a jury of peers, and greater rights by women and minorities, to name a few.

The type of society we live in is fundamental to who we are. Moreover, the level of technology and economic complexity calls forth different types of social organization and relationships. In industrial, and postindustrial society, these social relations are quite complex. The culture we live in is greatly influenced by technology and economy.

Think for a moment about how your life has been affected by the culture you live in. When you think about what you want to do with your life, which largely means what occupation you aspire to, you must also think about the social relations of production. That occupation requires, in all likelihood, an education. Moreover, not just any education but a specialized one. You will, of course, connect the occupation you desire to a certain standard of living. This standard of living, in turn, is associated with material goods, such as cars, television sets, computers, and so on. Perhaps you will desire certain clothes to help you establish the appropriate identity. You will even learn a "lingo," or linguistic terms associated with your occupational specialization. Even how many children you desire to have is influenced by the social norms under which you live. It is difficult to overstate the degree to which the type of society in which you live determines what choices are available to you, what standard of living you will enjoy, how long you will live, and what degree of health you will enjoy. In fact, without culture and social organization it is hard to imagine how you could aspire to be anything. Even how you feel about life itself and reality are influenced by culture, technology, social complexity, and economic and political arrangements.

7 | Society: Thinking Large.
by Frank O. Taylor, IV, Ph.D. and Ivan M. Chompalov, Ph.D.

Although in the United States people like to think of themselves as autonomous individuals who are personally responsible for every advantage they enjoy, a moment's reflection will convince you of just how dependent upon others you really are. Could you drive a car, wear the clothes you like to wear, live in your dream home, and use a telephone, stereo, television, computer, or even electric lights without the specialized activities of others? Certainly not.

Postindustrial Societies. To a large extent many industrial societies have been experiencing **deindustrialization**, shifting from industrial economic activities to service and information economies. For instance, steel and the production of spare auto parts have, for all purposes, vanished from the economic landscape of the United States. The new microchip technology is primarily responsible for the sweeping changes occurring in industrial societies. The change is so great that sociologists agree that a new type of society is emerging, **postindustrial society** (Bell 1973).

Production in industrial societies is based on factories and machinery and used to make consumer goods. However, postindustrial production relies on computers and other electronic technologies to produce, store, analyze and apply information. While workers in industrial society develop skills that allow them to work with machinery, workers in postindustrial society develop skills that will allow them to work with computers and other forms of electronic, information-based, communication.

The shift in skills in postindustrial society has dramatically altered the occupational structure. Fewer people are employed in manufacturing and the ranks of white-collar workers, clerical staff, managers, advertising and marketing agents, academia, and so on, grows quite large. Over seventy percent of the workforce of the United States works in the service sector of the economy, such as education, health, research, counseling, government, mass media, law, banking, or investment. The basic component is no longer raw materials but information. Teachers, bankers, lawyers, and physicians pass on and use specialized knowledge. In industrial societies workers produce material goods. Postindustrial workers do not really produce things. Instead, they analyze, use, or otherwise communicate information and provide services for which others are willing to pay. This trend away from manufacturing is occurring in Western Europe, Japan, and other industrial countries. However, the effect of this new technology is not confined to industrial countries. Its influence is so great that it affects the entire world.

The changes are so fundamental and extensive that many suggest we are in the midst of a fourth social revolution. As new technologies transformed agrarian and industrial societies, so will the new microchip technology transform our society. We are just beginning to witness the changes. Today people drive their cars while talking to others on the phone, perhaps on the other side of the world (this is probably not conducive to safe driving), work at home, or attempt to vanquish imaginary video enemies. Old established ways of life and perspectives are being replaced by new ones. Electronic mail, for example, allows people to communicate by using the written word almost as fast as talking on the telephone, and it is much cheaper.

Microchip technology, for better or worse, is bringing about dramatic changes in our lifestyle, law enforcement, medicine, education, and the workplace. et due to **cultural lag**, the process by which some elements of culture, such as technology, change faster than others, such as values and norms, the changes will not take place uniformly. For example, our economy may be based on information technology but our legal system is the relic of an older era.

ECONOMIC SYSTEMS AND TRANSFORMATION

When we think of a market one might envision a scene in which farmers are selling fruits and vegetables, as well as domestic animals, blankets, and other handicrafts such as baskets. People may be cooking food for customers. Others may be socializing or perusing the available goods. The picture that comes to mind may be that of a farmer's market or a bazaar. A very colorful picture indeed. These are common in non-industrialized societies. Thus, a market can be a forum for buying and selling goods.

Markets also establish the price of goods and services or their value. A market can also be a mechanism by which goods are produced and distributed. Without it, especially in industrial societies, we would all be hungry in short order. Somehow, people must be induced to produce the things we want and need. In other words, the output question must be answered. If the price is right, someone will produce those goods. In the simplest terms, that is the market process. We are all involved, one way or the other, in the productive process, producing what others want. This is how we get what we want.

133

The input question must also be answered: What resources should be used in the production process? When producing things for others we tend to use the cheapest resources available that will get the job done. In the end, greater profits will be generated. Scarce resources are very expensive. This expense tends to be a conserving mechanism for society's most valued resources. People who produce a lot of what we need and desire tend to make a lot of money, or income, especially when they use the cheapest inputs.

Earning an income allows people to purchase their share of society's output. This answers the distribution question, or who gets which distributive share. We all get our income by producing things other people are willing to pay for. People who produce goods or services at higher prices tend to earn more income. This is called the productivity principle of distribution: the value of what is produced determines income. We will return to market mechanisms in more detail later.

Sociologists refer to the dynamics of the market as the **economy**. The economy is a system of production and distribution of goods and services. There are different types of economic systems. A **subsistence economy** is one in which human groups live off the land with little or no surplus. Many sociologists hold that of all social institutions the economy is most important. Today's economic system is greatly different from all but the most recent past.

There is no doubt that today economic systems are global. If you own and drive a car, for example, the parts out of which it was produced come from different parts of the world, are assembled in different parts of the world, and are shipped to the points of distribution from various parts of the world. This is referred to as the global assembly line.

Like it or not, the economy is related to almost every aspect of our existence: the food we eat, the clothes we wear, and the home we live in. It would be hard to claim an identity or self without economic activity. Our health and welfare are related to employment, inflation, economic recession or economic expansion, and supply and demand. The economy affects our chances of owning a car or home, getting an education, and whether or not we obtain a good job or a dead-end job.

by Frank O. Taylor, IV, Ph.D. and Ivan M. Chompalov, Ph.D.

Hunting and Gathering Economic Systems. The earliest human societies, hunting and gathering societies, lived under a simple subsistence economy. They lived off the land, in small groups of twenty to forty individuals, with little or no economic surplus. They gathered what they could and when food availability ran low, they moved to a new site. Technological knowledge was based on the weapons they developed for hunting and storing meat. With little surplus there was no trade with other groups and no excess to accumulate. In this earliest of human societies, there was a high degree of similarity and social equality.

Pastoral and Horticultural Economic Systems. Pastoral and horticultural societies created a more dependable food supply when they began to breed animals and cultivate plants. This led to the development of one of the most important events in human history, a surplus. Human relationships and existence were fundamentally changed. Human groups increased in size, formed permanent settlements, and developed a specialized division of labor. For the first time in human history, some people were involved in activities not specifically related to obtaining food. Some people became specialists in other productive processes. The new division of labor, based on food surpluses, soon created useful products that, in turn, became the basis for trade. Additionally, surpluses and trade also meant that material wealth could be accumulated. Some members of the group accumulated more possessions than others, fostering the social inequality that is still present today.

Agricultural Economic Systems. The creation of surplus products for trade, social complexity, and inequality, and the division of labor were all magnified by the invention of the plow. As more people were freed from the production of food, the division of labor became even more complex. Trade expanded and goods moved over greater distances to far away markets. Soon trading centers developed into cities. Power hands as the heads of families and chiefs were replaced by ruling elite who forged new economic, political, and social relations. Inequalities in these new social realms became even greater.

Industrial Economic Systems. Industrial technology, based on machines and powered by fuels, created unprecedented surpluses. A handful of people could produce all the food necessary for a given society, and then some. As the industrial revolution proceeded, social inequalities were magnified. Exploiting the labor of others and the political system, some individuals were able to amass great wealth. Workers labored under conditions that would seem abhorrent by today's standards. In response, workers unionized and engaged in a violent and often bloody struggle to improve their working conditions. Their successes are largely taken for granted today. The surpluses soon led to improved standards of living for entire societies, as people were able to purchase consumer goods.

Postindustrial Economic Systems. By 1973, sociologist Daniel Bell was writing about the emergence of postindustrial society. This new type of society has six defining characteristics, according to Bell:

1. extensive trade network among nations;

2. a tremendous surplus of goods;

3. a service sector which employs the majority of workers;

4. diversity of goods available to ordinary citizens;

5. an "information explosion;" and

6. a "global village" of instantaneous worldwide communications.

News of economic forecasts and changes travels around the world quickly affecting economic conditions everywhere. Trading occurring at the New York Stock Exchange echoes on the Japanese Nikkei Stock Exchange, and visa versa. Nations, which formerly had only internal markets or only a handful of trading partners, form economic unions. In Europe, for example, seventeen nations have formed such a union. The United States has formed economic alliances with Mexico and Canada.

Continued Social Inequality. Postindustrial technology and economy allows the average citizen to live within a standard of living unheard of only a few generations ago. Yet, in spite of all of the wealth generated by the societies social inequality remains. Indeed, in the United States the gap between the top ten percent of earners and everyone else widens with each passing year. Forty-six percent of the income of the nation goes to just the top fifth of Americans, while only four percent goes to the bottom fifth of Americans. Hunger, malnutrition, unemployment, functional illiteracy, childhood diseases long thought to be vanquished, such as measles, and homelessness are all persistent problems in the United States and seem to be on the rise. Therefore, income distribution remains unequal, and may in fact be worsening, at the same time as the nation is experiencing tremendous economic growth and women and minorities have made many political, cultural, and economic gains. We shall return to these issues in detail later on in the book.

TRANSFORMATION IN THE MEDIUM OF EXCHANGE

The means by which individuals exchange goods and services is called the medium of exchange. We are all familiar with money as a medium of exchange but this is not the single medium. All societies must have this vital necessity, although the medium of exchange depends upon the level of social development.

Early Mediums of Exchange. In hunting and gathering societies, there is little or no surplus and almost no trade. **Barter** was the medium of exchange for whatever trade did occur. Barter is the direct exchange of one item for another.

Agricultural Mediums of Exchange. Bartering certainly continued during agricultural social development. However, a new medium of exchange soon made its appearance: money. Money can essentially be anything, from seashells to coins, to currency. Money reflects the value of goods. Early in its use, money was made of gold or silver and its value depended upon the weight and purity of the coins. In some areas, purchases could also be made with deposit receipts. In this case, the receipt is used as money and it is used against goods on deposit in a warehouse or bank. These deposits could be in the form of gold, wheat, or other trade goods. By the end of the agricultural period, deposit receipts had been formalized into currency, or paper money. Each bill represented a specified amount of gold or silver deposited in a central warehouse. No more currency could be issued than the stored value that it represented.

Industrial Mediums of Exchange. By the time industrial society developed, bartering was a thing of the past. In the United States, gold was replaced with paper currency and was backed by reserves of gold at Fort Knox. This policy was called the gold standard, each dollar representing a specified amount of gold. The number of dollars that could be issued was limited. By the end of the industrial period, the gold standard had been replaced by **fiat money**, currency issued by the government, guaranteed by the government, but not backed up by stored gold or silver.

Governments using fiat money still have practical limits as to the amount of money that can be in circulation. If the government prints too much money, in relation to the available level of goods and services, the result will be inflation. **Inflation** occurs when each unit of currency purchases fewer and fewer goods and services. Inflation is a destabilizing force in society and governments attempt to control it. The issue of inflation will be another topic we shall look at in depth further along. The value of the United States dollar has been declining rapidly since about 1973.

Checking accounts held in banks also became prevalent during the industrial period. A check is a type of deposit receipt. It is a promise that the person writing the check has enough funds in their bank account to cover the check.

A more recent development is the credit card, which allows users to make purchases up to a pre-approved limit without the exchange of money. Cardholders are later billed for the purchases. This recent development, it must be said, has lead to an extreme amount of debt among credit card holders and has fueled more personal bankruptcies any either other period in the history of the United States.

THE TWO FORMS OF SOCIAL LIFE

All these developments speak of an underlying deep change in the way people relate to one another. Sociologists have long observed the shift in what creates order in human groups and what holds society together. At a very fundamental level, the radical transformations that accompanied the switch from one society to another could be described as the transition from a traditional to a modern kind of society, or, in other words, the way pre-industrial societies were organized and functioned saw a radical departure with the advent of industrialism and the post-industrial society.

The two sociologists who extensively analyzed this transformation were Ferdinand Tonnies and Emile Durkheim.

by Frank O. Taylor, IV, Ph.D. and Ivan M. Chompalov, Ph.D.

Ferdinand Tonnies (1855-1936): Gemeinschaft and Gesellschaft

In *Community and Society (Gemeinschaft and Gesellschaft)* the German sociologist Ferdinand Tonnies spelled out two forms of social life. The first one is what he called *Gemeinschaft*, or community type that characterizes rural life, while the second is what he termed *Gesellschaft*, or social life based on association, which characterizes city life. For Tonnies, these two concepts are opposites, and all human social relationships can be seen as divided between these two different types.

Gemeinschaft relationships are found in the relationships within the family and kinship groups and between physically close friends or neighbors who work or live together with the utmost understanding and cooperation. These relationships are deep, warm, intense, satisfying, and are most typical of small rural and agricultural communities. People there have a unity of purpose, they know one another, do things together, take interest in each other's wellbeing, and help each other. People in such societies are like a big family. They form strong bonds and think in terms of "we." These are more or less the so-called traditional societies. The community based form of social life happens at different levels, for example the house, village, and town. The town is the highest and the most complex form of social life in a *Gemeinschaft*. Its local character, in common with that of the village, contrasts with the family character of the house. Both the village and the town retain many characteristics of the family, the village to a larger extent than the town. Only when the town develops into the city are these characteristics almost entirely lost. One contemporary instance of a *Gemeinschaft* society in the midst of a postmodern nation are the Amish, who still persist to old ways of life.

With modernization, industrialization, and urbanization (the mass movement of people from the villages and small towns to the large cities) another type of society came to the fore. This is what Tonnies called the *Gesellschaft*. It is a stark contrast from the community type.

Gesellschaft relationships are more impersonal, bonded by social contract rather than natural will, and tend to separate individuals and groups from one another by creating isolation, tension, and conflict. These relationships dominate the modern city. There people think more often in terms of "I" than "we," they are more self-centered and utilitarian. People are part of society because they realize that they need each other's expertise but the traditional bonds based on kinship and friendship are in decline. People are strangers to each other and often suffer from alienation and isolation. As the urbanization process expands, *Gesellschaft* relationships will grow more dominant and will eventually replace *Gemeinschaft* relationships.

Thus, the rise and growth of the city at the expense of the countryside induces a major transformation in social relations from traditional and communal to modern and associative, from more personal to more impersonal, from supportive and collective to utilitarian and individualistic (selfish).   In short, Tonnies probably laid the foundations of urban sociology proper by distinguishing between the two types of social life and analyzing urban life as a distinct way of relating to other people in a modern and industrialized society.

Emile Durkheim's (1858-1917): Mechanical and Organic Solidarity

In his early seminal work *The Division of Labor in Society*, the French sociologist Emile Durkheim saw preindustrial societies as characterized by what he called "mechanical solidarity" and industrial societies as characterized by what he called "organic solidarity."   The names are somewhat misleading, since **mechanical solidarity** is used to describe what Tonnies called *Gemeinschaft* and **organic solidarity** is used to describe what Tonnies called *Gesellschaft*.

Durkheim developed his ideal types no doubt in trying to make sense, pretty much like Tonnies, of the rapid industrialization and the urban revolution that Europe was experiencing. Thus, in major ways the two typologies are quite similar and reinforce each other. Societies based on mechanical solidarity achieve social unity, or solidarity, from the fact that everyone does essentially the same kind of work and there exists only simple division of labor. In contrast, as the nature of work becomes more differentiated and specialized with the more complex division of labor in modern urban industrial societies, mechanical solidarity becomes gradually displaced by "organic solidarity."

Organic solidarity refers to the social integration of society based on the recognition that individuals in highly specialized occupational roles are highly dependent on other individuals in other highly specialized but unlike roles to supply goods and services that they cannot supply themselves. Thus, organic solidarity is necessary for the functioning of modern, urbanized societies.

The main point of departure in the case of Durkheim is that he viewed urbanization and modernization as an inevitable result of the development of the productive forces, especially the division of labor and that he suffered from less nostalgia for the loss of traditional community social life than did Tonnies. In other words, Durkheim considered both the rural and the urban environments as normal and argued that it is simply that urban communities achieve a new form of cohesion and order that expresses interdependence based on contractual and not familial obligations.

At the same time, Durkheim recognized that organic solidarity did not come about automatically, and that social integration of societies characterized by an increasing division of labor was threatened by the following possibilities:

1. anomie, or a sense of normlessness and isolation, may increase with the division of labor;

2. individuals may be reluctantly forced to perform tasks that are not of their own choosing; and

3. the division of labor may be so minute that any given work task does not seem to be relevant or meaningful, thus leading to a sense of alienation.

POPULATION AND THE ENVIRONMENT

The overview of the development of human society so far highlights the importance of population growth and the use of natural resources for shifting social relations. Rapid population growth has been a fact of life for thousands of years. It is associated with crucial questions about the existence of humankind, like: will the planet be able to accommodate the ever increasing population? Are we going to have enough space for everybody? Are chronic famine, wars, and diseases our sorry fate or can we do something to both avoid them and curb the unchecked population growth? Will the depletion of earth's resources and environmental pollution doom us in the future? Such questions have been at the heart of an area of sociology, called demography, or

141

by Frank O. Taylor, IV, Ph.D. and Ivan M. Chompalov, Ph.D.

the study of the size, composition, growth, and distribution of human populations and their relationships with the environment (Weeks 2005).

Demography is one of the oldest and best developed social science specialties. Its origins can be traced to antiquity; for instance in Egypt in 2500 B.C. when the pharaohs began counting their population and property. However, the first comprehensive demographic undertaking, known as a **census**, according to some experts was conducted shortly after William the Conqueror, Duke of Normandy invaded England in 1066. Suspicious that his subjects were not paying enough taxes, William sent men all over the country to count the number of subjects and to find out what land and cattle they possessed. It took approximately two years to complete this massive undertaking and compile what came to be known as the "Doomsday Book." In short, this is generally considered as the first systematic *census*, or a complete population count, often broken down by such categories as sex, age, occupation, marital status, and the like. Later governments, realizing the usefulness of this procedure and the need to repeat it periodically because of population fluctuations, encouraged inquiry into how and why such fluctuations occur. Thus came into existence the science of *demography*.

The term ***demography*** itself is of Greek origin and is comprised of two parts—*demos*, or people, and *graphy*, or description. Thus, demography means describing people or populations. Its main concern is with documenting and explaining human population changes, as well as the interrelations of human populations with their environment. It studies processes such as population growth, mortality, fertility, the marriage rate, the divorce rate, migration, and similar issues by applying a variety of statistical and historical techniques. Currently, the development of demographic knowledge has led not only to better understanding of population processes, but also to a more scientific public policy, both short-term (as a result of the census and "snapshot" population surveys) and long-term (as a result of population projections and forecasting).

The three measures of population change are respectively the birth rate (fertility), the death rate (mortality), and migration. **Fertility** is another word for child bearing. The **fertility rate** (sometimes called total fertility rate) is how many children the average woman bears. The highest total fertility rate is in Sub-Saharan Africa (about 6), the lowest (1.4) in Europe. The lowest such rate is in Bulgaria and Latvia (1.1), the highest in Niger (7.5). In the United States, it is about 2 children. Another measure used by demographers is the **crude birth rate**, or the number of live births per 1,000 population. **Mortality** is simply another word for the number of deaths. The most commonly used measure of mortality is the **crude death rate**, or the number of deaths per 1,000 population. The highest death rate is in Niger (24), the lowest (2) in Kuwait, Qatar and UAE (all are oil rich countries). The third major demographic variable is **migration**, or the movement of people in and out of geographically and politically defined areas. The difference between in-movers and out-movers is known as **net migration**. Typically, however, migration is measured as net migration rate, or simply the difference between immigrants (people moving in) and emigrants (people moving out) per 1,000 population.

The Demographic Equation. The basic demographic equation measures population growth and involves all the three major variables. Simply put, *Population Growth = births – deaths + net migration.*

It is important for public policy to have accurate projections of population growth. The basic pattern here is that *as a country industrializes, it experiences a decline in population growth.* We have **zero population growth** when every 1,000 women give birth to 2,100 children.

What are the implications of demographic analysis for our society?

The short answer is that the study of population characteristics and fluctuations, which is the subject matter of demography, directly and indirectly affects practically all spheres of social life. On an individual level, you will probably experience most of the demographic processes in your lifetime (birth, death, migration). On a macro-social level, crucial developments and policy decisions are based on demographic trends. For example, census data is used to determine how many electoral college votes each state gets, or how congressional seats will be apportioned (e.g., as a result of the 2000 Census Georgia gained two seats in Congress, while Pennsylvania lost two), to carry out congressional redistricting, to estimate revenues from taxes, to compile the federal budget, to allocate federal funds to individual states, to monitor trends in immigration and formulate respective policies, and so on.

Moreover, census data permit the study of trends and feed into future projections that have wide-ranging implications. For instance, the 2000 Census data showed that, for the first time, Hispanics surpassed Blacks as the largest minority group in the United States (35.3 million

Hispanics, or 12.5 percent of the total population versus 34.7 million Blacks, or 12.3 percent of the total population of 281 million). The driving force behind that was that in Mexico fertility declined slightly, whereas mortality dropped precipitously. As a result, the high population growth in our southern neighbor meant that the economy could not generate a similar growth in jobs, so people try to migrate to where the jobs are (the United States). On the other hand, the low growth rates in the United States were accompanied with the opening up of low-skilled, underpaid jobs especially in the seasonal agricultural sector and the lower end of the services sector. More importantly, the Hispanic population increased from 1990 to 2000 by 57.9 percent, while overall the United States population increased by 13.2 percent. This means that, if the growth rates stay the same, in about 2060 Hispanics will constitute half of the total population. It is not a stretch to imagine that at that time, or even earlier, Spanish will become the second official language in the United States.

However, population changes in and of themselves do not reveal the full picture. It is also important to see what the implications are for our interaction with the environment. A short example will suffice. It is largely believed, although estimates vary, that human activity, especially after the industrial revolution, has contributed to increased emissions of the so-called "greenhouse gases" (mainly carbon dioxide, water, and methane) and hence, to **global warming**. By 2100, average temperatures are expected to increase between 2.5 and 10.4 degrees Fahrenheit and the effects from this, though debated, will undoubtedly be significant.

World Population Growth. As mentioned earlier in the chapter, historically there have been five types of human societies—hunters-gatherers, horticultural and pastoral societies, agricultural societies, industrial societies, and post-industrial societies. In each one of these evolutionary stages, the world's population has grown. At the dawn of civilization, there were probably several thousand humans. Hunters and gatherers slowly started pushing their **carrying capacity**, or the available resources to support a certain number of people, given their lifestyle, because they were using resources extensively, rather than intensively. On the eve of the agricultural revolution about 10,000 years ago, there were approximately 4 million humans. This population began to grow more noticeably after the agricultural revolution was in full swing. By the turn of the first Millennium A.D., there were approximately 200 million people and that number was growing by 300,000 each year. On the eve of the industrial revolution (about 1750), the population of the world was nearly 1 billion and was increasing by 2.6 million every year. What happened after that was an even more spectacular increase in the world's population, characterized by an ever accelerating growth. These events have been described as a population explosion. It took humankind tens of thousands of years to reach 1 billion people and then in about 250 short years (from the point of view of human history) the world's population exploded to reach 6 billion people. We reached the 1 billion mark in roughly 1804, then it took 123 years (1927) to reach 2 billion, only 33 years to hit 3 billion (1960). It took only 14 years to add another billion people (1974), we then reached 5 billion in 13 short years (1987), and 6 billion in 12 more years (1999). Currently, the population of the world has exceeded 6 billion and 500 million people and the population of the United States is almost 300 million people.

The Theory of Malthus. The first influential theory of population change, which prompted some observers to label demography as the *grim science* was developed at the end of the eighteenth century (1798) in a book titled *An Essay on the Principle of Population* by Thomas Malthus—a Scottish thinker educated in England. *In capsule, he argued on the basis of analysis of data about population changes throughout the history of mankind that there is a gap between population and subsistence.* Thus, while the human species grow at geometrical rates (i.e., involving multiplication or power, for instance 2, 2 x 2 = 4, 2 x 2 x 2 =8, 2 x 2 x 2 x 2 = 16, etc.), subsistence or resources grow at arithmetic rates (i.e., involving addition, for instance, 1, 1 + 1 = 2, 1 + 1 + 1 = 3, 1 + 1 + 1 + 1 = 4, etc.). Malthus's theory states that populations will rise to the level of their subsistence and when food supply becomes scarce in the face of a population growing out of proportion, the so-called "positive checks" will inevitably set in to restore the balance. Ironically, what he referred to as positive checks were calamities such as famine, epidemics, natural disasters, and wars. From Malthus's standpoint, mortality is the crucial factor in regulating population size, as he believed that fertility could not be controlled and that it will always remain high.

Recently, another theory of population change, which challenges the arguments of the followers of Malthus, has gained greater recognition as being more accurate. These researchers call themselves "Anti-Malthusians" and think that Malthus's theory and the arguments of his followers are dead wrong, since people do not blindly reproduce until there is no room left for them on earth (Julian Simon 1981, 1992). They claim that the so-called **Demographic Transition Theory** better describes the changes in the world's population. Transition theory describes population changes in terms of several stages. During stage one, there was high fertility and high mortality, just as Malthus has predicted. Then, due to industrialization and advances in medicine from roughly 1700 to the mid-1800s Europe entered stage two, the fairly high fertility was combined with fairly low mortality. The <u>third stage</u> started around the turn of the century and was in full swing at about 1930. It is characterized by declining fertility and declining mortality, which leads to a stabilized, but lower level of growth. This has not been predicted by Malthus's theory (he held fertility constantly high).

How Fast Are We Growing? Although the rate of population increase has slowed since the 1960s, we are still worried about rapid population growth, because in absolute numbers the world is still producing too many humans. The reason is that we are building on a very large population base. Thus, even the fairly slow growth rate of 1.2 percent per year translates into 77 million additional people every year. Projections are that the average annual rate of growth in about 2050 will go back to the levels of 1800. Projections, however, are a tricky business. For example, nobody predicted that the growth rate in 1960 would dip below the rate in 1950. That happened because of Mao's Great Leap Forward (industrialization), which led to 30 million people dying of famine in China. In addition, nobody predicted the Post-World war II Baby Boom.

How Fast Can We Grow? The short answer is "Faster than is desirable." This is because human populations (and other animal populations, for that matter) have the potential to grow at an exponential rate (something that Malthus warned about). In short, the time for doubling of the population becomes shorter and shorter as the rate of increase accelerates. Another way to think about it is that if growth doubles at approximately equal periods of time, it suddenly accelerates (e.g., 4 million doubles in 10 years = 8, then 8 million doubles in 10 years = 16, then 16 million doubles in 10 years = 32; if the increase was the same as the initial 10-year increase (4 million), in 30 years we would have achieved 3 x 4 = 12 + the initial 4 = 16 million, instead of 32 million).

Early populations grew extremely slowly, if at all. One major reason was that for hunter-gatherers was mortality was high and the life expectancy was extremely short (about 20 years). Later on (during the agricultural revolution) the high density of populations contributed to the spread of infectious diseases, but birth rates probably went up due to better nutrition, as did life expectancy.

A major reason for the acceleration of population increase after the mid-eighteenth century was the drop in death rates, accompanying the industrial revolution. This was due to both higher standards of living and to medical advances. The important thing to remember is that the drop in fertility rates lagged behind the drop in mortality rates, which caused a "population explosion." Recently, the growth rate has slowed down and many developed countries are experiencing zero population growth or even negative population growth (although the latter is an oxymoron).

Naturally, the question arises: Have we slowed population growth so much that the world will begin to lose population, or be "downsized"? The answer is that this is mostly rhetorical, based on projections that many European countries and Japan will lose population. However, the less developed countries are projected to grow from 4.9 billion in 2000 to 8.2 billion in 2050 (medium projections of the United Nations), which means that this will probably spill over via migration to the 39 countries expected to see a dwindling of their populations.

Population and the Environment. The relationships between human populations and their environments are the domain of **ecology**, or human ecology. These relationships were at the heart of centuries old demographic concerns, including Malthus's dire predictions that, since the population grows at a geometrical rate and the food supply increases only arithmetically, "positive checks" on population growth are inevitable. Thus, dangers of the population growing too fast and thus outstripping the availability of resources (food, water, energy, land) have often come to the fore in demographic discussions.

One factor that limits our future food production is the destruction of the environment. The erosion of top soil, the exhaustion of fresh water resources, the pollution of the air and the soil all portend difficulties ahead. The danger is summarized by the Canadian geographer of Czech origin Vaclav Smil, who estimated that there is no way under even an increased capacity to produce food to sustain even the more than 6 billion people alive today if they all consume at the rate of the average United States citizen, which is approximately as much as 50 individuals in the Third World. In short, in America we have already surpassed our carrying capacity (the resources available to maintain a human population at a given standard of living). The danger is that according to reasonable estimates, by the middle of this century the population of the world will be not 6 but about 9 billion people or more.

About 50 years ago, a true social movement, known as environmentalism, arose out of dissatisfaction with our practices that lead to endangering the environment in which we live. It seeks to transform existing cultural beliefs and values and to alter societal practices and institutions so that a new, ecologically informed person-environment relationship can be achieved. What are the negative effects of our population growth and unharnessed economic development? Our **biosphere** (the zone on the earth where life is found) consists of three elements: the lithosphere (land, or upper part of the earth's crust); atmosphere (a mixture of gases surrounding the planet, or the air layer above the earth); and hydrosphere (surface and ground water).

We have already done and are doing much damage to the thin crust of the earth's surface. The damage consists of soil erosion, soil degradation, loss of biodiversity, deforestation, desertification, strip-mining for energy resources, dumping of hazardous waste. One example is deforestation, about 80 percent of which is due to population growth. The problem with deforestation is that we disrupt the hydrologic and carbon cycles, thus contributing to soil erosion—the top soil is lost since we have removed the natural barriers that protect it against the elements.

We are also doing a great deal of damage to the atmosphere, which consists of various gases and determines weather patterns, as well as the quality of air we breathe. One example of such damage is "global warming." It is largely believed, although estimates vary, that human activity, especially after the industrial revolution, has contributed to increased emissions of the so-called "greenhouse gases" (mainly carbon dioxide, water, and methane, but also ozone, nitrous oxide and chlorofluorocarbons [CFC]) and hence, to global warming, or increase in the global temperature due to these gases trapping heat which cannot escape back into space (light and infrared radiation from the sun goes through the layer but not all of this heat goes back, when it rises back from earth). This is expected to lead to rising ocean levels because of melting of the polar ice caps and unimaginable consequences that defy reason. Increased energy use (emissions of carbon dioxide and methane) is the main culprit for global warming and the United States, China, and Russia are by far the main polluters. Another untoward consequence of our destructive ways that affects the atmosphere is the thinning of the ozone layer, which protects us from deadly UV light. This is mainly due to emissions of CFCs. A by-product of burning coal is the so-called acid rain (sulfur particles trapped in the air that can cause a lot of damage when it rains). Moreover, of course, we all know the disastrous health effects of "smog."

148

by Frank O. Taylor, IV, Ph.D. and Ivan M. Chompalov, Ph.D.

According to many demographers and environmental scientists, we are also depleting the hydrosphere. The depletion of fresh water resources and fresh water scarcity loom large on the horizon and may be our most immediate danger that perhaps has to be averted in order to avoid an ecological disaster. This argument is bolstered by facts. Fresh water constitutes only 3 percent of the world's water availability and only one-thousandth of this 3 percent is readily available in lakes, soil moisture, streams, atmospheric water vapor, and exploitable groundwater. The magnitude of the water issue further becomes clear when we take into account the fact that it takes half a million gallons of water to grow an acre of rice and that irrigated agriculture accounts for 70 percent of consumed water. Desalination of salt water, which is in abundant supply, is one solution, but this turns out to be very expensive.

A useful concept to measure whether we are <u>overshooting</u> our carrying capacity is the so-called **ecological footprint,** or the land and water area that is required to support indefinitely the material standard of living of a given human population, using prevailing technology. Thus, the average United States ecological footprint is 10.3 hectares per capita, whereas the available ecological capacity for the world is 2.0 hectares per capita and that of the United States—6.7 hectares. No wonder that, according to some reliable estimates, if everybody in the world was using resources at the rate of the average American, we will need two additional planets the size of the Earth to support the current population of the world.

ॐ ଔ ॐ ଔ

DEFINITIONS

Agrarian Society. A society based on using the plow to cultivate large areas of land and increase productivity.

Barter. The direct exchange of one item for another.

Biosphere. The zone on the earth where life is found.

Carrying Capacity. The available resources to support a certain number of people, given their lifestyle.

Census. A complete population count, often broken down by such categories as sex, age, race, occupation, and marital status.

Crude Birth Rate. The number of live births per 1,000 population.

Crude Death Rate. The number of deaths per 1,000 population.

Cultural Lag. The process by which some elements of culture, such as technology, change faster than others, such as values and norms.

Deindustrialization. The shifting from industrial economic activities to service and information economies. Decline in the share of manufacturing industries in the country's economy. Typically, industrial plants are closed down and not replaced, and service industries increase. Refers to the movement of labor-intensive work to the Third World, where unions, pro-labor legislation, and environmental protection laws are non-existent and works are often paid mere pennies a day.

Demographic Equation. The basic way demographers figure out population growth: Population Growth = Births – Deaths + Net Migration.

Demographic Transition Theory. A demographic theory describing the major change in world population as a transition from high fertility and high mortality to low fertility and low mortality.

Demography.   The study of the size, composition, growth, and distribution of human populations.

Division of Labor. The dividing up of tasks among members of a human group.

Ecological Footprint. The land and water area that is required to support indefinitely the material standard of living of a given human population, using prevailing technology.

Ecology.   The study of the relationships between human populations and their environments.

Economy. The system of production and distribution of goods and services.

Fertility Rate (Sometimes called Total Fertility Rate). How many children the average woman bears.

Fertility. Another word for childbearing.

Fiat Money. A currency used by the government, guaranteed by the government, but not backed up by stored gold or silver.

Gemeinschaft. According to Ferdinand Tonnies, a society that is based on community relations that characterize rural life.

Gesellschaft. According to Ferdinand Tonnies, a society where social life is based on association, which characterizes city life.

Global Warming. The gradual rise of average temperatures due to increased emission of carbon dioxide, water, and methane.

Hunting and Gathering Society. The historically first human society in which members relied on simple technology for hunting animals and gathering vegetation.

Industrial Society. A society in which machines powered by fuels are used to manufacture goods and create tremendous surplus.

Inflation. A state of the economy when each currency purchases fewer and fewer goods and services.

Mechanical Solidarity. According to Emile Durkheim, the traditional type of society, where solidarity is achieved from the fact that everyone does essentially the same kind of work and there exists only a simple division of labor.

Migration. The movement of people in and out of geographically and politically defined areas.

Mortality. Another word for death and dying.

Net Migration. The difference between in-movers and out-movers.

Organic Solidarity. According to Emile Durkheim, the modern type of society, where solidarity is based on a complex, functional division of labor where individuals perform highly specialized but unlike roles.

Pastoral and Horticultural Society. A primitive human society in which members domesticate animals and plants.

Patriarchy. A social system in which men are the dominant group and occupy positions of power over women. The subordination of women to men. Male dominance in society and the family.

Postindustrial Society. The highest stage of development of human society in which microchip technology is used and services become the dominant sector of the economy.

Slavery. A system where some people are owned and exploited by others.

Subsistence Economy. Living off nature with little or no surplus.

Theory of Malthus. A demographic theory by Thomas Malthus that argues that human populations have the potential for explosive growth due to subsistence growing arithmetically and population growing geometrically.

Zero Population Growth. When the population does not change, or when every 1,000 women give birth to 2,100 children.

REFERENCES

Bell, Daniel. 1973. *The Coming of Post-Industrial Society: A Venture in Social Forecasting*. New York: Basic Books.

Chagnon, Napoleon A. 1992. *Yanomamo: The Fierce People*. 4th ed. New York: Holt, Rinehart, and Winston.

Durkheim, Emile. 1964. *The Division of Labor in Society*. New York: Free Press.

Endicott, Karen. 1992. "Fathering in an Egalitarian Society." Pp. 281-96 in *Father-Child Relations: Cultural and Bio-Social Contexts*, edited by Barry S. Hewlett. New York: Aldine.

Fisher, Claude W. 1984. *The Urban Experience*. 2nd ed. New York: Harcourt Brace Jovanovich.

Gerth, H. H. and C. Wright Mills, eds. 1946. *From Max Weber: Essays in Sociology*. New York: Oxford University Press.

Hewlett, Barry S. 1992. "Husband-Wife Reciprocity and the Father-Infant Relationship among Aka Pygmies." Pp. 153-76 in *Father-Child Relations: Cultural and Bio-Social Contexts*, edited by Barry S. Hewlett. New York: Aldine.

Leacock, Eleanor. 1978. "Women's Status in Egalitarian Societies: Implications for Social Evolution." *Current Anthropology* 19(2) (June):245-75.

Lenski, Gerhard, Patrick Nolan, and Jean Lenski. 1995. *Human Societies: An Introduction to Macrosociology*. 7th ed. New York: McGraw-Hill.

Malthus, Thomas Robert. 1798 (1965). *An Essay on the Principle of Population*. New York: Augustus Kelley.

Marx, Karl. 1959. Excerpt from "A Contribution to the Critique of Political Economy." In Karl Marx and Friedrich Engles, *Marx and Engles: Basic Writings on Politics and Philosophy*, Lewis S. Feurer, ed. Garden City, NY: Anchor Books.

Simon, Julian. 1981. *The Ultimate Resource*. Princeton, NJ: Princeton University Press.

Simon, Julian. 1992. *Population and Development in Poor Countries: Selected Essays*. Princeton, NJ: Princeton University Press.

Smil, Vaclav. 2000. *Feeding the World: A Challenge for the 21st Century*. Cambridge, MA: MIT Press.

Stavrianos, L. S. 1983. *A Global History: The Human Heritage*. 3rd ed. Englewood Cliffs, NJ: Prentice Hall.

Tonnies, Ferdinand. 1887 (1988). *Community and Society (Gemeinschaft and Gesellschaft)*. New Brunswick, NJ: Transaction Books.

Weber, Max. 1958. *The Protestant Ethic and the Spirit of Capitalism*. New York: Charles Scribner's Sons.

Weber, Max. 1978. *Economy and Society*. G. Roth and C. Wittich, eds. Berkeley, CA: University of California Press.

Weeks, John. 2005. *Population: An Introduction to Concepts and Issues*. 9th ed. Belmont, CA: Wadsworth.

8 | Sociological Methods: How We Know What We Know.
by Ivan M. Chompalov, Ph.D.

SOCIOLOGICAL RESEARCH

Sociologists, just like other social scientists, prefer to examine social reality in a systematic manner by collecting accurate and reliable information, following a systematic procedure. Thus, they carry out sociological research to base their conclusions and theories about society on a more solid foundation. The main reason for engaging in rigorous research rather than relying on common sense or popular wisdom is that common sense is not trustworthy. For example, common sense tells us that the longer you have known a potential life mate by, let us say, living together (cohabiting) the better the chances that a marriage will last, if the two of you decide to "tie the knot." However, it is well-documented by marriage and family sociologists that cohabitation prior to marriage leads to higher chances of divorce, once the two partners do get married, as compared with not cohabiting before marriage. This highlights the usefulness of sociological research.

There are many ways to do sociological research. In this chapter we will cover the most frequently used methods of research about society.

SURVEYS

Surveys are the "bread and butter" of empirical sociology, just as experiments are "the bread and butter" of empirical psychology. A **survey** is a research method that relies on collecting data from a large group of people by asking them a series of questions. When the questions are asked in a written format, we call that a *questionnaire survey*. A questionnaire is a set of written questions, also called an instrument, that we administer to **respondents** or people who answer the questions. The most common questionnaire surveys are surveys administered by interviewers who read the questions to the respondent and then check off the appropriate answers, and the self-administered questionnaires, where the respondents are given a questionnaire to complete on their own either by mail, or e-mail, or via the web. When the questions are asked orally, we speak of an **interview survey**. Interview surveys are either conducted face-to-face or by telephone.

Surveys are especially appropriate when we gather demographic information, or elicit people's opinions and attitudes, but also when we want to assess people's familiarity with an issue or knowledge of facts. There are several typical steps in carrying out survey research: develop hypotheses; choose a type of survey; design the questionnaire or the interview protocol; do a pilot test of the instrument; finalize the instrument; decide on an appropriate sampling design; select the members of the sample; contact the respondents; conduct the interviews or administer and collect the questionnaires; enter the data and statistically analyze it; and share the findings by writing a report, presenting a paper at a conference, or publishing an article or a book.

When choosing the participants in a survey, we need to determine the **population**, or the target group we intend to study. However, it is typically impractical because of limited funds or resources, as well as because of time constraints, to survey the whole population. For that reason, we select a **sample**, or a subgroup from the population that we use to generalize about the population. There are two types of sampling: probability and non-probability. In a **probability sample,** all elements of the population (or units of analysis) have an equal and mathematically known chance of being picked for the sample. This is so, because we do the selection at random (like picking numbers out of a hat). This assures that, given a large enough size of the probability sample, we are confident that our sample is closely representative of the population, which allows inferences about the population based on our sample findings. In non-probability sampling the probability to be selected is not equal (some cases are more likely to become a part of our sample than others are, which introduces bias).

Surveys employ different random (probability) sampling designs. One common type of probability sampling is **simple random sampling**. This entails the listing of all elements in the population (also called sampling frame) and then randomly selecting the desired number to reach the sample size we are aiming for. The random selection was done by using a Table of Random Numbers in the past, but nowadays the computer can automatically perform this random selection for us. For example, if we want to conduct a survey of 8,000 university students by way of simple random sampling and are targeting a 10 percent sample, we would get an alphabetically arranged list of the population of all 8,000 students numbered in ascending order and then let the computer randomly pick 800 numbers.

If we decide to resort to another type of probability sample, a **systematic random sample**, then every K^{th} student is chosen for inclusion in the sample, where K is the so-called sampling interval, determined by dividing the population size by the sample size (in our hypothetical example K = 10). Thus, we will pick a random number between 1 and 10 and then choose every 10th student afterwards. If this random number happens to be, let us say 5, then we get students number 5, 15, 25, 35, 45, etc. until we get 800 students altogether.

A third option would be to take a **stratified random sample**, which randomly chooses cases from subpopulations of interest, so that the proportion of the sub-sample is the same as the proportion of the subpopulation. This ensures better representativeness and smaller error. In our hypothetical example, we might want to make sure we obtain an accurate representation of students by sex. Then, since the relative share of female students in the population is 60 percent and the relative share of male students is 40 percent, we divide the student population into two subpopulations. Thus, we compile an alphabetical list of all 4,800 female students and randomly select 10 percent or 480 women. Then we repeat this procedure for male students and end up with 320 men. In this way, we still have randomly chosen 800 students but the proportion of male and female students in our sample mirrors exactly their proportion in the population. There are other types of probability samples (cluster sampling, ratio estimation, probability proportional to size sampling) but they go beyond the scope of this text.

In designing the set of questions, or questionnaire, we should take great care to minimize bias and to avoid ambiguity. There are two types of questions—open-ended and closed-ended—and, hence, two types of questionnaires, corresponding to these questions—unstructured and structured. A third or intermediary type of questionnaire is the semi-structured questionnaire, which is a mixture of the two kinds of questions. A purely unstructured questionnaire contains only **open-ended questions**. Such questions seek a free response. For example, you can ask the respondent, what is your favorite TV program or show? The respondent is free to elaborate and can give any answer. A structured questionnaire contains only **closed-ended questions**. These questions give the respondent a list of fixed answers from which he/she can choose the option that best reflects their opinion. An example here could be a question such as, how would you evaluate the president's performance on foreign policy? (Please circle one answer.)

Excellent   Very Good   Good   Fair   Poor

Conducting surveys is a skill that sociologists hone over a number of years. One of the authors had the good fortune to work as a post-doc with a true expert in the art of interviewing, who is currently a Regents' Professor of Public Policy at Georgia Institute of Technology, Dr. Barry Bozeman. Here are some of Prof. Bozeman's "rules of thumb" for conducting effective semi-structured interviews:

WHAT IS SEMI-STRUCTURED INTERVIEWING?

- An approach to eliciting information through face-to-face questioning, relying on pre-determined question themes, "probes" and spontaneity

But how do *I* obtain an interview with a busy, important person?

- Exude confidence!

- Use (at your peril) the 60 Minutes technique

- "I just happen to be in town"

- Make most of institutional affiliation and other status appurtenances

- Reverse strategy: "just a poor, humble student (beginner, assistant professor, etc.)"

- Plan ahead

- Be persistent after cancellations, changes

- Rely on network resources

- Make a compelling pitch

- Flatter, honestly

WHAT ARE THE ADVANTAGES OF SEMI-STRUCTURED INTERVIEWING?

- Richness of data, depth

- Use of probes

- Respondent can help guide the study

- Chain interviewing

- Informs choice of other research approaches

DISADVANTAGES?

- Difficult to code data

- Relies heavily on skills of interviewer

- Interview results often not comparable

- Can be costly (travel and time)

When should we use semi-structured interviewing?

1.   Hypotheses not as precise, still exploratory

2.   Seeking "grounded theory"

3.   Supplement other approaches

4.   Context and nuance vital

5.   Need great depth in questioning

6.   Unique or distinctive respondents

7.   Need "flexibility" not offered by structured questions

Scheduling techniques:

■   Ask for 15 minutes, hope for more

■   Allow overrun

■   Schedule for geographic proximity

■   Check route ahead of time

■   Leave time for organization of notes, for human comfort

■   Keep phone numbers in case you are late

THE BEST SETTING FOR THE INTERVIEW?

■   Not lunch

■   Your site or neutral, preferably not the respondent's office

■   If respondent's office, ask to hold calls

- Others? Depends, but often a bad idea

- For important interviews, be flexible and accommodate respondent

What is the best **medium** for the interview?

- Tape recorder is *hazardous!*

- Take minimal notes, flesh out later

- Use portable computers with select subjects (with partner if possible)

- If more than one interviewer, use specialized roles

- Do not appear to be writing furiously

- Have pre-determined retreat for writing and recapitulation

QUESTIONING TECHNIQUES

- *How do I cut off a respondent?*

- "That is a really good question,...moving on"

- Stop giving cues (nods, uh-huh) but still listen

- Understand reason for expansiveness

- *How do I draw out a respondent?*

- Judicious use of silence

- Verbal cues, physical cues, probes

- Long questions usually get longer responses

- <u>Never</u> stop respondent for your problems in note taking or tape recording

DEVELOPING THE PROTOCOL

- Develop both themes and probes, not too many of either

- Give thought to reasons for question sequencing

- Do not ask for information easily obtained from other sources

- Pictures may be useful supplement

- Begin with full details on place, person, time, address, impressions

- Use a template if you record by computer

Lessons from Bozemanic Experience

- Culture matters. The rules are different in Japan

- No amount of care makes interviewers comparable

- It is always difficult to discard; information overload is a constant problem

- The interview data never leaves

- Ego is everything, there is no such thing as a humble elite

CHECKLIST FOR ASKING NON-THREATENING QUESTIONS ABOUT BEHAVIOR:

- Determine whether threatening

- Make sure choices are exhaustive

- Develop recall aids if necessary

- Make the question as specific as possible, provide time span or discrete event

- Relate time span to salience of topic

- Permit use of records when possible

- Avoid jargon, consider vocabulary of the respondents

TO DETERMINE LEVEL OF THREAT:

- Consider published results. From Bradburn, Sudman, Assoc., 1979:

    Table 8.1   Percentage of People who Feel "Very Uneasy"

Topic	Percent "Very Uneasy"
Sports activities	1.3
Drinking alcohol	10.3
Gambling with friends	10.5
Income	12.5
Intoxication	29.0
Use of marijuana	42.0
Sexual activity	56.4

TO ASSESS LEVEL OF THREAT:

- Ask the respondent!

- Make post hoc inference from missing data.

- In addition to threat, consider "socially-desirable response"

TECHNIQUES FOR ELICITING VALID RESPONSES ON THREATENING QUESTIONS:

- Use Open Questions (e.g., "How many packs of cigarettes do you smoke per week"), do not require "judging by grouping"

- Use Long Questions which set context

- Use Familiar words, less sharp in tone (e.g., "make love" v. "engage in sex")

- Deliberate loadings (e.g., "Even good parents get upset with their kids, sometime striking them..." "Many people in this country drink beer...")

- Assume the behavior; ask about frequency (e.g., "How many bottles of whiskey did you purchase this week?")

AIDED RECALL

- Use lists.

- For example, not "What magazines do you read?" <u>But</u> "Do you read any of the following magazines, *Time, Newsweek, New Yorker...*"

- However, SDR involved in long lists ("I should read *some* of these!")

- Make question specific, refer to discrete events (e.g., "What brand of soft drink do you buy?" is a <u>poor</u> question. When? Where? Generally or last time? And, What is a soft drink?

- Avoid ambiguous terms for periodicity (e.g., "usually," "generally," "regularly").

- Determine saliency. A function of: (1) unusualness of the event, (2) economic and social cost-benefit, (3) continuing consequences.

- *Telescoping*: respondent remembers event but not date. Usually leads to overreports.

- *Bounded Recall*: repeated interviews with same respondent (panel study), reminding respondent of previous responses.

- Diaries and records.

One of the best examples of a professionally designed and executed survey of national importance that is considered by many sociologists the "golden standard" in the field is the General Social Survey, designed and administered by the National Opinion Researcher Center at the University of Chicago.

GSS Study Description

This study, begun in 1972, was supported in its first year by grants from the Russell Sage Foundation and the National Science Foundation. NSF provided support for 1973 through 1991, with surveys in 1973-1978, 1980, 1982, 1983-1993, 1994, 1996, 1998, 2000, 2002, 2004, and 2006.

The Principal Investigators are James A. Davis, formerly Director of NORC and now a Senior Lecturer in the Department of Sociology at the University of Chicago, Tom W. Smith, Director of the General Social Survey (GSS), NORC and Lecturer in the Departments of Sociology and Political

Science at the University of Chicago, and Peter V. Marsden, Department of Sociology, Harvard University.

The National Data Program for the Social Sciences (General Social Survey) is both a data diffusion project and a program of social indicator research. Its data collection instrument, the General Social Survey (GSS), is being fielded for the 26th time this year. Previously an annual survey, the GSS became biennial in 1994. The questionnaire contains a standard core of demographic and attitudinal variables, plus certain topics of special interest selected for rotation (called "topical modules"). Items that appeared on national surveys between 1973 and 1975 are replicated. The exact wording of these questions is retained to facilitate time trend studies as well as replications of earlier findings.

NORC also incorporates methodological experiments into each year of the GSS data collection. These have involved question wording, context effects, use of different types of response scales, as well as random probes and other assessments of validity and reliability.

For the baseline items in the initial survey, some 150 social scientists reviewed drafts of the questionnaire, suggested revisions and additions, and expressed their preferences by vote. Topic and question selection is monitored annually by a Board of Overseers, composed of distinguished social scientists.

Items include national spending priorities, drinking behavior, marijuana use, crime and punishment, race relations, quality of life, confidence in institutions, and membership in voluntary associations.

Since 1985, the GSS has taken part in the International Social Survey Program, a consortium of social scientists from 40 countries around the world. The ISSP asks an identical battery of questions in all countries; the United States version of these questions is incorporated into the GSS. GSS co-Principal Investigator Tom W. Smith served as the ISSP Secretary General in 1997-2003.

The basic purposes of the GSS are to gather data on contemporary American society in order to monitor and explain trends and constants in attitudes, behaviors, and attributes; to examine the structure and functioning of society in general as well as the role played by relevant subgroups; to compare the United States to other societies in order to place American society in comparative perspective and develop cross-national models of human society; and to make high-quality data easily accessible to scholars, students, policy makers, and others, with minimal cost and waiting. Since 1988, the GSS has also collected data on number of sex partners, frequency of intercourse, extramarital relationships, and sex with prostitutes.

The GSS is the largest sociology project funded by NSF and has been described as a national resource. In use by sociologists, it is second only to the Census. Through 2005 over 12,000 research uses in articles, textbooks, monographs, dissertations, etc. have been documented.

Average Length of Interview

About 90 minutes.

Response Rates

1975—76 percent	1989—78 percent
1976—75 percent	1990—74 percent
1977—77 percent	1991—78 percent
1978—74 percent	1992 *
1980—76 percent	1993—82 percent
1982—78 percent	1994—78 percent
1983—79 percent	1996—76 percent
1984—79 percent	1998—76 percent
1985—79 percent	2000—70 percent
1986—76 percent	2002—70 percent
1987—75 percent	2004—70 percent
1988—77 percent	

* While there was no 1992 GSS, there was a special survey in which respondents to the 1991 GSS were recontacted by mail or telephone, with a response rate of 84 percent.

Key Findings

As a trend study, the GSS does not have "findings" as such because the data collection is ongoing and the purpose of the data analysis is to study ongoing social trends. Certain important trends the GSS has noted have been a dramatic increase over the past thirty years in support for racial equality and integration, and a steady increase in support for civil liberties.

Uses of the Data

As indicated above, the GSS data are widely used by social scientists—to date, over 9,000 known research uses of the data. The GSS is also widely used in college and graduate-level classes. In addition, the news media make continual use of these data in the popular press, in stories on a very broad range of topics.

Source: The National Opinion Research Center (NORC). Web site accessed on 3/14/2006 at: http://www.norc.uchicago.edu/about/index.asp

EXPERIMENTAL RESEARCH

One of the most effective methods of conducting sociological research is the experiment. Experiments are appropriate when we want to discover **causal relationships**. Causality presupposes at least three things: 1) That two variables are correlated. One property has to systematically vary with another to assume this prerequisite for cause and effect, 2) That the cause should precede the effect. For instance, we can infer that age may cause childbearing ability in women because they have to mature in time to the point of being able to conceive and give birth, 3) There should not be any spuriousness. In other words, we have to verify that the observed correlation between two variables cannot be explained by the effect of a third variable. A well-known example is when we observe a high positive correlation between the number of storks and the number of newborn babies. We might wrongly conclude that storks bring babies. However, if we take into account the type of place (rural versus urban), we will quickly realize that this is a spurious relationship that rules out storks as the cause of new babies. In reality, people living in villages and small towns tend to have more babies and storks prefer the unpolluted countryside, where there is more food and cleaner air and water.

Thus, we prefer experimental research when we are seeking an explanation and trying to eliminate alternative accounts. Experiments are best when we have a limited number of concepts, when the researcher has a fair degree of control over the set-up, and when we try to formally test a research hypothesis. It inherently presupposes quantitative analysis and rigorous procedures that we do not deviate from. In that sense, it is probably the most purely empirical approach.

Each true experiment consists of several elements. These parts include: the treatment, or **independent variable** (this is the modification of the situation, which we are trying to find out whether it is effective, for example a new job training program); the dependent, or outcome variable (for example GPA, job skills, prejudice) which is commonly measured at least twice; pretesting and posttesting (the subjects are usually measured in terms of the **dependent variable** before the treatment (**pretest**) and after the treatment (**posttest**); experimental and control group (in a true experiment we have at least two groups—one that is exposed to the treatment (**experimental group**) and another one that is not (**control group**); random assignment or matching (when we randomly assign subjects to either an experimental or a control group, this ensures that the subjects in various groups are similar and avoids bias and self-selection, but when this is not possible the second best solution is to match cases in groups on certain demographic characteristics such as age, sex, social class, race/ethnicity, marital status).

Typically, we follow several steps in carrying out an experiment. First, we have to formulate a **hypothesis** (a statement of the expected relationship between two variables). Next, we have to decide which experimental design is the most appropriate for the task at hand (the different experimental designs are briefly presented below). Third, we need to select the subject by either random choice or matching. Fourth, we gather the data for the pretest on the dependent variable. Five, we expose the experimental group subjects to the treatment (the independent variable). Then we collect data on the posttest measure of the dependent (outcome variable) for both groups. The seventh step is to debrief the subjects at the conclusion of the experiment. Finally, we analyze the collected data and test the hypothesis by statistical comparisons between different groups.

Types of Experimental Designs

There is a variety of different experimental designs that we either can choose from, depending on our research purpose, or are forced to resort to, if we cannot have full control over the selection of subjects and/or the collection of data. Here is a sample of some of the 16 different designs that Campbell and Stanley identified (1963). The symbols used below stand for the following concepts: R = random assignment; X = the independent variable, or treatment; O = the outcome variable, or the dependent variable; row = group.

> ➤ Classical experimental design

```
              O          X          O
    R
              O                     O
```

An example of this design could be a study of the effectiveness of a University remediation course. One group of freshmen students with low academic preparedness (measured by SAT, high school rank, and high school GPA) is randomly selected to take the remediation course (the experimental group). Another group of freshmen with a similar academic unpreparedness does not take the remediation course. Both groups are compared one year after the first group has completed the remediation course to see if the experimental group has developed better academic coping skills as measured by a standardized scale.

> ➤ Pre-experimental design (no random assignment)

> • *One-shot case study design*

```
         X                    O
```

An illustration of this design could be a single group of people watching an educational video about sexual harassment in the workplace to find out whether this increased their awareness of the phenomenon occurring in their work organization.

- *One-group pretest-posttest design*

  O   X   O

An example of this experimental design could be a single group of bad drivers taking a defensive-driving course to see if this improves their driving.

- *Static-group comparison*

  X   O
                       O

To illustrate how this design might come in handy, imagine a situation where two groups of workers are compared in terms of their awareness of sexual harassment happening in their work place, where one group is shown an educational video about the phenomenon of interest but the other is not.

➢ Quasi-experimental and special designs (better control of the causal relationship; used when classical design is inappropriate)

- *Two-group posttest-only design*

          X   O
  R
                                        O

This is the same as the static group comparison, except that the two groups of workers have been randomly chosen.

- *Interrupted time series*

  O O O O X O O O O

169

An example of the use of this design is given by Neuman (2000). In 1979, taxes on cigarettes were increased by 35 percent. If we measure consumption of cigarettes 10 years prior to 1979 and 10 years after 1979, we can use this design to test a hypothesis that a higher price of cigarettes will lead to a reduction of smoking.

- *Equivalent time series*

O X O X O X O X O X O

Again, Neuman (2000) gives an apt example of when we can employ this experimental design. In 1975, a law was passed that required motorcyclists to wear helmets. The law was repealed in 1981 but reinstated in 1989. We can use the equivalent time series design to see whether wearing helmets resulted in fewer deaths from head injuries in motorcycle accidents.

- *Latin Squares design*

$$
\begin{array}{ccccc}
 & O & Xa & O & Xb & O \\
R & & & & & \\
 & O & Xb & O & Xa & O
\end{array}
$$

Imagine that you are a statistics instructor and are trying to find out which method of teaching the subject is more effective. You can design a Latin Squares experiment by randomly choosing one class where you teach concepts rather than formula derivations and choosing another class where statistics is being taught more mechanically (emphasizing formula derivations and mechanically doing a lot of problems). Then you compare the two classes to see how they will do on your final exam.

- *Solomon four-group design*

				Groups
	O	X	O	1
R	O		O	2
	O	X	O	3
			O	4

This is one of the best ways to control for causality and any potential threats to the **validity** of the experiment, because this design combines the classical experiment with the two-group posttest-only design. For example, a mental health worker wants to determine whether some new training method (X) can improve the clients' coping skills (O). If groups 1 and 3 are similar to each other but different from groups 2 and 4, which, in turn, are similar to each other, then pretest learning is not a problem. If, on the other hand, groups 1 and 2 are similar to each other but different from groups 3 and 4, which, in turn, are almost identical, then we know that the pretest is a problem for the dependent variable (Neuman 2000).

- *Factorial design (used when more than one independent variable is necessary)*

	X1	Z1	O
R	X1	Z2	O
	X2	Z1	O
	X2	Z2	O

This is a rather complicated design but is effective when we have more than one independent variable (treatment). Neuman (2000) gives an example with a researcher trying to find out how two independent variables (X and Z) can affect a dependent variable of interest (O). In this case, the independent variables could be level of cooperation (X) with two categories (high = X1 and low = X2) and level of stress (Z) with two categories as well (high = Z1 and low = Z2), and the dependent variable—productivity of work groups. Thus, the research hypothesis is that high cooperation (X1) in combination with low stress (Z2) will lead to the highest productivity (O). In other words, group two is expected to show the greatest productivity of all four work groups.

UNOBTRUSIVE RESEARCH

Typically, sociologists conduct their studies of society by doing surveys, carrying out experiments, or directly observing people's behavior. Surveys, experiments, and direct observations of social interactions are *reactive*; i.e., the people being studied are aware of that fact. In contrast, *unobtrusive* or *nonreactive* research involves research techniques (either quantitative or qualitative) that are *nonreactive*; i.e., those being studied are unaware that they are part of a sociological study. In short, the gist of nonreactive or *unobtrusive measures* is that the researcher examines traces of human activity without the knowledge of the people who produced these traces.

Unobtrusive (or nonreactive) measurement begins when a researcher notices something that indicates a variable of interest. The critical thing about nonreactive or *unobtrusive measures* (i.e., measures that are not obtrusive or intrusive) is that the people that are being studied have no clue of this fact; they cannot react to it, but leave evidence (traces) of their social behavior or actions "in a natural way." The observant researcher infers from that evidence the behavior or attitudes without disrupting the individuals under study.

Social scientists have been resourceful in figuring out new ways to analyze social behavior without letting the people or groups of interest know that they are being a part of a systematic study. Unobtrusive measures are varied and researchers have been quite ingenious in inventing indirect ways to measure social behavior. Some examples of using nonreactive research are:

1) examination of the contents of garbage dumps to learn about life-styles from what is thrown away. Based on garbage, it has been found that people underreport their liquor consumption by 40 to 60 percent;

2) a study of reams of paper purchased by a college dean's office for 10 years when student enrollments are steady to see when bureaucratic paperwork has increased;

3) a study of the listening habits of drivers by checking what stations their radios are tuned to when cars are repaired;

4) a study of bumper stickers in support of different political candidates to see if one candidate's supporters are more likely than another's to obey traffic laws;

5) a study of tombstones to find out if there was a disproportionately large number of deaths in a particular period and why;

6) measurement of how long men and women pause in front of a painting of a nude man or woman;

7) a study of ads by psychics in the yellow pages of telephone books in different parts of the country (it turns out that Seattle, WA registered the largest number).

An interesting application of unobtrusive research is a cemetery study of Roman tombstones, as reported by Dorsten and Hotchkiss. The study illustrated both the strengths and pitfalls of this method. It found good evidence that children's deaths were underrepresented, as were younger women's ages at death, whereas ages at death beyond 50 were definitely exaggerated. Thus, the best data of mortality (death) estimates turned out to be inscriptions of males dying between the ages of 15 and 42. Relying on the latter, the authors of the study approximate the average life expectancy of Romans in the first and second centuries AD between 25 and 30 years. Such analysis shows both the usefulness of historical data that is nonreactive and the need for careful scrutiny, since the sources of error are obviously numerous.

Often, unobtrusive research relies on physical traces left behind by people who never expected them to become sources of sociological interpretations and conclusions. **Physical traces** are commonly divided into *erosion measures* and *accretion measures*.

Erosion measures are those where we look at the wear and tear of objects to draw sociological inferences. An example would be when a sociologist tries to categorize toys at a day care center depending on how new or worn-out they are, if all toys were bought at the same time.

Preserved toys are obviously not very popular and the toys children like will tend to be worn-out from frequent use.

Accretion measures are those whose greater accumulation suggests stronger preference. They can also be thought of as "deposits" that tell us something about human behavior. Thus, examining the brands of cans in dumpsters in front of male and female dormitories will allow us to draw conclusions about gender differences in consumption of certain foods and beverages.

Doing unobtrusive research often follows the logic of quantitative measurement, although qualitative research is by no means precluded. There are several measures that fall into that category but the four most commonly used techniques of doing unobtrusive research are: content analysis; existing statistics and secondary analysis; historical-comparative analysis; and indirect observation.

CONTENT ANALYSIS AS A FORM OF UNOBTRUSIVE RESEARCH

A common and popular unobtrusive research technique is content analysis. What was the most frequently covered topic in the media in 2005? What is the most common theme in political blogs? What is the typical language in internet dating sites profiles? What are the predominant messages in country songs and how do they enlighten us about human relations? These are all questions that can be answered by careful use of content analysis. But what is content analysis?

Content analysis is a technique for revealing the semantics (i.e., the meaning) of the products of communication. Most researchers perceive it as a somewhat laborious and repetitive coding and interpretation of texts. Thus, it has been suggested that "textual coding" might be a better name than content analysis. It has also been called "the quantitative semantics of a text."

According to Neuman, content analysis can be applied to study a wide variety of issues: themes in pop songs; trends in newspapers coverage; the ideological content of newspaper editorials; sex-role stereotypes in textbooks or feature films; the representation of race in TV commercials and programs; enemy propaganda during war; images on the covers of popular magazines; personality characteristics from suicide notes; gender differences in conversations; public speeches of politicians and corporate executives.

There are several advantages in doing content analysis: it is fairly cheap and not time consuming—a single individual can do it in a couple of days; you can always go back and redo the analysis since it is nonreactive (you cannot do that with surveys and experiments); it allows you to study trends over time; it does not bother the subjects you are studying; it is fairly reliable (you can code and recode numerous times). Among its disadvantages are the difficulty with revealing meaning; the limit to recorded communication; it tends to be a bit tedious; and sometimes there are problems with different people coding in the same way.

Content analysis may involve either probability or nonprobability sampling. It further requires precise measurement, and fairly accurate operational definitions for abstract concepts. Coding turns aspects of content that represent variables into numbers. Then we can enter the numbers into computers and analyze them with statistics. Careful measurement is crucial in content analysis because texts are multidimensional and the diffuse, ambiguous, and murky symbolic medium has to be converted to precise and explicit quantitative data. The four commonly measured attributes of a text content are frequency, direction, intensity, and space. Neuman gives an example of how a researcher might try to determine how frequently TV dramas portray elderly characters in terms of negative stereotypes. He or she develops a measure of the construct "negative stereotypes of the elderly." This may include attributes such as senile, forgetful, cranky, argumentative, conservative, set in their opinions, inflexible, slow, ill, frail, inactive, in nursing homes, etc.

A decision usually has to be made of whether to employ what is called manifest coding (focusing on the surface content of a text) or latent coding (coding the implicit or connotative meaning of a text). Finally, as Neuman and Babbie point out, the constructs in content analysis are operationalized with a **coding system**, or in other words a set of instructions or rules on how to systematically observe and record content from text. If several coders use the same coding scheme to analyze the content of the same set of texts, we need to ask them to code independently of each other and then check for agreement among them. This agreement is called **intercoder reliability** and can be measured with a statistical coefficient that tells us the degree of consistency among coders.

Thus content analysis can and has been used as a powerful teaching tool. It can serve a variety of purposes and help achieve a better understanding of basic sociological concepts, methods, and trends.

Two of the authors have experienced its effectiveness on "both sides of the fence," in a manner of speech.

The first example describes how the use of content analysis in higher education appears from a student perspective. When one of the authors was a graduate student at Louisiana State University, his first assignment in the Research Methods class was to do a content analysis of the trends in American sociology by examining the three major sociological journals (American Sociological Review, American Journal of Sociology, and Social Forces). The author focused on looking at two things: theoretical paradigms (structural-functionalism, symbolic interactionism, conflict theory) and research methods (quantitative v. qualitative; surveys v. experiments v. field research; primary v. secondary analysis of data; etc.). Since it was decided to cover a 75-year period, it was prudent to limit the exercise to research articles only (research notes, discussion papers, book reviews and the like were excluded).

Often content analysis involves sampling simply because it is impractical to analyze everything. That was the case here. There were still too many research articles left—over 5,000 articles in the thus defined target population. So, a decision was made to resort to probability sampling. In probability or random sampling each element or unit of analysis has an equal and mathematically known chance of being selected. An appropriate type of random sampling design turned out to be systematic sampling. Thus, the author ended up picking about 270 articles overall (taking a sample once every 5 years = 15 x 3 journals = 45, 2 issues per journal per selected year = 90, 3 articles per issue, 3 x 90 = 270). Then all abstracts were read and a count was taken of the articles in the various categories.

Naturally, in order to do that you have to construct variables and specify what codes will be used. In this content analysis assignment, there were two variables. One variable was theoretical paradigm, with categories corresponding to the major theoretical perspectives in sociology. Of course, you also have to decide how to determine those (e.g., conflict theory is associated with a focus on differential access to and distribution of resources, class struggle, power relationships, exploitation, alienation, and the like). The other variable was "research methods" with several categories (survey, experiment, observation, historical-comparative research, secondary data analysis, etc.).

Finally, a line graph was produced, showing the different trends in American sociology over the time of interest.

The second example illustrates how to make effective use of content analysis when teaching introductory sociology courses at a four-year liberal arts university. We will briefly recap an exercise used by Frank Taylor in his introductory sociology classes. The goal was to do a content analysis of children's books in order to reveal gender stereotypes embedded in the narrative and pictures.

The theoretical background for the exercise is that children are unaware of the hidden gender specific messages in the books they read or are read to them. Thus, they learn certain gender codes and stereotypes that later structure their lives in particular ways. The traditional gender role ideology prevalent in our culture and reflected in many of these children's books is to depict women as possessing to a higher degree the so-called expressive traits (submissiveness, dependency, weakness, sensitivity, cooperation, supportiveness, compassion, weakness, being more emotional, and so on) and to portray men as possessing to a greater extent the so-called instrumental traits (aggressiveness, assertiveness, strength, bravery, rationality, analytical ability, ambition, independence, confidence, dominance, and so on). In short, women are perceived as *feminine* and men as *masculine*. Additionally, gender-colored narratives and pictures may be interpreted as a test of the Sapir-Whorf hypothesis that language not only expresses our thoughts and feelings but also shapes our ways of thinking and feeling about people, inanimate objects, and behaviors in powerful ways.

The learning objectives for this exercise were:

1) To familiarize the students with content analysis as a fairly common and easy to learn technique for analyzing the meaning of communications messages;

2) To show how gender stereotypes and ideology are embedded in even such innocuous texts as children's books;

3) To link the gender ideology present in these books to gender-related inequalities in the workplace, income, education, politics, and occupation;

4) To discuss whether these children's books contribute to gender stratification in society instead of just merely reflecting some biological differences between men and women;

5) To set the stage for a more informed discussion in the classroom of important sociological topics such as gender discrimination, sex typing, patriarchy, domination, and oppression of minority groups.

The sampling design was a type of nonprobability sampling, namely **purposive sampling** which is well suited for this exercise. Overall, the units of analysis were taken from the Dr. Seuss series and the Berenstein Bears series, because the vast majority of the 1,357 students from four separate universities and colleges who completed the exercise indicated they were familiar with them.

The coding frame was fairly simple and included two lists of words associated with male and female gender stereotypes, respectively. The words describing feminine traits were submissive, unintelligent, receptive, weak, content, cooperative, sex object, dependent, emotional, intuitive, timid, passive, sensitive, and attractive. The words associated with masculine traits were dominant, intelligent, assertive, strong, ambitious, competitive, sexually aggressive, independent, rational, analytical, brave, active, insensitive, and achievement.

Based on the findings from this exercise, Taylor reached the conclusion that content analysis proved to be a very effective tool to teach students about the social construction of gender in society, which people in the United States learn at a very early age by being exposed to gender stereotypes in children's books. This early process of gender role socialization is insidious because people do not realize that they are being fed stereotypes that are later augmented by the mass media and the reality of social life.

Summarizing the results from five years of administering this exercise to students in his introductory sociology classes, Taylor noticed that the students invoke <u>three general conclusions</u>: 1) these are just books and we are over-interpreting—children are probably not much affected by gender ideologies; 2) children's books have changed a lot in recent years and do not seem to reflect the old gender stereotypes; 3) it is possible that the books just reflect reality.

Overall, student remarks after the completion of the exercise show that an overwhelming majority find the exercise very helpful in recognizing gender stereotypes and scripts in popular children's books. They come to realize that society's gender role expectations are quite pervasive not only in the adult mass media world but also in the seemingly innocent media of children's books. Indeed, some students were shocked to discover that many of these well-known stories are permeated by denigration of little girls and the frequent casting of female characters in secondary and inferior roles.

QUALITATIVE FIELD RESEARCH

Unlike experiments and surveys, which are quantitative methods of research, field research is a qualitative research method. Sometimes it is also called **ethnography** or **participant observation**. This is not entirely accurate, since there are other modes of qualitative field research. Nevertheless, these two modes highlight important features of the field style of research. It is: 1) qualitative, using texts or images rather than numbers; 2) involves observation of behavior in real time, 3) focuses on the natural setting of human behavior, and 4) it is often not only a data collection activity, but also typically a theory-building activity.

Neuman (2000) defines field research <u>as a qualitative style in which the researcher directly observes and participates in small-scale social settings in the present time and the "natural" context of behavior of the observed people.</u>

Of course, it is difficult to incorporate all the various activities and approaches that fall under "field research" in a simple and neat definition. Perhaps it is easier to describe what researchers do when they carry out field research. In field research, the individual researcher directly talks with and observes the people being studied. Through interaction over long periods of time, the researcher learns about their lives and activities, opinions, beliefs, preferences, and aspirations. Some topics can only be studied in this manner but this could be cumbersome, time consuming, stressful, and sometimes downright dangerous.

Typically, field research proceeds in the following sequence: loosely formulate a topic or area of research interest; select the site or social group to be studied; gain access to the site; make observations; take detailed field notes; analyze the observations and field notes. A special form of field research is the participant observation, i.e. when the researcher becomes a part of the group under study, without letting the group know his real purpose (e.g., Laud Humphreys' study of homosexual encounters).

As Neuman (2000) points out, field research appeals to those who like watching people and prefer a more loose approach of doing research. It can be fun because it involves hanging out with some exotic group of people instead of using cold mathematics or complicated statistics. Instead, there is a direct, face-to-face interaction with "real people" in a natural setting.

Research Questions and Topics Appropriate for Field Research

There are a variety of topics that can be studied using qualitative field research techniques.. This method is sometimes the only option available for certain groups and research topics. For example, it is used when other methods (e.g., survey, experiments) are not practical as in studying street gangs, or drug addicts, or prostitution, or gambling. Field research offers the advantage of examining social life in its natural habitat. It can involve studying practices, episodes, events, encounters, groups, organizations, social worlds, statuses, roles, relationships, subcultures, or lifestyles. Here is a sample of actual topics that have been explored by field researchers, according to Neuman (2000):

<u>Settings and subcultures</u>: Laundromats; waiting rooms; shopping malls; battered women shelters; social movements; social welfare offices; bars; retirement communities; urban ethnic neighborhoods; working class communities.

Occupations: doctors; cab drivers; cocktail waitresses; police officers; door-to-door salespeople; social workers; jazz musicians; factory workers; airline attendants; artists; car dealers.

The culture of children's social worlds: Children's playgrounds; Little League baseball; schoolchildren.

Medical sociology contributions: intensive care units; emergency rooms; pregnancy/birth; death; AIDS patients.

Especially valuable for studying deviant behavior: nude beaches; gambling; drug-dealing; drug addicts; street gangs; street people, tramps, or hoboes; prostitutes; hippie communities; homosexuals; cults; swingers.

Special Problems in Field Research

Earl Babbie (2002) identifies some special problems and hurdles that face sociologists who attempt field research. Here is a brief summary of the most challenging issues.

Since the emphasis in field research is on authenticity and the "naturalness" of the setting, we have some special advantages, as well as some specific problems to deal with. One big advantage is flexibility.   Field researchers rarely follow fixed steps.   It allows the researcher to shift direction, follow leads, and discard unproductive avenues.

Various roles: The researchers often perform a variety of roles in the field. The basic tension here is between being a participant and being an observer. The danger in being a participant is that you may go "native," thus failing to detach yourself and objectively evaluating what is happening. On the other hand, being only an observer makes it much more difficult to gain an intimate and deeper understanding of why people behave in certain ways, what "makes them tick," in a manner of speech. Associated with these two basic roles is a host of ethical dilemmas which the researcher needs to resolve:

- Do you let the subjects know that you are studying them by participating in their activities?

- Is it ethical to deceive the people you observe?

- How can you get an "insider understanding" of their behavior, if they most likely will modify their behavior, once they know they are being studied?

- Do potential scientific benefits of your research offset some degree of deception?

- How far can you go in becoming "native" (e.g., The Chronicle of Higher Education reports in its October 25, 2002, issue that a professor lost his job at CUNY, because he tried heroin in order to better understand addiction and withdrawal in a three million dollar study of drug addiction and trade)?

Gaining access, entering the field site, exiting the field site: Gaining access to the study site can be notoriously difficult. Sometimes a researcher's ascribed characteristics can limit access (if you study the KKK or neo-Nazis, obviously you will have a problem with access if you are African-American).

- How do you become an "insider"?

- Is it proper to use informants and pay them?

- How do you negotiate with the so-called "gate keepers," who control access to the site?

- When you enter the field how much do you have to disclose?

- How do you assure a natural entry without making the subjects suspicious of your motives?

- How do you present yourself?

- Do you emphasize qualities you do not possess but that will make you more acceptable?

- Do you help the subjects in difficult or life-threatening situations?

- When do you leave the field site and how?

- What does this entail for your study?

Building rapport: A field researcher establishes rapport by getting along with members in the field. A field researcher needs social skills and personal charm to build rapport. Rapport helps field researchers to understand members. Once he or she attains an understanding of the member's point of view, the next step is to learn how to think and act within a member's perspective. This is empathy, or adopting another person's perspective, or putting oneself in someone else's shoes.

Context is critical: The context is important in understanding the social world. Nowhere is this more evident than in field research. This is because we are dealing with meaning and connotations, which depend on the circumstances. Therefore, special attention is paid to what surrounds the focus of the study, or the context in which social action unfolds.

Qualitative Field Research Paradigms

Field research can be done from different epistemological (= concerned with how we know and what is the status of knowledge claims) perspectives. There is no single particular method or technique specific to a particular perspective (paradigm). Babbie (2002) summarizes the most important paradigms in conducting field research.

A. **Naturalism**. Naturalism is the stance whereby we assume that social reality is objective, out there, and the researcher can observe and report it almost as an exact correspondence to what "really exists." This is also known as positivism, or positive science. This tradition was started in American sociology by the Chicago school of sociology. At the beginning, these researchers focused on describing neighborhoods and community life in an urban setting. Participant observation was developed as a distinct technique. Three principles emerged:

1) Study people in their natural setting, or in situ.

2) Study people by directly interacting with them.

3) Gain an understanding of the social world and make theoretical statements about the members' perspectives.

Later on, more emphasis was put on theoretical analysis. Often the naturalistic approach is applied in what is known as **ethnography**, or a study that focuses on description of people and their culture. It has its origins in cultural anthropology. *Ethno* means people or folk and *graphy* means description. In essence, ethnography is describing a culture and understanding another way of life from the native point of view.

B. **Ethnomethodology**. This is a sociological offshoot of the philosophical tradition of phenomenology. Literally, it means "describing the methods of the people," or how people make sense of their everyday life. In essence, this is the study of people's commonsensical knowledge. It strives to reveal people's "background assumptions" when they take certain beliefs and behaviors for granted. Harold Garfinkel had his students try to shock ordinary people to get to the bottom of these "everyday rules of behavior" (for instance by asking his students to negotiate prices at department stores and observe the shop assistants' reactions). Such field researchers are guided by profound skepticism about how people report their experiences of reality and everyday life situations.

C. **Grounded Theory**. This theory was developed by Barney Glaser and Anselm Strauss and it combines two traditions: positivism and interactionism. This is an inductive method, meaning that theory is built from data or grounded in the data. The researcher begins with a research question, not even a hypothesis. Then he follows certain procedures of collection and analysis and extracts the theory from that. In short, theory develops during the data collection process. **Conceptualization** (developing concepts and ideas) and **operationalization** (specifying the rules of how variables will be measured) occur simultaneously with data collection and preliminary data analysis. Theory is built by making comparisons. The researcher should maintain a healthy skeptical attitude and should periodically step back and reassess the discoveries from the study. Modifications are introduced as necessary. In a sense, this is "opportunistic research."

D. **<u>Case Studies</u>**. There is little consensus as to what constitutes a case, but in simple terms cases are the same as units of analysis, or what we are trying to study (organizations, groups of people, events). This approach is case-oriented in that it places cases, not variables, at the center of research. It examines a wide variety of aspects of one case (The Chernobyl disaster or the Challenger disaster) or a few cases (several recent Fortune 100 companies that experienced corporate scandals, serial killers, etc.).

E. **<u>Institutional Ethnography</u>**. This approach tries to bridge the micro level study of everyday life interaction and the macro level influence of social institutions. For example, a qualitative field study of mothering, schooling, and child development by Alison Griffith (1995) found that child development discourse in schools reproduces class distinctions by adopting a middle class ideology for family-school relations and trying to impose these ideas on parents and children of lower classes.

F. **<u>Participatory Action Research</u>**. PAR is a recent approach that aims at doing away with the inherently unequal power relations that exist in traditional field research (and other methods of research, for that matter). PAR tries to include the participants in a study as more or less equal partners with the researcher. Thus, the researcher is NOT perceived as an expert of some sort, who should observe and explain, but as a facilitator who should get the subjects (typically from disadvantaged groups) involved on an equal footing, try to educate them and educate himself/herself in the process by tapping the subjects' better familiarity with their own situation. It is thus a <u>collaborative</u> type of research. The consultant/facilitator learns as much from the subjects as they learn from him/her. Everything is negotiated (methods, findings, better strategies, writing a report, recommending solutions).

Modes of Qualitative Field Research

There are several ways of collecting data in qualitative field research. Babbie (2002) emphasizes that the most common of these are three: qualitative interviewing, focus groups, and observation.

A. <u>**Qualitative Interviewing**</u>. This is a common mode of field research. It is often used to supplement observations of behavior, especially if you have not gone native and it is difficult to make sense of why the members of a community are doing something. The easiest way is to ask them a series of questions. These are often loosely structured and contain exclusively open-ended questions. A lot of probing is necessary. This type of interview is flexible, often iterative, and evolving. It is more like a conversation and interaction than a systematic, structured interview. Historians often use qualitative interviews, called Oral History Interviews. There you have several general topics and then let the respondent elaborate. In these interviews, it is important to maintain a steady flow of the conversation. In addition, the interviewer needs to be a very good listener and to subtly direct the flow of the conversation. A big advantage is the richness of detail and insights that you obtain. The difficulty is to analyze these interview transcripts, or notes.

B. <u>**Observations**</u>. This is the bread and butter of qualitative field research. There are usually two types of field observations: <u>direct</u> and <u>participant</u>. In a direct observation, the observed individuals are aware that they are being studied. In a participant observation, the researcher goes "under cover" and becomes a part of the studied group. Regardless of whether you conduct a direct or a participant observation, essential here is to take full and adequate field notes, especially if you cannot videotape the behavior. It is always a good idea to jot down certain headings (variables) beforehand and to try to fill these in (e.g., social class, race, age, etc.). In addition, the researcher needs to not only keep records of what actions took place but in what context. A rule of thumb is to jot down your detailed notes immediately after the observation was carried out, while the details are still fresh in your memory. If there are two observers, they need to compare their field notes at the end of the day.

C. **Focus Groups**.   Sometimes, the researcher prefers to bring several people in one place (university, office hall) and group interview them. This is called a *focus group*. They are similar to "town hall meetings." The researcher invites between 10 and 15 people to a room for a group discussion of a topic of interest. He serves as a moderator of the discussion. This is pretty much what you have seen journalists do on TV when they convene "town hall meetings." Focus groups are often used for marketing research or for gauging political attitudes during a campaign. They have the advantage of giving quick results and being low-cost. Among their disadvantages are dubious representativeness, differences between groups, difficulty in analyzing the data, dangers that the discussion can be usurped by a few individuals.

Validity and Reliability

Field research is touted as having higher validity (accuracy) than experiments and surveys. Their superior validity comes from the observation and interviewing of people in their natural settings (experiments and surveys are somewhat artificial). **Reliability** (repeatability, replicability), however, is more problematic in field research as compared with surveys and experiments. The main reason is that field research is somewhat unstructured, interpretative, and unrepresentative.

Ethical Issues

More than any other type of research, with the exception of experiments, in qualitative field research we have to worry about ethical and moral issues such as: deception, misleading, studying people you despise, using informants, lack of anonymity, problems with confidentiality, not helping people in severe need of help, paying people to gain access to their "dirty laundry," learning secrets that may expose a participant to criminal prosecution, etc.

EVALUATION RESEARCH

Evaluation research is not a separate research method but rather one particular application of various research methods (such as the survey, experiment, case study, content analysis, secondary data analysis, focus groups, etc.). More generally, it is applied social research, typically an instance of applied sociology.

The simplest definition is that the purpose of **evaluation research** is that it tries to determine whether social interventions or programs have had their desired effects. In short, it tries to evaluate or assess whether programs designed to solve or alleviate social problems have been effective in achieving their intended goals (Posavac and Carey 2003).

More formally, <u>evaluation is the systematic assessment of the operation and/or the outcomes of a program or policy, compared to a set of explicit or implicit standards, as a means of contributing to the improvement of the program or policy (Weiss 1998)</u>. As you can see, there are five key elements to an evaluation: systematic assessment (1), the focus of the investigation (operation (2) and outcomes (3) of the program), standards for comparison (4), and the purpose for which evaluation research is done—contribution to the improvement of the program and policy (5).

The possibilities to evaluate are almost limitless. Examples of evaluation research questions are:

- Does a teaching technique that is more interactive improve learning over lecturing?

- Does a law enforcement program of mandatory arrests reduce spouse abuse?

- Does Head Start help children from disadvantaged backgrounds to get a fair chance at a decent education?

- Does a flextime program increase employee productivity?

- Does the three-strikes law reduce crime?

- What are the consequences of liberalized marijuana laws?

- Do no-fault divorce laws increase the number of divorces?

- How effective was the Social Welfare Reform of 1996?

- Has no-fault automobile insurance brought down car insurance policy premiums? (Babbie 2002).

Evaluation research measures the effectiveness of a program, policy, or way of doing something. It is frequently descriptive but can be exploratory or explanatory.

Types of Evaluation

There are two main classifications of evaluation studies: outcome versus process evaluation, and formative versus summative evaluation (Weiss 1998).

A. Outcome and Process Evaluation. From the time it became a recognized activity in the 1930s, the main question evaluators tried to find an answer had to do with outcomes: Is the program attaining the goals that it was created to accomplish? More broadly: What are the results of the program? This focus on outcomes is still what most people associate with doing evaluation research. Outcome refers to the result of the program for the people it was intended to serve. The term outcome is used interchangeably with result and effect. Outcomes can be *intended* and *unintended*. *Thus, evaluating the outcomes of a program or social policy (= intervention) is called outcome evaluation.*

An emphasis on program outcome would direct the evaluation to the consequences of the intervention for its clients. Has the program positively changed the clients' situation (knowledge, behavior, earnings, health status, drug use, etc.)? Questions about attributions have to do with figuring out whether any changes that are observed over time are due to the program. The evaluation of a job training program, for example, may find that participants who completed the training increased their earnings as compared with the amount they had earned before entering the program. However, it is possible that their earnings would have gone up anyway, even if they had not enrolled in the program. The economy might have improved and thus better paying jobs might have become available. This highlights the difficulties in conducting outcome evaluations.

189

Another concept that sometimes is mentioned when people discuss the focus of evaluation is impact. Most of the time, the word means the same as outcome. Sometimes, impact is construed as long-term outcomes. Occasionally, writers use the word *impact* to mean effects of the program on the larger community.   In this sense, analysts use the term social impact assessment, i.e., the estimation of the likely consequences of a planned change (e.g., community service; social conditions [crime rates, the ability of the elderly to feel they can take care of themselves]; economic impact [changes in income levels, business failure rate], environmental consequences; demographic consequences; health outcomes; psychological wellbeing). Yet another meaning of impact is the net effects of the program, after taking into account what would have happened in the absence of a program. In operational terms, this means looking at the outcomes for program participants (say, nine percent hold jobs after the training program) and looking at the outcomes for an equivalent population of nonparticipants (say, three percent hold jobs at some point). Then the net impact of the program would be estimated to be nine percent - three percent = six percent (Weiss 1998).

Although outcomes were and still are the main emphasis in evaluation research, another interest is in whether the program is functioning as it was intended to function. Thus, as Weiss (1998) points out, evaluators need to study what the program actually does. This type of evaluation is called process evaluation.   One reason to study program process is that evaluators have to know what the programs really are before they can draw conclusions about whether they are successful or not. Second, sometimes the key questions that the program community has about the program have to do with its process. For example, what kind of service are participants being given? Is the service following the prescriptions of the program developer? How often are participants (say, in a drug treatment program) showing up? What kinds of problems are staff encountering? Are clients happy with the program? Is the program understaffed or overstaffed? A third reason to study program process is to complement the understanding of outcome data. The evaluator may find that, while certain participants in the program did extremely well, others deteriorated. There are many possible reasons for such a finding, but one possible reason is that different clients received different quality of service.

B. Formative Evaluation and Summative Evaluation. In discussing potential uses of a program, one of the top evaluation researchers in the world, the Australian Michael Scriven (1967) distinguished between formative and summative evaluation. Giving the example of an educational curriculum, he stated that **formative evaluation** produces information that is fed back during the development of a curriculum to help improve it. **Summative evaluation**, on the other hand, is done after the curriculum is finished to supply data about the effectiveness of the curriculum so that other school decision makers can introduce it in their schools. To illustrate this distinction, Scriven offers the following definition: "When the cook tastes the soup, that's formative evaluation; when the guest tastes it, that's summative evaluation."

Evaluation Research Designs

To reiterate, evaluation research is not a separate method but rather "applied social research" that can utilize a compilation of various techniques or any of several research designs. Two of the most widely used tools by evaluation researchers are needs assessment and cost-benefit analysis. We will only mention these briefly and then focus on two other designs used in evaluation studies: experiments, and qualitative evaluations (Weiss 1998; Babbie 2003; Posavac and Carey 2003).

In a **needs assessment**, a researcher collects data to determine what the community really needs and how badly it needs it. Often, this is a required preliminary step before a government agency or charity decides to spend resources and implement a program to help people. This is, however, no easy matter because we have to decide what the most important need is and try to involve various segments of the community. Thus, if homeless people say they need housing, unemployed may need jobs. After examining the situation, the sociologist may decide that housing would be available if the homeless had jobs. Thus, it may turn out that the two needs are related, with one causing the other. Furthermore, people often have multiple needs and it is quite complicated to decide which is the most pressing. Finally, influential political and business groups may not want some need to be studied and publicized in the mass media.

Social impact studies to justify certain public policy frequently include a **cost-benefit analysis**. Economists developed and elaborated cost-benefit analysis, where the researcher estimates the future costs and benefits of one or several proposed actions and gives them monetary values. Then costs are compared to benefits and policymakers decide whether the benefits exceed the costs, which most likely will lead to adoption of a given policy. The difficulty with cost-benefit analysis is that some measured outcomes do not yield themselves to an exact financial evaluation (reduction in crime, less fear, health, love, happiness, human dignity, respect, optimism, self-sufficiency).

<u>Experiments</u> in their various forms are often useful in evaluation research (Babbie 2002). For example, we can set up a classical experiment to find out if a new psychotherapeutic treatment for sexual impotence is effective. We would then select 100 patients treated at a clinic for sexual impotence and assign randomly 50 of them to an experimental group and 50 to a control group. The experimental group will get the stimulus, or intervention, or the new therapy (e.g., pornographic movies), while the control group will continue getting the conventional therapy. After some period of time, we will compare the two groups and see if there is any difference. Based on these results, we will evaluate the effectiveness of the new treatment.

Users and Uses of Evaluation Research

Evaluation research is often difficult and extremely challenging because you are dealing with important decisions that affect a large number of people (Weiss 1998). Therefore, contextual issues, political considerations, moral dilemmas, logistical problems, funding, interest group pressures often come to the fore. One set of problems concerns the users and uses of such studies.   There is a great variety of potential <u>users</u> with their specific interests and ideas, questions and concerns (the funding organization, national agencies, local agencies, politicians, clients of the project, program designers, directors and managers of similar programs elsewhere, scholars, program consultants, community leaders, concerned citizens, affected interest groups, the public, and so on). The set of all people with a possible stake in the evaluation are often called <u>stakeholders</u>.

Although findings from evaluation research can be used for many purposes, there are at least <u>three barriers</u> to practically implementing the recommendations of an evaluation: 1) The findings may not be presented in a way that makes them easy to interpret or apply (too technical, esoteric language, extensive use of sophisticated statistics, etc.); 2) sometimes evaluation findings contradict deeply held beliefs; and 3) vested interests often get in the way of the recognition and potential use of evaluation results.

by Ivan M. Chompalov, Ph.D.

ൠ ൃ ൠ ര

Definitions

Accretion Measures. Refers to those whose greater accumulation suggests stronger preference. They can also be thought of as "deposits" that tell us something about human behavior.

Case Studies. A research design that focuses on a single example rather than a representative sample.

Causal Relationships. A link between two things in which one event occurs as a result of another event. For a causal relationship to exist there needs to be a distinct and factual link between an initial event (A) and its result (B) (i.e., cause and effect, or A causes B).

Closed-Ended Questions. Questions on an instrument that have a fixed set of answers from which respondents must choose.

Coding System. A set of instructions or rules on how to systematically observe and record content from text.

Conceptualization. The development of concepts and ideas that are used in a study.

Content Analysis. An empirical examination of the frequency of a particular social characteristic or feature of a society. This can also be done on books, magazines, journal articles, newspapers, etc.

Control Group. A group of people in an experiment who are not exposed to the experimental stimulus under study.

Cost-Benefit Analysis. The process of weighing the total expected costs v. the total expected benefits of one or more actions in order to choose the best or most profitable option.

Dependent Variable. The consistent variable that depends on the experimental input to be changed.

Erosion Measures. Refers to those where we look at the wear and tear of objects to draw sociological inferences. An example would be when a sociologist tries to categorize toys at a day care center depending on how new or worn-out they are, if all toys were bought at the same time.

Ethnography (*participant observation*). A research method in which researchers observe behavior in real-life settings in which they are participants. Describing a culture and understanding another way of life from the native point of view.

Ethnomethodology. A sociological offshoot of the philosophical tradition of phenomenology. Literally, it means, "describing the methods of the people," or how people make sense of their everyday life. In essence, this is the study of people's commonsensical knowledge.

Evaluation Research. Tries to determine whether social interventions or programs have had their desired effects. In short, it tries to evaluate or assess whether programs designed to solve or alleviate social problems have been effective in achieving their intended goals (Posavac and Carey 2003).

Experimental Design. A research design using a positivist paradigm that attempts to control for internal and external validity, has a probability sample, uses a valid and reliable instrument, and tries to keep controls on the design that allow for conclusions of cause-effect relationships and generalizability to other people, places, and events.

Experimental Group. The group receiving the treatment input.

Focus Groups. A randomly selected group of subjects who discuss, in a group context, specific issues determined by the researcher.

Formative Evaluation. Produces information that is fed back during the development of a curriculum to help improve it.

Grounded Theory. Barney Glaser and Anselm Strauss developed this theory and it combines two traditions: positivism and interactionism. This is an inductive method, meaning that theory is built from data or grounded in the data. The researcher begins with a research question, not a hypothesis.

Hypothesis. An educated prediction of what a study will find based on what similar studies have found in the past. May be stated in a neutral way (a null hypothesis), a positive, or a negative way suggesting that the study will find either what other studies have found or the exact opposite of what other studies have found.

Independent Variable. The treatment variable within a research design that may affect the dependent variable.

Intercoder Reliability. The agreement among several coders to use the same coding scheme to analyze the content of the same set of texts.

Interview Survey. A method of gathering data through which people are asked a series of questions.

Medium. A means or instrumentality for storing or communicating information.

Naturalism. The stance whereby we assume that social reality is objective, out there, and the researcher can observe and report it almost as an exact correspondence to what "really exists." This is also known as positivism, or positive science.

Needs Assessment. In this type of design a researcher collects data to determine what the community really needs and how badly it needs it.

Open-Ended Questions. Questions on an instrument in which the answers are not pre-determined and the subjects can write anything they believe to be relevant.

Operationalization. Specifying the rules of how variables will be measured.

Participant Observation (*ethnography*). A research method in which researchers observe behavior in real-life settings in which they are participants. Describing a culture and understanding another way of life from the native point of view.

Physical Traces. Sources of evidence left behind by people who never expected them to become sources of sociological interpretations and conclusions. *Physical traces* are commonly divided into *erosion measures* and *accretion measures*.

Population. A collection of people who share a geographic territory. In research, any precisely defined set of objects, people, groups, or societies.

Posttest. Subjects are usually measured in terms of the dependent variable after the treatment.

Pretest. Subjects are usually measured in terms of the dependent variable before the treatment.

Probability Sample. A sampling approach in which every member of the larger population has an equal or random chance of being selected.

Purposive Sampling. A sampling approach that targets a particular population because those populations have a special quality related to the particular study.

Qualitative Methods. Research that provides more leeway than quantitative research in the flexibility of designs and sampling. Not felt to permit cause-effect relationships or the ability to generalize to other people, places, or situations.

Quantitative Methods. Research that uses a positivist paradigm, experimental designs, and the scientific method to produce findings that may show relationships that are generalizable to other people, places, and events.

Questionnaire Survey. A method of gathering information in which respondents complete a written form.

Reliability. The degree to which a measurement instrument gives the same results with repeated measurements (assuming that whatever is being measured does not change).

195

Respondents. Subjects that are being questioned in an interview or survey.

Sample. A subgroup of a population.

Simple Random Sampling. Choosing a large and diverse group of people at random in the hope that we will select a sample that closely represents the larger population.

Stratified Random Sample. Randomly chooses cases from subpopulations of interest, so that the proportion of the sub-sample is the same as the proportion of the sub-population.

Summative Evaluation. Is done after the curriculum is finished to supply data about the effectiveness of the curriculum so that other school decision makers can introduce it in their schools.

Survey. A method of gathering data through which people are asked a series of questions either by an interviewer or in questionnaire form.

Systematic Random Sample. A sample drawn by selecting a random starting point in a list of a population and skipping through the list at regular intervals.

Unobtrusive Measures. The researcher examines traces of human activity without the knowledge of the people who produced these traces.

Validity. The degree to which a measurement instrument measures what it is intended to measure.

REFERENCES

Babbie, Earl. 2002. *The Basics of Social Research.* 2nd ed. Belmont, CA: Wadsworth.

Campbell, Donald and Julian Stanley. 1963. *Experimental and Quasi-Experimental Designs for Research.* Chicago, IL: Rand McNally.

Dorsten, Linda Eberst and Lawrence Hotchkiss. 2005. *Research Methods and Society: Foundations of Social Inquiry.* Upper Saddle River, NJ: Prentice Hall.

Griffith, Allison. 1995. "Mothering, Schooling, and Children's Development." Pp. 108-121 in *Knowledge, Experience, and Ruling Relations: Studies in the Social Organization of Knowledge,* edited by M. Campbell and A. Manicom. Toronto, Canada: University of Toronto Press.

Neuman, W. Lawrence. 2000. *Social Research Methods: Qualitative and Quantitative Approaches.* 4th ed. Boston, MA: Allyn and Bacon.

Posavac, Emil and Raymond Carey. 2003. *Program Evaluation: Methods and Case Studies.* 6th ed. Upper Saddle River, NJ: Prentice Hall.

Sedlack, R. Guy and Jay Stanley. 1992. *Social Research: Theory and Methods.* Boston, MA: Allyn and Bacon.

Taylor, Frank. 2003. "Content Analysis and Gender Stereotypes in Children's Books." *Teaching Sociology* 31:300-311.

Weiss, Carol. 1998. *Evaluation.* 2nd ed. Upper Saddle River, NJ: Prentice Hall.

9 | Marriage and the Family: How We Come Together and Stay Together … Sometimes.
by Ivan M. Chompalov, Ph.D.

A recent ranking of the 36 countries with the highest divorce rates in the world showed that the United States leads all nations with almost 5 divorces per 1,000 people. This "grim distinction" is surely something we as Americans would not like to brag about, although in recent decades being divorced has become an acceptable way of life that does not raise many eyebrows. In fact, it has become quite common to hear in the mass media debates about American family values, the state of marriage, whether same-sex marriages should be legalized, the high divorce rate and whether it presents a problem for our society, domestic violence, abortion, the use of reproductive technologies, whether stepfamilies are destined for trouble, out-of-wedlock births, and similar issues. What they all have in common is that they are all concerns about marriage and the family as social institutions; Institutions that have been in existence since the dawn of humankind and are still an integral part of our society.

Why should we care about studying marriage and the family? Because typically we are born, live, and often die in a family and our life is intricately connected to marriages. These are **institutions** (established activities, beliefs, and values to satisfy social needs).

What is marriage? The Census definition says that **marriage** is "a legal contract between a woman and a man who are above a legal age and are not already legally married to someone else." This definition is too narrow and restrictive, so Schwartz and Scott propose a broader definition of marriage as "a union between people (legally recognized or not) that unites partners sexually, economically, and socially." The problem with this definition is just the opposite—it is too inclusive. For example, it will consider any cohabitation as "marriage," as well as any homosexual partnership as belonging to the same category, although the law currently does not allow same-sex marriages. Researchers commonly distinguish several types of marriages. **Monogamy** is when one person of one sex is, at any given point in time, married to only one person of the opposite sex. **Serial monogamy** describes a repeated pattern of monogamous marriage, divorce or widowhood, remarriage, another divorce or widowhood, another remarriage, and so on. We speak of **polygamy** when one person of one sex is simultaneously married to several people of the opposite sex. A special term for group marriage is **cenogamy**.

by Ivan M. Chompalov, Ph.D.

What is a family and how does it differ from marriage? According to the Census, a **family** is two or more persons living together and related by blood, marriage, or adoption. Again, the official definition is too narrow. There are families who do not live together—a number of academic couples maintain separate residences, often in different states, and are commonly referred to as "commuter marriages." Other definitions have been proposed, such as "any stable group who simply live together and provide one another with economic and emotional support," or "a group of people who define themselves as family." Again, this is a problematic definition. For instance, while in Graduate School one of the authors shared an apartment with a roommate who was also a graduate student. They lived together and supported each other but did not consider themselves a "family."

Table 9.1   Divorce Rates

SOURCE
divorcereform.org
DEFINITION
Divorce rate per 1,000 people

Rank	Country	Amount (top to bottom)
#1	United States	4.95 per 1,000 people
#2	Puerto Rico	4.47 per 1,000 people
#3	Russia	3.36 per 1,000 people
#4	United Kingdom	3.08 per 1,000 people

#5	Denmark	2.81 per 1,000 people
#6	New Zealand	2.63 per 1,000 people
#7	Australia	2.52 per 1,000 people
#8	Canada	2.46 per 1,000 people
#9	Finland	1.85 per 1,000 people
#10	Barbados	1.21 per 1,000 people
#11	Guadeloupe	1.18 per 1,000 people
#12	Qatar	0.97 per 1,000 people
#15	Portugal	0.88 per 1,000 people
#16	Albania	0.83 per 1,000 people
#17	Tunisia	0.82 per 1,000 people
#18	Singapore	0.8 per 1,000 people
#19	China	0.79 per 1,000 people
#20	Greece	0.76 per 1,000 people
#21	Brunei	0.72 per 1,000 people
#22	Panama	0.68 per 1,000 people
#23	Syria	0.65 per 1,000 people
#24	Thailand	0.58 per 1,000 people

#25	**Mauritius**	0.47 per 1,000 people	
#26	**Ecuador**	0.42 per 1,000 people	
#27	**El Salvador**	0.41 per 1,000 people	
#28	**Cyprus**	0.39 per 1,000 people	
#29	**Jamaica**	0.38 per 1,000 people	
#30	**Chile**	0.38 per 1,000 people	
#31	**Mongolia**	0.37 per 1,000 people	
#32	**Turkey**	0.37 per 1,000 people	
#33	**Mexico**	0.33 per 1,000 people	
#34	**Italy**	0.27 per 1,000 people	
#35	**Brazil**	0.26 per 1,000 people	
#36	**Sri Lanka**	0.15 per 1,000 people	
	Weighted average:	1.3 per 1,000 people	

Source: divorcereform.org.

9 | Marriage and the Family: How We Come Together and Stay Together … Sometimes.
by Ivan M. Chompalov, Ph.D.

There are different types of families. A **family of orientation** is the family where one was born and grew up. When we marry and have our own children, we start the so-called **family of procreation.** Another division is between a nuclear and an extended family. A **nuclear family** includes the mother, the father, and their children. An **extended family** builds upon the nuclear family and is comprised of parents, siblings, and other relatives (typically grandparents). Then there are also the families we create after remarriage. These are alternatively called **reconstituted, or blended, or stepfamilies.** Several other categories have gained popularity through the mass media, among them single-parent families; gay and lesbian families; racially mixed families; foster families; and surrogate family (roommates). Traditionally, the United States has had **patriarchal families** (where the male is the head of the family) as opposed to **matriarchal families** (where the female is the head of the family).

Sociologists have identified a number of functions, or positive consequences, of the family:

1. Regulation of Sexual Behavior. In most societies, sexual behavior is governed by norms that favor such behavior occurring within the family. On the other side of the coin, the majority of cultures around the world adhere to the **incest taboo**—a strong social norm that prohibits sexual relations with and marrying a blood   relative.

2. Reproduction. This is one of the primary social functions of the family. Some societies encourage reproduction (for example, the United States gives tax exemptions for kids); others discourage or limit reproduction (e.g., China's one child policy).

3. Social Placement. The family facilitates the placement in the **social structure** (i.e., the set of patterned social relations), composed of **statuses** (positions) and **roles** (behavioral expectations associated with statuses). Think of the opportunities you will be afforded if born in the Bill Gates family as compared with the constraints you will face throughout your life if you were born a "crack baby."

201

4. <u>Socialization</u>. This is the process through which people learn norms, values, and roles, the process through which they internalize the norms, values, and roles that constitute the culture of a society. Your family is considered the primary agent of socialization, alongside school.

5. <u>Economic Cooperation</u>. Children need to be fed, clothed, and provided with shelter. In addition, spouses need to cooperate economically.

6. <u>Care, Protection, and Intimacy</u>. Families supply their members with warmth, affection, love, emotional support. They also care for children and the elderly. Nowadays care has largely been taken over by public and private organizations (childcare; nursing homes).

<u>Images of families in contemporary United States society</u>. Baca Zinn and Eitzen identify three such images:

1. Family as a <u>haven</u>. Family provides love and protection (e.g., when a daughter gets mistreated or stood up at a date, she comes back home and her father, upon learning this, offers to beat the jerk up, while her mother cooks something and provides sympathy. So, the family takes care of you;

2. Family as <u>fulfillment</u>. In contrast to (1) or the "protective image," this is a "compensatory image." It involves self-fulfillment and enjoyment of joint activities. This is when your family is perceived as fun rather than an obligation (e.g., you and your family go to Disney World, spend holidays together, watch movies);

3. Family as <u>encumbrance</u>. This is a negative image as opposed to (2). In this image, the family is viewed as inhibiting through monogamy and childrearing of your self-expression and personal freedom. Typically, you see your family as hampering your career.

9 | Marriage and the Family: How We Come Together and Stay Together … Sometimes.
by Ivan M. Chompalov, Ph.D.

In recent years, there has been a heated <u>debate over family values</u>. Some researchers (e.g., Christopher Lasch) say that government encroachment has led to the family function being taken over, which disrupts families and leads to a number of ills (drugs, delinquency, teenage pregnancy, etc.). There are two problems with this view:

a) it treats the family as a causal agent rather than a reflection of social conditions;

b) it ignores the reasons for family breakdown.

Others view the family as the foundation of society and recognize changes in the meaning of family and the current diversity of arrangements (e.g., feminists). The opposite stance, adopted by "traditionalists" or conservatives focuses on the decline of family values, associated with feminism, the sexual revolution of the 1960s, and gay and lesbian lifestyles. Thus, Norvell Glenn chides feminists for not focusing enough on the "positive aspects" of traditional marriage and family (parents and their kids).

In our society, certain <u>myths about marriages and families</u> are still being perpetuated. Thus, Stephanie Coontz in *The Way We Never Were* argues that much of today's political "family values" debates idealizes the past, which leads to the creation of **myths** (false, imaginary beliefs about something). She identifies <u>five</u> such myths:

1) <u>The universal nuclear family</u>. This myth maintains that some form of nuclear family is found in all societies. The reality is that this is not true, since we witness a great diversity of family arrangements (children outside of marriage; different family functions).

2) <u>The self-reliant traditional family</u>. This myth says that in the past families through hard work and determination made it on their own, without depending on the state. Looking at the historical evidence, this turns out to be false. Early American families had an extended network of neighbors, friends, churches, and slaves living with them.

203

3) <u>The naturalness of different spheres for wives and husbands</u>. This happened with industrialization but before the mid-nineteenth century men shared childrearing and the family was also an economic unit (Baca Zinn and Eitzen 1998). Unemployment leads to increased violence and mixing of spheres. Nowadays, very often it is women who "wear the pants in the family."

4) <u>The unstable African American family</u>. Andrew Billingsley (1968) demonstrated that the class division of African American families is important in their analysis. Only the "underclass" experiences chronic and persistent poverty and the negative processes (single mothers, teenage pregnancy, welfare dependency, low marriage rate, etc.) associated with this stereotype. In addition, this myth disregards **institutional racism** (systematic discrimination within society).

5) <u>The idealized nuclear family of the 1950s</u>. Many TV shows from the 1950s (e.g., "Ozzie and Harriet," "Father Knows Best," "Leave It to Beaver") tend to idealize the "normal nuclear family." In the 1950s marriage rates soared and people were getting married younger and having more children because of a reaction to the hardships of World War II. Nevertheless, 20 percent of couples said they were "unhappy" and 20 percent reported "medium happiness." In addition, families have always changed and in times of prosperity (1950s) they are different than in times of economic crisis (the Great Depression).

Additionally, Baca Zinn and Eitzen (1998) have identified several more myths such as:

6) <u>The myth of undifferentiated family experience</u>. This myth assumes that family members have common needs, interests, and experiences. Sociological research, however, shows great differentiation within a family along gender and age lines.

7) <u>The myth of family consensus</u>. This myth assumes that families operate on principles of harmony and love. It disregards power struggles and competition within the family, which are quite common.

9 | Marriage and the Family: How We Come Together and Stay Together ... Sometimes.
by Ivan M. Chompalov, Ph.D.

Marriage is a watershed event in our life cycle. Few decisions are as important (school, getting a job, having children). Today marriage is still popular, although many marriages end up in divorce. Why do people still prefer marriage to being single? There are a variety of reasons why people still find the marriage option attractive. A summary of findings from various studies yields the following ranking:

1) Love;

2) Companionship;

3) Desire for children;

4) Happiness;

5) Money;

6) Convenience; and

7) Others.

Once the reality of marriage sets in, however, things get more complicated. <u>What makes a successful marriage</u>? The authors of this book may not be considered by many people to be the best experts when it comes to practical advice, since they have all, unfortunately, been serial monogamists and have personally experienced divorce. Thus, they can surely inform the student about what does NOT work, but not so much so, based on their personal experience, of what works. However, people have done studies that reveal certain patterns.

Most studies agree that the reasons to marry and the factors contributing to a successful marriage depend on cultural traditions. In <u>Japan</u>, love and commitment are not the most important factors for a durable marriage. Many couples believe that love marriages are more fragile. Japan has the lowest level of compatibility of marriage partners on politics, sex, religion, and ethics. Still, the Japanese enjoy very durable marriages. They tend to be much more reserved than Americans are when it comes to publicly expressing love and affection. In India, too, people think of marriage and love differently than in the United States. Since marriages in India are arranged, the motto is: marriage comes first; love comes later. If it happens, fine, if not, that is how it goes. Here in the United States, the situation is just the reverse. Love comes first, marriage comes later. In other words, the *mantra in India is "we love the ones we marry." The mantra in the United States is "we marry the ones we love."* That might explain partly the higher divorce rate in the United States (since love can fade away). <u>Other factors</u> that affect the decision to marry tend to be more sociological in nature: the economic situation (during the Great Depression people delayed marriage) and race are two such factors.

Of course, although marriage is ultimately a personal decision that involves feelings, emotions, preferences, and reasoning, sociologists are also interested in the structural factors affecting mate selection and the choice of a future marriage partner. What are these?

1. **The Marriage Market and the Pool of Eligibles**. Sociologists of marriage and family often describe the process of mate selection as rational and taking place in what is being called "the marriage market." Just like any other free market for goods and services, when we try to select a mate we "shop around." We have resources—money, attractiveness, abilities, future prospects—and we trade them for the best offer we can get. In some societies, *dowries* in the form of money or property are exchanged by the woman's family for high status of the male. One resource is also *virginity*. Women are still in a poorer bargaining position—men can get childcare, housework, and sex outside of marriage. The *pool of eligibles* is the group of acceptable potential marriage partners. When people of the opposite sex are similar to us in terms of class, race, age, or education, we talk about **homogamy.** In addition, two rules that govern the marriage market and pool of eligibles are **exogamy** (marrying someone from outside of your own ethnic or racial group) and **endogamy** (marrying someone from your own ethnic or racial group).

2. **The Marriage Squeeze and the Marriage Gradient. Marriage squeeze** is a term to describe an unfavorable imbalance in the sex ratio of marriage-aged men to marriage-aged women. Briefly, one sex has a more limited pool of eligibles than another does. Demographically, in the United States women are at

a disadvantage. This is especially evident among African-American women, where the man to woman ratio is 90:100. The **marriage gradient** refers to the fact that because women tend to marry upward and men downward, men at the top have a much larger pool of eligible women, whereas women at the top have a much more limited pool of eligibles. This, too, is a very prominent pattern among African-American women.

3. **Race**. Although there is some increase in intermarriages, still 98 percent of marriages in the United States occur within the same racial group.

4. **Social Class.** Since people of the same class share similar wealth, lifestyle, norms, and values, it is an important factor in mate selection. Typically people marry within the same class, although men more so than women can break this barrier.

5. **Age**. This factor operates more strongly when people marry for the first time and at a younger age. It is less important for remarriage.

6. **Religion**. About 90 percent of people select partners similar to them in terms of religious beliefs.

7. **Propinquity**. It is easier to meet people of the opposite sex in your place of residence or place of work. Thus, proximity facilitates mate selection. Now, with the advent of electronic communication this factor is less salient than in the past.

8. **Family and peer pressure**. Perhaps in the United States, these factors are not as strong as in some other countries (India, China, and most African countries where arranged marriages are still common, especially in rural areas).

People think in a variety of ways about their marriages and this differs by social class, culture, race, gender. Nevertheless, there are <u>three common notions of what it means to be married</u>:

1) **A Commitment**. Many researchers have argued that people understand marriage as a long-term commitment only when they enter it. It is considered a crucial factor in a durable relationship. For some couples this means a vow, a promise to stay together and help each other through thick and thin. This requires readiness for <u>sacrifices</u>. For others, it also stems from their family and religious background. In any event, commitment contributes to stability.

2) **A Sacrament**. This is the religious meaning of marriage as a <u>sacred union or rite</u>. About 75 percent of first marriages and about 60 percent of remarriages in the United States are conducted by clergy in church. Therefore, many people consider marriage to be "holy matrimony," or a holy institution. Some denominations are more flexible as to the dissolutions of marriage (Unitarians) while others are more strict (Catholics).

3) **A Legal Contract**. The Census definition places emphasis on marriage as a contract. <u>Legal marriage</u> is a contractual agreement—getting a marriage license—regulated by the states. <u>Social marriage</u> is not legally binding (common-law marriage and cohabitation), unless the two parties sign a prenuptial contract. State laws cover residents of the respective states, as well as who can perform a wedding and marry two people. In order to enter marriage as a legal contract, people have to meet certain conditions.

   a. **Sexual Orientation**. States typically define marriage as a commitment to have progeny and carry on the lineage. Therefore, same-sex marriages are still illegal in all states, except in Massachusetts. However, other legal aspects put that into question. Marriage is a legal union that has consequences for inheritance, health benefits, life insurance, pensions, tax returns, etc. Therefore, from that point of view homosexuals are discriminated against legally. Now only four countries allow by law "domestic partnerships." This has been a very contentious issue in the United States. Many of the opponents do not mind gays and lesbians having all other rights, but <u>marriage is the last bastion</u>. What is at stake is not just of academic interest (e.g., the case of Hawaii) but has financial and legal implications (taxes, property inheritance, funerals, and benefits).

b. **Bigamy and Incest Taboo.** Both are prohibited under the law. Marrying a second person while you are still legally married to the first spouse and marrying relatives.

c. **Age Restrictions**. You have to be considered old enough to marry. In all states, without parental consent you can marry when you are 18 (with the exception of Georgia, where you are allowed to do so at the age of 16). With parental consent states allow young people to get married at 16.

d. **Blood Tests.** In most states when you file an application to obtain a marriage license, you have to have a blood test for STDs.

Men and women have somewhat different experiences of marriage, which led sociologist of marriage and the family Jessie Bernard (1972) to talk about <u>his marriage and her marriage</u>:

1) **"Her" Marriage.** Wives were less happy with their marriages than husbands were. Married women experienced higher anxiety, phobia, and depression than any other group, except single men. Wives tend to complain more about their marriage life than husbands do primarily because the imbalance of power is in favor of husbands and too many chores alienate wives. Often women lose their identity and become very dependent on their husbands. Having children only exacerbates the situation for wives.

2) **"His" Marriage**. Some men feel trapped, but most prefer marriage to being single. Married men live longer and are healthier and happier. Additionally, being married and having children typically helps a husband's career but typically hurts a wife's career.

After they marry, people experience what is called a *marital adjustment*, or how they learn to get along with each other and live together. This period is very different from dating: the early marriage means that, unlike dating, you share many things: the good, the bad, and the ugly. There is no single model marriage, but there are several types, according to John Cuber and Peggy Harroff:

1) <u>The Conflict-Habituated Marriage</u>. This kind of marriage is characterized by extensive arguing, disagreements, and conflict, although things are still under control—the situation does not get out of hand.

2) <u>The Devitalized Marriage</u>. Once the spouses were deeply in love but over time, that intense feeling has faded away. As a result, the husband and wife pay little attention to each other.

3) <u>The Passive Congenial Marriage</u>. This type is similar to 2), but it was so from the beginning, not with time.

4) <u>The Vital Marriage</u>. The two spouses are highly involved with each other, they spend a lot of time together, and they share a lot.

5) <u>The Total Marriage</u>. These spouses are like Siamese twins. Unlike the vital marriage, the spouses do not even have individuality. This last type is extremely rare.

A large body of sociological literature deals with marital satisfaction. Married people are generally more satisfied with their lives, healthier, and happier than unmarried individuals are. <u>What keeps a marriage going</u>? Jeanette Lauer and Robert Lauer analyzed responses of 351 couples married for 15 years or more in 1986. The <u>top seven reasons in order of frequency of occurrence were</u>:

1) My spouse is my best friend;

2) I like my spouse as a person;

3) Marriage is a long-term commitment;

4) Marriage is sacred;

5) We agree on aims and goals;

6) My spouse has grown more interesting; and

7) I want the relationship to succeed.

All these things seem to contribute to satisfaction with the marriage and hence, lead to longevity of this institution. In recent years, there has been an increase in divorce rates and decline in marital success. The main reason could be that people have grown more <u>selfish and materialistic</u>. Therefore, often they have unrealistically high expectations. Although marital satisfaction has also declined, still married people are more satisfied with their lives than unmarrieds are. Several factors lead to higher satisfaction:

1) <u>Effective Communication</u>. This is very essential. Close to one-half ($\frac{1}{2}$) of households seek counseling or therapy.

2) <u>Self-Disclosure</u>. This refers to sharing with another person with expectation of reciprocity. Women practice self-disclosure more often than men do. If the spouses are understanding and willing to communicate and compromise, there marital satisfaction increases.

3) <u>Conflict Resolution</u>. The key is to manage conflict through negotiation. Destructive behaviors to marriage are criticism, contempt, defensiveness, and stalling.

When things do not go well, marriages are often dissolved through **divorce**. According to some researchers, approximately 50 percent of all marriages in the United States will eventually end in divorce. In the 1990s, roughly 1.2 million married couples became divorced each year. Some researchers regard this as a symptom of the disintegration and decline of modern American families. This is probably a myth, since divorce is not exactly a new phenomenon. The truth about the consequences of divorce is also difficult to establish—for some people it works out okay, for others it leaves permanent scars. How has divorce and the meaning of divorce fluctuated throughout the years? Schwartz and Scott (2003) distinguish several historical periods of the evolution of divorce in the United States:

1) **Divorce in Early America.** In 1639 a Massachusetts court gave the first legal divorce decree in America. That was the beginning. Although in the seventeenth and eighteenth centuries divorce was legally permitted in New England, the reasons for divorce varied. The most common pattern, though, was finding one of the spouses at fault (adultery, battering, sexual abuse). The "guilty party" was punished severely: fines, incarceration, public whipping, ban on remarriage, even banishment from the colony. Fault was also the basis for awarding **alimony**, or payment by the husband of a monetary allowance to the wife. If the wife was found guilty, she lost the right to alimony. Among the reasons for divorce in early America were the migration westward, industrialization, and the emergence of a market economy. All this led to greater mobility, more time outside the home and weakening of marriage as an institution.

2) **Divorce in Nineteenth Century America.** After the American revolution, rapid industrialization and urbanization occurred. This led, among many other things, to a greater relaxation of divorce laws. As a result, divorce rates went up, although the statistics are not very systematic. The critics of this trend proclaimed that divorce undermined American values and led to many social ills, thus disrupting social life and order. The other side in the debate claimed that it was not divorce that needed to be perceived as the problem, but marriage, which needed reform. Efforts here focused on widespread wife <u>abuse</u>, especially in the 1850s. Women's groups were especially active, in many cases ascribing fault with the husbands because of violence and abuse against their wives. In the nineteenth century, the negative consequences of divorce were becoming more evident—the impoverishment of divorced women with children. Alimony was often granted, but difficult to enforce. Judges started awarding

split custody, with girls and younger children being placed in the custody of the mother, while husbands were given custody of boys and older children.

3) **Divorce in Twentieth Century America.**   The twentieth century again saw heated debates over divorce, which by some was seen as an evil force, tearing apart the fabric of American society. Others pushed for a more liberal approach. Divorce rates again went up after WWI under the stress of economic hardship and uncertainty.   During the Great Depression, this trend was exacerbated. By the 1960s, attention began to shift toward the deleterious effects of divorce on wives and children. As a result, various proposals were put forward for a reform of divorce laws. This culminated in 1969 in California's no-fault divorce bill, which was signed into law by then governor Ronald Reagan. This was somewhat ironic, since as a Republican you would expect him to defend "family values" but then again, he himself was divorced. The next 20 years saw most states following California's example.   The most common reasons for divorce now are "irreconcilable differences" or "irretrievable breakdown of the marriage." Studies have provided controversial evidence regarding whether the new divorce law has diminished marriage problems and negative consequences of divorce. In any event, what is important is that this historical detour shows that the dissolution of marriage cannot be properly understood without studying the social context.   Nowadays, the divorce rate in the United States is the highest among all industrialized countries. In 1980, it was 23 per 1,000 married women, or 5.2 divorces per 1,000 people. In 1998 it declined somewhat to 3.6, using this last measure, and by 2005, as you can see from Table 9.1, it went back up to 4.95.

Divorce rates are not uniform across population subgroups. Women are more likely than men to be divorced. In addition, African Americans have the highest divorce rate, while Hispanics have the lowest. For African Americans one possible reason is, according to some researchers, the legacy of slavery. Other analysts argue that this is a more recent phenomenon, which took epidemic proportions after the 1960s with the economic hardships for many African American families. Some conservatives (Murray 1984) blame this on the War on Poverty and AFDC in particular. Most differences between African Americans and whites can be attributed to the different level of

213

income and education, as well as the higher unemployment rate amongst African Americans. There is evidence that unemployment and divorce are correlated. The low divorce rates among Hispanics are generally attributed to the high value they place on the family. Here, Catholicism also plays a role because it prohibits divorce. However, there are differences in this group among Puerto Ricans (high divorce rate) and Cuban Americans (low divorce rate). Native Americans have extremely high divorce rates, probably due to unemployment and poverty, as well as high rates of alcoholism. Asian Americans have a somewhat lower divorce rate as a group than the average. However, this rate is high (22 percent) among Cambodians and Laotians and fairly low (7 percent) among Asian Indians and the Japanese and Chinese (11 percent).

Naturally, the question arises: Who gets divorced and why? There is a variety of factors affecting marital stability, or marital instability. What are they?

1. **Age at First Marriage.** Younger people are more likely to be divorced after their first marriage than those who are 25 to 35 years old. At the same time, spouses over 35 at first marriage are also likely to experience high rates of divorce. For the younger group the reasons are inexperience, lack of material resources, pressures of early childbearing. For the middle-aged group the most likely factor is that they are established professionals with strong personalities, quite independent, and possibly too particular since they have delayed marriage for so long.

2. **Education.** The relationship between educational attainment and divorce is a bit more unclear. Nevertheless, women who drop out of high school have the highest divorce rates. Financial pressures and early childbearing may increase the likelihood of divorce in this category. However, surprisingly, divorce rates among women with five and more years of college education are higher than among those with fewer years of college. Researchers have been puzzled by why this should be the case.

3. **Income.** Generally speaking, the lower the income the higher the likelihood of divorce. However, some studies have found contradictory evidence that women earning a lot of money are also more likely to get divorced.

214

4. **Religion.** A well established fact here is people who are more religious are less likely to divorce. In addition, sharing the same faith makes you more stable in your family life and less likely to divorce. Membership in religious organizations has been known since Emile Durkheim to promote social cohesion and integration, so this is not that surprising. There are distinct patterns among the various nominations: Protestants are more likely to divorce, followed by Catholics and Jews. Among Protestants, Baptists and Pentecostals have higher divorce rates than Presbyterians and Episcopalians. The usual explanation is that the first two denominations have lower levels of education than the last two. We will add that Presbyterians and Episcopalians also have higher average income levels. Therefore, here we see some interaction of various factors on the probability of divorce.

5. **Parental Divorce.** The overall pattern here is that children of divorced parents are more likely to experience divorce than those from intact families. The difference is small, however. Nevertheless, some analysts argue that children of divorced parents learn that divorce can be one solution to marital problems.

6. **Presence of Children.** Marital dissolution is most likely if the marriage is childless, or at least when the child is younger than three years. Increasingly, couples are more likely to refrain from divorce because of the presence of children.

Divorce is a process—it usually does not happen abruptly or overnight. Ahrons and Levinger have identified three stages:

1) a period of marital conflict and unhappiness,

2) the actual marital dissolution, and

3) a post-divorce period.

9 | Marriage and the Family: How We Come Together and Stay Together … Sometimes.
by Ivan M. Chompalov, Ph.D.

Anthropologist Paul Bohannan (1970) has found six types of divorces that couples experience. He has called those the six *stations of divorce*:

A. **Emotional Divorce.** That happens when the spouses withdraw emotionally from the relationship. This is accompanied by a loss of respect, trust, and affection. This typically precedes the actual divorce.

B. **Legal Divorce.** This is when the marriage officially has ended with filing for divorce and obtaining it. Women plan longer for the legal divorce than men. The length of deliberation is 22 months for women and 12 months for men, on average.

C. **Economic Divorce**. This stage involves property settlement and is often acrimonious and bitter. Things like who gets the house, the car, the bank accounts, furniture. It is more difficult to decide how to figure the earnings potential of each individual.

D. **Co-Parental Divorce.** This involves decisions of child custody, visitation rights and legal and financial obligations of each former partner.

E. **Community Divorce.** This is the loss of friends and relatives, the loss of social contacts. It tends to be quite a painful period.

F. **Psychic Divorce.** This involves distancing from and acceptance of the breakup and going back to being single.

Divorce is caused by a variety of factors. There are several groups of causes but most sociologists zoom in on societal factors. The main macro-social factor is the change in attitudes. Divorce today is much more acceptable than it was in the past. Also, the advent of industrialization and urbanization has weakened family ties (the economic function was taken over by society from the family; also socialization occurs more outside of the family; child care is now provided in institutional settings). Changing gender role attitudes also played a part. Women have started spending more time working outside the family. This is not only a United States phenomenon. A cross-cultural study found that 25 out of 27 nations experienced increased divorce rates between 1950 and 1985. Rising divorce rates are furthermore not only confined to the Most Industrialized Nations.

From the perspective of the divorced people, there are some common reasons that merit attention. Paul Rasmussen and Kathleen Ferraro (1991) interviewed 32 divorced persons asking them about the common reasons for divorce. There was not a single overwhelming reason. Among the reasons pointed out were poor communication, extramarital sex, constant fighting, emotional abuse, and alcohol and drug addiction.

There are some common consequences of divorce for spouses. Of course, divorce is generally the last resort when marriages do not work. It has both positive, but mainly negative effects on the ex-spouses. On the positive side, people can get out of abusive relationships, can feel self-respect again, and can focus on their life without conflict. On the negative side, it may be painful; people can suffer emotionally and financially, can feel guilt and uncertainty. Interestingly, according to some studies most consequences tend to be positive. Among the negative effects are <u>health problems</u>. Thus, research has shown increased stress and depression after divorce. Another consequence is <u>loneliness—only 11 percent of the former partners keep good relations with their exes</u>. <u>Social and sexual adjustment</u> can be difficult for some divorced people, especially if it happens in middle age or old age. That is because such divorcees have to again get "into circulation," start over in the "dating and mating game."

As you remember from the previous discussion on marriage, Jessie Bernard (1972) in *The Future of Marriage* talked about "his" marriage and "her" marriage. The same holds good for "his divorce" and "her divorce."

1) **"Her" Divorce.** For women the most obvious and startling difference in experiencing divorce is the loss of income. The living standards for women and their children, despite alimony, drop sharply. Women suffer a 30 percent drop in their income in the year after divorce, whereas men enjoy a 15 percent increase. Furthermore, courts award alimony in only 15 percent of all cases and it is received in much fewer cases. Women also typically get custody of the children, which increases the burden and responsibilities. Due to a large part of

217

the "no-fault divorce laws" which demand that women and men are treated equally, women end up being at a disadvantage, unless their husbands were extremely rich.

2) **"His" Divorce.**   Men are typically better off financially after the divorce than women.   However, there are some negative consequences.   The main negative consequence is that men feel they have been victimized by the divorce process, since women get custody of the children in 90 percent of the cases.   Opportunities for remarriage are greater for men. In addition, they need to pay child support, which is normally not that high a proportion from their income.

Recovering From Divorce.   Judy Wallerstein and Sandra Blakeslee (1989) found that for women the average period of time to recover emotionally and to reestablish a sense of external order is on average from three to three and a half years, whereas for men it is from two to two and a half years. Most men and women eventually remarry. Men do so more often than women do.

The Impact of Divorce on Children.   About 90 percent of black children and 70 percent of white children will spend some time in a single-parent family due to divorce or births to unwed mothers.

1) **Short-Term and Long-Term Effects.**   In the short term, children experience anger, stress, denial, sadness, and grief. They frequently feel guilty and think it is their fault. Therefore, they try to bring the ex-spouses together. There is also a decline in living standards and some anecdotal evidence of increased incidence of illness. It is difficult to say what the long-term effects really are. One consistent finding is that children from divorced families engage in more deviant behavior and experience sex earlier, but this might be related to poverty as well. Boys typically have more difficulty than girls do in adjusting to divorce.

2) **Child Custody.**   Until recently, the preferred type of custody was sole custody, with mothers getting custody 90 percent of the time. The father had to prove that the ex is an unfit mother. Sexual orientation has also been used in custody

battles to deprive homosexuals from custody by arguing they are not good role models. Another form is joint custody. Again, California was the first state to pass such a law in 1979, due to a movement in defense of father's rights. Typically, this means only joint legal custody, NOT joint physical custody. Legal custody means that both parents are involved in childcare and decisions about the wellbeing and education of children together. Joint custody rarely works, since it requires cooperation, which is in short supply for divorced parents. Another source of stress involving divorce settlement concerning children is visitation rights. They can be a problem not only for the noncustodial parent, but also for grandparents. What matters about visitation rights is not so much the frequency of visits but the extent to which the child feels valued in the relationship (Wallerstein and Blakeslee 1989).

No period in life is without the potential for marital crisis. Sociologists argue that parenthood is often experienced as a crisis, that people tend to experience low levels of marital satisfaction 10 to 15 years after marriage, and that being married often entails role conflict. These are all crises but the most severe crisis involves domestic violence and spousal abuse. We will first focus on <u>what produces crisis</u>. These are the so-called "stressor events." <u>Reuben Hill (1958)</u> defines stressor events or crisis-provoking events as situations for which families have little or no prior preparation. Why do families respond differently to stressor events? Why does unemployment, divorce, or death severely cripple some persons, while others take them in stride? Hill proposed as an explanation the so-called **ABCX model of stress**. This formula refers to A (the event)—interacting with B (the family's crisis meeting resources)—interacting with C (the definition the family makes of the event)—producing X (the crisis). Events come in a variety of forms and consequences are likely to differ. From sociology, we know that events outside a group (e.g., wars, floods, and economic depression) tend to solidify the group internally. <u>Thus, although stressful</u>, events that are <u>external</u> tend to unify the family into a more cohesive unit. In contrast, <u>events within the family</u> that are defined as stressful may be more disruptive, because they arise from troubles that reflect poorly on the family's <u>internal adequacy</u>—e.g., nonsupport, marital breakdown, <u>violence</u>, suicide, and alcoholism among others. These, of course, may be exacerbated, when combined. <u>What factors make for crisis proneness and freedom from crisis proneness</u>? The explanation lies in B and C in Hill's formula. B is whether the family has resources to meet the crisis. Resources are income, family adaptability, kin support system, friends, education, good health, etc. C is the value system of the family, the definition of the event. <u>Crisis proneness is therefore both the deficiency in family resources (factor B) and the tendency to define hardship as crisis (factor C)</u>. *One major stressor event is violence.*

Violence in Families or among Intimates refers to any act among legally related individuals or those in close primary relationships that is carried out with the intention of causing physical harm. It includes spanking, beating, rape, murder, and so on. A number of myths, stereotypes, and distortions about family violence exist. Richard Gelles and Murray Straus (1979) identified seven such myths:

1. <u>Family violence is rare</u>. Evidence shows that this is not the case. Between 85 percent and 95 percent of parents use some form of physical punishment at some point in the child's life. Acts of family violence occur every 9 to 12 seconds.

2. <u>The abusers are mentally ill</u>. It turns out that only 10 percent of abusive incidents in the family are caused by mental illness.

3. <u>The abuse is confined to poor, minority families</u>. Actually, it is true that most violence occurs in such families, but is by no means confined to them. It cuts across classes and races.

4. <u>Alcohol and drugs are the real causes of violence in the home</u>. There is a link between alcohol or drug consumption and violence. However, the myth suggests that violence ends when the alcohol/drug problem is eliminated, or that drinking and drugs are the *cause* of violence. Research does not support such claims.

5. <u>Children who are abused grow up to be abusers</u>. Not all abused children become abusers themselves. The evidence here is contradictory.

6. <u>Battered women like being hit</u>. Since women stay at home and do not leave, they must like being hit; or that women must have done something to provoke the

abuse and thus have a desire to be beaten. Interviews with women show that the vast majority of women actually dread being beaten or raped.

7. <u>The last myth reported by Gelles and Straus is that violence and love are incompatible</u>. Many battered spouses have strong feelings for their partners and most battered children love their parents.

Family violence comes in many shapes and forms. What are the most common types of family violence?

1) **Violence against Women**. <u>Battering</u> is the single, most common cause of injury to women. This includes a range of behaviors such as beating, kicking, choking, the use, or threat of use of knives and arms. The pattern of battering against women is a recurrent behavior often referred to as the battered-woman syndrome. It is defined in terms of frequency and severity of the beating or physical assault (another synonym of battering). Over one-third of domestic violence incidents against women require hospitalization or a doctor's intervention. Over two-thirds of violence against women is perpetrated by husbands, boyfriends, relatives, or acquaintances. Over 50 percent of homeless women and children are trying to escape an abusive relationship. There are a variety of reasons that contribute to the widespread physical abuse of women—poverty, alcoholism, stress, and dependency. It is difficult to leave such relationships because of threat of even greater harm—fear is the primary factor why women stay in abusive homes. Seventy-five percent of women murdered by abusive partners are killed when they try to leave or after they have left. Also, women often decide to stay in an abusive relationship because of fear of economic hardship.

Another form of violence against women is sexual assault, or behavior, either physical or verbal, to coerce women into sexual activity against their will. <u>Rape is the most extreme form of such assault</u> being committed every two minutes in the United States. Although rape is the most frequently committed violent crime in the United States, it is the least reported. Most rape victims are white. Victims of marital rape are often described as the "hidden victims," because they rarely report it. Until the mid-1970s, marital rape was not considered a crime in the United States. What compounds the problem is that women are victimized <u>twice: once by the assailant and a second time by the criminal justice system</u>. Many of the cases never reach trial. There is a lot of insensitivity. A rape prosecution is twice as likely to be dismissed as a murder prosecution. You may have seen the movie <u>The Accused</u> with Jody Foster. If you remember, she was as much on trial there as were the gang rapists (for being drunk, for smoking, for wearing a mini-skirt, for behaving provocatively, for the language she used, for leading the men on, although she was just trying to get back with her boyfriend, not to get raped). There is a growing trend to deal with violence against women in a new way. Now women who have been exposed to domestic violence are not only considered "victims," but also "survivors."

2) **Child Abuse**. In the 1960s, Dr. Henry Kempe and associates drew national attention to child abuse. He defined the **battered-child syndrome** as "a clinical condition in children who received severe physical abuse primarily from a parent or foster parent." Child abuse is often more difficult to deal with than woman abuse. We tend not to take what children say seriously. Often even both parents testify against the child. Child abuse is often fatal. Parental violence is among the five leading causes of child mortality (between 1 and 18). Some high-profile cases have focused attention on the pervasiveness of child abuse and especially on the murder of children. <u>Especially, the rape and murder of the 6-year old beauty pageant queen Jon Benet Ramsey; the drowning of her young children by Susan Smith in North Carolina; the recent case of a Houston, TX woman (Andrea Yates) who killed her five children</u>. It is estimated that as high as one-third of all cases of child abuse go unreported, especially when they involve middle class and wealthy families. Children are also victims of sexual abuse, or the use of a child for the sexual gratification of an adult. One form of sexual abuse is incest—the sexual abuse by a blood relative. Sexual abuse of children is not so rare—incest, for example, occurs in 14 percent of United States families and can be found in all races and social classes.

3) **Sibling Abuse.**   Interestingly, children are most often abused by <u>their siblings</u>.   More than 29 million siblings abuse each other.   This is perhaps the most common form of family violence.   The most common type of sibling abuse is emotional abuse, followed by sexual abuse, and physical abuse.   The highest rate of sibling abuse occurs in all-male children families.

4) **Elder Abuse**, or the physical, psychological, and material maltreatment and neglect of old people is not an isolated phenomenon. One out of every 25 elderly people are victimized annually, but only one in six incidents are ever reported. Part of it is the difficulty to prove neglect and abuse that occurs in nursing homes. In addition, the most often type is spousal abuse, followed by abuse by children, especially adult daughters. The victims are mainly women 75 years and over.

What are the *current trends in marriages and families* in America? We have talked about a number of distinct trends and, although it is difficult to trace all of the interesting patterns, here is a summary:

1)   There is a wider variety of family forms and marriage arrangements nowadays in the United States than at any time in our history. This variety is determined by the composition and the relationship of members to one another;

2)   Modern views of the family emphasize its role in fulfilling personal needs for emotional security and companionship;

3)   Although historically the American family was patriarchal, there has been a gradual shift to a more democratic power structure;

4)   The marriage rate has declined since 1980;

5)   The median age at first marriage is increasing for both men and women, resulting in an increase in unmarried young adults in the population;

223

6) The proportion of people who cohabit has been going up steadily for the past several decades;

7) Declining birthrates since 1965 have resulted in smaller families;

8) The percentage of married women in the work force has been increasing steadily;

9) The number of one-parent families, especially mother-child families, has risen considerably in recent years;

10) Divorce rates increased steadily from 1958 until 1979, at which time they leveled off. At present, about 50 percent of new marriages are expected to end in divorce. The United States has the highest divorce rate among industrialized countries;

11) Most divorced men (about four-fifths, or 80 percent) and divorced women (about three-quarters, or 75 percent) will eventually remarry. This and the high divorce rate have led to the increase of reconstituted or blended families in recent years;

12) The number of babies born to single mothers in the United States has been growing;

13) The number of gay and lesbian families has been going up; and

14) There is a pronounced trend of "feminization of poverty."

৪০ ৫৪ ৪০ ৫৪

DEFINITIONS

ABCX Model of Stress. This formula refers to A (the event)—interacting with B (the family's crisis meeting resources)—interacting with C (the definition the family makes of the event)—producing X (the crisis).

Alimony. Payment of a monetary allowance to a spouse.

Battered-Child Syndrome. A clinical condition in children who received severe physical abuse primarily from a parent or foster parent.

Cenogamy. A special term for group marriage.

Divorce. The legal dissolution of a marriage.

Endogamy. Marrying someone from your own ethnic or racial group.

Exogamy.   Marrying someone from outside of your own ethnic or racial group.

Extended Family. Builds upon the nuclear family and is comprised of parents, siblings, and other relatives (typically grandparents).

Family of Orientation. The family where one was born and grew up.

Family of Procreation. When we marry and have our own children.

Family. Two or more persons living together and related by blood, marriage, or adoption.

Homogamy. Refers to marriage between individuals who are, in some culturally important way, similar to each other. Homogamy may be based on socio-economic status, class, ethnicity, or religion.

Incest Taboo. A strong social norm that prohibits sexual relations with and the marrying of a blood relative.

Institutional Racism. Those accepted, established, evident, visible, and respected forces, social arrangements, institutions, structures, policies, precedents and systems of social relations that operate and are manipulated in such a way as to allow, support, or acquiesce to acts of individual racism and to deprive certain racially identified categories within a society a chance to share, have equal access to, or have equal opportunity to acquire those things, material and nonmaterial, that are defined as desirable and necessary for rising in an hierarchical class society while that society is dependent, in part, upon that group they deprive for their labor and loyalty.

9 | Marriage and the Family: How We Come Together and Stay Together ... Sometimes.
by Ivan M. Chompalov, Ph.D.

Institutions. Complex social structures that meet basic human needs. "Sets of roles graded in authority that have been embodied in consistent patterns of actions that have been legitimated and sanctioned by society or segments of that society; whose purpose is to carry out certain activities or prescribed needs of that society or segments of that society." - C. Wright Mills, *The Sociological Imagination* (New York: Oxford University Press, 1959), p. 30.

Marriage Gradient. Refers to the fact that because women tend to marry upward and men downward, men at the top have a much larger pool of eligible women, whereas women at the top have a much more limited pool of eligible men.

Marriage Squeeze. A term used to describe an unfavorable imbalance in the sex ratio of marriage-aged men to marriage-aged women.

Marriage. A legal contract between a woman and a man who are above a legal age and are not already legally married to someone else. Schwartz and Scott define marriage as a union between people (legally recognized or not) that unites partners sexually, economically, and socially.

Matriarchal Families. Family situation in which the female is the head of the family.

Monogamy. When one person of one sex is, at any given point in time, married to only one person of the opposite sex.

Myths. False, imaginary beliefs about something.

Nuclear Family. Includes the mother, the father, and their children.

Patriarchal Families. Family situation in which the male is the head of the family.

Polygamy. When one person of one sex is simultaneously married to several people of the opposite sex.

Reconstituted, or blended, or stepfamilies. The families we create after remarriage.

Role. A role is the expected behavior associated with a particular status position—What the individual or group occupying a particular status position is supposed to do.

Serial Monogamy. Describes a repeated pattern of monogamous marriage, divorce or widowhood, remarriage, another divorce or widowhood, another remarriage, and so on.

Social Structure. Societies are "divided" generally into two components—social structure and social processes—that interpenetrate each other; i.e., are dialectically interrelated. The key to understanding social structure in a society is understanding its social institutions and their intertwining combinations. Social structure is the institutional framework that makes for order in daily, weekly, and yearly interaction between people. It is social institutions that promote the necessary order to make social structure possible.

Status. Status is a socially defined position in a social structure. It is a position that an individual occupies in a group, such as leader or follower; doctor or nurse; mother or son; student or professor, etc. A status can also be a specific position of one group in relation to another group, such as executives and secretaries in a large office.

REFERENCES

Baca Zinn, Maxine and Stanley Eitzen. 1998. *Diversity in Families*. 5th ed. New York: Longman Publishing Group.

Baca Zinn, Maxine and Stanley Eitzen. 2004. *Diversity in Families*. 7th ed. Boston, MA: Allyn and Bacon.

Bernard, Jessie. 1972. *The Future of Marriage*. New York: World.

Billingsley, Andrew. 1968. *Black Families in White America*. Englewood Cliffs, NJ: Prentice Hall.

Bohannan, Paul. 1970. *Divorce and After*. New York: Doubleday.

Bohannan, Paul. 1985. *All the Happy Families*. New York: McGraw-Hill.

Cherlin, Andrew. 1981. *Marriage, Divorce, Remarriage*. Cambridge, MA: Harvard University Press.

Coontz, Stephanie. 1992. *The Way We Never Were: American Families and the Nostalgia Trap*. New York: Basic Books.

Cuber, John and Peggy Harroff. 1966. *The Significant Americans*. New York: Random House.

Gelles, Richard and Murray Straus. 1988. *Intimate Violence: The Definitive Study of Cases and Consequences of Abuse in the American Family*. New York: Simon and Schuster.

Glenn, Norvell. 1997. *Closed Hearts, Closed Minds. A Report from the Council on Families*. New York: Institute for American Values.

Hill, Reuben. 1958. "Generic Features of Families under Stress." *Social Casework* 39 (February/March):139-150.

Hill, Reuben. 1972. *The Strength of Black Families*. New York: Emerson Hall.

Lasch, Christopher. 1977. *Heaven in a Heartless World: The Family Besieged*. New York: Basic Books.

Lauer, Robert and Jeanette Lauer. *The Quest for Intimacy*. Dubuque, IA: Brown.

Murray, Charles. 1984. *Losing Ground: American Social Policy, 1950-1980*. New York: Basic Books.

Popenoe, David. 1996. *Life without Father: Compelling New Evidence that Fatherhood and Marriage Are Indispensable for The Good of Children and Society*. New York: The Free Press.

Rasmussen, Paul and Kathleen Ferraro. 1991. "The Divorce Process." Pp. 376-388 in *Marriage and Family in Transition* edited by J. N. Edwards and D. H. Demo. Boston, MA: Allyn and Bacon.

Schwartz, Mary and Barbara Scott. 2003. *Marriages and Families: Diversity and Change*. 4th ed. Upper Saddle River, NJ: Prentice Hall.

9 | Marriage and the Family: How We Come Together and Stay Together ... Sometimes.
by Ivan M. Chompalov, Ph.D.

Tischler, Henry (ed.). 2001. *Debating Points: Marriage and Family Issues*. Upper Saddle River, NJ: Prentice Hall.

Wallerstein, Judy and Sandra Blakeslee. 1989. *Second Chances: Men, Women, and Children A Decade After Divorce*. New York: Ticknor and Fields.

10 | Religion as a Social Institution: Dealing With the Sacred.
by Lawrence J. Mencotti, Ph.D.

The Functions of Religion: Marx and Freud.   One of the richest traditions in the sociological study of religion has been to examine the functions that religions play for individuals as well as entire societies. For example, the conflict theorist Marx asserted that religion offered the downtrodden a psychic opiate that promised eternal happiness in the next world while deflecting attention away from their oppressors [and thus distracting them from their oppression] in this world. Thus, the major function of organized religion for Marx was one of diversion but its real effect ultimately was as an impediment to the full realization of the humanity of people.

Freud, though politically at the opposite end of the spectrum from Marx, made a similar point.   If Marx emphasized the institutional, Freud stressed the individual but does so in a surprisingly sociological fashion. Starting from depth psychology Freud locates individual wants, needs, frustrations, and fears in a distinctly sociological context. An extensive quote from Freud's The Future of an Illusion will help illustrate this point. It should not surprise us

> "[t]hat the suppressed should develop an intense hostility towards a culture whose existence they make possible by their work, but in whose wealth they have too small a share. In such conditions no internalization of the cultural prohibitions among the suppressed people is not to be expected. On the contrary, they are not prepared to acknowledge the prohibitions; they are intent on destroying the culture itself, and possibly even on doing away with the postulates on which it is based... It goes without saying that a civilization which leaves so large a number of its participants unsatisfied and drives them into revolt neither has nor deserves the prospect of a lasting existence... This identification of the suppressed classes with the class who rules and exploits them is, however, only part of a larger whole. For the suppressed classes can be emotionally attached to their masters; in spite of their hostility to them, they may see in them their ideals; unless such relations of a fundamentally satisfying kind subsisted, it would be impossible to understand how a number of civilizations have survived so long in spite of the justifiable hostility of large human masses."

So then what does Freud say about how people resolve their ambivalence toward oppressors? Well, first of all this ambivalence is not quite the whole story since in his classic *Civilization and Its Discontents* he stresses how in an even more fundamental way we must somehow control our instinctual needs and desires in order to have civilization at all. In other words, neurosis is the price humans pay for civilization. A neurosis-free society is not possible. With that as backdrop we can see how, from a Freudian perspective, it can be argued that religion is a way of not just dealing with the frustrations and terrors of the world [belief in God as the belief in an all powerful father; indeed, God AS the ultimate father-figure] but religion functions as a salve from oppression. In the last analysis though Freud is no more sympathetic to religion than is Marx because after centuries of religion humans are still not contented satisfied beings despite their tenacious beliefs in God, redemption, and an afterlife.

Therefore, it is readily apparent that Marx and Freud were very critical of religion. Marx indicted organized religion as buttressing oppressive economic and political structures and Freud chimed in with the idea that religious beliefs per se do not necessarily make people happy.

However, neither of them specifically addressed more contemporary concerns such as the sexual abuse of children by some clergy but probably neither would be surprised. Dismayed yes; surprised no. In their ideal worlds, religion would be no longer needed. However, independent of the truth or falsity of Marxism and Freudianism regarding the place and function of religion in society it is interesting to remember that two very powerful theorists starting from very different positions on the political spectrum and traveling much different analytic paths arrive at a surprisingly similar destination.

Social Structure and Social Belief: The Durkheimian Tradition. Though each addressed sociological concerns, neither Marx nor Freud were sociologists. Sociologists approach the study of religion in a respectful and [hopefully] objective way. Sociologists do not pass judgment on the **supernatural** claims of any religion but rather try to understand the claims with a naturalistic approach that treats religion as a social phenomenon. For example, throughout history there have been thousands of religions and a cynic would point out that given the tremendous disparities in ritual and belief that they all cannot be correct in their claims. True believers would agree but probably assert that theirs is the "correct one." Sociologists would sidestep the truth and falsity debate about religions and instead try to figure out why there has been [and continues to be] such variety in religious belief and practices.

Building on the work of one of the great founders of sociology, Emile Durkheim, many sociologists have concluded that rather than being divine revelations, god-concepts are essentially group projections. Rather than God revealing himself to the group the process is actually reversed: the group projects its deepest desires, hopes, fears and the like out from itself and ascribes these to its conception of God in particular and all things supernatural in general. Thus, *when the group worships God it is really the disguised worship of itself*—in idealized form. To a Durkheimian, it is not so much that God made man in His own image but rather the group/society makes their god-concept in their own image. One potential benefit of extending Durkheim's position is that it gives an insight into variety of religious beliefs and practices. Different groups will project their profane social structures unto the sacred realm.

This perspective sees any given religion like a movie with producers, directors, and scriptwriters [the clergy], screen stars [the personages to be worshipped/revered], and the audience [reverential worshippers]. Every so often, the movies are remade [religious reforms]. Sometimes the audience does not like the movie or tires of it and goes shopping for a new religion in a new theater [e.g., religious conversion] or stops going altogether [agnosticism/atheism]. Much of the time the religious audience's attention is less than rapt and of course, there are those among any audience who really get into the movie [true believers]. Those that so believe in the movie that they decide to take their beliefs outside of the theater [church/temple/mosque] and act on them in the presence of others we might term missionaries and, occasionally, fanatics.

An interesting extension of Durkheim's thought: that there is a relationship between structure and belief comes from the work of Guy Swanson. In *The Birth of the Gods*, Swanson examines a sample of various and sundry societies representing many different types and levels of social organization. Two of his findings are particularly intriguing. In one, he finds a strong relationship between societal complexity and belief in god[s]. More specifically, there is a strong positive correlation between societal complexity and monotheism. Put in layman's terms, societies that are more complex are much more likely to believe in one high all-powerful god [such as the God of Christianity, Judaism, and Islam] than are so called simpler, more primitive groups that tend to be **polytheistic**. It is not too much of a stretch to argue that a very important function of

monotheism for complex societies is that as the degree of complexity increases so does the possibility of the complexity overwhelming the commonality of all of the people of the society. Monotheism helps since all can relate to a single all-powerful supreme being rather than having the society splinter by having each group going its own way and worshipping its own deities. Thus, monotheism can function as social glue when the diversity of a society threatens to splinter it.

Now if we assume that more complex societies such as those found in [but not just in] western civilization evolved over quite a long period from what were originally much less complex societies then from a social evolutionary perspective it is not unreasonable to guess that the original state of religious nature was polytheistic.

Among many others, one more example of Swanson's research is particularly noteworthy. Swanson also looked at the social structural correlates of belief in a supernatural morality and found a strong relationship between the existence of social classes and the belief in a life after death including rewards for the righteous and punishments for evildoers. Upon a moment's reflection, it should not be difficult to figure this out. A supernatural morality—i.e. one that emphasizes rewards in the next life for adherents to God's law and punishments to those who disobey God's law is very functional for the maintenance of a stratification system. Those who do not do particularly well in this life at least have the hope of eternal bliss if they only keep their faith, follow the rules, and do not rock any boats. Of course, if the established religions either pledge allegiance to the prevailing political and economic order the clergy of established religions are, for the most part, not going to rock any boats themselves. In addition, political and economic [and other establishment] elites will not come under undue pressure if they, while benefiting immensely from the present arrangement, also demonstrate [sincerely or not] that they too are committed to the prevailing religious norms. A Durkheimian perspective on this function of religion is not so different from that of a Marxist though once again Durkheim and Marx had very different political views and agendas.

Therefore, adherence to established religions by large numbers of the populace is, all things being equal, very functional for the maintenance of the social system. It is no wonder that religion is so often seen as a conservative religious institution. Note that sociologists are not saying that religious beliefs are true [or not true] and they are not saying the people as individuals are better off [or not] for being serious adherents to a particular religion.

In an extraordinarily complex society such as that of contemporary America, one wonders if any one religion or even any single religious tradition could function as a "social glue" to help hold American society together. With such incredible diversity, how does America cohere? How do we stick together and identify ourselves as something more than an aggregate of shoppers who speak the same language [sort of].

Civil Religion.   The sociologist Robert Bellah came up with an intriguing interpretation of religious evolution in contemporary society. He has argued that past a point of secularization religion per se does not die so much as it takes on new forms one of which he calls a "civil religion." Our civil religion has sacred symbols: Old Glory; **"sacred"** hymns: The Star-Spangled Banner; sacred prayers: the Pledge of Allegiance; a sacred totem: the American eagle; sacred places: e.g. Gettysburg, the Lincoln Memorial; and sacred times: Fourth of July, Thanksgiving, Memorial Day, etc. Interestingly, America's civil religion not only functions as to give a common identity to nearly 300 million people in a highly pluralistic society but it does so with rather minimal demands while making appeals to the relevance and salience of American democracy for our lives. Strictly speaking, America's civil religion is not specifically Christian as much as it is western: belief in an activist monotheistic god who when push comes to shove is "on our side"—especially in foreign and military affairs. Granted that some of the more passionate adherents and interpreters of this religion of Americanism shout that to deny God is tantamount to treason or to believe in God is to believe in a God who has a special place in his heart for America [the promised land] and in exchange for obedience will deliver America and Americans from evil and destruction.

Thus, with civil religion, though the separation of church and state is blurred it is done so without institutionalizing any particular religion while allowing all Americans [whether they be Catholic, Protestant, Jewish, Muslim, Hindu, Buddhist, **agnostic** or **atheist**] to be nominally equal in the sight of one another.

Social Position and Belief.   The sociologist-priest Andrew Greeley once remarked that "...instead of Americans belonging to churches because they believe in religion, there may be a strong tendency for them to believe in religion because they belong to churches." With so many Americans living such mobile lives where in many cases family and many close friends are hundreds of miles away, religious groups often function to provide support during times of crisis. In a very

233

important sense, many Americans join churches and their beliefs follow. One can, and often does, "shop" for the right group: a religious community with whom one can feel comfortable. From this perspective, belief follows from membership; it does not necessarily precede it. This can explain why many people do go "shopping" for a church where the members are in the shoppers' comfort zone and the religious experience offered is sufficiently palatable to merit their allegiance: if only temporarily.   This observation by Greeley has been supported by much empirical research and illustrates a larger theme of the sociology of religion: what you believe is in no small part a function of where you are located: both geographically and socially.

The Social Structure of Morality.   As disconcerting as that is for some an even more provocative interpretation of the social structural argument of morality comes from the philosopher Nietzsche. In Nietzsche's view, there are two moralities/moral codes/value systems worthy of investigation: "master morality" and "slave morality." Master morality cuts up the moral world into good and bad. What powerful masters adhere to is good because it is noble and what the weak do/believe in is bad because...well, it is the weak that do these things and therefore they are not worthy. Alternatively, slave morality is based on good and evil and what the "slaves" see as evil is what the masters value most and what the masters despise is what the slaves exalt. Thus, to a master, humility, mercy, submission and the like are traits to be held in contempt whereas from a slave's viewpoint they are the means whereby some semblance of survival is possible. The slaves look at the master and because of their structural weakness define the master's virtue as evil and their own values as good. Note that the slave morality is a negation of the master morality grounded initially in weakness. Should a slave morality ever become an official moral code [as Nietzsche argued happened with Christianity as the Roman Empire crumbled and the Christians moved into the power vacuum] then we could speculate that there would be a great tension within those who would profess allegiance to a slave morality while occupying positions of authority.

It is tempting to apply Nietzsche's insights in different directions. For example, one could argue that in reaction to a dominant male ideology there would arise a female moral code that would stress just those values that males would despise and from a woman's point of view exalt the feminine ideals as being of greater virtue/worth than that of those beastly males.

In any case, it is important to remember that Nietzsche's schematic shows that at a given time and place there is more than one **moral code** operating; that moral codes are in large part defined and enacted in reaction to one another; and that what you believe is in no small part a function of where you are located in a power structure.

Social Structure and Moral Progress.   So, one of the more obvious [and obviously important] ways in which groups hold together is their adherence to a moral code. The question is still begged: Can moral progress occur with religion as the vehicle? Certainly, true believing adherents to a variety of faiths would answer in the affirmative always given that they believe, deep down, that their particular faith is the one true one. For help addressing this issue let us turn once again to Durkheim and his famous thought experiment. Durkheim asks us to imagine a society of saints.   Would you conjecture that because the group was composed of saints that transgressions and thus guilt would disappear? While that would be a reasonable guess, Durkheim answers differently: transgressions would not disappear since deviance is essential for the health and longevity of any group. After all, deviance marks the boundaries of group behavior: where one can go but no further. In addition, what holds the group together is their joint pursuit of moral perfection and so what would most likely happen is the group, to keep its members in line, would require them to feel guilty about transgressions about which you and I would give hardly a thought. Put another way, the group in order to morally "progress" would feel more and more guilt over smaller and smaller moral infractions. After all, that is what moral progress is, feeling guilty about conditions that a generation or two ago would not have raised an eyebrow let alone a second thought. Therefore, the pursuit of moral perfection does not lessen let alone eliminate group-imposed guilt; it merely changes the matters about which we are to feel guilty. As such, guilt is built in to the human condition—a conclusion with which Freud would definitely not disagree. Note that, as with the comparison with Marx and Freud, here Freud and Durkheim reach an agreement but from very different paths. With both theorists—the pessimistic Freud and the cautiously optimistic Durkheim—the fundamental tension between group demands and members' wishes is illustrated. Where Freud begins with the individual in society and concludes that neurosis and guilt are prices to be paid for a civilized life, Durkheim begins with the group and argues that for the group to survive [let alone flourish] sacrifices by the group members are vital.

Protestantism, Capitalism, and Beyond.   One of the most famous instances of classical sociological research has been Max Weber's work on the connection between religion and capitalism. Though written a century ago we shall see that it still inspires fresh original work. Weber saw that protestant Europe was more capitalist than was catholic Europe thus rendering the protestant

235

districts more economically advanced. While rudimentary capitalism had been found in several of the late medieval Italian city-states, it was left to protestant Europe to become the area where fully developed capitalism came into its own.

As Weber argued it, capitalism is not the greedy accumulation of money: that has been found in many societies over a long range of time. No, capitalism under Weber's scrutiny was a moral imperative. With fully developed capitalism one no longer worked to live; rather, *one lived to work.* The point was not just to work, not just to make money. Rather, it was one's duty to work hard, work smart [meaning working in a rational manner] and dedicate one's labor to the glorification of God. In so doing, religiosity was tamed [sublimated if you will] and directed toward hard work and its fruits: the accumulation and reinvestment of wealth. Weber believed that the ideology driving capitalism was not just Protestantism but also a particularly demanding variant: Calvinism, that preached that our eternal fate is predetermined by an omniscient, omnipotent, and emotionally distant God. If that was believed then what followed was terrifying. God knew what your destiny would be but you did not. Would YOU be one of the few to be saved [the elect] or part of the many that would be doomed to perdition?

Weber felt that capitalism was, in effect, a forum whereby protestant asceticism was expressed in a productive manner and coincidentally as an engine whereby society progressed rationally. The rational use of one's time, one's money, one's labor becomes paramount and the success that you would reap in this life by your dedication to your work becomes an outward sign not just of inward grace but a marker that you are part of the elect—the chosen few whom God has signified to be saved for all eternity. After all, would God waste his grace on the unworthy? Thus, success in this world marked one's worthiness for entrée into the divine next world.

Certainly, Weber's work has been controversial and has not gone unchallenged. Though it is beyond the scope of this essay to do justice to this continuing issue it is noteworthy to realize the obvious: that modern capitalism did not stay married to Calvinism forever. Suffice it to say that contemporary capitalism decoupled from its religious underpinnings by the modern emphasis [some might say, obsession] with rationality and this rationality is symbolized on the one hand by that most modern—and soulless of organizations—the bureaucracy and on the other by that most modern—and equally indisposed to soulful matters—the institution of science. Both bureaucracy and science exemplify the principle of how means supplant goals. Put another way, the means [rationality] become ends in themselves and the practice of rationality for its own sake becomes what is important—regardless of its ultimate use. Certainly, science can be a way of life in which the pursuit of science for its own sake is pleasurable and career enhancing. Whether anything lasting and important comes of it is problematic. The other major way that capitalism and religion separated is in the pursuit of wealth [greed] for its own sake and the mindless consumption of "stuff" [material gluttony] for its own sake.

Well, maybe NOT totally for their own sakes since from another angle one might argue that wealth and consumption as modern obsessions are two very obvious secular alternatives to a spiritual void. Both accumulating money and things mark one as a "success" devoid of a religious component. In this instance, the outward markers are used to communicate to others that one is a "worthwhile" person while they communicate to the accumulators that one's life has been "worthwhile." Thus, one of the great virtues of Weber's work is how he teases out social changes as internally generated phenomena and the latent functions that derive from these changes.

Christianity and Reason. Very recently, the preeminent sociologist of religion, Rodney Stark, has taken the Weberian thesis in a new direction in his book *The Victory of Reason.* Stark argues that certain important characteristic traits of Christianity were particularly favorable to the rise of capitalism. These traits include believing that reason is a gift of God that allows people to understand and possibly improve themselves and the world. Another trait was that Christianity [both in apocalyptic and non-apocalyptic versions] orients itself to the future. Still another trait, according to Stark, is that Christianity encourages tolerance and egalitarianism [e.g., all are equal in the sight of God].

While Weber emphasized a particular variant [Calvinism] of a more general variant [Protestantism] of Christianity, Stark points to the beginnings of capitalism in the Middle Ages and he does so by tracing the Christian emphasis on the necessity of reason and its most characteristic religious use in theology which is the rational pursuit of the nature of God and in things divine. Baldly put, if God is rational and we are made in his image then reason is a hallmark of the human being in living his/her life. Put still another way and a point on which both Christian creationists and secular evolutionists might agree, if God gave us a brain—then use it!

Getting back to Stark's main theme, the origins of capitalism are traceable to the so-called Dark Ages with Catholic monks attempting to improve the economic security of their estates via specialization of activities. Thus, rationality became applied to this-worldly activities as well as to other-worldly concerns. Capitalism then found its next phase in the northern Italian city-states and only later does it flourish in protestant northern Europe. Why then does England become the great expression of pure capitalism? Because it is in England, where there is the least degree of structural impediment to the development of capitalism: tyranny and it is tyranny and not Catholicism per se that blocks capitalist development.

Stark goes further in his book and argues that reason, a bedrock trait of Christianity, led ultimately to the political and intellectual as well as economic freedoms that have allowed so much of what we call progress to develop in western civilization. Stark's argument is at once a qualification as well as an extension of Weberian thinking and is an important contribution to macro-level sociology.

Love it or hate it religion has been one of the most important institutions invented by humankind. It continues to give solace to many while its effects have been less than salutary for others. That religion has been downright harmful for many is not disputed but something that has existed so widely for so long must have, in a Darwinian sense, much adaptive value. When all is said and done sociologists will say that organized religion does tend to create, maintain, and reinforce social order and as such benefit individuals—as members of society.

৪০ ৫৪ ৪০ ৫৪

DEFINITIONS

Agnostic. A person who argues that there is no known proof of the existence of god but does not deny the possibility that god might exist.
Atheist. A person who denies the existence of god.
Monotheism. Believing that there is only one god.

Moral Code. Prescriptions of how to behave based on an understanding of what is right and what is wrong.

Moral Progress. A group that keeps its members in line by requiring them to feel guilty about transgressions that a generation or two ago would not have raised an eyebrow let alone a second thought. Put another way, the group in order to morally "progress" would feel more and more guilt over smaller and smaller moral infractions.

Morality. A system of ideas of right and wrong.

Polytheism. Believing that there are many gods or goddesses.

Profane. Everything that pertains to everyday life on earth.

Religion. A social institution that separates the sacred from the profane and unites believers into a moral community (the church).

Sacred. Things that pertain to the supernatural, to life beyond this world.

Social Structure. Societies are "divided" generally into two components—social structure and social processes—that interpenetrate each other; i.e., are dialectically interrelated. The key to understanding social structure in a society is understanding its social institutions and their intertwining combinations. Social structure is the institutional framework that makes for order in daily, weekly, and yearly interaction between people. It is social institutions that promote the necessary order to make social structure possible.

Supernatural. Something that is divine, that is out of this world.

REFERENCES

Bellah, Robert and Philip E. Hammond. 1980. *Varieties of Civil Religion*. San Francisco, CA: Harper and Row.

Durkheim, Emile. 1954. *The Elementary Forms of Religious Life*. New York: The Free Press.

Durkheim, Emile. 1982. *The Rules of Sociological Method*. New York: The Free Press.

Freud, Sigmund. 1939. *Civilization and Its Discontents*. New York: Hogarth Press.

Freud, Sigmund. 1989. *The Future of an Illusion*. New York: W. W. Norton.

Greeley, Andrew. 1989. *Religious Change in America*. Cambridge, MA: Harvard University Press.

Marx, Karl. 1983. *The Portable Karl Marx*. New York: Penguin Books.

Nietzsche, Friedrich. 2000. "On The Genealogy of Morals." in *Basic Writings of Nietzsche*. Modern Library Edition.

Stark, Rodney. 2005. *The Victory of Reason: How Christianity Led to Freedom, Capitalism, and Western Success*. New York: Random House.

Swanson, Guy. 1960. *The Birth of the Gods*. Ann Arbor, MI: University of Michigan Press.

Weber, Max. 1905. *The Protestant Ethic and the Spirit of Capitalism*. New York: Charles Scribner's and Sons.

11 | Education as a Social Institution: Preparing to Get Your Share.
by Frank O. Taylor, IV, Ph.D.

In this essay we consider the role education plays in the reproduction of social class in United States society. First, let us note that the process of education is very broad and includes learning that takes place in a variety of settings. For example, the transmission of values and beliefs, which occurs in the family, from generation to generation is a form of education. What children learn about a deity and other related religious beliefs, is usually learned in church or through interaction with pastors, priests, and Sunday school teachers. Many children, for example, grow up to have religious and political beliefs similar to their parents. The concept of **education** broadly refers to the transmission of skills, values, beliefs, knowledge, and facts to members of society in a variety of settings. This is different from **schooling**, a more formal process. Schooling takes place in the United States under the supervision of teachers with a college education and takes place within large bureaucratic social settings. Schooling is considered essential for an industrial society with thousands of occupations and jobs requiring specialized knowledge and skills.

In the United States society, citizens generally subscribe to the ideology of equal opportunity, which assumes that educational opportunities should be available to all citizens. This value underlies public education in our nation. In addition, as a nation we generally believe that an informed citizenry is a necessity for informed voting, the cornerstone of any democracy. Many people, if not most, assume that educational attainment is somehow equal to a person's talent or ability. In other words, a person with a Ph.D. is often seen as having more intelligence or academic ability than a person who has only a high school degree. It is possible that the person with the Ph.D. was born into a family higher up in the stratification system and that family had the resources to send the individual to college, whereas the family of the other student did not. In any case, the ideology of meritocracy is highly valued in United States society.

Many people also subscribe to the ideology of meritocracy, which holds that some people in our society are more deserving of a greater share of social rewards than others. For example, many people would agree that college professors are more important to society than are garbage collectors and therefore, college professors should earn more income than garbage collectors. The same may be said of doctors and shoe shiners. Actually, garbage collectors are extremely important to society. In a true meritocracy, social rewards would entirely be a matter of individual effort. However, with just a little thought we can dismiss the idea that a meritocracy actually exists. Some people work hard all of their lives and never get ahead. If you have ever actually hauled garbage around you know what I mean. Other people inherit fabulous wealth and essentially live lives of leisure, producing nothing of social value whatsoever.

When considering social mobility and education two important factors come into play. One factor is related to individual characteristics. As a society, we seem to be fixated with the individual and tend to think less, if at all, about the influence of social structure, the second important factor. In addition to individual effort, social factors greatly influence educational attainment and social mobility. Motivation, desire, will power, striving to achieve, and so on, characteristics associated with the individual, absolutely are very important. After all, if you are not willing to help yourself very few others will. On the other hand, important variables such as the family you are born into and its social class position are also very important. If you are a somewhat lazy individual with low motivation, but happen to be born into a very affluent and politically powerful family, you may receive certain benefits and advantages other individuals do not. In general, two things are necessary for educational attainment. First, educational opportunities must be socially available. Second, you must be motivated to take advantage of existing educational opportunities. You cannot create educational opportunities out of thin air, only society and collective action can create an educational system. Let us now consider what positive and negative consequences a formal system of education creates for society. In other words, what are the functions of education for society?

Functions of Schooling. From the structural functional perspective, formal schooling contributes to the stability of society and provides many positive benefits for society. There are at least three major manifest functions of schooling, including socialization, social integration, and social placement. A **manifest function** refers to intended operation of a social institution. For example, one manifest function of schooling is the formal transmission of knowledge. That is what school is designed to accomplish. Most people consider the transmission of knowledge from one generation to another a positive accomplishment. **Latent functions** refer to unintended but generally positive outcomes. Lastly, when the social system is producing negative outcomes sociologists speak of **dysfunction**.

241

by Frank O. Taylor, IV, Ph.D.

Perhaps the most important function of schooling is that of **socialization**. Socialization refers to the lifelong process of learning your culture. Education is considered to be one of the major institutions associated with secondary socialization, that which occurs outside of the home. Think back on all the things you learned in school associated with learning about the values, beliefs, language, history, symbols, and ideologies of our culture. Saying the pledge of allegiance, for example, is related to the value of patriotism. Receiving grades for the work you turned in is related to the value of competition. You learned the history of your culture. You practiced reading and writing English. In addition to reading, writing, and arithmetic, you were exposed to a great number of norms, such as not jumping in line, being polite, raising your hand before asking a question, and so on. Homework, in addition to helping you master subject material, is indirectly related to the ethic of hard work. Many nontraditional students report how difficult it is to be re-socialized into the academic environment.

Additionally, one major function of education has always been the socialization of large numbers of immigrants who migrate here. This is the **assimilation** function of education. If there is only one institution in which immigrants, and the children of immigrants, are exposed to Anglo values, beliefs, ideologies, symbols, norms, and language, it is that of formal schooling. Second and third generation immigrants, including many of you reading this essay, often, have become so assimilated they can no longer speak their native languages and feel they have more in common with the dominant group than with their grandparents. I witnessed a Japanese family at the shopping mall one day with two small children who spoke perfect English, while the parents spoke to each other in Japanese.

Social Integration is another major function of schooling. Social integration refers to a sense of social unity, or sense of belonging. Not only do schools teach the norms, values, and beliefs of the broader society, but they also strive to create a sense of togetherness. The move toward multicultural education has been in part due to perceived overemphasis on Western history. The goal is to celebrate the diverse backgrounds from which students come. On another level, schools have been charged with the task of transmitting the knowledge and skills necessary for every child to have a place in our society. The other side of a "place for everyone," of course, is "everyone in their place," which refers to social placement.

Social placement is a third major function of schooling. Schools go to great lengths to evaluate and assess student performance. On the face of it, student performance seems to be entirely a matter of individual achievement. However, social class background plays an important role in the process of social placement. Schools employ a process called **tracking**, in which students who achieve the highest marks are placed in the college prep track, students who achieve average marks are placed in the general studies track, and students who achieve modest marks are placed in the vocational education track. Our society employs a complex technology, which requires a formal system of education due to the wide range of specializations in our occupational structure. In general, schools attempt to assess the student's aptitude and train them for an appropriate position in the occupational structure. At least that is the goal.

In addition to the manifest functions of schooling, there are a number of latent functions that seem to be operating. A latent function is one that generally has positive benefits for society but which were clearly not intended or designed to operate in such a fashion. School provides cheap child-care for working parents, for example. While not having to pay for daycare is a plus for working parents, it is not an intended function of education. School age children have a place to be while their parents are at work, at least if their parents work during the daytime. Middle class parents, who generally work traditional hours, have an advantage over working and lower class parents who often earn a living working shifts and weekends. School also keeps potential cheap labor, at least during the school year, out of the labor market. In addition, potentially disruptive youngsters are kept under supervision for a major portion of the day.

Schools also provide a venue for a great deal of anticipatory socialization with respect to the future roles students will play in life. We refer here to the roles of work and family. Students will form friendships and peer groups. School can be very helpful to individuals in that lifelong social networks, which may be helpful in providing career opportunities later in life, are formed. One latent function of schooling is that it creates opportunities for young adults to meet future spouses. Most people would agree that school boards were probably not specifically concerned with dating when creating a curriculum for their school. However, dating provides the opportunity for anticipatory socialization—the socialization of children for future roles in life.

Schooling and the Reproduction of Social Class. Let us now turn to an analysis of the manner in which schooling is related to the reproduction of social class. Imagine for a moment that we live in a small society with just fifty essential occupations. The **division of labor**, in other words, is not too complex but as a society, we are still interdependent. This means that in order for me to earn a living at one of the fifty occupations the remaining forty-nine occupations must also function. Each occupation is functionally dependent upon the others in order for society to operate. Everything may function normally until we begin to age. At some point, we may want to retire. The question is who will replace us?

It should now be clear that every society is faced with the **educational functional requisite**. What this means is that every society must have in place educational systems and institutions that pass on the essential skills and knowledge from one generation to the next regarding the **occupational structure**. However, this is only half of the picture. Some jobs may be rewarded with more income, power, status, prestige, and leisure time than other jobs, which implies some type of stratification system. Since every known society is stratified in some manner, it is highly likely that our small society will also be stratified, even though we only have fifty distinct occupations. Thus, every society must establish educational institutions to train members of society to replace workers when they retire or die. Since the occupations we are training people to occupy are stratified, as each successive generation occupies positions in the occupational structure, social inequality is reproduced. To be more precise, some occupations in our society are associated with great social rewards; other occupations garner only meager social rewards.

If our society were stratified strictly upon the principle of meritocracy, minor inequalities might be bearable. However, no modern society is stratified in such a way. The idea that every individual who works hard will be rewarded with upward **social mobility** can be dismissed with a minor amount of thought. How many people do you know who work hard every day, and aspire to greater things in life, but who are simply struggling to make ends meet? I remember working in the meat packing industry when I was younger. I earned minimum wage and the work was dull, repetitive, and dangerous, not to mention odiferous. I eventually quit and joined the Navy, with the idea in mind that I would receive educational benefits upon completion of my term of service so that I could, and eventually did, take advantage of that opportunity. In United States society, for working and middle class people, education is the key to upward social mobility. Today, many people who have only a high school education and no special skills are finding it difficult to join the armed forces. The point is, there are millions of people in the United States who are highly motivated to improve their lot in life, but their jobs only pay poverty wages, or worse.

Consider the case of two women who recently took courses from me, Mary and Bonita. Both Mary and Bonita were highly motivated to succeed in college. Both had very respectable SAT scores. Both women came from the top ten percent of their high school class and had very good high school grade point averages. On the face of it, both Mary and Bonita seemed to have very similar personal characteristics. While in college, both women had good attendance in my courses, studied hard, and earned good grades. However, remember, personal attributes such as motivation and hard work are only part of the story. What important differences were there between Mary and Bonita that may have suggested that Mary would fare better in college than Bonita from the very first day?

First, you may have guessed that Bonita is a Latina. Bonita attended an inner city school in Philly, while Mary attended a public high school nearby with extremely high per pupil spending. In other words, Mary's school had more money for resources, since the average property values in the neighborhood where her school was located were much higher than in the inner city. In addition, Mary's school could afford teachers with advanced degrees, superb sports facilities, science and computer labs, a modern library, and other educational amenities. Bonita's school had no such facilities. Even though both Mary and Bonita achieved good grades in high school, Mary's school had advanced courses in mathematics, science, languages, and the arts, while Bonita's school could only offer a few such courses.

There are many hidden advantages related to social class we almost never think of when we consider only the individual merits of students. Mary comes from a long line of college graduates, while Bonita is the first person in her family to attend college. Just imagine that for a minute. If Mary had questions regarding the college experience, she could turn to her parents for guidance. Bonita, on the other hand, would have to figure things out for herself. None of this necessarily means that Bonita was doomed to failure. It only indicates that Bonita would have to struggle harder than Mary did even though they are of similar intellectual ability. Mary could rely on her family to supply her with the additional money that she needed beyond what she could get in loans and grants. Bonita had to work part-time in order to earn the extra money. In the end, Bonita was forced to leave college for financial reasons even though she was a good student. In this case, the opportunity structure favors the children of the middle class and upper class over the working and lower classes.

The Self-Fulfilling Prophecy and Social Inequality. At this point, we consider the intersection of social class, gender, social psychology, and social inequality. Before children ever step foot in a school, they complete a significant amount of learning in their family. Thus, a child's social class background is extremely important. Both working class and middle class parents value education and want their children to do as well as possible in school. One important difference is that working class parents are likely to view teaching their children as the job of the teacher and the school, whereas middle class parents are more likely to be highly involved in their child's learning. Middle class parents often have the ability to take time off for important educational events, such as parent-teacher conferences or sporting events. Working class parents often find it difficult to take time off from work for such activities, especially if they are working poor and the loss of hours equals the loss of significant income. Additionally, college educated middle class parents may be better prepared to be involved in a child's education.

Consider some important social class characteristics that are related to education before the child even gets through the door of the school. Imagine you are a kindergarten teacher. What questions would you be likely to ask about a child you know will be attending your class? Some come to mind immediately, usually related to basic knowledge. Can the child count to ten? Does the child know his or her alphabet? Can the child spell his or her name? Can the child tie his or her shoes? Does he or she know their address, telephone number, and so on? Other questions might also occur to you if you think about it long enough. What does the child's father do for a living? Does the child's mother work or does she stay at home with the children? Where does the child live? How many children are in the family? Are the parents divorced? Is there adequate nutrition in the home? Are there school supplies in the home to which the child has access?

We refer to all of this as **cultural capital**. Cultural capital amounts to objects, knowledge, and experiences that are like money, which can be spent on education. Cultural capital includes dictionaries, encyclopedias, computers, art, books, toys associated with learning and cognitive skills, such as building blocks, which help children visualize objects in three dimensions, and even experiences such as vacations, trips to the museum, art gallery, opera, or travel abroad. Some children have more cultural capital than others do. Cultural capital is highly correlated with social class. Affluent children have access to greater amounts of cultural capital than poor children do. Imagine what an educational advantage it must be to have both a mother and a father who are college graduates. This certainly does not mean that children with working class parents cannot help them with their homework. It does mean, however, that as the difficulty of schoolwork increases over time, children with college-educated parents have a hidden advantage over children of high school graduates.

When children first come through the door at school, teachers assess their basic level of preparedness. Unfortunately, how well prepared children are for school is often correlated with the social class background of their parents. At this point children are often sorted into ability groups. Some children are identified as "gifted," usually those children whose parents have already invested a lot of time in teaching them the basics. Other children are identified as "average," and still other children are identified as "below-average." It is clear that there is no way to disconnect social class background from these assessments. This process of sorting children into similar ability groups is known as **tracking**. It seems entirely logical that teachers would do this. In order to meet the learning needs of average and below average students, they must first be identified. Thus, the goal is to bring the ability of the below average students up to at least the average level. Children with greater access to cultural capital are more likely to be placed in the higher tracks than are children with less access to cultural capital.

Tracking is a system that is meant to enhance the **cognitive development** of children. Cognitive development refers to the growth and acquisition of mental skills. Learning to thinking independently, to think abstractly, to weigh evidence, consider what would invalidate a claim, and to develop independent judgment are all forms of cognitive ability. Cognitive ability and development is enhanced if the teacher has high expectations of the student, and the work is complex and demanding, without close supervision. Thus, when the teacher has high expectations of you, especially if you are a child who looks up to the teacher as a good role model, you are more likely to strive for greater educational attainment. Additionally, when the teacher sets goals for you, but allows you some degree of freedom to achieve those goals, you will experience greater cognitive development. Its simple, children who learn to solve problems with little or no help from the teacher are better problem solvers than students who have a teacher standing over them the entire time. This is also a major value of the workplace for middle class employees, who are often given a set of goals to achieve without much direction or supervision and expected to achieve those goals. Lastly, children who consistently are given more and more complex work to complete, incrementally, learn more.

11 | Education as a Social Institution: Preparing to Get Your Share.
by Frank O. Taylor, IV, Ph.D.

When my son was in the fourth grade, he had a friend from the mobile home park across the street named John. We lived in a single family home and John lived with his family in a mobile home. They both had the same fourth grade teacher and she visited the families of many of her prospective students about a week before class. Teachers are human beings and I often wonder if their perceptions of students' cognitive abilities are influenced by such home visits. Here is a story of two social classes. When my son went to kindergarten, he could read at the third grade level, count to ten, write the alphabet, his verbal skills were highly developed, and he could perform simple addition and subtraction. As you know, his father is a college professor. His mother also has a college degree and worked as the manager of a restaurant. John's parents, on the other hand, were working class. His father was a truck driver and his mother was a waitress. Neither parent had a high school degree. Consequently, John, although a very bright child, was not as academically prepared as my son. Even worse, John's mother baby talked when she spoke to John. John, of course, had difficulty pronouncing words correctly. In terms of education, my son was light years ahead of John before one hour of schooling had taken place. That is cultural capital. When the teachers visited our two homes, which they all did for each grade, did the social environments influence their assessment of each child's global ability? My son was identified as "gifted," whereas John was identified as suffering from a speech impediment and placed in the below-average track.

Recall the reason for tracking. Below average students must be identified, if not grouped into one track, in order to help bring their cognitive development up to average—a laudable goal. Imagine if I divided this class arbitrarily up into three tracks. Students in the high ability track are exposed to fairly complex and demanding work, both within the classroom and for homework. I also have very high expectations for them and heap lots of positive rewards upon them. I constantly remind them how smart they are. Students in the average ability track are not required to do much homework and as long as they achieve average grades, I do not pay much attention to them or worry too much about them. Students in the low ability group spend a lot of time with tutors and I assign a graduate student to work with them. Because of the "special" treatment they receive in terms of tutoring, outside the classroom study sessions, and so on, they are constantly reminded that they are "below average." It does not take a large amount of imagination to understand which group of students will do better and which will do worse.

I recall one day when my son and his fourth-grade friends were studying for their spelling test. They received their words on every Monday and took the test every Friday. They were practicing writing their words on a chalkboard he had in his room. Until that day, I had never noticed that they actually had different words to learn. Being a "gifted" student, my son had multiple syllable words assigned to learn and memorize, which were quite difficult. John, on the other hand had very simple two and three letter words. Upon inquiring of the boys, I learned that John's list almost never changed while my son's list changed every week! I suspect that John's parents were not even aware of this situation. Both children were in the same grade with the same teacher but both children were not receiving the same education. I decided to experiment a little and quickly learned that John was capable of learning to spell words that are more difficult. Obviously, once he had been identified as having a speech impediment, teachers had also believed that he was learning disabled.

There is evidence that the track assignment students are placed in is highly correlated with the amount of material they are exposed to, the complexity of that material, and the amount of homework required. In other words, students in the high-ability group learn more because they are taught more. Students in the low-ability group learn less because they are taught less. Tracking is also related to self-esteem and a student's perception of their ability. Students in the high-ability group tend to have positive self-assessments of their abilities and tend to think highly of themselves. Students in the low-ability group have self-assessments that are more negative as well as a lower opinion of their abilities. This is the social psychological aspect of tracking—children begin to internalize characteristics associated with the track in which they are placed. Students in the low-ability group begin to think they are stupid. This will certainly hinder any effort to help them improve academically.

There is another important aspect to the issue of cognitive development and tracking—the issue of **social distance**. Social distance refers to the gulf between the experiences of the affluent and the poor. I remember watching a story on the evening news one day when George Bush Sr. was running for reelection. He was in a grocery store and marveled about bar codes on the products and cash registers that scanned those codes. Clearly, President Bush had not spent much time doing something as mundane as shopping for his family. Other people did his shopping, a reality far removed from the lives of average families. That is social distance. Social distance also refers to the self-imposed boundaries people often maintain. I once watched a white woman actually move her purse from one side of her body to the other as a black male approached her. That is social distance. Choosing not to interact with someone because of race, class, gender, or other characteristics is social distance.

Research indicates that cognitive development is enhanced when teachers have high expectations of the students. Teachers are most demanding when they are from the same social class as their students. Imagine what an advantage it must be to have visited the same museums, cities, art galleries, and nations that your teacher has discussed in class. This is why teachers are fond of students from a similar social class background—their experiences are more likely to mesh. When there is great social distance between the teacher and the students, teachers are more likely to rigidly structure the classroom and make fewer demands on the students. When students are from the lower class and the teacher is from the middle class, they are more likely to learn less then when both the students and teacher are from the same social class. This is a major disadvantage for poor children.

Researchers have found that being assigned to the high ability group has positive effects for students. Conversely, assignment to the low ability group has negative effects. Students in low ability groups have teachers who do not have very high expectations of them, they are not exposed to very complex material, are required to complete little or no homework, have fewer opportunities to learn, and are just taught less. These students also suffer from lower self-esteem. Once powerful persons, such as teachers and principles, label a student below average, the label is very hard to reject. The danger is that the student will internalize the label. This means that the student begins to see themselves as below average and act as if they are below average. They will have lower and lower expectations of themselves. On the other hand, students in the high ability group receive strong affirmation and feedback regarding their academic ability. Teachers have high expectations of them, they are exposed to complex and demanding work, have many opportunities to learn, and generally have higher self-esteem than students in the low ability track. Students in the college prep track begin to see themselves as smarter than other students. The danger here is that these students will begin to believe that they "deserve" more out of life than poor students.

We now consider the relationship between gender and tracking. Traditional gender norms steer women and men into different social spheres. Women are supposed to be concerned with childcare and homemaking. Men are supposed to be concerned with breadwinning. There has been some change in traditional gender roles recently, giving women especially a broader range of choices. However, there is evidence that traditional gender norms continue to influence men and women. About sixty percent of married women are in the labor force. Forty percent of married women are entirely dependent upon their husband's earnings. Married women who are employed usually have incomes lower than their husbands do. Since income is generally related to power in marriages, men continue to enjoy more of it. Family obligations force many married women who are employed to work part-time, rather than full-time. Additionally, the division of household labor, in most marriages, continues to favor the men, who spend about 14 hours per week on household labor compared to the 33 hours on average employed women spend on such labor. Although women have made great progress in terms of labor force participation this does not necessarily imply that women and men are now equals.

In 1972, Congress passed Title IX of the Educational Amendments Act, which was supposed to make gender discrimination in public schools illegal. However, there is evidence that gender discrimination, in curriculum, textbooks, school sports, counseling, and student-teacher interaction continues to remain a problem. Schools educate boys and girls differently. Let us first consider curricular differences for girls and boys. In 1992 the American Association of University Women discovered that differences in test scores between boys and girls for math are minor and have been steadily declining, but girls are still less likely than boys to take advanced courses in mathematics. Only fifteen percent of girls, compared to twenty-five percent of boys, take physics in high school. Gendered tracking in high school results in girls being steered into secretarial and vocational courses, such as cosmetology or home education. Boys tend to be tracked into math and science, for the high ability groups, and vocational courses in woodworking and auto mechanics for the lower ability groups. From about the fifth grade on, girls are overrepresented in courses related to education and the humanities, while boys are overrepresented in courses related to physical science, engineering, and law. These trends continue into college, where women tend to major in English, humanities, fine art, education, and social science, and men tend to major in mathematics, physics, chemistry, biology, and computer science.

The issue is whether such different educational trajectories are a matter of natural difference between women and men or the result of tracking. School guidance counselors help students choose their career and then suggest a sequence of courses designed to help students achieve their career goals. The guidance students receive is partly based on gender stereotypes, a form of tracking. This results in boys being steered into mathematics, science, and vocational study such as carpentry and auto mechanics while girls are steered into humanities, art, social science, and vocational study such as home education. Thus, it is not surprising that when young women and men enter college they tend to major in that which they have some experience. Since engineers and scientists generally earn more than elementary school teachers and social workers, after college men fare better than women do in terms of income.

When children go to school, and in particular, when they learn to read, they are being exposed to society's status structure, indeed, our entire culture. In other words, the textbooks children read are a reflection of society and its gender roles. There is a considerable amount of gender bias in school textbooks. It hardly matters what the subject is, women and minorities are underrepresented in school textbooks. This is true for subjects ranging from history to science. When women are mentioned, they are usually connected to traditional gender norms and stereotypes. Men are associated with politics, war, inventions, discovery, and so on, in spite of the scientific achievements and contributions of women and minorities to these fields. Children in school can hardly be aware that the roles of women and men in their textbooks are biased toward traditional gender norms and not an accurate description of what women and men do in the real world. The danger is that girls and boys will internalize these stereotypes and accept them as appropriate gender roles. I suspect that in large measure this is in fact occurring.

I remember attending a parent-teacher conference with my son when he was in the fourth grade. In the entire school, there were only two male role models, the principal and the janitor. Women comprised the remainder of the role models in his elementary school. He did not have a male teacher until he was in junior high school and was enrolled in a pre-algebra course. Steadily, as he progressed from elementary school through high school, the ratio of women to men began to favor male teachers the older he became. Since women tend to occupy the lower level positions throughout the workforce, we should not be surprised that women teach our children in elementary school. In higher education, women represent only about thirty-one percent of full-time faculty in the nation's colleges, and even here they tend to be concentrated in the lower ranks and are less likely to be tenured.

Here is what seems to be going on with respect to the self-fulfilling prophecy in education. First, children are tracked into ability groups based partly on social class and gender. Second, the curriculum differs, based on the child's social class background and gender. Upper class boys are tracked into college prep courses that emphasize mathematics, computer science, and physical science.   Upper class girls are tracked into college prep courses that emphasize social science, English, and the humanities. Lower class boys are tracked into vocational educational courses, such as auto mechanics and carpentry.   Lower class girls are tracked into vocational courses such as homemaking and cosmetology.   Third, teachers tend to have higher expectations for the children of the upper classes and lower expectations for children of the lower classes.   Fourth, tracking ensures that children in the higher tracks will be exposed to more complex and demanding work with greater levels of homework. The reverse is true for children in the lower tracks, who will receive boring, mundane, and less complex work with little to no homework. Fifth, the high ability group will develop the cognitive skills necessary to be successful in college. The average ability group will develop the cognitive skills sufficient for dead-end **McJobs**. Some in the low ability group will have cognitive skills related to blue-collar vocations.   Sixth, the perpetrators and proponents of tracking then point to the outcomes that they largely created, artificially, as "proof" that gender and social class stereotypes are real and continue to track students. It is a little like saying, "see, I told you girls are predisposed to be nurses because of their care giving genes," after spending twelve to thirteen years training them to be caregivers.

Even though tracking is commonly found in eighty percent of classrooms in the nation's educational system, making it part of the social structure of education, we cannot forget the other side of the equation—individual motivation. Discussion of the self-fulfilling prophecy should not be taken to mean that only children of the affluent, who have lots of cultural capital, would go to college and be successful. Some of my best students over the years have been nontraditional students who come from less-advantaged backgrounds. I suspect this in true, in part, because nontraditional students who major in sociology have already experienced a lot of the sociology curriculum in their daily lives—people struggling to overcoming poverty and oppression tend to do well in courses in which the subject matter is poverty and oppression. However, it is true that in terms of rates, children of affluent parents make up the greatest percentage of college students while children of the less affluent are a minority. It boils down to this: even if you did not take college prep classes while in high school you can be successful in college, you will just have to work a little harder at it. As much as it is anything else, college is an exercise in will power and determination. Having said that, if you are functionally illiterate, as many graduates of the nation's inner city schools are, college will be a daunting task. Even if you are reasonably intelligent, if you lack the academic socialization children of the affluent receive in the high ability track, you will still struggle to be successful in college.

Disadvantaged children face a broad range of hardships that work against them every day while in school. The importance of cultural capital cannot be stressed enough. Children with little cultural capital, who do not have access to literature, computers, dictionaries, encyclopedias, and other important school supplies, are at a severe handicap. When my son was in the seventh grade, he was required to take a science course. His biology teacher required a major project that asked students either to build a model of a cell or to draw one. However, only children who constructed a model could receive an A for the project. Children drawing a picture of the parts of the cell could do no better than a B for the project. When I inquired as to the reason for the difference in grading, the biology teacher informed me that "anyone" could "draw" a picture of a cell and that constructing a model of a cell was much more challenging, and therefore deserving of the higher grade. The projects were presented during the school's science fair. There were several very intricate drawings, completed very cheaply with color pencil and whiteboard among a majority of models, some of which were expensively elaborate. This is a base form of discrimination widely practiced in our educational system. I suspect that the drawing option was only grudgingly allowed when poor parents complained to the principal that they could not afford the expense of components for the model.

Poor children are more likely to have parents who must devote a lot of time to struggling from day-to-day to survive. People who are worried about putting food on the table, and who may have little education themselves, find it difficult to meet the educational needs of their children. This, under certain circumstances, extends to even parents who are educated. During every life cycle, there are periods of stress, when parents cannot attend to their children's educational needs. The death of a spouse, divorce, loss of income due to downsizing or factory closings, bankruptcy, mental or physical illness, among a host of other problems, may force people into a coping mode where just surviving from one day to the next is a challenge. Poor parents are much more likely to be under daily stress related to economic hardship. Consequently, they are more likely to feel it is the school's job to educate their children, are less likely to attend parent-teacher conferences, and less able, as schoolwork gets more complex, to help their children with their homework. Some blue-collar workers may not even be sure school is necessary in the first place. On more than one occasion, I have heard a father remark, particularly to sons, that he did not need a college education and neither should they. I think these blue-collar fathers forget that jobs in the industrial sector of the economy, which pay middle class wages, are disappearing.

Cooling Out the Mark. From this discussion, it is clear that in spite of individual levels of motivation or ability, schooling is systematically biased to favor the children of the affluent. Our educational system tends to provide vocational education for the children of the working class and a curriculum of college preparation for the children of upper class professionals. However, if this is the case why is there not a social outcry to prevent it? After all, meritocracy and equal opportunity are two major values in our society. On the face of it, tracking and inequalities in resources based on property taxes appear to violate the spirit of meritocracy and equal opportunity. The interesting question is why more people do not complain.

One group of United States families, of course, has no interest in complaining because they reap the benefits of the educational system—the affluent. The system of private high schools and elite Ivy League colleges ensures that the children of the affluent will obtain the knowledge and skills necessary to move into the professional occupations of their parents, thereby reproducing their social class, as a class. In addition to the knowledge and skills attained by the affluent children, elite private schools also try to instill a sense of leadership in their students. These children are made to understand that they will be the movers-and-shakers of society from a very young age. They are raised and educated to believe that they will be the political, economic, and cultural leaders of the nation. Education in the nation's elite private schools is designed to turn social class advantage into personal merit. In other words, after this type of education affluent students are more likely to point to their grades and hard work rather than to social class advantage when explaining their educational success. It is usually these people, who enjoyed every advantage money could buy in their childhood and education who claim money is not important, effort and motivation is the key. However, if money is not important why do affluent parents send their children to private schools instead of public schools?

Public high schools and colleges also help reproduce the existing social class system by providing the training necessary for both white-collar professional occupations and blue-collar occupations. This is an important point: every society must reproduce the knowledge and skills necessary for people to move into the jobs of its occupational structure. This is how social class is reproduced. Private schools educate the children of the elite, preparing them for the highest paid jobs in the economy. Middle class children mostly attend flagship state colleges and universities, where they are prepared for middle class professional jobs. Children of working class parents, if they go to college, are more likely to attended community colleges or vocational schools. Children of the lower class, although some do eventually make it to college and eventually graduate, mostly attain only a high school education, if they do not drop out of school entirely.

We employ the concept of "cooling out the mark" to explain why more people do not complain about the lack of educational opportunities, in spite of their level of intelligence. As noted, people who benefit from the existing arrangements are not likely to complain. That leaves those who are disadvantaged by the educational system. Children are "marked" from birth. The mark is that of social class.   Children of the lower class are "marked" for jobs in the lower rungs of the occupational structure. These jobs are primarily low-skill manual labor. Society has prepared a course of education appropriate for such jobs. Advanced degrees are not necessary to prepare anyone to work at a McJob. Functional literacy and the ability to perform simple math and follow directions is all that is necessary, along with other components of the **hidden curriculum**, such as obedience to authority, following instructions, being punctual, raising you hand before asking a question, and other norms associated with a life in the workforce as an order-taker. A large amount of education has very little to do with knowledge or learning and a lot to do with accepting a position of subservience in society and the occupational structure.

When we say children are "marked," we do not mean to imply a rigid social system that tracks every single child into certain types of education depending on their social class. The point is that certain types of education are set aside for groups of occupations in the occupational structure. Some positions in the occupation structure require order-givers, while others require order-takers. This implies different types of education. Order-givers will need a college education. For order-takers, a high school education will suffice. There are professional jobs, menial jobs, clerical jobs, and so on, each of which requires different types of education.

When you are born, you are born into a family already located somewhere in the social class structure. Your family will have a certain amount of cultural capital. Your parents' education and their occupations will influence you in incalculable ways. For example, parents with financial resources may choose to find a home near a better school, which will benefit you in many ways you will largely be unconscious of. Other parents have no choice but to remain near a failing school because they lack financial resources. Society has prepared education in advance of your arrival and you are tracked into different types of education depending upon your gender, the neighborhood you live in, the value of the homes in your school district, your parent's economic resources, and the amount of cultural capital you have. This is what we mean by being "marked." Many other people have already made decisions about the nature and type of education you will receive, including parents, teachers, school board members, politicians, and even religious leaders, who may run for school board office. Your contribution will be to be "motivated" to learn what is placed before you.

Some people, depending upon their family background, are marked for more education and a greater share of social rewards; other people are marked for less education and fewer social rewards. The elites, who control the economic, political, and cultural institutions of society, use their power to ensure that their children will follow in their steps. The question is what keeps the have-nots in their place? Socialization, particularly in the educational setting, goes a long way toward answering this question. We are socialized to believe that we are bounded individuals, each somewhat distinct from everyone else, with certain innate talents and abilities. Children are taught in school to value and respect the existing economic and political system; This in spite of the fact that they may be victims of the very system. Additionally, the ideologies of meritocracy and individualism encourage people to internalize failure. At a very young age, you accept as fact ideologies that encourage you to think everyone is different from each other in important ways and that some people are smarter than others are. Therefore, if you fail it must be your fault.

We encounter the mechanism that encourages the internalization of failure very early in life. Perhaps you remember, as I do, the very first day you discovered that every child was not equal. For most of us, that day occurred at school when we received our first grade, for one assignment or another. I distinctly remember wondering why I had a bell instead of a star on my spelling paper. Imagine a school system that relied upon a strategy of "mastery of skills," in which children move from one set of skills to the next depending upon mastery of the previous skills, and no grades are involved whatsoever. There are varieties of methods to assess what children have learned that do not necessarily involve grades. Grades are one way to assess progress. However, grades also have a latent function that a mastery strategy does not; grades rank children, from exceptional to below average. Indeed, even the word failure is incorporated into the standard grading system in our educational system. From a very early age, children are taught that they have no one to blame but themselves for failure by mechanisms such as grading. This is why, as adults, it is so hard for students in sociology classes to think about all the other components of educational success, especially if you are an affluent student.

I have visited schools that do not have a library at all. I visited a school once in a lower class neighborhood that did have a library but no new book had been purchased, due to funding cutbacks by the state, for nearly fifteen years! In Ohio, I recall that Cleveland's political leaders preferred to be more concerned about building a new football stadium for the Browns than rebuilding the schools downtown. In some classrooms, if the teacher did not purchase books and materials the children would simply go without. Can you imagine not even having a textbook? Once, while visiting with a teacher in a rural Kentucky school, a teacher told me that most of the parents of her students were waiting for the "crop" to come in, so they could buy new clothes and school supplies. I inquired as to what crop she was referring; mistakenly believing it must be tobacco. They were waiting on the marijuana crop. That is a reality most affluent students will never know. One time when I was visiting a school in St. Louis and asked directions to the restroom I was directed to a port-a-pot outside. Elite parents would not tolerate such circumstances for one second.

Even children, at a very early age, can figure out when the deck is stacked against them. In this case, kids are told to "motivate themselves," to try harder, and they will succeed. I teach college classes to socially disadvantaged adults in the evenings at a local high school. In place of computers, indoor football fields, art and music classes, an up-to-date library, and the like, there are posters everywhere encouraging students to get motivated—to pull themselves up by their bootstraps. Having a positive outlook on life hardly puts opportunities back into the opportunity structure that have evaporated. As you look out the window of that classroom, you can see the demolished buildings and parking lot of the factory that used to employ hundreds of people, some of the very students in that class. All that remains are the smokestacks. The guard shack is still there and someone is always on duty, as if people in the neighborhood might try to break into the empty parking lot and steal back their jobs! When we encourage poor schoolchildren to try harder, we are still encouraging them to think in individualistic terms. If they fail to achieve it is still their fault, not the complete lack of opportunity and economic resources.

Eventually, more likely than not, poor children become poor adults. When they come to me as college students they know who is limiting their opportunities, and they are not likely to look in the mirror and blame themselves for the trade imbalance, deindustrialization, war, military spending, the federal debt, or any of the other major problems our economy faces. Poor people know that when the government cuts taxes, it has less revenue. Less revenue means less government spending. Less government spending means cuts in programs that serve the poor. In recent years, there have been massive cuts to health care, food stamps, aid to families with dependent children, school breakfast and lunch programs, head start programs, and a host of other educational programs that help the poor. These cuts to educational and social programs are the result of political policy; policy that political and economic elites have decided to change regardless of the effects it will have on children. You may say that it is the job of the parent to feed children, not the government. However, when families are out of work because the factory closed, the result is that children go hungry. Hungry children do not make good learners. When the economy is expanding government programs for the poor tend to expand also. When the economy contracts it is the poor who must bear the cuts.

As the social disturbances that followed the Rodney King verdict demonstrated, sometimes people get angry and take to the streets in protest. Frequently, the lives of the poor become so desperate that they develop an **injustice frame**. When these types of protest happen, it is usually because people feel victimized and want something to be done about it. There are many examples of such behavior, including the women's movement, the green movement, and the civil rights movement, among others. It is important to realize that when people become truly desperate the legitimacy of the government begins to fail, particularly when the government is taking away a benefit formerly supplied. The manifest function of government welfare programs is to help people meet their basic housing and nutrition needs. A latent function of government welfare is to support the legitimacy of government.   When poor people become unruly and start protesting, the government expands the welfare roles. When poor people are just alienated and withdrawn, and relatively passive, government contracts the welfare roles. This is known as cooling-out-the-mark.

People who are marked for poverty and a marginal education are kept passive by a variety of techniques. First, through the process of socialization children are taught two major ideologies, meritocracy and individualism. School reinforces both of these ideologies. Children are treated as individuals who compete against each other in school. Children are taught that failure is a personal attribute and not an outcome associated with the system. Grading and tracking children into ability groups reinforces the idea that children who earn higher grades are somehow also better, and consequently, more deserving of better teachers and more educational resources. Children who believe they are worthless are not likely to complain. Second, children in poverty-stricken neighborhoods are more likely to become alienated and to withdraw from school. Third, when poor people become unruly and begin to protest publicly, the government extends aid, until stability returns and the aid can be cut back. The best way to keep people marked for poverty calm is to get them to internalize failure. Socialization in our educational system goes a long way toward achieving that goal.

We began the discussion of education by noting that our social class system is reproduced by education. Every society, especially one with a complex division of labor, must find systematic ways to train members to occupy positions in the occupational structure. In our society, social class is closely correlated with occupation, since we earn a living based on income we receive for paid labor. It is with this income that we obtain a higher or lower standard of living. Individual motivation aside, there is a correlation between social class and education. The children of the affluent tend to attend private high schools and Ivy League Colleges, after which they move into high-powered occupations in business, law, and medicine. Middle class children tend to attend high quality public schools and enroll in the better state colleges and universities. Following college, the children of the middle class tend to find jobs in the professional occupations. Working class children tend to enroll either in community colleges or in vocational schools, moving into blue-collar employment or clerical work.

We noted that family background and cultural capital is highly influential in determining who will be educationally successful. Affluent children are more likely to have books, computers, educated parents, and a host of other experiences, materials, and advantages related to educational success. Lastly, we noted that some students were "marked" for educational success while other students were "marked" for poverty and a circumscribed education.

A latent function of socialization in our educational system is the internalization of failure, which indirectly forces the children of the poor to blame themselves for the structural failure of society. When the poor become conscious of the ways in which they are systematically disadvantaged, or just plain tired of poverty, and become socially active, the state extends welfare and expands the roles, which usually has the effect of cooling off tempers. At other times, the state allows a large number of poor to remain alienated and disaffected, so long as they are not disruptive. We also noted that systematic disparities in education, such as tracking and basing per-student spending on local property taxes, violates the values of meritocracy and equal opportunity.

ဆ ᏟᏗ ဆ ᏟᏗ

DEFINITIONS

Assimilation. A process by which a racial or ethnic minority loses its distinctive identity and lifeways and conforms to cultural patterns of the dominant group.

Cognitive Development. Refers to the growth and acquisition of mental skills.

Cultural Capital. Objects, knowledge, and experiences that are like money, which can be spent on education. Cultural capital includes dictionaries, encyclopedias, computers, art, books, and toys associated with learning and cogitative skills.

Division of Labor. The delegation and assignment of certain specified tasks, jobs, or work (or parts of them) to be completed by certain specified individuals, groups, categories, and classes of people. Sex, age, education type and level, and the occupation area of one's family are the most traditional bases for differentiating occupational activities.

Dysfunction. The interference (or negative outcome) of an aspect of a social system with the maintenance or adaptation of that system or its values.

Education. Broadly refers to the transmission of skills, values, beliefs, knowledge, and facts to members of society in a variety of settings.

Educational Functional Requisite. Every culture requires educational systems and institutions that pass on the essential skills and knowledge from one generation to the next.

Hidden Curriculum. An aspect of education designed to teach dominant norms and values, such as obedience to authority, following instructions, being punctual, raising you hand before asking a question, and other norms associated with a life in the workforce as an order-taker.

Injustice Frame. A collection of ideas and symbols that illustrate both how significant the problem is as well as what the movement can do to alleviate it.

Latent Functions. Unintended and unrecognized operations of a social institution with generally positive outcomes.

Manifest Function. Anticipated and intended operation of a social institution.

McJobs. A new term sociologists have coined for jobs in the lower tier of the service economy. Referred to as dead-end jobs or jobs with low pay and limited advancement possibilities.

Occupational Structure. The classification of occupational categories in the labor market. Each category includes detailed occupation(s) according to job duties, skills, education, or experience.

Schooling. A more formal process of education. Schooling takes place in the United States under the supervision of teachers with a college education and takes place within large bureaucratic social settings. Schooling is considered essential for an industrial society with thousands of occupations and jobs requiring specialized knowledge and skills.

Social Distance. Refers to the gulf between the experiences of the affluent and the poor. Also refers to the self-imposed boundaries people often maintain.

Social Integration. The bringing together of people from diverse backgrounds so that they share common social experiences and develop commonly held norms, attitudes, and beliefs. A sense of social unity or sense of belonging.

Social Mobility. The movement of people from one social position to another in the stratification system.

Social Placement. This function involves determining what roles and statuses, or positions, the child will occupy in society.

Socialization. The lifelong process of learning culture. During the process of socialization individuals learn and internalize the norms of our culture, attitudes, values, beliefs, ways of thinking and learning, social expectations of society, and develop a sense of self.

Tracking. The placement of students into courses based on their performance in standardized achievement tests and/or IQ tests and in previous courses in the same discipline. In simpler terms, it is the practice of placing students in different classes based on perceived differences in their abilities.

REFERENCES

The ideas expressed in my essay on education and the information presented are based on the following works:

Alexander, Karl L., Doris Entwisle, and Maxine Thompson. 1987. "School Performance, Status Relations, and the Structure of Sentiment: Bringing the Teacher Back In." *American Sociological Review* 52:665-82.

Alexander, Karl L., Gary Natriello, and Aaron M. Pallas. 1985. "For Whom the School Bell Tolls: The Impact of Dropping Out on Cognitive Performance." *American Sociological Review* 50 (June):409-20.

Alexander, Karl, Doris Entwisle, Doris Cadigan, and Aaron Pallas. 1987. "Getting Ready for First Grade: Standards of Deportment in Home and School." *Social Forces* 66:57-84.

American Association of University Women. 1992. "How Schools Shortchange Girls." Executive Summary. *AAUW Report*. American Association of University Women Educational Foundation.

Bowles, Samuel, and Herbert Gintis. 1976. *Schooling in Capitalist America: Educational Reform and the Contradiction of Economic Life*. New York: Basic Books.

Bowles, Samuel. 1969. "Toward Equality of Educational Opportunity." *Harvard Educational Review*. Cambridge, MA: Harvard University Press.

Bowles, Samuel. 1977. "Unequal Education and the Reproduction of the Social Division of Labor." Pp. 137-153 in *Power and Ideology in Education*, edited by Jerome Karabel and A. H. Halsey. New York: Oxford University Press.

Chase, Bob. 1997. "All Children Are Equal but Some Children Are More Equal Than Others." *The Washington Post National Weekly Edition*, April 28, pp. 20.

Cookson, Jr., W. Peter and Caroline Hodges Persell. 1985. *Preparing for Power: America's Elite Boarding Schools*. New York: Basic Books.

Cose, Ellis. 1995. "Teaching Kids To Be Smart." *Newsweek*, August 21, pp. 58-60.

Eitzen, Stanley D. and Maxine Baca Zinn. 2006. *Social Problems*. 10th ed. New York: Allyn and Bacon.

Gamoran, Adam and Robert Mare. 1989. "Secondary School Tracking and Educational Inequality." *American Journal of Sociology* 94:1146-83.

Gamoran, Adam. 1992. "The Variable Effects of High School Tracking." *American Sociological Review* 57:812-828.

Gardner, Howard. 1983. *Frames of Mind: The Theory of Multiple Intelligences*. New York: Basic Books.

Hallinan, M. 1988. "Equality of Educational Opportunity." *Annual Review of Sociology* 14:249-68.

Hallinan, Maureen T. 1994. "Tracking: From Theory to Practice." *Sociology of Education* 67(2) (April):79-84.

Hallinan, Maureen T. and Aage B. Sorenson. 1986. "Student Characteristics and Assignment to Ability Groups: Two Conceptual Formulations." *Sociological Quarterly* 27(1):1-13.

Hancock, Lyn Nell. 1995. "The Haves and the Have-Nots." *Newsweek*, February 27, pp. 50-53.

Horn, Miriam. 1987. "The Burgeoning Educational Underclass." *U.S. News and World Report* (May):66-67.

Jencks, Christopher, et al. 1972. *Inequality: A Reassessment of the Effect of Family and Schooling in America*. New York: Basic Books

Jencks, Christopher, et al. 1979. *Who Gets Ahead? The Determinants of Economic Success in America*. New York: Basic Books.

11 | Education as a Social Institution: Preparing to Get Your Share.

by Frank O. Taylor, IV, Ph.D.

Jensen, Arthur R. 1969. "How Much Can We Boost IQ and Scholastic Achievement?" *Harvard Educational Review* 39 (Winter):1-123.

Jensen, Arthur R. 1980. *Bias in Mental Testing.* New York: Free Press.

Kagan, Jerome. 1973. "What is Intelligence?" *Social Policy* 4 (July/August):88-94.

Kempton, Murray. 1979. "Arithmetic of Inequality." *The Progressive* 43 (November):8-9.

Kozol, Jonathan. 1967. *Death At An Early Age.* New York: Penguin Books.

Kozol, Jonathan. 1991. *Savage Inequalities: Children in America's Schools.* New York: Crown.

Kozol, Jonathan. 1995. *Amazing Grace: The Lives of Children and The Conscience of a Nation.* New York: Harper Perennial.

Leslie, Connie. 1995. "You Can't High-Jump If the Bar Is Set Low" *Newsweek*, November 6, pp. 81, 83.

Mansnerus, Laura. 1992. "Should Tracking Be Derailed?" *New York Times*, November 1, pp. E14-E16.

Merton, Robert K. 1957. *Social Theory and Social Structure.* 2nd ed. Glencoe, IL: Free Press.

Miller, Karen A., Melvin L. Kohn, and Carmi Schooler. 1985. "Educational Self-Direction and the Cognitive Functioning of Students." *Social Forces* 63 (June):923-44.

Miller, Karen, Melvin Kohn, and Carmi Schooler. 1986. "Educational Self-Direction and Personality." *American Sociological Review* 51:372-90.

Minnich, Elizabeth Kamarch. 1990. *Transforming Knowledge.* Philadelphia, PA: Temple University Press.

Oaks, Jeannie. 1985. *Keeping Track: How Schools Structure Inequality.* New York: Yale University Press.

Orenstein, Peggy. 1994. *School Girls: Young Women, Self-Esteem, and the Confidence Gap.* New York: Anchor Books.

Piven, Frances Fox and Richard A. Cloward. 1971. *Regulating the Poor: The Functions of Public Welfare.* New York: Random House.

Piven, Frances Fox. 1996. "Welfare and the Transformation of Electoral Politics." *Dissent* 43 (Fall):61-67.

Rachlin, Jill. 1989. "The Label That Sticks." *U.S. News and World Report*, July 3, pp. 51-52.

Taylor, Frank. 2003. "Content Analysis and Gender Stereotypes in Children's Books." *Teaching Sociology* 31 (July):300-311.

Weitzman, Lenore J., Deborah Eifler, Elizabeth Hokada, and Catherine Ross. 1972. "Sex- Role Socialization in Picture Books for Preschool Children." *American Journal of Sociology* 77 (May):1125-50.

Williams, J. Allen, JoEtta A. Vernon, Martha C. Williams, and Karen Malecha. 1987. "Sex-Role Socialization in Picture Books: An Update." *Social Science Quarterly* 68 (March):148-56.

12 | Power: Forcing Us to Give Them What They Want.
by Frank O. Taylor, IV, Ph.D.

THEORETICAL PERSPECTIVES ON POWER

What is power? Although many sociologists were interested in the topic, Max Weber is the sociologist most closely associated with power. According to Weber, power is multidimensional. Power is the ability to control the behavior of other people against their will. Understanding power, and how it works, is necessary for any policy analyst. After examining the different levels of power the chapter moves on to the national power structure and different theoretical perspectives, and then on to the political system, paying particular attention to the problems our democracy faces.

THE NATURE OF POWER

Weber noted that there is a distribution to power—some individuals and groups have more of it than others do. According to Weber, power is essentially the ability of the individual (or group) to force their will upon others systematically. Weber was talking about community action (policies and programs) that involves people against their will. Nearly all definitions of power are based on the Weberian definition. One type of power is associated with one's position in the authority hierarchy—**legitimate authority**. Presidents and school principals wield this type of power. All systems of stratification are really only institutionalized power differentials. Thought of in this way, stratification systems are differential access to valued outcomes in life that are based on some social criteria, such as gender or race. Those with more power have greater access to resources related to life chances.

Another way to view power is to remove the locus of power from the individual and examine social structure. Power can be examined, structurally, as a network of independent/dependent relationships that occur in the social setting. Several conditions must exist for a social relationship to exhibit power over an individual: 1) the individual cannot reciprocate with anything of value, 2) there are no other suppliers of the valued resource, 3) the individual does not have the power to force others to give up the resource, and 4) the resource is essential for survival. These conditions clearly point to the social setting in which the power relation exists. The government, or national

265

power structure, is the major source of social policy, social programs, and legislation. The average citizen is dependent upon the others with political power. Those with political power have the means to help or harm others.

Consider the case of someone living below the poverty line. This is a good example since the stated goal of the president and congress is to move people off the welfare roles and into the paid labor force. If the poverty-stricken individual wishes to petition the government for relief, the type of aid and the conditions under which it will be granted are entirely dependent upon the whims of the government. The individual does not have the power to force the government to give the aid. Why? First, the poor person has nothing of value to give back to the government. This is even more interesting when the person seeking aid is a mother with young children. In the present political environment, the government is essentially adopting the position that the labor of raising and nurturing children is of no legitimate value. In other historical periods, some mothers of young children were seen as deserving of aid.

Secondly, there are precious few other suppliers of financial aid. Some respond to this claim by referring to the many charitable organizations. However, if all poor people had to rely upon charity these organizations would be quickly swamped. Indeed, they are already swamped even with government aid. If charity could solve the poverty problem, why are there so many poor people?

Third, poor people lack the power with which to force the government to give adequate aid without stigmatization. Some people clearly are able to influence the government, but not poor people. They lack the necessary resources. They have not the money to make political donations. They do not have a lobby in Washington. They would find it very difficult to "March on Washington" in protest, lacking adequate transportation. No, the poor are reduced to begging politicians on whatever terms will be granted.

Lastly, and most importantly, the aid is absolutely necessary for survival. Who can live without food, shelter, and other basics such as heat, electricity, and clean water? Imagine having the power to decide, virtually, whether the people in your charge will eat, or have a place to live, or heat in the winter, or clothes. The conservative argument is that people should be responsible for themselves. However, as a society, do we expect children, the elderly, and disabled persons to be responsible for self-sufficient?

Whether or not the poor person can remove the condition of dependence upon the government depends greatly on the manner in which the surrounding social environment is structured. Poor people lack the networks of influence others frequently take advantage of: voting, partisanship, interest groups, political action committees, family background, institutional position, or money. Social power is embedded in and characteristic of the social structure. Therefore, the organization of the social setting is of paramount importance if the analyst is to understand how power works. We will consider the issue of whether or not everyone has equal access to voting later in the chapter.

Political policy, then, is not only inevitable; it is a necessity. After all, if poverty is an aspect of capitalism, and it is, then dealing with its worst effects will be a matter of government social policy. Actors and charities without the power of the government are not likely to systematically end poverty or alleviate its effects for large numbers of poor.

Let us begin with a simple two-person discussion of power. In this situation, the "**ordinate**" is the sender or user of power and the "**subordinate**" the receiver. The subordinate experiences the effects of power when forced to do something they would not ordinarily do. A common situation of this sort arises in the teacher-student social setting. In fact, the ordinate may not even realize that they are forcing the subordinate to do something they normally would not. In order for graduate students to complete their Ph.D. program successfully, they frequently must write a thesis. They depend upon the advice and input of their faculty advisers. This is a **power-relationship**. Students are commonly prevailed upon to help their advisors complete research. Although they may be busy working on their dissertation and be under strain trying to fulfill all their other roles, they often hesitate to refuse. Why? One, they need the advisor's help and cannot graduate without the advisor signing off. Two, they have nothing else to reciprocate except their labor. Three, there are no other faculty to advise them and perhaps they cannot choose another because it would violate the rules and regulations. Four, without the help and consent of the advisor they cannot graduate. Perhaps a little extra research would not be that much of a burden, but small tasks quickly become larger ones. What if the ordinate preferred sexual access rather than help with research? The conditions of dependency would still apply.

267

When power is used, it involves a transaction rather than choices freely made by both the ordinate and subordinate. It may appear, especially to the ordinate, that the student voluntarily acquiesces to the request. It may even appear to the student that the arrangement is equitable. However, this is only an illusion. None of the four conditions is fundamentally altered. If the four conditions are clearly coercive when the ordinate wants to trade grades for sex, they are no less coercive when the issue is a little research. The fundamental basis of the relationship does not change—the student has less power than the teacher does. Moreover, the disparities of power are likely to be more apparent to the subordinate than they are to the ordinate. Thus, it is not possible to understand power by examining only either the ordinate or subordinate. Neither can power be understood as people only making choices on a more or less equal footing. Clearly, in the educational social setting teachers have more power than their students do. These power differentials exist in every social setting, at church, at work, in the home, and at school. If there is a choice for subordinates, it may be to risk dire consequences. People can and do make these choices. However, it is hard to see how power can be understood as subordinates having the "power" to choose job loss, demotions, hunger, or even death. These are not really choices in the sense that one could choose to accept or reject a promotion at work.

The sociologist Simmel noted that the simplest power-relationship is a **dyad**. It takes at least two people for a power-transaction to occur. Without slaves there are no masters; without sinners there are no saints. A considerable amount of politics goes into power-transactions. For instance, the teacher must be careful in using power. There are some important considerations to ponder. A take-it-or-leave-it or do-it-or-else approach may result in the student choosing or-else. How should the request be framed? How much power is enough? What type of power expenditure is appropriate or sufficient? These are important questions which ordinates are faced with whether they realize it or not. Power is frequently wielded in transactions involving more than two people.

Person-to-Person Power. One particular type of micro-level power is known as **person-to-person power**. This type of power involves the use of expertise, coercion, reward, charisma, and authority, in face-to-face social settings where someone is trying to exert power over another individual. Ordinates may use their expertise and (presumed) knowledge when trying to convince others to adopt their position. Of course, it is always helpful if subordinates believe the ordinate *is* an expert. **Coercive power** is the threat of or use of sanctions. For example, a teacher may suggest that the student who balks at completing the research requested will get a poor or failing grade, or not receive funding or an assistantship. In other situations, the threat may entail the loss of a job, promotion, or pay-raise. Again, this type of power-transaction can only be successful if the subordinate believes that the ordinate actually has the power to enforce the sanction. In addition to this, the threat must truly be threatening. The threat to look unfavorably upon someone who refuses to grant the request to complete research is likely to cause less fear than the threat of a poor or failing grade.

Sometimes ordinates decide to use **reward power**—the use of attractive inducements, such as promotions, pay-raises, or even a pat on the back to achieve their goal. Frequently these are quid-pro-quo arrangements in which a favor or request is granted by the subordinate for a reciprocal favor from the ordinate in the future. These types of arrangements are common among relative equals. Politicians are particularly fond of reward power. For example, one legislator may agree to support someone else's bill in return for support for his or her own. Presidents may reward legislators who display a pattern of supportive votes with financial backing for favored programs or other similar arrangements.

Charismatic power exists when the personal attributes of an individual, such as persuasiveness or leadership ability, is the basis of their power. A good many political leaders have displayed this particular quality. Adolph Hitler, Franklin D. Roosevelt, Martin Luther King, and John F. Kennedy, for example, all were charismatic leaders. Charismatic leaders frequently consolidate other types of power in their hands. Additionally, some people may be awed by the fact that an individual simply occupies a very high social position. Presidents may be admired simply due to the charisma of the office.

Person-to-person power can also be used when the ordinate gives instructions or presentations to the larger group. A teacher may say to the class "this is an important point to take note of and those who do will get a better grade" (reward power). In addition, the teacher may say, "test scores are falling and this negatively affects our national standing" (coercive power). Sometimes person-to-person power flows through third parties. This is the case when one legislator asks another to find others to support a piece of legislation he or she has written.

The successful use of person-to-power depends upon some important factors. It is most effective when the ordinate selects the type of power the subordinate is most likely to respond to. For instance, a subordinate may be more likely to acquiesce to an ordinate's request if they are receptive to the ordinate's expertise. The same person may be unreceptive to coercion. Additionally, knowing which type of power to employ requires that the ordinate know the subordinates whom they are seeking to influence. To be successful, the ordinate not only has to choose the appropriate type of power but must also apply it skillfully. Power transactions can frequently be used in tandem—reward power may be reinforced with expertise power, for instance.

Substantive Power. **Substantive power** refers to the ability of policy makers to shape the content of social policy or to appeal for support from others. This type of power is used on a daily basis in the Congress of the United States. Frequently people either support or oppose a social policy due to its substantive content. For example, it is well documented that the nutrition program Women-Infants-and Children (WIC), while intended to help poor women and their children, reaches women of even moderate income. The program has been truly successful. Some might argue that one of the reasons for the success is precisely because it benefited middle class women. Consider this—a social policy may be proposed that is intended to help provide good nutrition to impoverished mothers and their infant children. The "content" of such a social program would, as you may guess, immediately appeal to the champions of the poor. On the other hand, to those who feel that such forms of welfare are a disincentive to work, the "content" of the social program may be offensive. One way around this dilemma is to write the program such that it benefits a wider range of the population. The broader the popular support for a program is the less able politicians are to defeat it. Another way around the substantive content issues is to leave the wording vague, so that the intended beneficiaries are harder to label. It should be noted that both conservatives and liberals frequently employ these tactics.

Policy makers use substantive power when they add or delete content to a social policy in an effort to win support. Policy makers often insert content deliberately designed to gain support from the opposition. Such tactics can occur during the drafting process, during the discussions and debates, and even on the floor of the Congress. Give-and-take is characteristic of substantive power. One component of the policy may be rescinded in order to win over opponents of another component. Conversely, policy makers may decide to include a component they are not really in favor of in the process of making compromises. Frequently, these deals are reciprocal—opponents agree to support a social policy if some of their components are included.

One rather obvious problem with substantive power is that the deal making and concession granting may dilute the social policy to the point where it bears little resemblance to the original program. When this happens, the legislation is merely symbolic. Often such social policies lack sufficient "teeth" to be effect and frequently lack any specific requirements. Such criticism is often aimed at agencies created by politicians in Washington. The Environmental Protection Agency and the Food and Drug Agency have both been accused of being staffed by the people and corporations they are supposed to regulate. Another criticism is that they lack sufficient enforcement power. It is not at all uncommon to discover that the officials in charge of such regulatory agencies are drawn from the very sectors of the economy they are supposed to regulate. Another problem with substantive power is that excessive compromising may alienate one power block or another. To avoid these pitfalls, it is necessary for policy makers to stick to their original content unless specific compromises are needed to ensure its passage.

An all too common tactic that involves the use of substantive power is the attachment of riders to other legislation Congress either is in a hurry to finish or is of great importance. These riders are often relatively unpopular proposals that the author's attempt to attach to important bills. President Clinton often vetoed very popular bills sent up by Congress due to the attachment of riders he felt were not in the best interests of the nation or otherwise could not be passed on their own merits. Indeed, one such attempt by the Republican controlled congress led to the shutdown of the federal government for a number of days. The Republican strategy backfired when they lost their overwhelming majority in the House of Representatives in the following election. Apparently, the average voter was able to see through the naked use of substantive power they attempted. President Bush has yet to veto a single piece of legislation, possibly because, as of this writing, his political party controls all branches of the national government.

The political struggles involving substantive power can become quite ridiculous, in spite of the seriousness of the issues they deal with. Newt Gingrich, perhaps the most detested politician who ever presided over the House of Representatives, was extremely adept at using substantive power. The author of the "Contract with America," or "Contract on America," depending upon who one listened to, was able to pass sweeping tax and welfare reforms. Although it helped that

Republicans held an almost veto-proof majority in Congress, one tactic was simply to name the bill in as inoffensive manner as possible. Even today, several years later, most people do not realize that Welfare, or Aid to Families with Dependent Children, no longer exists as a federal entitlement program. Many people do not realize that women who have children out-of-wedlock can never receive federal assistance, or use subsidized housing. Most people might feel that punishing children for the bad judgment of their parent is pushing the matter too far. However, if you call the legislation the "Wage Enhancement and Personal Responsibility Act" people may not bother to look at the details. After all, who is not for higher wages and personal responsibility? With such a broad based title, the public is not apt to figure out that the already affluent would have their taxes cut and wages increased, at the expense of average wage earners, and that the act would be punitive to children. The ink was hardly dry on the bill before 1.2 million additional children were pushed into poverty due to the loss of their federal entitlements.

This legislation elicited a debate almost never heard in modern politics—basic principles of each party. Captivated audiences watched with horror, or perhaps elation, depending, as fistfights broke out in the halls of Congress, involving Congressmen no less. After many years of languishing, Democrats were proudly talking about democratic principles. Something the "new" democrats, such as President Clinton, eschewed, given the conservative mood the nation seemed to be in. Unfortunately, the Democrats failed to convince the president to veto the Welfare reform act. This brings up two related points. First, the president had campaigned on a policy of welfare reform and he would seem to be backing down if he vetoed the bill. Therefore, the Republican timing was right. Secondly, successful policy makers almost never talk about basic principles. It is beyond doubt that valuable allies, in this case moderate Republicans, were alienated by the indignant behavior of the Democrats. Remaining noncommittal concerning basic principles often allows politicians and policy makers to focus on the details of the legislation.

Procedural Power. In the political realm, **procedural power** is perhaps the oldest type of power. The course of a bill making its way through Congress can be quite complex, involving a mapped out chain of discussions. On the way to becoming a law, a bill passes through a sequence of committees and numerous discussions. For example:

- When legislative proposals are introduced in the House, the bill is assigned to a specific committee.

- This committee assigns the bill to a subcommittee.

- When the subcommittee's work is finished, the committee approves a final version of the bill. If a conflict cannot be resolved, the bill is returned to the subcommittee until a resolution is reached.

- The rules of debate are decided.

- The committee version of the bill is forwarded to the full House.

- The bill is considered, amended, and, if passed in the House forwarded to the Senate.

- Steps 1 – 7 are repeated in the Senate and if the bill is passed, it is forwarded to the conference committee, which attempts to resolve the differences between the House and Senate versions.

- A House-Senate conference committee is established.

- The House-Senate version of the bill is established.

- The bill is sent back to the House and Senate to ratify the conference version.

- If both the House and Senate pass the bill, it is forwarded to the President to sign.

- If the President signs the bill, it becomes law.

One can only marvel that any proposed legislation becomes law. No wonder, then, that by the time a bill becomes law it can be so diluted as to be merely symbolic.

There are numerous openings in this complex process for the use of procedural power. Many parliamentary strategies exist for circumventing some of the steps along the way. One strategy is to attempt to route the proposal to more favorable committees and try to bypass certain people and committees who may be unfavorable to the legislation. A "steering committee" may attempt to follow such a plan. Frequently, then, specific proposals can be considered by any number of committees. The trick will be to "steer" the legislation to a committee that is favorably disposed to it. In these situations, person-to-person power can be used to good advantage by locating, in the procedural power hierarchy, strategically located individuals who can make such decisions.

A chairperson, or other important person on a specific committee, can be instrumental to a bill's success or defeat. Some chairs prevent bills from moving through the process if they are opposed to them. Frequently, this happens when the president has nominated someone to head a branch of the government and the Congress needs to confirm the candidate. Thus, the chairperson can obstruct the bill, place the bill in favored subcommittee, put it in a favored place on the agenda, and even shorten discussions concerning the bill. Simply being aware of the parliamentary procedures involved is also a form of procedural power. Procedural strategists can be quite adept at maneuvering bills, outflanking opponents, amending, sidetracking, and blocking opponents by manipulating parliamentary procedures.

One important aspect of procedural power is that when one party or the other holds the majority they are able to capture important seats on the various committees. During the early years of the Regan administration, for example, Republicans occupied the chairs of the important committees due to their majority. As already mentioned, the various committees can establish the rules by which they operate and the rule under which debate concerning legislation will occur. This situation inherently gave the Republicans greater procedural power than the Democrats. Thus, the Republicans in Congress and the Republican President were able to cooperate closely and pass bills that were favored by the administration. It is not surprising that legislation proposed by Democrats frequently failed to make it out of subcommittees even when the bills had popular support. This is why it is of primary importance to each party to control the Congress—the party that has the majority captures the important positions and the power that goes with them.

In every agency, not just Congress, the procedures for decision-making run the gamut from simple to complex. In a simple situation, a chief-executive-officer may simply institute a new policy. In a more complex situation, a staff member may propose a new program for the agency. In this case, a subcommittee may be formed to look at the proposal and make recommendations. The subcommittee may report back to the full committee before the proposal is presented to the board. The board may refer it to a board subcommittee. In many situations, therefore, the complex procedures found in the political arena are mirrored in the public and private arenas as well.

Process Power. **Process power** is used by policy makers when they try to shape the give-and-take of policy deliberations. This refers to the tenor, tempo, and scope of policy discussions. Tenor describes the level or intensity of conflict; tempo describes the pace, timing, and duration of the discussions; and scope of conflict refers to the numbers and types of individuals involved in the policy discussions. Process power, then, is used when policy makers attempt to control the tenor, tempo, and scope of policy discussions in ways that are to their advantage.

The parties involved in a dispute, for example, must give some thought to the process itself. In any conflict, the parties must develop their positions and decide how they want to resolve their difficulties. At what level of intensity should one press their point or position? Should the debate be resolved relatively quickly or should a lengthy battle ensue? Shall the opponent be bullied or finessed? How many people should be involved in the conflict?

If you are a parent, perhaps you have already experienced most, if not all, of the elements of process power when you attended parent-teacher conferences. It would be surprising if more than a handful of parents recognized that the conference is as much a power struggle as anything else. The struggle is essentially over **defining the situation**—the educational experience of your child. Think about the situation itself. Legitimate authority is granted to the teacher, not the parent or child. Most discussions center on such issues as the child's motivation, where the child can improve, behavior problems, and so on. The mere mention that the fault may lie with the teacher or school system is enough to invoke a conflict. Teachers and administrators, having legitimate power over your child, do not like to have their failings pointed out. It is not supposed to work that way—the child is supposed to be to blame for his or her failings.

On the other hand, teachers and administrators are quick to take credit for success, and discussions about the motivational levels of students hardly enter the debate. In the case of success, the focus is not on highly motivated students but on successful programs. In the case of failure, the focus is always on students rather than teachers, administrators, or programs. It seems rather obvious that if a good educational program can produce successful students a poor educational program may produce individual failures. Conversely, if some students succeed regardless of the educational program, good or bad, highly motivated students may still succeed when the educational program is flawed.

The point is that before a parent ever sits down to a conference with his or her child's teacher, the situation, which is inherently conflictual, has already been manipulated to favor the teacher's definition of the situation. The conflictual aspects of the interaction never become apparent to most people due to the adeptness of teachers at managing the tenor, tempo, and scope of the conference. A teacher skilled at using process power will make sure that the interaction occurs very quickly; say within ten minutes. This ensures that there will not be enough time for either the parent or the teacher to cover potentially sticky issues. By "sticky," we mean issues on which the parent may question the teacher's definition of the situation. If everything happens rather quickly, the likelihood that significant conflict will arise is greatly reduced. Moreover, no topic will be covered substantially, again, reducing the likelihood of conflict.

Secondly, teachers skilled in process power maintain an authoritative tone (tenor)—they are the experts. A teacher who is good at using process power will turn the parent into a student. If there is a problem they will try to teach the parent how to parent, how to help their child, or if there is a behavioral problem what to do about it. Most parents willingly accept the role during the conference. Thirdly, teachers will try to restrict the scope of the conference by focusing on only one or two things that your child either does very well or needs to improve. Most parents may think that attending parent-teacher conferences gets them involved in their child's education. Nothing could be further from the truth.

A parent who bucks the process and insinuates that the blame lies either with the teacher or with the system is likely to face the full weight of the education system as the administration closes ranks to protect the teacher. The teacher may express surprise at your attitude (tenor). Very quickly, the principal will get involved in the conflict. Usually the principal will adopt a tenor that suggests that they are reasonable but the parent is not. They may point out that no one has complained before or that the community supports the educational program, in general, and thus, the particular teacher specifically. Additionally, the scope of the conflict is likely to increase, as the school will involve the teacher, the principal, a counselor, and perhaps even a lawyer, if your tone warrants it. Once again, they will try to manipulate the process to marginalize the parent and protect themselves. Imagine yourself in such a situation, you will be on one side of the table, nearly helpless, and they will be on the other. You could decide, of course, to change your tone, say by yelling at them. You could increase the scope by hiring a lawyer to sue them. Either side could increase the duration of the interaction through litigation. Usually, however, the parent will be dismissed as abusive or irrational and most parents lack the power to do much about it.

The timing of a policy proposal may be crucial. The success of the Republicans in getting President Clinton to sign a welfare reform act, which was not much to the liking of the Democratic Party, was largely a matter of timing. The Republicans were able to capitalize on one of Clinton's campaign promises. Not to pass the act would have been to surrender the debate to the Republicans in spite of the fact that social programs have been associated with the Democrats for decades. On the other hand, if a program is proposed at the wrong time no matter how skilled its backers or what its merits are, it will probably be doomed to fail. Background factors such as budget deficits, an uncooperative executive, or a full agenda can provide a harsh environment for a policy proposal. However, policy proposals, which may not have had much of a chance of success in earlier periods, may find the going easier at a later time.

Most policy makers have only limited ability and power to influence the political process. A policy maker may try to use process power by limiting conflict but this goal could be sabotaged when opponents escalate conflict. No doubt, the Bush administration has tried to limit the scope of conflict by attempting to keep the media in the dark about the various scandals swirling around the White House. President Clinton attempted the same thing in relation to the Lewinski scandal. However, both were unable to keep the scandals from escalating or to stop their detractors from making an issue out of them. In President Clinton's case, the Health Care Reform task force faced the same problem with the insurance industry, which stood to lose a great deal of their profits. The insurance lobby was successfully able to turn a national debate concerning the quality of health care into a debate as to whether or not the nation would be saddled with a "Canadian" style health care system. Additionally, the Clinton administration was unable to stop the momentum the insurance lobby built. Before long, the scope of the conflict increased and the task force came under fire from every quarter, the media, doctors, and special interest groups. Most of these groups had nothing to gain from health care reform, although the average citizen did, and everything to lose. Thus, when the status quo is likely to be upset on a grand scale by social policy it is hard to maintain control of the debate, it quickly devolves into polarization between groups.

Autonomous Power. Sometimes an individual can be said to have power when they resist another's attempt to control them or influence their actions and behavior. This is called **autonomous power**. It is one thing to talk about the power to create social policy at the national level and the power to set the agenda at the level of the agency, but at the micro-level, for example, individuals have more leeway than one would imagine when it comes to "interpreting" the rules. The theory of social-construction holds that no one is simply a blank slate upon which to write rules. Social workers in the field may decide to *interpret* the rules in a manner that favors their clients even though national politicians are trying to get people off the welfare roles. The field is a long way from Washington and many policy practitioners are going to be relatively autonomous in situations where they object to the stated policy objectives and goals. We now consider the many ways in which power operates at the national level.

THE NATIONAL POWER STRUCTURE

There are numerous theories regarding the national power structure of the United States. One theory holds that the majority can only ignore various minorities at their own peril. In other words, minorities can force the majority to be sensitive to their issues. Another theoretical perspective indicates that there is a "power elite" or "ruling class" which uses national politics as a tool to ensure that their interests are protected. Others believe that the United States is more pluralistic, a number of power-blocs which must form coalitions in order to gain power and no one bloc can maintain control for very long.

Three perspectives dominate the debate concerning the national power structure:

1) the pluralist,

2) the power elite, and

3) the ruling class perspectives.

The major issue and point of difference between the three perspectives is the degree to which power is concentrated.   There are, thus, two basic views regarding the power structure—the pluralist version and the elitist version, the power elite and the ruling class being somewhat similar. The analysis now moves to a discussion of each and the empirical evidence.

The Pluralist Perspective.   In civics classes, high school students are taught that in the United States the people have ultimate power.   They elect politicians to represent them.   In this view the will of the majority prevails, people are equal before the law, and decisions are made in the interest of the common good.   The United States is not a direct democracy—it is a representative democracy.   In our political system, decisions are made by some very powerful people at the top of the political hierarchy.   The pluralist position argues that there are a large number of groups and organizations in the nation that compete for power and that no one group holds power all of the time.   Each group is relatively autonomous and pursues interests independently of the others. Rather than cooperating with each other they compete for power, thus there is no dominant inner circle or select group of powerful individuals.   The goals of each group are narrow.   The important point is that since their goals differ, even if a group has a great deal of power over a narrow set of issues, there are many other issues and groups over which they have no particular power. Therefore, while it is possible that such groups have contact with each other their contact deals with specific issues rather than political cooperation.   Balance is maintained because power shifts from one group today to another tomorrow.   Individuals, who wish, may become members of one or another of the competing groups.   The notion that power is shared among competing interest groups is widely held.

Most pluralist theories share the following four core ideas:

- Power is not concentrated in the hands of a few elites but shared by a plurality of groups, individuals, and organizations.

279

- These groups enjoy relative autonomy—they have influence over a narrow set of issues and are interested in national policy, which directly involves their issues.

- Through membership in such groups, average citizens can enjoy input in national politics. Additionally, individuals can count on journalists and academics to keep them informed.

- Balance is achieved because power is distributed among different groups.

The major assumption, which underlies the pluralist view, is that society is based on a broad set of shared values—i.e., consensus on important issues. However, pluralism pays scant attention to the issue of power. Thus, powerlessness, and the related social ills, does not appear to be a major concern. If the institutions of society, particularly the political institutions, are regarded as providing major benefits for society the assumption is that they should not be toyed with in any significant fashion, according to pluralism. The focus will be on reform of social systems rather than revolutionizing them. Thus, pluralism tends to be rather conservative.

Perhaps pluralism is popular because it offers something to everyone. There is a dualistic picture offered by the pluralists—on one side is the tough world of politics where different interest groups compete for power, and on the other are the relatively content and amicable citizens. The complexity of United States society allows for numerous examples of competition between powerful groups in different circumstances. The extremely public battles between the pro-life and pro-choice faction regarding abortion is a good example. This type of pluralism postulates that there are indefinite numbers of interest groups dispersed throughout the population that can exert power—not just political, economic, or military elites.

Another variation of the pluralist model suggests that the existence of **strategic elites** is inevitable, considering the high degree of complexity and differentiation in modern society. Strategic elites perform coordinating functions for society that serve the common good and achieve collective aims and goals. What prevents strategic elites from becoming power elites is their narrow knowledge specialization—they have social impact only in a small arena of social life. Strategic elites are to be found in the military, politics, and economy, naturally, but also in academia, journalism, cultural occupations, and a host of other fields. The sheer number, specialization, and narrow interests of strategic elites preclude the possibility of cooperation and the formation of a power bloc. However, this does not account for the degree of importance each of the strategic elites enjoys, or what happens when strategic elites find themselves either united by an issue or at odds over an issue.

The most modern versions of pluralism attempt to recognize that certain social agents, large corporations in particular, hold inordinate power, while at the same time preserving the four major postulates of pluralism. There is no denying that corporations have become so powerful as to challenge most groups in competition for power. Clearly, some groups are more powerful than others are. New-pluralism, however, stresses that what is more important are the "veto-powers" of the various competing power blocs. These power blocs exist within every institution of society—the military, police, armed forces, government, industry, business, law, education, medicine, and so on. Each group primarily seeks to achieve their goals and protect their interests. Thus, the issue at hand determines which group (or groups) is active. Balance between the competing groups is achieved when each group moves into action to protect its interests from encroachment by other groups. Each group appeals to the citizenry for support on their issues.

Worker and civic consciousness concerning the power of corporations has increased. More and more, people are calling for equity in the distribution of power and increased control over corporations, especially multinational corporations. This new type of pluralism is critical of the distribution of power, stresses major structural reforms, a redistribution of wealth and income, and more government ownership of private enterprise.

Modern pluralists are convinced that equity in the distribution of power is a necessity for democracy. However, in the final analysis, the "new pluralism" still refuses to recognize the importance of social class in discussions of power differentials. Without an analysis of social class, the ironic result is that modern pluralism winds up supporting many of the aspects of the present system which lead to the conditions they are concerned about, i.e., the growing power of corporations.

The new-pluralist model does not deny the existence of a number of sectors of power, or that the upper class controls each sector. However, pluralists insist that the upper class is not a unified group of people. Because each power sector has different interests, there is plenty of room for conflict and competition. This is the basis of their claim that power is not concentrated within one social class but is correlated with issues and shifting coalitions.

Detractors and critics of pluralism abound. Perhaps the most important criticism of pluralism is the question of whether or not democracy is really alive let alone well in the United States. As evidence that something is amiss, critics of pluralism often point out that the government is not really representing everyone's interests. Many people are not in a position to make their interests known to the government, while, on the other hand, economic elites command vast power and influence over the government. People who hold economic and social positions of power, and share a value-system with those in Washington, stand a much better chance of having their interests heard and protected. Large groups of people, such as the homeless, the poor, and children, are nearly invisible to policy makers in Washington.

Other serious criticisms are related to the idealistic aspects of pluralism. Does power really shift from one power bloc to another, or is one power sector more likely to be in control than the others are? Do interest groups really balance each other out? For example, is the Children's Defense Fund, one of the only national-level organizations that represent the interests of poor children in Washington, equal in power to American Association of Retired Persons (AARP)? Are family farmers and the voluntary associations that represent their interests equal to the power of Allied Fruit or Archer Daniels Midlands? It does not seem legitimate to claim that the power of multinational corporations is balanced by the interests of small voluntary associations.

Another criticism of pluralism notes that the voluntary associations, which were once effective in representing the interests of average citizens, have themselves become oligarchic in nature. In other words, even in these organizations power is concentrated at the top among a handful of individuals. Thus, those in positions of power in organizations are not very representative of their membership. The membership lacks any significant power. Lastly, pluralism ignores the values and biases that are built into the political system.

It is probably not logical to dismiss pluralism entirely. Even a cursory examination of the Civil Rights Movement, for example, will highlight the ability of coalitions of voluntary associations to seek power and compete with other powerful agents in society. We must conclude that it is indeed possible for competition between different sectors of power to exist. Sometimes legislators do attempt to represent the interests of their constituencies. Nevertheless, the most resounding criticism of pluralism is that the leaders in each sector of power overwhelmingly come from the elite classes.

The Power Elite Perspective. The elitist versions of the national power distribution are similar to Marx's theoretical positions. Marx held that every society needed an economic foundation and that the unequal distribution of rewards created the stratification system. Private ownership of property allows the economic elite to control the economy and, in turn, to influence government decisions and actions. According to Marx, this constitutes a ruling class. The elite have many tools at hand by which to control the masses, including religion, the mass media, and control of the state. Perhaps the most effective type of control, however, is achieved through ideology. The elite class attempts to present their particular class interests as the general interest, that which is in the best interests of society as a whole. There is general agreement among Marxists that the elite class controls the state. What Marxists are less likely to agree on is how it is accomplished.

From the **instrumentalist perspective**, the ruling class becomes dominant by using money and institutional and social influence to control politicians. Those at the top of the corporate power structure and those at the top of the political power structure share a common social background and worldview. The instrumentalist view notes that people in positions of power, strategically located in the political power structure, can manipulate state policies, directly or indirectly by virtue of their positions. Power, then, is instrumentally exercised. The government is an instrument used by the elites to achieve their goals.

The **structuralist perspective** is another way Marxists theorize about the ruling class. From this perspective, the location of individuals in the political power structure who serve the interests of the elites is not important. Structuralists point to the nature and organization of the economy as the primary manner in which elites control the government. Regardless of whether or not corporate leaders act to directly or indirectly influence the state, the state has no choice but to serve their interests since the economy is structured such that a small concentration of families and individuals virtually owns it. Ownership of the means of production is highly concentrated. Thus, almost any action the government takes to safeguard the health of the economy, indirectly at least, serves the interests of the elite. This does not mean that the elites do not actively seek to influence the state. The structuralist perspective points out that elites need not play an active role in seeking to preserve or widen their interests—the system is biased in their favor in any event.

C. Wright Mills.   Mills was very critical of Marxism. Nevertheless, his views concerning the power elite fall within the structuralist camp. Mills held that three sectors in society were very important in terms of their power: the military, the executive branch of government, and the corporate rich. According to Mills, the leaders of these three sectors of power combine to form a **power elite** that makes all the important decisions.

The position of Mills has perhaps never been as crystal clear as currently. The discussions and ultimate decision to invade Iraq, as it turns out, were made largely out of view of the public and intimately involved select members of the executive branch of the government, corporate leaders, and military leaders. In addition, the invasion of Iraq is not the only recent incidence of a power elite directing political decisions behind the scenes. It is now common knowledge that select members of the energy sector of the economy met with Vice-President Cheney and had a direct hand in writing the nation's energy policy. The recent conviction of several prominent legislators for fraud, in relationship to lobbying, is strong evidence that a power elite of well-placed individuals attempts to control public policy in secret.

The notion of a power elite differs radically from the pluralist conceptions of power. This idea of a power elite has a rich history in social science, dating back to the works of Mosca and Pareto. Mosca wrote that an elite group dominates every society. Therefore, democracy, in which power is distributed throughout the citizenry, is unattainable. In large societies the ruling group could be very small because the larger the political community the smaller the numbers of representatives, proportionally. This makes it difficult for ordinary people to organize against the elite. Mosca is clearly referring to the "structure" of democracy and political representation. A society with a large population that relies on representative democracy will elect only a tiny minority of the population to govern. If those political representatives are chosen from one stratum in society, the upper class, then the obvious result will be the formation of a power elite.

The **"Iron Law of Oligarchy,"** which every social organization succumbs to, guarantees that an elite will rule. Oligarchy is necessary because of the complexity of society and the need for efficient government and social organization. Democracy cannot escape oligarchy any more than other forms of government. Additionally, political leaders tend to possess unique qualities and skills, learned while governing, which are irreplaceable. Pareto's theory, known as the "circulation of elites," held that there is always a small group of elites who rule. Elitism, according to Pareto, referred to those who were best in their respective fields. Pareto held that the ruling group usually contains both elite and non-elite members.

The power elite theory developed by C. Wright Mills represents the best example of a theory intended to oppose pluralist ideas. Mills' central thesis is quite easy to understand—power is centralized in the offices of a select group of people at the top of the power hierarchy, a **power elite**. Mills did not buy the pluralist argument that a system of checks and balances existed in the United States. To adopt the pluralist position, according to Mills, was to neglect the fact that power is unequally distributed and disputes over power can be quite confrontational. Two essential assumptions on which pluralism is based, which define social relationships, are consensus and harmony. The pluralists tend to emphasize that there is a large degree of harmony of interest and consensus about what those interests are. Mills rejected those assumptions.

Mills felt that the development of a power elite was the result of historical processes and changes. As society develops, its institutions become more complex. Additionally, the business of governing becomes more centralized in specific institutions—the military, the economy, and the polity. Mills pointed out that the tasks in the most powerful positions of these institutions have become so similar that those in the top positions are interchangeable. The people at the top of the three power hierarchies have coalesced into one power elite, due to the historical processes of centralization and interchangeability. Thus, the power elite is composed of the most powerful actors located in the military, political, and economic institutions, who move in the same circles, have a set of overlapping concerns, share decision-making, and reach decisions with national implications. The heart of the power elite are those individuals who hold high positions in more than one of the three major institutions, along with the lawyers and financiers who knit the three institutions together.

Some individuals come to mind—the President, the Secretary of Defense, the Secretary of State, and the Secretary of the Treasury, to name only a few. The Secretary of the Treasury, for example, is typically chosen from the ranks of financiers and frequently from the nation's top universities. It is not at all unusual for high-ranking officers from the Pentagon, who have experience in awarding lucrative weapons contracts to certain industries, to find themselves on the corporate boards of those very same industries. Many legislators who have political expertise in one area or another related to defense or the economy, upon leaving public office, waste no time finding jobs in the consulting industry. The phenomenon of interchangeability of top positions in business, defense, and government is called the **revolving door.**

The power these individuals have is associated with their positions in the national power structure, rather than any particular personal characteristics. Nevertheless, these individuals do share some important social similarities. For one thing, they tend to come from the same social and educational backgrounds. That is to say that they spend a lot of time intermingling with each other. They come from the upper class, attend the same private boarding schools, and go on to attend the same Ivy League universities. Not everyone in public service, of course, comes from this particular background. However, the higher up in the power echelons analysts look the more likely powerful individuals share important social characteristics.

Mills felt that the power elite is composed of individuals who not only know they are powerful, and are therefore conscious of their power, but are also relatively cohesive. They share three important characteristics: psychological similarity, social interaction, and coinciding interests. Institutions have a way of shaping the values of the people who are positioned within them. Military personnel, obviously, are socialized by their interactions within the institution. However, every institution has customs and norms that shape its members. In addition to their institutional roles, elites also share similar social origins and lifestyles. Since the elite are involved in institutions that have overlapping interests, they move in the same circles. They are conscious of themselves as an upper class. The bond that glues the elite together is their common economic interest. The most basic interest is maintenance of the capitalist system, which infers a requisite interest in keeping their dominant positions. The government, as well as multinational corporations, depends upon the military for defense. Corporate interests are very willing to sell weapons systems to the military for a profit. Other corporations have large holdings abroad and expect the government to make decisions beneficial for them. For these reasons, according to Mills, the powerful actors in the three sectors will coordinate their activities and efforts.

Mills believed that the higher reaches of the power structure were more corruptible. This is because, given the way institutions are structured, certain individuals have the opportunity to take advantage of others. In other words, highly placed individuals can take advantage of their positions to seek their own goals. In the relationship between campaign financing and wealth, for instance, there are structural paths that allow the funneling of money to candidates. Money, when combined with the structural paths (legal mechanism and campaign finance loopholes), can influence the political and intellectual position of people in power. Additionally, Mills believed that mediocrity and cynicism had replaced talent, skill, and independent thinking. Increasing urbanization and improved transportation and communication have shifted power away from the local level to the national level.

Mills placed Congress on a lower level in terms of the national power scale. After the executive branch, the corporate rich, and the military, are the leaders of special interest groups. Below these individuals, but above the unorganized masses, are congressional leaders. Those in Congress, particularly in the House of Representatives, are concerned with local issues and constituencies, not to mention reelection, rather than issues of real national importance. Other groups, such as those associated with labor unions and professional organizations, also have little to do with national policy. Mills assigned these groups and Congress specifically, to the middle-levels of power. If pluralism exists at all, according to Mills, it is at the level of power, where competing interest groups come together in an effort to influence the political process. However, above this level of power exists a much more profound type of power. The power to control the economic growth of the nation, the power to wage wars and conduct covert, sometime illegal, operations against sovereign nations, and the power to make decisions which affect every single citizen.

At the bottom of the power structure are the majority of ordinary citizens. The masses are on the receiving end of the political decisions and, for the most part, have no voice in the discussions that concern them. This is easy to see for people on public assistance and children. The powerless have long been excluded from debates concerning their needs. However, Mills felt that even the middle class lacked any significant outlet for their political aspirations or desires. This is accomplished by the mass media, which tells the masses how to interpret political policy. This does not mean that people fail to think critically about issues. It does mean that ordinary citizens are increasingly isolated and detached from the political decision making process and have no outlet for effective action.

12 | Power: Forcing Us to Give Them What They Want.
by Frank O. Taylor, IV, Ph.D.

One sure sign of political detachment and alienation is the declining rates of voting. Mills felt that an education, far from improving the situation, only helped the alienated middle class adjust to their new circumstances.

Mills did not believe that there was a conspiracy being conducted by a handful of very powerful individuals who wanted to control the political process. The development of a power structure is the result of specific historical and structural events. These events occurred after the New Deal. One important reason for the development of the power elite was World War II. The war required a reorganization of the military, polity, and economy. The national government practically had dictatorial powers. Indeed, Mills is not alone in voicing concerns regarding the power elite. Before leaving office, President Eisenhower voiced much the same concern as regards to the military-industrial complex. After WWII, the cold war and fear of communism kept the nation from shifting back to a peacetime economy. Due to such factors, then, the military, polity, and economy became more centralized and decisions made in each domain, while affecting every citizen, also affected the other domains. Therefore, the key leaders of each domain felt it in their best interests to cooperate.

Two important and related factors helped bring about the emergence of the power elite. First, the means of power and violence are much greater and more concentrated than at any time in the past. Second, they are more centralized. In the military, decisions are more and more centralized. The economy, through mergers, interlocking directorates and takeovers, has shifted from large numbers of relatively autonomous businesses to higher levels of concentration. Today, a mere 200 giant corporations dominate the economy. The advances in transportation and communication have made it possible for people in the political, economic, and military spheres to be in constant contract. Thus, all of these social processes and historical factors led to the development of a power elite.

Much of Mills' argument actually fits the realities of modern politics in the United States. There is little doubt that those at the top of the power hierarchies he described do indeed exercise a great deal of power. If he succeeded in nothing else, he certainly raised the debate to an entirely new level of analysis. Mills was the first major social scientist to note that power relationships vary with the issues at hand who anchored his analysis in specific major institutions.

The Ruling-Class Perspective. Another structuralist perspective is that of G. William Domhoff. While Mills felt that a small cohesive group of powerful individuals occupied positions of power, Domhoff, on the other hand, views power as more broadly based in a "governing class." According to Domhoff, the governing class consists of the top 0.5 percent of individuals and families who own most the nation's wealth. The important institutions and decision-making groups are disproportionately staffed by members of this class. The governing class is made up of wealthy businesspeople and their families. Domhoff presents a convincing argument that the members of this group are united through stock ownership, intermarriages, private schools, exclusive social clubs and summer resorts, and service on interlocking corporate boards. Moreover, he argues that the core of the ruling class is politically active, working in high-level positions in profit and nonprofit institutions. Similar to Mills, Domhoff does not believe the ruling class is conspiratorial. Nevertheless, he does stress that the ruling class is more unified, conscious, and manipulative than the pluralists have thought.

In Domhoff's view, the power of the ruling class lies in the fact that they control a hugely disproportionate share of the national wealth. This group has four defining characteristics:

1) they are extremely well off, compared to the rest of the population,

2) they control over eighty percent of the wealth of the nation,

3) a wide array of social and economic institutions are under their control, and

4) they dominate the political process.

In addition, they dominate the political arena through a variety of political processes and specific techniques. First, they are particularly adept at using the special interest process. To insure that their class interests are preserved in the political system they use lobbyists, lawyers, and membership on regulatory commissions and Congressional committees. The ruling class is directly involved in the policy formation process. Frequently, members of the upper class are to be found on important committees that formulate national policies. These commissions, councils, and policy planning groups include the Business Council, Committee for Economic Development, National Security Council, National Industrial Conference Board, and the Council on Foreign Relations.

Another manner in which the ruling class attempts to influence the political process is through the candidate selection process. Through campaign donations, political party influence, and control of the media a candidate is selected who can serve their interests.

Lastly, Domhoff mentions **ideological hegemony** and the Marxist concept of "the general interest." Ideological hegemony refers to the institutions of socialization, such as education and the mass media, through which the values and beliefs that support the interests of the elite class become generally accepted. These institutions are owned and controlled by the ruling class. Domhoff's argument, then, is that the structure of United States institutions has been penetrated by the upper class who have a good understanding of how power operates.

According to Domhoff, the ruling class controls the executive branch of the federal government, the mass media, foundations, universities, major corporations and they are represented on many important policy setting councils. Control of the executive branch grants the ruling class control over the important regulatory agencies. This is important because the ruling class also owns most of the businesses regulated by these agencies. Additionally, the executive branch makes nominations to the judiciary, the military, and the law enforcement agencies. In Domhoff's view, state, local, and congressional bodies are only influenced by the ruling class, rather than controlled. These elements of the formal power structure are more open to a broader range of citizens. Nevertheless, effective control of the executive and judicial branches of government means that congress can easily be thwarted if it attempts to pass legislation detrimental to the interests of the ruling class.

Therefore, important foreign and domestic policies are initiated and executed by members of the power elite that serve the interests of the ruling class. These issues usually revolve around a strong defense, economic growth, and social stability. Certainly, these goals are beneficial to everyone, but the policies are nonetheless designed to favor the affluent. The military might of the United States and economic muscle protect United States corporations abroad, foreign trade agreements, such as NAFTA and GATT, favor corporations, and the tax structure has become increasingly regressive, shifting the tax burden onto the middle and working classes.

Comparison of Mill and Domhoff.   In many ways, Domhoff can be seen as improving on Mills. Both Mills and Domhoff view the power structure as a pyramid, with the elite class occupying the top positions. Both also view the affluent, particularly the corporate rich, as the most powerful group. Most interesting is the fact that both see Congress as relatively ineffectual and not in control of any appreciable degree of power. In Mills's view, the Congress amounted to "structured stagnation." In both theories, the executive and judicial branches of the federal government, along with the important regulatory agencies and policy-making councils, have the real power. Lastly, both Mills and Domhoff view the masses as essentially alienated and powerless with no real ability to mount a sustained grass-roots movement. A quick glance at the literature regarding the Women's movement, the Civil Rights Movement, and the Peace Movement will disabuse most of the notion that ordinary people are completely powerless. Both theorists can legitimately be criticized for failing to take much note of powerful social movements. The major point of difference between the two is that Mills stressed cooperation between three power sectors while Domhoff asserts the complete ascendancy of the upper class.

Domhoff's position has a lot to recommend in spite of some minor criticisms. He was able to demonstrate fairly clearly the manner in which the ruling class interacts. He notes that the evidence regarding the candidate selection process and the nomination of presidential candidates is straightforward: candidates without large sums of money rely upon the backing of the wealthy. Without ties to the ruling class, ordinary citizens cannot develop a national presence or compete in the primaries. Secondly, he notes that both political parties are controlled by the ruling class. Even the Democratic Party, traditionally the party of the common person, is controlled by wealthy aristocrats.   Lastly, he documented the common social background of almost all-important appointive governmental positions, including judges, diplomats, cabinet members, and members of regulatory agencies and advisory councils.

Parenti's System-Bias Perspective.   Far from being a neural agent concerned with the general welfare, the state can be organized to benefit the affluent, repress opposition, make and enforce laws, control information, and determine the distributive share of output accorded to the different social classes. This is the point of view of Michael Parenti. Since power is an attribute of positions within the social hierarchy, power tends to be associated with the government and large corporations. Thus, decisions made by the powerful, such as the president, cabinet, the Federal Reserve, the Supreme Court, and others in similar positions, can greatly influence the lives of all citizens. These individuals make decisions concerning health care, public transportation, business and industry, the economy, interest rates, and taxes. Economic decisions, in particular, are no longer made by a vast multitude of entrepreneurs and small business owners—they are made by a small handful of mega-corporations that dominate the market.

The point is that personal wealth is not the basis of power in the structural paradigm. Although the power elite tend to come from affluent backgrounds, power is a manifestation of decision-making that takes place in relation to positions in the social hierarchy. These decisions tend to benefit the wealthy more than the other social groups. It is the nature of social organization that is important. The bias toward the elite occurs due to their influence over the candidate selection process and government officials, through control of the laws, courts, and administrative decisions, and through ideological control.

Systemic control refers to ability of the power elite to achieve control without having to mobilize or take any direct action whatsoever. The institutions of society operate under systematic norms, which produce prearranged results in spite of who the decision maker is or what their predispositions are. There is an old saying among conflict theorists—"the master's house cannot be disassembled with the master's tools." This means that although some elected officials, for instance, may intend to bring about great changes upon taking office, the rules of government systematically work against them. The government is structured to do certain things and achieve certain goals and not other things and other goals. This bias favors the status quo. Moreover, because the current political and economic systems appear to work to everyone's benefit, they tend not to be questioned critically in the first place. The laws, customs, and institutions of society not only are resistant to change, they benefit the elite class and disadvantage the poor.

Another example of systemic control centers on defense spending. The government can rely upon the support of the vast majority in terms of protecting the nation against its enemies, real or imagined. The result of this is that large sums of money are apportioned to the defense industries. Of course, this generates a tremendous amount of profit for such industries. Additionally, United States multinationals operating abroad need a profitable business climate, which can certainly be guaranteed by the might of the nation's military. A healthy and profitable business climate within the United States borders is also essential. The government tends, therefore, to squash dissidence, even when such dissidence may improve the lot of ordinary citizens.

Another aspect of power is related to ideology. People who do not realize they are being discriminated against are unlikely to be upset about it. The best way for the power elite to achieve control is to ensure that members of society internalize a set of values consistent with their interests and goals. This is the arena of ideology. Parenti notes that those who control the definition of interests also control the agenda of issues. In Marxist terms, the working and poorer classes are cooled out by internalizing a set of values that support the power elites' claims to a greater share of resources and power. This ideological control is largely achieved in the family, the schools, and the church. In these institutions, and particularly in the educational setting, children learn that the only correct economic system is capitalism—the natural economic system. Children are taught to accept the present economic and political situation as just, right, good, and natural. As Parenti puts it, the interests of an economically dominant class are enshrouded in the flag, legitimated by the law, enforced by the police, nurtured by the media, taught by the schools, and blessed by the church.

Power is defined in this essay as the ability of one individual or group to force others to do their will. We experience power as coercion. Often we comply with the wishes of others when we would rather not. Frequently we are under the control of those in legitimate authority. We do favors for those who can reward or help us. Working women often succumb to the sexual advances of their employers or superiors because they are in the inferior position and risk losing their job if they complain. Most people obey the traffic laws, for example, because they do not want a traffic citation. Fear of the use of force by those in authority in large measure explains why people comply most of the time.

This essay also explores the issue of how power operates in a democracy. Do "we the people" really have power? We have the right to vote, and voting is the primary act in any democracy. Unfortunately, even that right has been called into question by recent events in the last two presidential elections, with serious voting problems occurring in Florida and Ohio. The pluralists recognize that even though average people have the right to vote, we tend to elect people who are either wealthy or who have obtained the necessary funds to run for office from the wealthy. Thus, at the national level at least, most elected politicians come from a small minority of United States families—the elite. The issue is whether these elite constitute a "power elite" of individuals who control the reigns of power. The pluralists argue that they do not.

293

Pluralists believe that power is not concentrated in the hands of a few wealthy individuals but shared by a plurality of groups, individuals, and organizations that have narrow interests and who compete with each other for power. Anyone is free to join these groups. Thus, average citizens can try to influence national politics through voluntary participation in a variety of interest groups. The essential claim is that no single interest group ever achieves complete power. Therefore, power elite cannot exist.

However, a little quick reflection may convince us that pluralism is not entirely correct. For example, there are many people in society who are not represented by any interest group. Very few special interest groups represent children, the disabled, the poor, or the disenfranchised. For example, many professors are represented by their professional organizations, which give money to politicians, political parties, and political action committees in pursuit of their interests. However, are college students similarly represented? Do the homeless have a political action committee? Does every interest group have the same amount of influence and resources? These questions call into question the validity of the claims made by the pluralists.

ഇ ය ഇ ය

DEFINITIONS

Autonomous Power. When a person individually resists another's attempt to control them or influence their actions and behaviors.

Charismatic Power. Exists when the personal attributes of an individual, such as persuasiveness or leadership ability, is the basis of their power.

Coercive Power. The threat of or use of sanctions to exert power over another individual.

12 | Power: Forcing Us to Give Them What They Want.
by Frank O. Taylor, IV, Ph.D.

Definition of the Situation. Conveys who is present in terms of roles, and thus, how a situation is organized. For symbolic interactionism, the concept of role provides a key link between the perspective and behavior of individuals and the social situations in which they find themselves.

Ideological Hegemony. Refers to the institutions of socialization, such as education and the mass media, through which the values and beliefs that support the interests of the elite class become generally accepted.

Instrumentalist Perspective. A perspective that posits that people in positions of power, strategically located in the political power structure, can manipulate state policies, directly or indirectly by virtue of their positions.

Iron Law of Oligarchy. Michel's' theory that all states inevitably become ruled by the privileged elite.

Legitimate Authority. Power that is associated with one's position in the authority hierarchy.

Networks of Power. The distribution of power in social systems. Those who occupy the command posts of power in our society include corporation heads, political leaders, and military leaders.

Ordinate. The sender or user of power in a simple two-person discussion of power.

Person-to-Person Power. Type of power that involves the use of expertise, coercion, reward, charisma, and authority, in face-to-face social settings where someone is trying to exert power over another individual.

Power Elite. A small group of top corporate, political, and military leaders who dominate American politics.

Power Relationship. A relationship between two parties that establishes who will determine the goals the work serves and the means that will be used to do the work.

Power. The potential to have an effect on ourselves, others, or our environment in spite of opposition.

Procedural Power. A series of steps used by many of those in power that systematically routes bills, proposals, among other legislation, to more favorable committees and tries to bypass certain people and committees who may be unfavorable to such legislation.

Process Power. Used by policymakers when they try to shape the give-and-take of policy deliberations. This refers to the tenor, tempo, and scope of policy discussions.

Revolving Door. The phenomenon of interchangeability of top positions in business, defense, and government.

Reward Power. The use of attractive inducements, such as promotions, pay raises, or even a pat on the back to achieve their goal.

Ruling Class. Domhoff's perspective of the governing class that consists of the top 0.5 percent of individuals and families who own most of the nation's wealth. The important institutions and decision-making groups are disproportionately staffed by members of this class.

Strategic Elites. Those who perform coordinating functions for society that serve the common good and achieve collective aims and goals.

Structural Perspective. From this Marxist perspective, the location of individuals in the political power structure who serve the interests of the elites is not important. Structuralists point to the nature and organization of the economy as the primary manner in which elites control the government.

Subordinate. The receiver in a simple two-person discussion of power.

Substantive Power. Refers to the ability of policy makers to shape the content of social policy or to appeal for support from others. This type of power is used on a daily basis in the Congress of the United States.

REFERENCES

The ideas, facts, and information presented in my essay on power can be found in the following references:

Bachrach, Peter, and Morton S. Baratz. 1962. "Two Faces of Power." *American Political Science Review* 56:947-52.

Beeghley, Leonard. 2000. *The Structure of Social Stratification in the United States.* Boston, MA: Allyn and Bacon.

Blau, Peter M. 1964. *Exchange and Power in Social Life.* New York: John Wiley and Sons.

Connolly, William E. 1969. *The Bias of Pluralism.* New York: Lieber-Atherton.

Coser, Lewis A. 1956. *The Functions of Social Conflict.* New York: Free Press.

Cunningham, Frank. 1975. "Pluralism and Class Struggle." *Science and Society* 39:385-416.

Dahl, Robert A. 1967. *Pluralist Democracy in the Unites States: Conflicts and Consent.* Chicago, IL: Rand McNally.

Dahl, Robert A. 1982. *Dilemmas of Pluralist Democracy.* New Haven, CT: Yale University Press.

Domhoff, William G. 1983. *Who Rules America Now?: A View for the '80s.* New York: Simon and Schuster.

Domhoff, William G. 2002. *Who Rules America?* 4th ed. Boston, MA: McGraw-Hill.

Eitzen, Stanley D. and Maxine Baca Zinn. 2004. *In Conflict and Order: Understanding Society.* 10th ed. Boston, MA: Allyn and Bacon.

Emerson, Richard M. 1962. "Power-dependence Relations." *American Sociological Review* 27:31-41.

Gamson, William A. 1975. *The Strategy of Protest.* Homewood, IL: Dorsey Press.

Hurst, Charles E. 1995. *Social Inequality: Forms, Causes, and Consequences.* Boston, MA: Allyn and Bacon.

Jansson, Bruce S. 1990. *Social Welfare Policy: From Theory to Practice.* Belmont, CA: Wadsworth.

Manley, John F. 1983. "Neo-Pluralism: A Class Analysis of Pluralism I and Pluralism II." *American Political Science Review* 77:368-83.

Martin, Roderick. 1971. "The Concept of Power: A Critical Defense." *British Journal of Sociology* 22:240-257.

McFarland, Andrew S. 1987. "Interest Groups and Theories of Power in America." *British Journal of Political Science* 17:129-47.

Michels, Robert. 1911. *Political Parties.* New York: Dover.

Mills, C. Wright. 1958. *The Power Elite.* New York: Oxford University Press.

Mills, C. Wright. 1968. "The Power Elite." Pp. 263-276 in *Reader in Political Sociology,* edited by Frank Lindenfeld. New York: Funk and Wagnalls.

Mosca, Gaetano. 1939. *The Ruling Class.* New York: McGraw-Hill.

Parenti, Michael. 1978. *Power and the Powerless.* 2nd ed. New York: St. Martin's Press.

Parenti, Michael. 2002. *Democracy for the Few.* 7th ed. New York: Bedford/St. Martin's Press.

Piven, Frances Fox and Richard A. Cloward. 1993. *Regulating the Poor: The Functions of Public Welfare.* New York: Vintage Books.

Weber, Max. 1920. *Economy and Society.* Totowa, NJ: Bedminster Press.

Weber, Max. 1947. *The Theory of Social and Economic Organization.* A. M. Henderson and Talcott Parsons (trans.) New York: Free Press.

Weber, Max. 1958. *The Protestant Ethic and the Spirit of Capitalism.* Talcott Parsons (trans.) New York: Scribner.

13 | Politics: Determining Who Gets What.
by Frank O. Taylor, IV, Ph.D.

THE BIAS OF THE POLITICAL SYSTEM

In a representative democracy, such as that which exists in the United States, the political system relies upon the electorate for its authority and legitimacy. This is the theory. The government holds elections; political parties endorse candidates who run for office, and people vote. Voting is the backbone of any democracy. On the fact of it, the United States certainly appears to be dramatic. However, recent disquieting trends may be threatening the democracy United States citizens' value so dearly. This chapter will explore the ways in which corporate wealth influences the system. Increasingly, corporate lobbies, special interest groups, political action committees, and wealthy individuals have been able to influence political policy. One disheartening result of this trend is that a lesser percentage of eligible voters actually vote for President. Ordinary people may feel that the political process no longer serves their needs.

WEALTH AND POWER

Interest Groups. The principle of majority rule is violated when interest groups intervene in the political process and try to overturn or deflect the will of the electorate. Special interest groups abound on the political landscape and run the gamut from liberal to conservative, although conservative interest groups far outnumber and outspend liberal groups. These groups are comprised of people who think alike on a particular issue or range of issues. The American Association of Retired Persons (AARP) and the National Rifle Association (NRA) are two well-known special interest groups.

These organizations attempt to influence government in a number of ways, including financial support of political candidates, campaign contributions to political parties, and propaganda campaigns that attempt to sway the public to their side of an issue. Interest groups have much to gain from such tactics, such as tax breaks, favorable rulings, subsidies, de-regulation, and so on. In addition to trying to influence specific politicians, interest groups also target congressional committees, regulatory agencies, and executive bureaucracies.

298

The tools such organizations have at hand to accomplish their goals are impressive indeed and include brochures, expert testimony, and technical reports. Moreover, many special interest groups can offer financial inducements ranging from slush funds and campaign contributions to exorbitant lecture fees, stock awards, stock tips, easy-term loans, and even high paying corporate jobs, which retiring politicians favor. If money and post-political-career jobs fail, interest groups can offer luxury vacation jaunts, hotels, private jets, and free housing.

Imagine that you are elected to public office as a Senator. For most of your life, you have been interested in educational excellence. You have noticed that public education in the United States is suffering from all manner of stresses and problems. Now you have a chance to do something about it. You sponsor a bill that, although raising taxes on the affluent and corporations, promises to repair old buildings, build new schools, hire new teachers, and decrease class size. To you, your proposals seem only logical and just and the program appeals to large numbers of the electorate who send their children to classes in the public schools.

As soon as your bill becomes public knowledge, and probably before, entire organizations of people rush into action with the sole purpose of defeating it. Those who stand to have their incomes or profits diminished by the legislation will not waste any time—they will send telegrams and electronic-mail, contact their supporters in the Senate and House of Representatives, call reporters, hold news conferences, and even pay for research which will demonstrate, supposedly, that the legislation is not only doomed to fail, but will cost too much and damage the educational system to boot. Opponents of the bill will marshal experts to rebut the logic of its propositions, demand congressional hearings, and send out spokespersons to appear on television news and talk shows. They will give financial support to politicians who oppose the bill and even support your opponent in the next election.

Most special interest groups also employ lobbyists, people who earn a living attempting to influence legislation on behalf of clients. Lobbyists maintain offices in Washington, D.C., and in the state capitals around the nation. Together, special-interest groups and lobbyists form a powerful political force. Most politicians, being interested in re-election, cannot afford to take them lightly let alone neglect them. Not only are such groups and organizations a financial resource for politicians and candidates, they represent a pool of voters. Frequently, the voters lobbyists represent have a **vested interest** in seeing particular legislation passed or defeated. Special-interest groups are well finance, represented by lobbyists, and able to deliver votes. Every politician's worst fear may be that the votes will be delivered to an opponent.

Should your educational bill prevail and make it into law the **special interest groups** will work tirelessly in the background to overturn it or deflect its effects. They may even decide to challenge it in court and seek an injunction to prevent it being implemented until the courts rule on the matter. The depth and breadth of power and resources many special interest groups wield is truly staggering. In all likelihood, if legislation is proposed which offends one or more major interest groups it has very little chance of success.

Another type of interest group is the **political action committee** (PACs). Political action committees came into existence in the 1970s after Congress, attempting to reign in the money interest groups were giving to candidates, passed legislation limiting the amount of money individuals and organizations could give to a candidate, and required donations of over $1,000 to be reported. PACs are able to get around the limits on donations by soliciting contributions from various donors and pooling the money. Today there are nearly four thousand PACs and they spent $400 million per election. Most PACs represent very narrow financial interests, such as the oil industry, the auto industry, the banking industry, and the like. The will of PACs may seem, to politicians, like the will of the people. Although all PACs and most politicians will deny it, once elected, politicians who accepted money from interest groups owe them favors. If not favors outright then at least access. When legislation that affects an interest group is on the table, their representatives contact the politicians to whom they lent their financial support—they tell politicians how they want them to vote.

Although they do not constitute an interest group, many wealthy individuals attempt to influence the political process. Long before the rise of political action committees powerful individuals, such as Henry Ford, John D. Rockefeller, and even Alexander Graham Bell, were able to gain access to politicians and influence the political process. These rich individuals, and others like them, clearly had a stake in legislation that could make or break them.

Criticism of Interest Groups. The average senator needs to raise about $1700 per day, over a six-year term, to finance a reelection bid—money is, thus, the "mothers milk of politics." It is no surprise that the major criticism leveled against special-interest groups and PACs is that they try to buy votes and influence the political process through campaign donations. The legitimate fear is that legislators will represent the interests of those who contributed to their elections, and help them remain in power, rather than their constituents. For example, the $60 million spent by the medical lobby on members of Congress may be one reason why the United States, alone among the industrial democracies, has no national health care insurance.

The recent flap over political donations made by the Chinese government to the Democratic National Commission (DNC) highlights another criticism of interest groups—foreign lobbyists spend over $150 million each year trying to influence votes. In 1993 Japanese interest groups alone spent $60 million pressuring Congress to reduce tariffs, duties, and quotas on the products Japan exports to the United States. Largely, the lobbyists who disperse the funds are former United States government officials. Japan attempts to influence legislation by supporting both candidates in presidential elections. Such activities, not surprisingly, are illegal in Japan. Of course, Japan is not alone in such activities—during the same year the Canadians spent $23 million trying to influence the United States political process, the Germans spent $13 million, the French almost $13 million, and Hong Kong, Mexico, Kuwait, Taiwan, Australia, and Ireland dumped funds ranging from $8 to $10 million each into the pockets of politicians. Interest groups, foreign or domestic, do not spent millions of dollars without expecting something in return.

TYPES OF POLITICAL PARTICIPATION

Researchers have begun to make a convincing argument that what exists in the United States today is a **"mock democracy."** According to some political analysts, the issue is not whether elites participate in the democratic process through political contributions, PACs, and interest groups, but the degree to which elected officials are accountable to their constituents. At the national level, ordinary citizens have little influence over decision- or policy-making, although they are greatly affected by the policies. What remains is the "shell" of democracy—middle class voters get enough benefits from the political system to remain happy and marginally engaged in the political process. Behind the scenes, however, the agenda is set by political partisans with huge sums of money to invest. Most of the interaction between affluent individuals, interest groups, PACs, and foreign interest groups, takes place out of the spotlight and out of sight of the public.

Those who receive little by way of benefits from the political system are much less engaged—the working class, the poor, the disadvantaged, and inner city minorities.

Voting. Representative democracy is based on elections. Elections provide the useful function of allowing citizens to express their political desires. The United States was founded upon certain pluralist principles. For example, the Declaration of Independence and the Constitution hold that political participation should be equal. Under the United States democratic system, all citizens are free to form associations that compete for political power. Pluralism is founded upon two basic principles:

1) attempts to influence the political process should occur within the rules; and
2) any group or person should have access to compete for political power.

Under such a system, politicians are accountable for their actions and decisions. Moreover, everyone has a multitude of different interests based on their religious, racial, ethnic, occupational, and social class affiliations. This helps ensure that a balance of power among competitors is maintained. For the most part, this text argues that pluralism exists only in theory and ideology. Nevertheless, for pluralism to exist in any meaningful fashion electoral procedures must maximize participation. For ordinary citizens, the major form of political participation is voting. Unfortunately, unlike other democracies, the United States makes voting difficult.

In a democracy the primary act of participation is voting. In spite of all the ways in which partisans attempt to influence the political process, candidates must still win the votes of ordinary citizens. Therefore, voters can hold politicians accountable for their actions and decisions—if voters are not happy they can vote for the challenger in the next election. The problem with this analysis is that many, if not most, eligible citizens no longer vote, especially in off-year elections. After plenty of unruly behavior—riots, protests, and demonstrations—the franchise, initially applying only to property owning white males, was extended to nearly everyone. Thus, while most adults are eligible to vote today relatively few exercise this right.

Prior to 1900, average national rates of voting hovered around eighty percent. Thus, in the last quarter of the nineteenth century most people voted. In some areas, such as Indiana, New Jersey, Ohio, New York, and Pennsylvania, densely populated states, voter turnout was close to ninety percent and in some of these areas more. In non-presidential elections, these same areas maintained voting rates of seventy percent or more. However, rates of voting experienced a decline from just after 1900 to 1992. In the presidential election of that year only 54 percent of registered voters went to the polls.

What explains this lack of political participation that has marked recent elections? It might be argued that those who do not vote, the working class and the poor, for instance, are either unmotivated or happy with the current state of public policy. However, such arguments hardly seem valid given that the working class and poor receive the least from the political process. The affluent and middle classes not only dominate the political process they receive most of the benefits.

A better explanation may be the introduction of laws requiring voters to register, introduced in the 1900 presidential election. Although voter participation dropped, rates remained stable between 1900 and 1972, hovering around sixty percent. After 1972, voting rates dropped even further, to around 50 – 55 percent. In the last two decades, the typical presidential election has seen voter turnouts of between 50 and 60 percent. This means that the necessary majority to elect the president is about 25 percent of eligible adults, hardly a mandate by voters. The rates of voting are even lower in an off-year election—many senators, representatives, governors, state legislators and local officials find their way into public office with less than 17 percent of eligible adults voting.

There are some important predictors of whether or not people vote. For example, although only 69 percent of the population was registered to vote in 1993, of those registered to vote about 90 percent did. This indicates that individuals registered to vote are more likely to do so. Thus, if more poor and working class people registered to vote they might increase their political participation. Additionally, as family income increases the percentage of adults reporting that they are registered to vote also increases. Not only does registering to vote increase with family income, so does the likelihood of actually going to the polls.

Partisanship. Partisans identify with, work for, and try to influence a party, candidate, or issue. Partisan involvement may be as simple as wearing a campaign button or as intense as volunteer work and financial contributions. Lobbying continues after the election as partisans attempt to influence legislators, bureaucrats, and others. Lobbying can be done by ordinary citizens who write to their representatives. These calls and letters from average people are important to politicians because people who contact them about an issue are highly likely to vote.

Money is the key to successful lobbying. Thus, contributions are a major issue. Individuals and political action committees funnel money to a candidate's campaign—sometimes both liberal and conservative candidates are both supported. The problem with money and elections is that, although both are types of political participation, not everyone who can vote can contribute money. Voting and partisanship work within the existing system to achieve change.

Unruliness.   Not everyone feels that voting brings about a sense of security. There are those who are so alienated and feel so powerless that sometimes they express themselves in unruly behavior. Violent and destructive riots have occurred periodically in the United States. The media usually portrays such outbursts as the actions of malcontents, deviants, and criminals. The civil unrest, which erupted in Los Angles after the acquittal of the police officers involved in the Rodney King beating, is a classic example. The media, politicians, and pundits focused on the destruction, looting, beatings, and other criminal behavior. Very little attention was paid to the fact that police brutality was for years a major complaint of the minority residents. Add to these feelings of social injustice a steady period of economic decline and high rates of unemployment and it becomes easier to contemplate the political motivations behind the "riots." Indeed, it is just as easy to define such situations as rebellions by oppressed people.

The Rodney King incident was certainly not the first time racial tension and alienation has erupted into violence. During the 1960s, a multitude of cities with large minority populations experienced racial unrest and violent riots, particularly following the assassination of Martin Luther King Jr. Social policy that deals with unruliness tends to focus on individual rioters, who are defined as criminals who should be prosecuted. Often however, violence and unruly behavior are more than just protests—they constitute collective grievances to be considered. Few legitimate political options exist for the alienated and disadvantaged. Collective violence can be a form of political participation that grows out of frustration. It is often a signal to those with power that the disenfranchised want to be included in the political process. Conservatives and liberals alike often forget that the United States was born out of just such political unrest and upheaval.

FINANCING POLITICAL CAMPAIGNS AND THE ROLE OF MONEY IN ELECTIONS

Campaign financing has to rank as the least democratic feature of the United States political system. It may seem like the political process is fairly straightforward with candidates presenting their ideas in political advertisements and debates with opponents, each trying to appeal to voters. However, the cost of winning has skyrocketed—in 1974 incumbents in the House of Representatives spent about $56,000 on their campaigns and challengers spent about $40,000; in 1992 incumbents spent more than $500,000 and challengers averaged almost $150,000 for their campaigns. The reality is much different than pluralist ideology would have us believe. Although candidates still try to win votes by using public forums and voters select winners on Election Day, behind the scenes are some very disturbing trends. The real business of campaigning is conducted with money. Those who have it have a source of power average citizens lack. Some critics of the role of money in the political process claim that the United States has the best Congress money can buy.

The Cost of Winning.   Not many average citizens realize what goes into a political campaign or how they are financed. Political campaigns need staff and volunteers, phones, consultants, advisors, researchers, computers and so on. In 1988, for example, the average senator winning a new seat spent $3.6 million. The same senate seat cost about $610,000 in 1976. This meant that the senator had to raise $12,000 a week for six years to bankroll the next election. Thus, both incumbents and challengers have become increasingly dependent upon PAC contributions. Being elected has never been easy, but today it is so expensive that candidates must either be wealthy, well connected, or both to campaign effectively.   Expensive campaigns, where success often depends upon the quality of the commercial rather than the quality of the candidate, are funded by individual contributions, funds donated from interest groups and PACs, and candidate's personal wealth. PAC donations have grown from $12.4 million, given to congressional candidates in 1974, to $45 million in 1980, and $181 million in 1992. Of congressional bids, senate races are extremely expensive. The average senator spent nearly $4 million to win in the 1990 election. The most expensive race was that of Jesse Helms', who spent over $17 million in 1990 to retain his seat.

305

PACs, which are formed to represent interests such as labor unions, teachers, corporations, retired persons, and others, can donate up to $5,000 to each candidate during the primary—and an equal amount during the election. What do PACs expect for their money? PAC money generally goes to candidates who have a history of voting the right way on their issues, or who will shortly. For example, it is well known that Robert Dole changed his position on whether or not tobacco was addictive, shortly after receiving a rather large political contribution from the tobacco lobby. After pocketing the contribution, Dole maintained that, perhaps, tobacco was not that addictive after all, since *he* had managed to quit.

Individuals and special interest groups also funnel money to candidates. Individuals can donate up to $1,000 per candidate. This may not seem like much but a popular manner in which the spirit of campaign finance regulations are violated is known as "bundling." Affluent people and corporate executive officers can bundle their donations together into one lump sum, effectively giving their candidate thousands of dollars. **"Soft money"** is another popular method of making political contributions. There are no limits as to the amount any individual or organization can donate to a political party at the local, state, or national levels. Moreover, many private organizations collect money for political uses. These organizations are supposed to be independent from political parties. The soft money loophole has been used extensively by affluent people to funnel huge sums of money to both Republican and Democratic national parties.

Presidential candidates often collect huge sums of money from private individuals. What do these affluent partisans receive for their generosity? Often these private donors have business interests pending with the federal government. It is highly likely that these people seek either access to the President or the ability to influence the President, once elected. When someone donates such a large sum to a political party, they are anything but anonymous and the amount of the sum guarantees they will be remembered for it.

It is hard to claim outright that campaign contributions buy votes. Nevertheless, there is indirect evidence that such contributions are advantageous. In the 1988 election 53 candidates running unopposed for seats in the House of Representatives received $8.4 million in contributions—Speaker of the House Wright also ran unopposed but still received more than a half a million from PACs. When a politician runs unopposed one would assume that their need for funding is somewhat less than would be the case if they had strong opposition.

PACs frequently give to both sides in an election and often to the candidate they opposed after the election but who won anyway. In 1992, Archer Daniels Midland gave $397,000 to the Republican Party and $76,000 to the Democrats; Atlantic Richfield gave $226,000 to the Republicans and $120,000 to Democrats; RJR-Nabisco gave $382,500 to Republicans and $231,500 to Democrats. The role of money in elections is a fundamental threat to democracy because only the interests of the affluent, powerful, and wealthy are served. If candidates do not have enough of their own money, they must rely upon the rich and contributions from interest groups, to whom they will be beholden.

Getting Reelected.   The evidence supports the assertion that the more money a candidate spends on their election the more likely they are to win. Examining the period between 1974 and 1992, it is clear that incumbents always outspend challengers. Over this period time, however, the amounts by which incumbents have outspent challengers have increased dramatically. In 1974, the incumbents spent, on average, $56 thousand and challengers about $40 thousand.   By 1992 incumbents were outspending challengers by ten to one, about $577 thousand to about $148 thousand respectively. Incumbents who outspend opponents, and incumbents always do, usually win. One reason why incumbents are able to outspend challengers is that they are very well positioned, by virtue of their political office, to collect donations from various interest groups.

In the Unites States House of Representatives and Senate, for the years between 1960 and 1992, an average of 93 percent of representatives and 80 percent of senators were reelected. Incumbents have some advantages over challengers in elections.   Most incumbents have an established network of individual contributors and PACs. One advantage, just mentioned, is that interest groups of every type and philosophy are interested in giving him or her money. As noted previously, most interest groups play both sides of the isle, democrat and republican, in order to hedge their bets. Additionally, incumbents have very high name recognition. They also provide services for their states and districts. A senator or representative who tries to preserve federal spending in their state, for example, may be highly regarded. This is referred to as pork-barrel politics—introducing bills which insure that federal funds, for military spending, military bases, highways, roads, bridges, and so on, is spent in the state of the politician who introduces the legislation. During the round of military base closings in the early 1990s, politicians who fought to save major installations in their states or districts can be regarded as heroes. The congressional franking privilege, another advantage incumbents have over challengers, allows mailings of newsletters and other items to constituents for free. It is particularly useful to incumbents to be covered by the local or national media. Challengers usually only make the local media during elections but incumbents may be in the media periodically for their entire term in office.

The Origins of Political Donations.   Precisely where does the money come from? Challengers lose because affluent individuals and PACs support incumbents with reams of money. Moreover, when analyzing the sources of this money certain patterns become apparent. In 1992, for example, senators relied on wealthy individual contributors for 39 percent of their campaign funds, on PACs for 29 percent, small individual contributions accounted for 17 percent, and the political party and others sources for the remainder. Representatives, on the other hand, relied more heavily on PACs—43 percent of their campaign funds were derived from Political Action Committees. Large individual contributions accounted for 27 percent of representatives' funds, small individual contributions amount to 18 percent, the party and other sources accounted for the remainder. Senators rely heavily on affluent individuals; representatives rely largely on Political Action Committees.

Getting Around the Limits.   With the exception of the office of president, candidates for federal office can legally spend as much as they can raise.

> Citizens can contribute $1,000 to a candidate during the primary.
> Citizens can contribute $1,000 to a candidate during the election.
> Citizens can contribute $5,000 to a PAC during a calendar year.
> Citizens can contribute $20,000 to a political party per calendar year.

However, these limits are easily avoided. Wealthy individuals often give money in the names of their children, relatives, and even friends. Corporations often direct employees to donate to their PACs, although not all employees subscribe to the political philosophies of the corporations for which they work. The largest sums of money go directly to the political parties, known as soft money, which is then disbursed to individual candidates. Hundreds of thousands of dollars can be funneled to candidates in this fashion. Lastly, Political Action Committees can spend money indirectly in support of candidates, in addition to what they give to the candidate's party or campaign organization. PACs frequently spend millions of dollars trying to educate the public on an issue and sway people to their side. Just as frequently, voting the right way, from the Political Action Committee's point of view, implies voting for a particular candidate.

What is wrong with all this spending? In a democracy, people and organizations should have the right to support candidates for office who represent their interests. Right? Campaign contributions are legally defined as "political speech," which is constitutionally protected. Nevertheless, one of the most fundamental principles of any democracy is that citizens should participate equally in the process of selecting those who represent them. If campaign contributions are regarded as "free speech," who can afford to participate in the debate?

Poor families obviously cannot. Whatever the average working class family can afford to contribute will not be much. If a householder is a member of a union, they might manage a few hundred dollars, but certainly no more. Middle class families are in a better position to "talk" politically. However, even these families may not be able to contribute very large sums. Many middle class professionals belong to professional organizations. Most of these organizations maintain lobbying operations. Thus, working class individuals may donate through their unions and middle class professionals may donate through their organizational lobby. However, the affluent that can give thousands of dollars to political campaigns. Since the basis of most wealth is capital, the rich tend to support candidates and parties that favor business interests. In the United States, this traditionally has been the Republican Party.

Researchers distinguish between three types of PACs, those oriented to business or labor, and those that are ideological. Business contributions come from every sector of the economy— agriculture, communications, defense, utilities, medicine, law, you name it. In the 1992 elections business oriented PACs contributed $126,800,000 and affluent business individuals contributed $168,600,000. These are truly staggering sums of money. Labor contributions, from unions associated with some of the same industries managed only $43,100,000 in contributions. Individuals oriented toward labor interests managed only $200,000. In spite of this disparity in political "speech" conservative politicians, largely Republicans, have recently been trying to limit the amount unions can contribute, usually to democrats, by requiring unions to get permission from each union-member before using some of their dues for such purposes. Ideological PACs are those associated with issues such as environmental protection, guns, abortion, and the like, from either side of the issue, liberal or conservative. Ideological PACs contributed $18,600,000 in the 1992 elections and individuals associated with one or another ideology contributed $10,700,000. Thus, when it comes to talking politically, and taking part in the political "debate," the speech of business clearly overwhelms labor and ideological PACs. In the 1992 elections business PACs literally roared, contributing 80 percent of the campaign funds. Labor, with 12 percent, and ideology with 8 percent, were barely audible. The poor, of course, were mute.

THE INFLUENCE OF SOCIAL STRUCTURE IN POLITICAL PARTICIPATION

Politicians are held accountable by only two constituencies: middle class people who vote and rich people with cash. This effectively violates the principle of equal participation in the political process. Additionally, the pluralist ideal of political participation within a framework of rules is violated if only certain groups in society are able to influence effectively political policy.

The Social Structure of Voting. Those who have learned anything at all about the political process have probably been taught that elections are events in which people vote their conscience—voting is purely a matter of individual choice among candidates. If this was, in fact, true, and everyone had equal access to the political process the role of money in campaigns would be much less important. In other words, if rates of voting were equal to what they were in the late 1800s and early 1900s, politicians would be accountable to voters for their decisions. In this sense, the word voter implies all citizens who can vote. In order to be elected, political candidates would have to appeal to interests that have a broader base of support.

However, when rates of voting are as low as they have been for several decades, slightly over 60 percent, the term voters cannot be applicable to everyone. Thus, who votes becomes more important. Generally, people who feel that their interests are not represented, or who are alienated, do not vote. The following analysis deals with the manner in which structural barriers prevent large numbers of people from participating, usually the poor. However, voting procedures are deliberately designed to limit participation by the poor and facilitate participation by the affluent. The rate of voting in the United States is impacted by:

Election Day.
Registration requirements.

Voting procedures.
Separation of elections.
Frequency of elections.

The Election Day itself is a limitation on voting for large numbers of people. Election Day in many European nations falls either on Sunday or a national holiday. This makes it easy for citizens to get to the polls because they have time off from their jobs. Electoral participation in most European democracies is between 80 and 90 percent, without the social class differences found in the United States. In the United States, however, Election Day falls frequently on a working day. This may not seem like such a big deal, at first glance. Nevertheless, for many people, taking time off work is not an option. They would lose a significant portion of their earnings. Thus, conducting elections on a working day is a structural barrier to voting. This barrier does not affect everyone. Doctors, lawyers, teachers, and other white-collar workers are certainly very busy people. Nevertheless, they have a great deal of autonomy when it comes to control of their time. Thus, there is a clear social class bias related to the election day—people in the affluent classes do not experience much difficulty making it to the polls, whereas working people may not have the time, energy, or ability to lose a portion of their pay to go out and vote.

Registration requirements make it harder for certain people to vote. Citizens in Western European nations are automatically registered to vote by their governments. Alone among the Western democracies, in the United States, citizens must register themselves. Requiring citizens to register before they vote is another structural barrier to full participation in the political process. Beeghley argues that this fact alone may explain why rates of voting are so low in the United States. Prior to the laws that required voter registration, the United States had rates of voting equal to the Western European democracies. Registration can be more difficult than voting, since citizens often must travel to a specific location, such as a city hall or county seat, during working hours and prior to the election. Registration requirements are a structural barrier to voting for the same reasons the Election Day is—working class and poor people find it difficult to take time off from work or to travel to registration office. Researchers have estimated that registration requirements may reduce voter participation by as much as 19 percent.

The reason for requiring voters to register is to reduce electoral fraud. Nations that make voting easy have the highest rates of voting. Nations that hold elections on working days make it

311

harder for some people to vote. Voter registration in the United States may be a prime reason that rates of voting are declining.

Along with the Election Day and registration procedures, voting procedures hinder rates of participation. Many citizens are faced with have to have a complex understanding of issues when they get in the ballot booth due to the Australian ballot. This ballot gives voters greater choices and the possibility of splitting their ticket. Voters today can easily be confused as to what a yes vote for a measure means compared to a no vote. Frequently, once in the ballot booth, voters must read through complex instructions explaining what a vote either way actually means. Add to this complexity modern computers and voting machines, and voting procedures become even more confusing. It is likely that the complexity of voting procedures hinders full participation by those who are less sophisticated, especially the poor. Nevertheless, even well educated people can easily be confused by the arcane wording of instructions.

Separation of elections may function as a structural barrier to full political participation. In the United States, it seems that there is no end to elections, as state, local, and federal may be held at different times. Thus, people must go to the polls at different times for different reasons. State gubernatorial elections coincide with presidential elections in only fourteen states. Local elections are usually separate from state and federal contests. Worse, only 17 percent of cities with populations greater than 25,000 hold concurrent state and federal elections. Bond issues may be voted on at still different times. Thus, if some people find it difficult to get to the polls for presidential and congressional elections, how much less likely are they to vote in state, local, or bond elections? Those who are most likely to vote in the myriad elections are usually the most partisan, have a stake in the outcome, belong to groups with a stake in the outcome, and have the time, money, and energy to participate. The majority of such people are the affluent and the rich.

Lastly, the frequency of elections can influence rates of participation. The frequency and separation of elections in the United States means that people must travel to the polls often. This means that many people who are elected to office will not represent the majority of their constituents. They win elections all right, but often with less than 20 percent of the electorate voting. Some states even purge their rolls of nonvoters every two years. This means that registered voters who have not voted in the last couple of elections, for whatever reason, must register to vote all over again.

Structural barriers to voting restrict the participation of the working class and the poor. This leads to a lower voting rate, which, in turn leads candidates to stress interests and policies that are favored by the more affluent. This alienates the working class and the poor even further and may reduce their participation again. Over time, as participation by the working class and poor drops off, candidates do not have to take account of their interests and fail to contact or mobilize the poor. This in turn means that the less-affluent do not develop unique political interests and attitudes, which reduces the rate of voting of the poor and working class even further. An additional consequence is that the more affluent defend the structural barriers to full participation. Indeed, they may fear to make voting any easier because they cannot predict how the less affluent will behave if they were to increase their participation significantly. Conservatives always fear change and may seek to perpetuate the structural barriers in order to maintain the status quo. A low rate of voting among the poor and less affluent virtually means that political decision-makers do not have to be accountable to the interests of the non-engaged. Because of this, the middle and upper class receive more benefits from the political system than do the less affluent.

Affluent Partisanship.   Structural barriers to political participation limits participation by the non-affluent.   The rich, unfortunately, have many more means of political partisanship and power. In a sense, everyone is a partisan. Average people may choose to vote, or not, and whom to vote for. That is the extent of it for most people. The policy battles and decisions of Washington D.C. are far removed from the lives of ordinary citizens. The goings-on in the capital, even though they may be gravely related to the average citizen's wellbeing, seem less important than the problems people face in their everyday lives. As mentioned, the partisans who have a stake in the legislative process are as involved as they can be, trying to influence the process. Money is the building block of their partisanship, but not the only one. There are three sources of partisanship by the affluent:

1) money,

2) family background, and

3) institutional location.

The foremost political resource in the United States is **money**. Beeghley describes politics as essential a series of exchanges between those who need votes and those who have money to donate as campaign funds. Raising money for a campaign is a daunting task. Thus, politicians need to pay attention to the interests of those who have money to give. Those who do not participate can be ignored, unless they become unruly. It is not necessary to view these exchanges as bribes. What the affluent desire in the exchange is access. Access serves the needs of the affluent because it gives them a forum to be heard in the policymaking and legislative process. In this sense, access to the political decision-making process equals power. Those from the upper class have greater ability to make large campaign contributions and, therefore, greater access to public officials. It goes without saying that average citizens will never go about their day with the unlisted telephone numbers of their congressmen or the president in their pockets. Access, of course, means influence. The affluent are able to influence the legislative, rule-making, and rule-enforcing process at every point along the way.

Even more insidious is the fact that politicians often rely upon special-interest groups and lobbyists for "expert" advice. Additionally, lobbyists often provide politicians with gifts, honoraria for "speeches" and personal favors. The norm of reciprocity calls for people to return favors and to be friendly with those who bestow favors upon us. It is no different for politicians and lobbyists; they become obligated to each other. Lobbyists can help politicians in other important ways too. For example, they can help use their political networks to mount telephone call-in campaigns or write-in campaigns to support a particular piece of legislation. Moreover, politicians and lobbyists come from the same social class, share interests, belong to the same organizations, and are generally compatible with one another.

Family background is a second source of power partisans can use to influence the political process. A person's family of origin may grant them certain social ties, which include people who are wealthy, have political influence, or are connected to the business world. This is a broader type of social influence than that associated with a particular interest group, lobby, or political action committee. Affluent families tend to share certain social characteristics. These individuals may have attended the same prep school, Ivy League colleges, fraternities or sororities, and be members in the same elite social clubs. Additionally, many people from this social class live in gated communities, share certain views about globalization, and have similar educational backgrounds—

they overwhelmingly major in business, law, and medicine while in college. Not only do they share important socialization experiences and world-views, they may sit upon the same corporate boards with each other. Thus, in various settings and in a multitude of informal settings these individuals have opportunities to make business deals and discuss politics. Indeed, they tend to frequent the same clubs and social events as political decision-makers. It is understood that the less affluent, the poor, and even the middle class are systematically excluded from such groups. The point is that political decision-makers and the affluent often come from similar social backgrounds. This fact, combined with the money the affluent can donate; combine to grant elites access to politicians.

A third source of partisanship the affluent enjoy is institutional location. Individuals of elite family background tend to occupy positions of power within the occupational hierarchy. Such positions may be located at the higher levels of universities, the mass media, the military, businesses, and even the government. It may be that the interests of the affluent are more likely to be met because they occupy many of the positions of power in the nation. It is estimated that about 7,300 positions of power exist in the United States and they are mostly filled by the elite. Of this number, 4,300 are in the corporate sector. Corporate positions of power include chief executive officers and the heads of major boards of directors. About 2,700 positions of power are to be found in the public sector, including the owners, CEOs, and heads of law firms, foundations, mass media companies, law firms, and civic organizations. Lastly, around 300 power positions are located within the government sector, which includes not only elected officials but also appointed officials. Without a doubt, the secretaries of the various government agencies, such as the Department of Defense, the Department of the Interior, the Department of Education, the State Department, and so on. Additionally, the power positions of the Federal Bureau of Investigation, the Central Intelligence Agency, and other law-enforcement agencies may be filled by the power elite. Thus, people who occupy these positions will be able to influence political decision-makers.

80 C8 80 C8

DEFINITIONS

Australian Ballot. A printed ballot that bears the names of all candidates and the text of propositions and is distributed to all the voters at the polls and also called *secret ballot.*

Election Day. The day appointed for an election in the United States. It is the first Tuesday after the first Monday in November.

Family Background. A type of social influence in which a person's family of origin may grant them certain social ties. This includes people who are wealthy, have political influence, or are connected to the business world.

Institutional Location. A source of partisanship in which individuals of elite family backgrounds tend to occupy positions of power within the occupational hierarchy.

Instrumentalist Perspective. A perspective that posits that people in positions of power, strategically located in the political power structure, can manipulate state policies, directly or indirectly by virtue of their positions.

Interest Groups. Groups of people who come together and organize in an attempt to achieve political change or to protect political advantages.

Iron Law of Oligarchy. Michel's' theory that all states inevitably become ruled by the privileged elite.

Lobbyists. Someone who tries to persuade legislators to vote for bills that the lobbyists favor.

Mock Democracy. To many analysts, the United States has become less democratic over time. Important policy issues are discussed without public input. The Patriot Act is undermining the civil liberties guaranteed by the Constitution and the Bill of Rights. Rates of voting continue to decline. In many ways, the United States appears to be only going through the motions of democracy. The installation of a president by the Supreme Court, rather than through an objective counting of votes is a prime example of mock democracy.

Money. The most common medium of exchange, functions as legal tender issued by a government or national bank.

Networks of Power. The distribution of power in social systems. Those who occupy the command posts of power in our society include corporation heads, political leaders, and military leaders.

Pluralist Principles. Belief that many different types of people, with different beliefs, opinions, and needs should be equal in political participation. Under the United States democratic system, all citizens are free to form associations that compete for political power.

316

Political Action Committee (PAC). Political action committees are formed by interest groups, particularly corporations, who want to influence political legislation and policy. Doctors, lawyers, corporations, environmental groups, retired citizens, and unions, among others, have formed PACs. A PAC may donate up to $5,000 to any candidate during the primary and another $5,000 during the election.

Pork-Barrel Politics. Introducing bills that insure that federal funds, for military spending, military bases, highways, roads, bridges, and so on, is spent in the state of the politician who introduces the legislation.

Procedural Power. A series of steps used by many of those in power that systematically routes bills, proposals, among other legislation, to more favorable committees and tries to bypass certain people and committees who may be unfavorable to such legislation.

Registration Requirements. Laws that require citizens to register before they vote. Registration requirements are a structural barrier that inhibits some people from voting such as working class and poor people. These individuals find it difficult to take time off from work or to travel to the registration office.

Separation of Elections. Elections, such as state, local, and federal may be held at different times. This usually has an effect on voter participation.

Soft Money. Political contributions made in such a way as to avoid the United States regulations for federal election campaigns (as by contributions to a political action committee).

Special Interest Groups. A group, however loosely or tightly organized, doing advocacy: those determined to encourage or prevent changes in public policy without trying to be elected.

Vested Interest. Many corporations have a "vested interest" in legislation before the Congress or policies under consideration by the agencies that regulate them. For example, the tobacco industry had an interest in supporting politicians who were opposed to lawsuits by people who had contracted cancer from smoking.

Voting Procedures. A complex set of established forms or methods for electing someone to office. These procedures hinder full participation by those who are less sophisticated, especially the poor.

REFERENCES

The ideas expressed in my essay on politics and the information presented are based on the following works:

Bachrach, Peter, and Morton S. Baratz. 1962. "Two Faces of Power." *American Political Science Review* 56:947-52.

Barlett, Donald L. and James B. Steele. 1994. *America: Who Really Pays the Taxes*. New York: Simon and Schuster.

Barlett, Donald L. and James B. Steele. 1998. "Corporate Welfare." *Time*, November 9, pp. 36-54.

Barlett, Donald L. and James B. Steele. 2001. "How the Little Guy Gets Crunched." *Time,* February 7, pp. 40-43.

Barlett, Donald L. and James B. Steele. 2004. "Has Your Life Become a Game of Chance?" *Time*, February 2, pp. 42-44.

Barlett, Donald L., and James B. Steele. 2000. "Soaked by Congress." *Time*, May 15, pp. 64-75.

Beeghley, Leonard. 2000. *The Structure of Social Stratification in the United States*. 3rd ed. Boston, MA: Allyn and Bacon.

Blau, Peter M. 1964. *Exchange and Power in Social Life*. New York: John Wiley and Sons.

Clark, Terry N. 1968. *Community Structure and Decision Making: Comparative Analysis*. Corte Madera, CA: Chandler and Sharp.

Connolly, William E. 1969. *The Bias of Pluralism*. New York: Lieber-Atherton.

Cunningham, Frank. 1975. "Pluralism and Class Struggle." *Science and Society* 39:385-416.

Dahl, Robert A. 1982. *Dilemmas of Pluralist Democracy*. New Haven, CT: Yale University Press.

Dahrendorf, Ralf. 1958. "Toward a Theory of Social Conflict." *Journal of Conflict Resolution* 2:178-83.

Dahrendorf, Ralf. 1959. *Class and Class Conflict in Industrial Society*. Stanford, CA: Stanford University Press.

Dahrendorf, Ralf. 1970. "On the Origin of Inequality Among Men." Pp. 3-10 in *The Logic of Social Hierarchies,* edited by E. O. Laumann, P. M. Siegel, and R. W. Hodge. Chicago, IL: Markham.

Emerson, Richard M. 1962. "Power-dependence Relations." *American Sociological Review* 27:31-41.

Gans, Herbert J. 1968. *More Equality*. New York: Vintage Books.

Gerth, Hans H. and C. Wright Mills, eds. 1962. *From Max Weber: Essays in Sociology*. New York: Oxford University Press.

Getter, Lisa. 2004. "Bush, Kerry Awash in Money." *Los Angeles Times*, May 4.

Gold, David A., Clarence Y. H. Lo, and Erik Olin Wright. 1975. "Recent Developments in the Marxist Theories of the Capitalist State." *Monthly Review* 27 (October):29-43 and 27 (November):36-51.

Greenstein, Robert and Issac Shapiro. 2003. "The New, Definitive CBO Data on Income and Tax." *Center on Budget and Policy Priorities* (September 23).

Higley, John and Given Moore. 1981. "Elite Integration in the United States and Australia." *American Political Science Review* 75:581-97.

Huffingtion, Arianna. 2003. *Pigs at the Trough: How Corporate Greed and Political Corruption are Undermining America*. New York: Crown.

Hurst, Charles E. 1995. *Social Inequality: Forms, Causes, and Consequences*. 2nd ed. Needham Heights, MA. Allyn and Bacon.

Ivins, Molly. 2000. "Capitalism Gets a Really Bad Name." *Progressive Populist* (May 15):22-23.

Jansson, Bruce S. 1990. *Social Welfare Policy: From Theory to Practice*. Belmont, CA: Wadsworth.

Jones, Del. 2003. "CEOs, Heirs to Stock Fortune Win big with CUT." *USA Today*, January 9, 3B.

Judis, John B. 1990. "Pulling U.S. Strings: Japanese Money Buys Influence." *Akron Beacon Journal*, January 21, E1 and E4.

Keller, Suzanne. 1969. "Beyond the Ruling Class – Strategic Elites." Pp. 520-524 in *Structured Social Inequality*, edited by C. S. Heller. New York: MacMillan.

Keller, Suzanne. 1987. "Social Differentiation and Social Stratification: The Special Case of Gender." Pp. 329-49 in *Structured Social Inequality*, edited by Celia S. Heller. New York: MacMillan.

Lindblom, Charles E. 1977. *Politics and Markets*. New York: Basic Books.

Manley, John F. 1983. "Neo-Pluralism: A Class Analysis of Pluralism I and Pluralism II." *American Political Science Review* 77:368-83.

Martin, Roderick. 1971. "The Concept of Power: A Critical Defense." *British Journal of Sociology* 22:240-257.

McFarland, Andrew S. 1987. "Interest Groups and Theories of Power in America." *British Journal of Political Science* 17:129-47.

Mills, C. Wright. 1956. *The Power Elite*. New York: Oxford University Press.

Mosca, Gaetano. 1939. *The Ruling Class*. New York: McGraw-Hill.

Parenti, Michael. 1978. *Power and the Powerless*. 2nd ed. New York: St. Martin's Press.

Parenti, Michael. 2002. *Democracy for the Few*. 7th ed. New York: Bedford/St. Martian's Press.

Phillips, Kevin. 1995. "Today's 'Gingrichomics' Echoes GOP Eras of Old." *Christian Science Monitor* (December 22):18.

Phillips, Kevin. 2002. *Wealth and Democracy: A Political History of the American Rich*. New York: Broadway Books.

Piven, Frances Fox and Richard A. Cloward. 1971. *Regulating the Poor: The Functions of Public Welfare*. New York: Random House.

Piven, Frances Fox. 1996. "Welfare and the Transformation of Electoral Politics." *Dissent* 43 (Fall):61-67.

Presthus, Robert. 1962. *The Organizational Society: An Analysis and Theory.*. New York: Vintage Books.

Solomon, Susan Gross (ed.). 1982. *Pluralism in the Soviet Union*. New York: St. Martin's Press.

Tanner, Robert. 2003. "$715 Million Spent Lobbying State Legislators." *Denver Post*, May 15, 8A.

319

The Sociology of Economic Life: How the "What" Gets Produced and Distributed.
by Frank O. Taylor, Ph.D.

THE ECONOMY

Sociologists are interested in the economy because it is fundamental to our lives and to the health to any society. We are confronted by a variety of economic issues and questions on a daily basis. You may wonder if you can afford a new car. Rising gasoline prices may have you wondering if you can afford to drive to work. Most of us expect to purchase a home someday. Increasingly, homeownership is out of reach for many Americans. The average price of a home in California, for instance, is over half a million dollars and only 14 percent of Californians can qualify for a home loan. You may notice that your paycheck does not seem to go as far as it used to. To ask yourself "what's for dinner," is to understand just how important the economy is to you.

Economic institutions are involved in the production and distribution of goods and services. Economic production is related to a number of complex issues. What resources will be used during process? Shall we build more weapons systems or shall we build more highways? Do we prefer public transportation or shall we build more automobiles. Will goods be produced by human beings or by robots? Production issues generally include the questions of what should be produced, by what means, and with what resources. Economic distribution refers to the complex ways in which goods and services are distributed throughout the population. Is it ethical for the Chief Executive Officers to receive a greater share of goods and services than their employees? What is an acceptable minimum wage? Should health care be universal? Distribution issues are related to who gets what share of social rewards.

TYPES OF ECONOMIC INSTITUTIONS

Every society must produce certain things. We may think of these necessities as **functional requisites**, or products and services needed for a society to survive. Economically speaking, while these requisites include both the production of food and water, shelter, and clothing and some institutionalized way of distribution, there are a variety of ways a society may go about fulfilling functional requisites.

14 | The Sociology of Economic Life: How the "What" Gets Produced and Distributed.
by Frank O. Taylor, IV, Ph.D.

Preindustrial Economies. Preindustrial societies include hunting and gathering, horticultural, and agricultural societies. In a preindustrial economy, individual families produce almost all the goods and services. Families may engage in small scale bartering but they consume most of the goods they produce. In these societies, work is closely integrated with every aspect of life. If the family does not harvest enough in the fall, in the spring they may experience malnutrition. Although these societies did give rise to great cities, such as Athens and Rome, in which there was enough surplus to support an artistic and scholarly elite, in truth, the vast majority of people were very poor and engaged in **primary production**. This type of production is based on extracting raw materials directly from nature and includes hunting, farming, herding, fishing, logging, and mining. In preindustrial economies settlements are small and dispersed. Humans and animals provide the labor power. Technology is relatively simple and may include irrigation systems, water wheels, and hand tools. One important aspect of preindustrial economies is that social responsibility dictates that families care for children, the elderly, and the sick. In preindustrial societies, families attempt to produce as many children as possible, because children provide labor and are viewed as old-age insurance when parents become elderly.

Industrial Economies. While preindustrial economies are based on primary production, industrial economies are based on **secondary production**. Secondary production is characterized by large bureaucratically organized units of production, heavy reliance on modern energy, such as gasoline, electricity, or nuclear power, and the processing of raw materials. All you have to do is imagine a modern automobile-manufacturing factory and you get the idea. Raw materials such as steel, rubber, and oil are turned into an automobile. Industrial economies use advanced technology to reduce the number of people involved in primary production, which produces a surplus and allows the number of people engaged in other productive activities to increase. This is known as the **division of labor**. Although substantial inequalities may still exist, industrialization generally leads to higher standards of living, better health care, and more education. Unfortunately, industrialization is also usually accompanied by considerable pollution, toxic waste, and environmental degradation.

Postindustrial Economies. Postindustrial economies rely on **tertiary production**, or the production of services rather than goods. Tertiary production does not rely upon the production of tangible goods. Postindustrial economies are characterized by a complex division of labor in which a

321

variety of occupations produce services. Doctors, lawyers, teachers, college professors, accountants, police officers, firefighters, social workers, nurses, and people involved in a host of other occupations provide services for others but do not produce or manufacture anything. In 1920, only 19 percent of the United States labor force was involved in tertiary production. By 2000, nearly three-quarters of the labor force was involved in tertiary production. Today only 3 percent of the labor force is engaged in primary production and secondary production has declined to 24 percent.

CAPITALISM AND SOCIALISM

Capitalism.   Capitalism is an economic system based on the profit motive and in which most wealth is held in the form of private property. Three conditions are necessary for capitalism to exist: private ownership of property, the pursuit of personal profit, and a market system based on competition. The first principle of pure capitalism is private ownership of the **means of production**. This means that individuals can own almost anything, a home, for example, or an automobile or other personal belongings. This principle also dictates that private individuals can own the means of production and distribution, such as major manufacturing and retail concerns. In a society characterized by pure capitalism, the public would not own anything that could potentially produce a profit. In a pure capitalist economy, there would be no state-owned mass transit system, public rail or subway system, or even national park system if corporations could make a profit providing those services.

In a capitalist society, the pursuit of personal profit is viewed as not only entirely natural but as a basic component of human nature. The Scottish philosopher Adam Smith held that individuals should be free to maximize their personal wealth and that the individual pursuit of self-interest benefits the entire society through the creation of jobs and economic growth.

Profit is derived from paying those who produce a good less than the cost of its production. Here is how it works. If you decide to go into business for yourself selling pizzas, you will personally make every pizza you sell. Your labor is part of the value of the pizza. Thus, the pizza is worth the raw materials you had to purchase, the overhead expended on the oven, lights, energy, heat and so on, and your labor. Your profit on the pizza is equal to whatever consumers will pay you minus labor, ingredients, and overhead to make it. If the business becomes successful, you will hire some workers to help make the pizzas and you will pay them a wage. However, you cannot pay the workers the same amount of money you paid yourself to make the pizza—you would not make any profit! Assuming that the amount of labor that goes into making a pizza remains constant, as do the costs of raw materials and overhead, the only way for you to derive a profit is to pay your employees less than the value of their labor. Of course, this arrangement disproportionately benefits you over your employees. Capitalism is characterized by the unequal distribution of social rewards.

The third principle of capitalism is competition. In a pure capitalist economy if a particular good or service can produce a profit any number of producers will enter the market and undertake its production. The price of the good or service will be determined by competition among a number of producers. If, for example, there are ten producers of a good or service of similar functionality, consumers will presumably be drawn to the most reliable and cheapest alternative. In practical terms, this means that the nine other producers of the same good or service cannot raise their prices much beyond the single most successful producer. Competition among producers acts like a break on corporate greed and socially irresponsible corporate behavior. The same is true for wages. If one employer attempts to pay workers with a particular set of skills less than competing employers pay, workers will migrate to the competitors.

Two principles are important here: competition and a free market. This free market system is called a ***laissez-faire*** economy. In theory, a laissez-faire economy, according to Adam Smith, is free from regulation and governed only by the **invisible hand** of supply and demand. The government does not need to set minimum wages, regulate the safety environment at work, or concern itself with consumer safety. In a free market economy, if wages are higher in a certain sector of the economy, workers will migrate to that sector of the economy and abandon the sectors that are low paid. Similarly, if a sector of the economy has unsafe working conditions workers will leave for other employment. Consumers will switch from unsafe products to safer brands. When the demand for a good is equal to the supply of that good prices are stable. If the demand for a good is less than the supply of the good, prices will fall. Conversely, if the demand for a good is greater than the supply of the good, prices will increase. In this way, a competitive market unencumbered by government interference will theoretically operate in a manner beneficial for everyone in society.

14 | The Sociology of Economic Life: How the "What" Gets Produced and Distributed.
by Frank O. Taylor, IV, Ph.D.

It is important to realize that a free market does not exist anywhere in the world (certainly not in the United States), and never has. We will return to this point later in the chapter. Since the economy is the foundation of all culture and civil life, no government can afford not to be involved. In modern nations, it is fruitless to think that political and economic systems are distinct and uniquely separate. In the United States there tends to be a connection between the political elite and the economic elite. When workers advocate for a living wage, economic elites like to trot out Adam Smith and *laissez-faire* economic theory and claim that they will go out of business if the government intervenes. However, when their businesses face bankruptcy, the economic elite tend to forget capitalist economic theory and expect the government to get involved and bail them out, even if the failure is the result of bad decision-making.

The vast majority of businesses are privately owned in the United States. However, the government plays an extensive role in regulating the economy. The board of Federal Governors (Fed), for example, attempts to regulate economic growth by raising or lowering interest rates. If inflation starts to become significant, the Fed tries to slow down economic growth by raising the interest rate. If the economy is growing stagnant, the Fed tries to encourage economic growth by lowering the interest rate. The federal government owns the United States Postal Service, the Amtrak railroad, and the United States military. Many colleges and universities as well as public school systems are owned and operated by state and local governments. The government also is involved in operating roads, parks, and museums. Additionally, the government is involved in student loans, veteran's benefits, Social Security and public support, and the regulation of industry. Not surprisingly, local, state, and federal governments are collectively the nation's largest employers, employing fully 14 percent of the nation's work force.

Any number of circumstances can work against a free market. If important goods and services are controlled by a monopoly, then there is no invisible hand working for the public good. Also, many services we all agree are necessary for the public good are not provided by any corporation for the simple reason that they cannot make a profit. Historically, the invisible hand was not very successful in forcing employers to pay higher wages, produce safe products, or look out for the safety and well being of their employees. Recently, we have seen what the result of deregulating the energy industry has yielded in the wake of the Enron debacle.

Labor is only mobile in theory. An unemployed single mother, for example, is unlikely to be able to simply pick up and move if no employer is willing to buy her labor where she lives. Many individuals and families simply lack the resources to move to where there are better jobs. As the United States, government and corporate America increasingly abandon health care and pension programs the debate as to what constitutes public wellbeing and the "invisible hand" that is supposed to provide for it will undoubtedly be revisited.

Socialism.   In marked contrast to capitalism, socialism is an economic system in which the means of production are collectively owned, managed, and operated for the good of the community, rather than private individuals.   Whereas capitalism is an economic system that emphasizes production, at the expense of distribution, socialism is an economic system that stresses distribution at the expense of production.   The key principles of socialism include collective ownership of property, pursuit of collective goals, and government control over the economy.

The first principle of socialism is collective ownership of property. In a capitalist economy only those who can afford it have health care, own homes, achieve an education. A socialist society defines work, health care, housing, and old age pensions as a right. Some socialist societies view transportation, communication, paid leave after the birth of a child, and even vacations as rights to which everyone is entitled. In a socialist economy, private property exists but the means of production is used to benefit everyone. The government controls major industries and ensures that health care, housing, and goods and services are available to all citizens, not just people with money.

The second principle of socialism is the pursuit of collective goals. In a capitalist economy, the demands of the marketplace, at least in theory, determine what will be produced. This can have seriously deleterious effects on a society. For example, in a capitalist society rising health care costs will result fewer and fewer people being able to afford health care. Socialist public policy would attempt to control the cost of health care through careful regulation, thus ensuring that every citizen has access to health care. Capitalist public policy would attempt to make individuals responsible for their own health care.   Obviously, placing limits on profit-taking and other regulations would limit the ability of health care organizations to make a profit, which is an anathema to capitalists. In a capitalist economy, health care is privately owned and operated on a for-profit basis. In a socialist economy, health care is viewed as a basic human right and the state has an obligation to ensure that people have a minimum level of care.

The same scenario can be seen in other areas of social life, such as housing, education, transportation, and communication. In a capitalist society developers focus on up-scale housing where profits are high. This may result in very few units of affordable homes or apartment complexes being built. Housing development would be controlled in a socialist economy to ensure that adequate housing exists for everyone.

The third principle of socialism is government control of the economy. The laissez-faire approach to the economy is rejected by socialism in favor of a **command economy**. In a command economy, a rational assessment of social needs is undertaken and the economy is directed and organized in a manner best aimed at achieving those needs. A command economy is organized to meeting the material needs of the population. Economic planning can also be extended such social goals as protecting the environment, research and development related to new technologies, and saving natural resources. Frequent, in a command economy prices and wages are set by the government rather than the invisible hand of the market. One advantage a socialist economy has over capitalism is that resources can be diverted from one industry or sector of the economy to another in order to pursue long-range goals in education or agriculture, for example.

One disadvantage of socialism is that production is usually lower in socialist economies than it is in capitalist economies. For one thing, capital is extremely mobile in a capitalist economy. Capital is held in fewer hands in a capitalist economy and individuals with large sums of money can make decisions about spending and investment very quickly, transferring large amounts of money from one account to another. In a command economy, the decisions to use capital in one way or another are made by large bureaucracies and money is concentrated in the hands of a greater number of people. Additionally, when incompetent and lazy workers are paid as much or more than competent and motivated workers, the work ethic tends to decline.

Mixed Economies. Most modern societies have a mixture of socialist and capitalist economic structures. Until recently, the trend in the United States since the 1930s has been toward creating a mixed economy, although currently conservatives are making a concerted effort aimed at undoing the **Great Society**. Most industrial democracies have gone a long way toward creating mixed economies. There are two main reasons for creating a mixed economy. First, in many instances industries key to collective welfare, such as education and public transportation, are not profitable and would not be provided under a capitalist economy. Second, many nations have deemed the social provision of health care, housing, education, nutrition, and pensions as a matter of ethics. Such nations do not deem it ethical to have high rates of homelessness and other social problems. Some nations therefore set social policy to eliminate homelessness. In the United States, unfortunately, many cities, most recently in Florida and Texas, are moving to criminalize homelessness.

Sweden is a good example of a mixed economy. The economy is largely capitalist with a generous social welfare system based on the principles of democratic socialism (discussed below). Swedish social and economic policy is aimed at leveling the extremes of wealth and poverty. The list of government programs designed to provide basic social services for the population is impressive. Sweden has a national health insurance program, a family program, a retirement program, and subsidized housing. Under the health care program, citizens pay $108 for an entire year of subsidized health care. The Swedish family program provides prenatal, delivery, and postnatal care free of charge and children receive free medical and dental care until age 20, after which they are covered by the health insurance program. Working parents receive 450 days of paid leave to care for newborns and 60 days of paid leave to care for a sick child. Children are entitled to three hours of free preschool per day. The elderly are entitled to receive free nursing care in their home and a housing subsidy. Lower income families have access to non-profit housing where rent is controlled and state-subsidized financing for new homes.

Sweden is able to achieve these results because of the high rate of taxation. Many United States citizens would see a 52 percent rate of taxation as intolerable, but that is because we do not get much in return for our taxes, which go largely to defense spending and social security. However, if you lived in Sweden you would have a guaranteed job and income, access to free housing, a free college education, free medical care, and security in your elderly years. The list goes on! Medical expenses for giving birth to children and day care are provided by the state. You would continue to receive 80 percent of your paycheck while you are taking family leave. While the future of Sweden's market socialism cannot be certain, the Swedes have managed to balance capitalism and socialism.

The Political Economy of Socialism. Many critics of socialism point out that it minimizes individual freedom and limits choices. These critics point to the human-rights abuses of the former

Soviet Union, the People's Republic of China, and Cuba as evidence of the superiority of capitalism over socialism and communism. However, many Marxists decry the policies of China and the former Soviet Union and reject, as a perversion of socialism, the type of communism that emerged in those states. **Communism** is a socialist economy combined with an authoritarian political system. It is a mistake to equate all socialist nations with the Soviet Union and China.

There are two types of socialism: **authoritarian socialism** and **democratic socialism**. Authoritarian socialism is characterized by a socialist economy controlled by a political elite kept in power through control of the military. Critics of authoritarian socialism argue that the economy is run for the benefits of the political elite at the expense of the workers. They also allege that the inefficiencies and inequalities of communism have nothing to due with socialist principles but are a result of authoritarianism and excessive bureaucratization. In many so-called socialist societies, people are denied basic civil liberties and freedoms and the government is controlled by a single authoritarian political party. In these nations, elections are a sham and citizens have no choice but to vote for candidates selected and approved by the government.

Democratic socialism, as represented by Sweden, for instance, has been achieved with the support of the people through democratic institutions. In Sweden representatives of the socialist state are answerable to the people they represent. These nations subscribe to the principle of **egalitarianism**: equality of opportunity for all. It is understood that equal opportunity is not the same thing as outright equality. Some inequality is acceptable. However, the huge differences in standard of living that characterize the United States are unacceptable to nations that practice democratic socialism. These nations are committed to leveling out inequalities of income, education, and opportunities.

The Political Economy of Capitalism. In the United States, pro-business conservatives continuously argue that government intervention in the economy is excessive and regulation has reduced the ability of capitalism to respond to the market. This argument became so pervasive that in the 1980s Ronald Reagan was elected on the slogan that "government is not the solution to the problem; government *is* the problem." In spite of conservative claims, there is mounting evidence that the government has been captured by economic elites, who pursue a pro-business agenda at the expense of the interests of the middle and working classes, not to mention the poor.

GLOBALIZATION

The United States economy, beginning in the 1970s and expanding rapidly in the 1980s has been characterized by **deindustrialization**. Deindustrialization refers to the movement of labor-intensive work to the third world, where unions, pro-labor legislation, and environmental protection laws are non-existent and workers are often paid mere pennies a day. **Multinational corporations** are large corporations that operate on a global basis and often wield more power and economic resources that the nations that host them. Although many nations, including Germany, Great Britain, and Japan, are home to multinational corporations, the majority of multinationals are United States corporations.   Ford, General Motors, International Telephone and Telegraph, and International Business Machines are included among the ranks of the largest corporations in the world.

Globalization has proceeded to such a degree that consumer goods are increasingly produced abroad. Can you purchase a television, DVD, video, or CD player, refrigerator, oven, microwave, toaster, or coffee maker manufactured in the United States? It is increasingly unlikely. The car you drive, even if manufactured by Ford, can at best be said to be "assembled" in the United States from parts manufactured all over the Third World. When you can purchase a product produced in the United States, the cost is often prohibitive. For example, Gibson guitars, still manufactured in the United States, often cost over $2,500.   A comparable guitar manufactured in Korea, Mexico, Japan, or China often costs less than $500. People of average means often have no other choice than to purchase a foreign made product.

One negative effect of deindustrialization is the resultant decline in standard of living of the American working class. As people's standard of living declines, they are forced to purchase cheaper foreign goods. Leaving individual corporations aside, as a nation, the United States must compete with other economies around the world. Whenever United States citizens spend their dollars on foreign products, money is removed from our economy. For example, when you buy a Honda Accord, you may get a car that gets excellent gas mileage, is extremely reliable, and American workers receive the wages, but the downside is that a Japanese corporation receives the profits. As more and more people buy foreign goods, more and more money is removed from our economy. This is called the **trade deficit**. The United States buys more goods from foreign nations than they buy from us. As money flows out of the United States to foreign banks, there is less and less money available for savings, investment, and loans in America.

Another negative effect of globalization is the imperialism it generates. As United States multinationals entered the Third World United States military might often followed. For example, in the 1920s the United States invaded 12 Latin American countries often in support of United States multinational corporations involved in agribusiness, mining, and oil production. As recent events in Iraq demonstrate, the influence of multinationals over United States foreign policy is problematic.

THE UNITED STATES ECONOMY

The Dual Economy. The United States economy is composed of two major parts: the **industrial core**, and a **periphery** of smaller competitive businesses. As discussed previously, in a pure market economy a large number of producers compete with each other for customers, labor, resources and raw material used in the production process, and capital. Competition disciplines the market and protects consumers from price gouging. In the industrial core, unfortunately, the competition that underpins a pure market does not exist, if it ever did.

A few corporate giants, such as Exxon, Ford, General Motors, and IBM, many of which are multinationals, dominate the core. Each of these corporations has economic assets running in the billions, more wealth than most nations of the world, and employs hundreds of thousands of individuals distributed around the world. These multinational businesses are so powerful that they have been able to bargain with local and state governments, and the federal government to attain tax advantages and other favorable legislation. Relationships among capitalists today are more characterized by interdependence than competition. This is because serving on the same boards, owning stock in the same corporations, and their relationship to the same financial institutions, links them to each other. This decrease in competition means that large firms have become more cooperative than competitive and efficiency is reduced.

The periphery is composed of competitive small businesses, most of which are family owned or operated by a small group of partners. If the core is characterized by large bureaucracies, relative job security, higher wages, benefits packages that include pensions and health care, and thousands of employees, the periphery is characterized by small businesses with a handful of employees, economic uncertainty, little bureaucratization, and lower wages and few benefits. Owning one's own business has long been part of the American Dream. Many Americans are able, through modest means, to begin a small enterprise, such as farming, repair shops, contracting, retail stores, and restaurants, among other businesses, such as beauty salons, or independent contracting. It is in the periphery that competition exists.   Many small businesses go bankrupt and fail. However, many small businesses succeed and thrive in the periphery.

For many years, I worked as a professional musician, traveling with a band all over the Midwest. Every week we earned wages but we were always paid in cash. Effectively, we were part of the **underground economy**. This informal economy is characterized by lack of recordkeeping and the state, although aware of the underground economy, is largely unable to regulate it. Those who participate in this type of work rarely pay taxes. A major drawback is that employers, since they do not keep records, do not pay into social security or unemployment insurance for workers they pay under the table. Thus, the underground economy is an important source of employment but those who are involved do not reap the benefits associated with work in the core or small business. During my years as a musician I became acquainted with lots of people involved in the underground economy, including strippers, drug dealers, gamblers, and prostitutes. However, the underground economy also employs a variety of people engaged in legal, if unofficial enterprises, including people in home repair, housecleaning, and construction.

The Segmented Labor Market. The dual economy creates a **segmented labor market**. The segmented labor market is based on different hiring procedures, credentials, promotion ladders, and job experiences for those who work in the industrial core and those who work in the periphery. To work in the industrial core, or the **primary labor market**, you must have the requisite credentials, either vocational training or a college degree. Once you are hired, you will embark on your "career" and, hopefully, move up through a promotional ladder that is explicitly defined. This is known as an **internal labor market**—upper-level positions are filled from the lower ranks. You credentials will help determine how far up the promotional ladder you are able to climb. In the core, employment is highly secure, career paths are stable, and the benefits are good. The larger the firm, the better the wages and benefits tend to be. If you find employment in the core, you will have to deal with a large impersonal bureaucracy that employs thousands of people, who you will never know personally, and is governed by lots of rules, regulations, and red tape. You will be evaluated regularly and promotion will depend upon you ability.

If you find employment in the periphery, or the **secondary labor market**, you will work in a smaller setting with less bureaucracy. Likely, you will know all your co-workers. The periphery is less dependent upon credentials. After all, it requires very little training or education to be a fry cook in a restaurant or a maid in a hotel. People who lack an education, who have poor work records, or who simply need to work part-time, find employment in the periphery attractive. Employment in the periphery is characterized by few, if any, promotional ladders, low pay, less job security, and few benefits. These are largely blue-collar jobs, in low-skilled assembly-line operations and service sector employment. The periphery employs large number of women, who are interested in part-time work, and large numbers of minorities, who lack the credentials to work in the core.

Work in the United States. In Western culture, employment is directly tied to social rewards. Although most Western societies provide social welfare for the ill, elderly, and disabled, most able-bodied people are expected to work for wages or a salary. In our capitalist economy, we use wages earned from paid-employment to purchase the necessities of life, including food, clothing, housing, transportation, communication, and healthcare. Of course, not everyone works, but generally someone in the household does and it is through their labor that household members have access to social rewards. Employment is a necessity for most people. Employment is also related to self-esteem, mental and physical health, and status. Unemployed people are more vulnerable to depression, alcoholism, and family violence. About two-thirds of all adults in the United States are in employed in the labor force at any given time. Historically, labor force participation for women has lagged behind men, but they are closing the gap and are expected to surpass men in the not too distant future. It is clear, therefore, that in United States society, employment structures our daily lives.

The unemployed are also considered part of the labor force. The unemployed are part of the **reserve pool of labor**—during an economic expansion, they can be pulled into the labor force and, alternatively, during an economic recession they are often laid off. The official unemployment rate reached a peak in 1983 of nearly 11 percent and stood at a low of 3.9 in 2000, which translates into about 5.7 million people. Over the last 40 years, the average unemployment rate has hovered around 5 percent.

Table 14.1   Unemployment Rate 2000

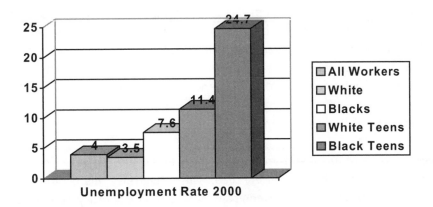

Referring to the table above, we can see that unemployment is not distributed equally. Minorities are twice as likely as Whites to be unemployed. The unemployment rate for Hispanics is nearly 5 percent and for Blacks nearly 8 percent. The White unemployment rate is only 4 percent. The unemployment rate for college graduates is a mere 1.7 percent. Black teens between the ages of 16 and 19 have an unemployment rate of a whopping 24.7 percent, which is extremely troubling. The rate of unemployment for White women is 3.6 percent compared to 7.2 percent for Black women, 3.4 percent for White men, and 8.1 percent for Black men.

The official unemployment statistics are badly flawed. The unemployment rate is underestimated because it only tracks people who actively sought employment in the last four weeks. The data do not account for the 60 million people who are not in the labor force. Who are these people? The unemployed include students, homemakers, the retired, the disabled, and about 1 million **discouraged workers** who have given up looking for a job. If the Bureau of Labor Statistics fails to accurately track the unemployed, a complete picture of the jobless is impossible to attain. For example, the will, on the part of the people or the government, to undertake public policy reform related to unemployment is undermined when the statistics are underestimated. An unemployment rate of only 3.4 percent seems quite small and people are unlikely to be much concerned about it. The reality is that the unemployment rate is closer to three times the official rate, which would place it at more than 10 percent.

By only tracking individuals who actively sought work in the previously four weeks, the Bureau of Labor Statistics is able to effectively mask major problems in the labor force. Many people are forced to subsist on odd jobs, day labor, temporary work, and part-time work. These people are counted as "fully employed" by the government. In fact, the government considers you fully employed if you were paid for even one hour of work in the week prior to being interviewed. **Underemployment** is also a problem for millions of people. Currently, about 30 million people work part time. Others hold jobs far beneath their educational credentials. Still others are employed seasonally. About 20 percent of the underemployed indicate that they are dissatisfied and would take full-time employment if they could find it.

Frequently, students believe that anyone who wants a job can get a job, if they are willing to look long enough and accept whatever is offered. Unfortunately, this is not true. Full employment is catastrophically inflationary. The government has built in monetary and fiscal policies designed to keep the economy expanding, but not too much. Big economic booms are followed by big economic busts. The goal is to manage the economy in order to sustain slow growth, around 3 percent. An economic expansion really boils down to investors and consumers spending more money. The government can slow down spending through taxation and raising interest rates. In addition, the government does just that when it looks as though inflation is about to set in. This has the effect of creating unemployment. When interest rates go up businesses will not borrow money and may even downsize. Conversely, if the economy looks as if it may go into a recession, the government cuts taxes and the interest rate, trying to encourage businesses to expand. If this works, people go to work.

Capitalists favor these policies. A high unemployment rate and low wages tends to increase their profits. How does this work? If minimum wages were higher, wage increases would occur all the way up the promotion ladder. Higher wages at the bottom lead to higher wages at the top. Thus, lower minimum wages tends to deflate wages throughout the wage structure. In addition, if there is a large pool of workers willing to work for low wages, those who have a job are less likely to agitate for higher pay out of fear that they will be replaced by cheaper workers.

Occupational Structure. We have noted that employment is directly ties to social rewards. However, if you are a college professor you income, status, job security, autonomy, and work satisfaction will be very different from people who work on an assembly line or in a restaurant. What is the difference between a job and a profession? Occupations that demand specialized skills, education, a high degree of personal involvement, creative freedom, work with the mind rather than the hands, and a sense of obligation to a professional community are **professions**. The professions include law, medicine, teaching, art, music, and a wide variety of related occupations. Some professionals, such as doctors, command higher incomes than others do, such as artists and musicians. However, income is only one aspect of the professions.

The most distinguishing characteristic about the professions is **autonomy**. Professionals, because they must rely on personal judgment and are involved in non-routine work that cannot be standardized, are substantially free from direct supervision. Employers trust that professionals can achieve the goals they are given, efficiently and in a timely manner, without direct supervision. Your college professor is a pretty good example of a professional with a very high degree of autonomy.   Although college professors are certainly evaluated and must teach their classes according to a schedule, they have a high degree of freedom in deciding exactly how to teach their classes. It would be extremely rare to see a department chair or a Dean show up to check on a professor.   The teaching community has a set of ethical guidelines to which most professors willingly subscribe.

Another good indication of the status of your job is whether you work with your hands or your mind. People who work with their hands, as farmers, assemblers, contractors, welders, and so on, are known as **blue-collar workers**. Some blue-collar workers earn very high wages but for the most part, blue-collar work is associated with work that is highly supervised, routine, less secure, and less well paid. Those who work their mind, are expected to think independently and typically work in a office setting or retail sales, are known as **white-collar workers**. **Pink-Collar** workers are women who work in low-status, low-skill, dead-end jobs in which women replicate in the work force the type of work they do in the home.

The **service economy** can be divided into two tiers, an upper tier and a lower tier. The **upper tier** of the service economy is comprised of occupations in fields of medicine, health care, insurance, communications, education, accounting, law, and the mass media among others. Positions in these types of occupations are typically white-collar. The **lower tier** of the service economy is comprised of low-paid, low-skill, no benefits, and no advancement jobs. Working as a maid, janitor, cooks, hamburger-flipper, or waiter, and so on, in the service economy are common jobs in the lower tier. Sociologists have coined a new term for jobs in the lower tier: "**McJobs**." The fastest growing occupations include food service, health service, and janitorial service in the future.

Your occupation is the main determinant of your location in the stratification structure. Again, work is the key to social rewards. Social rewards are more than just income and status. Your health, lifestyle, and happiness are all related to your occupation. Imagine all the ways in which work structures your reality. It structures where you spend the majority of your day. It is related to whom you work with, what you do, how you do it, and under what conditions you labor. Work is highly correlated with whether or not people find life fulfilling or miserable.

Two types of rewards are associated with work: intrinsic rewards and extrinsic rewards. **Intrinsic rewards** are related to the work itself—you obtain intrinsic rewards when you find the work satisfying and you feel pride in your creative abilities. **Extrinsic rewards** refer to the tangible benefits, such as income, benefits, or job security. The sense of fulfillment many college professors feel when their students graduate and go on to a good job or perhaps to graduate school is an intrinsic reward. Tenure, on the other hand, is a form of job security and therefore an extrinsic reward.

Job satisfaction is another dimension of the occupational structure. A truly satisfying job probably has some mixture of intrinsic and extrinsic rewards. Research on job satisfaction indicates that the most satisfying jobs are those that have good pay and benefits, a high degree of autonomy, opportunities for promotion, high occupational prestige, interesting work, and highly valued skills and abilities. The most satisfied workers tend to be in the learned professions—doctors, lawyers, and professors. These workers tend to be highly educated, have great freedom from supervision, are accorded great respect and status by society, and are involved in creative and interesting work. The least satisfied workers are those on assembly lines. Professionals and other skilled workers then to be more satisfied with their work than semi-skilled and unskilled workers.

Alienation is another dimension of the quality of work. **Alienation** is a feeling that develops when workers have no control over the process of work or their labor and the work seems particularly meaningless. I remember working on an assembly line. The work was boring, repetitive, frequently dangerous, and mind numbing. I repeated the same set of physical movements over and over for hours on end. Assembly line work, service work, especially in the lower tier, and work, which requires high levels of emotional stress, can all be alienating.

Another key aspect of the occupational structure is self-direction. **Self-direction** refers to the degree to which an employee is given a set of abstract goals and granted the freedom to achieve them. College professors have a high degree of self-direction. However, some blue-collar workers, such as carpenters and plumbers who have flexible jobs that require decision-making, also have a high level of self-direction. Self-direction has three components: low routine, low-supervision, and high complexity. Workers who are involved in creative, complex, enterprises without close supervision are the most satisfied and least alienated. Conversely, workers who are involved in assembly line work, or who work as checkout cashiers, are the least satisfied and most alienated.

CAPITALISM AND INEQUALITY

Clearly, capitalism has undergone a vast array of changes. Not the least of which is the regulation of the economy by the Federal Board of Governors. The ideas of Adam Smith are history—the present economy in the United States is far from a free market system. The ideal system of competition among many of more or less equal producers is corrupted by the economic market power of huge corporations. These corporations, rather than respond to changes in demand, control the market. Additionally, the trend toward globalization of capitalism is making profound changes in the economies of not only the United States but foreign nations as well. The rise of corporations begs the question of how economic policy should be derived in the modern world.

The rise of the modern corporation has changed capitalism fundamentally. A corporation is a business that is considered by law to be a person. Those who own a corporation are not responsible for its liabilities and obligations. Unlike you or me, the owners of a corporation cannot be held liable for its debts. A corporation can enter into contracts, buy or sell stocks and bonds, and sue and be sued.

Monopolistic Capitalism. Several inherent contradictions plague capitalism. One of the most significant contradictions in capitalism is the tendency toward monopolies. Without strict prohibitions against it, the free market system automatically results in businesses getting bigger and bigger, through mergers, takeovers, acquisitions, and unfair competition. The result is that smaller firms are either forced out of business or bought up by the giants. Eventually, every sector of the economy could be dominated by a monopoly. Imagine a situation in which one global corporation was entirely in control of the world's food supply. This is not as farfetched as it seems. Already the vast majority of the world's food production and distribution is controlled by a handful of major corporations, such as Archer-Daniels-Midlands.

There is a lot of evidence that competition has been severely diminished. There certainly are some titanic corporations in our economy—General Motors, Ford, General Electric, Coca-Cola, Du Pont, and American Telephone and Telegraph come to mind. Nevertheless, no sector of the economy appears to be completely dominated by a single monopoly. Instead, a small number of firms tend to dominate most sectors of the economy. **Shared monopolies**, or oligopolies, exist when four or fewer firms supply fifty percent or more of a given market. The automobile industry is a good example. A number of other important industries are also highly concentrated, including defense, brewing, breakfast cereals, and gasoline. The trend toward high concentration among corporations has accelerated due to two important trends: mergers and interlocking directorates.

Megamergers. The law forbids that any single producer dominant a market by establishing a monopoly. Oligopoly, on the other hand, the domination of the market by a handful of producers, has become an accepted reality. The 1980s saw a frenzy of mergers, encouraged by the federal government's relaxation of antitrust laws, the largest of which was the purchase of RJR-Nabisco for $25 billion. There are many examples of megamergers: Time and AOL joining with Warner Communications; Disney now owns ABC; Wells Fargo merged with First Interstate Banks; Phillip Morris joined with Miller Brewing; Citicorp merged with Travelers Group, to name a few. Some megamergers have combined United States and foreign firms. For example in the automobile manufacturing industry Daimler and Chrysler merged. In the oil industry, British Petroleum and Amoco merged.

There are four negative consequences of megamergers. First, the competition necessary to make the free market work is reduced. When capital is highly concentrated in the hands of a few corporations, competition is reduced and prices for consumers invariable go up. Second, the market power of huge corporations increases. As we know from earlier discussions, when a company's

338

market power gets more concentrated it is able to resist changes in demand. Thus, big corporations, rather than being controlled by market forces, are able to control the market. This gives these firms control over consumers, workers, unions, and even the government. Henry Ford was fond of telling Senators and other politicians that if Ford went under it would wreck the entire United States economy—so they had better do as he wished. Third, it diminishes the number of jobs. Since the 1980s, the supply-side philosophy of increasing worker efficiency has been adopted by large corporations. This has resulted in massive layoffs through corporate downsizing. Millions and millions of jobs are lost each year due to these policies. Mostly, these are mid-level white-collar jobs paying middle class wages. The result could very well be a reduction in total spending as these people fail to find jobs that pay similar wages. Lastly, megamergers are not productive investment. During the 1980s, thousand of corporations changed hands at a cost of trillions of dollars. This expense did not produce new factories, plants, products, or jobs but amounted to paper shuffling. In order to pay for poor management decisions many workers were laid off through downsizing.

Interlocking Directorates. In 1914 Congress passed the Clayton Act, making it illegal for a person to serve simultaneously on the boards of two corporations in direct competition with each other. **Indirect interlocks**, were companies are not in competition with each other, were allowed. In spite of the prohibition interlocking directorates are proliferate throughout United States industry. The wealthy use interlocking corporate directorates as a tool to wield political and economic power. Members of the elite serve as directors of several companies. It is like joining an exclusive club.

People who serve on outside boards are continually in contact with a built in panel of experts who meet regularly each month. A member of Ford's board of directors, for example, may also be a board member of Exxon's board of directors, along with a member from General Motors. The result is that competition is reduced because no director is going to approve a plan that will damage a company in which they have a vested interest. All parties will have access to valuable information about each other's marketing strategies and products. The top executives of the biggest corporations also meet frequently in recreational settings, where they develop a sense of solidarity and purpose. The atmosphere is more one of cooperation than direct competition.

What of the "invisible hand" of market processes theorized by Adam Smith or the social responsibility that competition would bring? Instead of a free market system, the United States economy is dominated by huge corporations. Without the threat of competition, these companies are free to increase prices regardless of what consumers do. Corporate power is so pervasive and competition between corporations so limited that government regulation may be the only way to protect the public good.

Politically liberal economists tend to be much more accepting of the idea that government needs to provide for the social welfare of its citizens. Sadly, it may be a moot point since government is corporate America's largest customer. Also, the 1980s and supply-side economics ushered in a period of deregulation of businesses which shows no signs of abating anytime soon. Quite contrary to Smith's ideas of pure capitalism and a free market system, the government frequently intervenes to support failing corporations, at taxpayer expense. The recent savings and loan bailout is an example. Within the past generation Chrysler was bailed out and Harley Davidson received protection by increased tariffs and duties on its direct competitors—Honda, Suzuki, and Kawasaki.

Corporate Capitalism. A significant aspect of modern corporations is the separation of ownership and management. Most mom and pop stores still compete with each other and the owners run the day-to-day affairs of their businesses. This is not true for corporations. The stockholders, who are the owners, leave the running of the corporations to managers.

The managers treat the businesses as if they were their own. Interestingly, this results in owners who do not control their wealth, and control of wealth without ownership. When a few owners hold all or most of the stock of a business they tend to dominate the board of directors and have a large hand in running it. When a firm's stock is highly dispersed, each owner has only a small fraction of ownership. This allows managers to fill the power void. Managers have a vested interest in setting their own goals and controlling their salaries. Management negotiates with unions, hires advertising agencies, and sets marketing strategies, and so on. Their duty is to produce profits for shareholders. It is common for the chief executive officer and others in upper management, to be awarded stock options. As long as managements reports good profits at the annual stockholder's meeting stockholders may be inclined to rubberstamp their recommendations.

Shared monopolies use their ability to dominate an industry and their political power to support legislation that gives them special tax breaks or protects their industry from imports, as in the case of Harley Davidson. Corporations have changed capitalism so dramatically that the term **corporate capitalism** is used to indicate that the economy is controlled by a handful of giant corporations.

Of the hundreds of thousands of corporations in the United States, a mere five hundred virtually dominate the market place. These firms' annual profits are equal to one-forth of the entire gross national product of the economy. The largest firms are giants composed of many other businesses—conglomerates.

Conglomerates emerge as corporations enter new markets or take over new companies. In 1996 Viacom, a gigantic umbrella corporation had revenues of $12.1 billion. Paramount, Blockbuster, MTV, Nickelodeon, and a host of other businesses and radio and television shows are all part of Viacom. In addition to interlocking directorates and social networks, corporations are also linked by owning stock in each other. For instance, Ford owns the English car manufacturer Jaguar outright and has a significant share of Mazda. General Motors has invested heavily in Isuzu, and Chrysler owns stock in Mitsubishi.

Multinational Corporations.   As we have seen, there is a tendency for corporations to increase in size and power, eventually resulting in huge conglomerates and monopolies. These corporations have enormous economic and political power. This power has grown even greater with the newest trend—the globalization of the largest corporations.

Today, giant corporations account for most of the world's economic output. The largest corporations, based in the United States, Japan, and Western Europe, have established production facilities all over the globe. Their production processes span national borders, making the entire world one big marketplace. Larger corporations focus on the "global economy" and have become more and more detached from the interests and values of the nations that spawned them. Corporate giants, such as General Motors for example, feel little or no allegiance to the cities in the United States that provided the infrastructure and labor force that made their success possible. When General Motors closed eleven plants in Flint Michigan and moved them to Mexico the city's economy was left in ruins. Exxon-Mobil, General Motors, and Ford have more annual revenue than all but seven nations of the world.

United States' Multinational corporations move investments and production from country to country in search of lower labor costs, without much concern for consequences other than profits. Most of the planet's resources and population is to be found in the less-developed nations. Multinational corporations are gaining access to their raw materials, markets, and labor forces. An autoworker in Mexico earns as little as fifty cents an hour. Not even enough to live on. An industrial worker in Taiwan must work all week to earn as much as an American worker earns in a single day. United States' multinationals have a variety of other reasons for investment in foreign markets. Many Third World nations have no laws protecting the safety of workers or the environment. United States' multinationals prefer Third World nations that ban labor unions, have no minimum wage wages laws, no worker-safety laws, no environmental protection laws, and cheap natural resources. They can build plants and factories in the Third World that would never pass safety inspections in the United States.

As the global economy has become more integrated, multinational corporations are playing an increasingly important role in global life. The decisions of these corporations can dramatically affect the economic health of the nations that host them. If a multinational corporation decides to close down operations in one nation and move to another location, in search of even cheaper labor, a nation's economy can suffer disastrous consequence. Additionally, multinational corporations have a long history of attempting to control the internal affairs of host nations in order to maximize their profits. The huge profit Halliburton is reaping in Iraq is a good example of this behavior. However, we must ask ourselves if sacrificing the lives of our sons and daughters to protect United States business interests is appropriate.

Modernization theorists hold that the nations of the world will achieve higher standards of living as multinational corporations bring the great productivity of corporate capitalism to bear on their economies. Corporations, theoretically, offer new jobs, better technology, capital investment, and accelerated economic growth. The Dependency theorists disagree and note that the effect of global capitalism has largely been increased inequality. Multinational investment crowds out indigenous industry and markets, shifts production to exports for consumption in first-world nations, rather than production for local markets, and removes profits from the host nations. Seen from this point of view, multinationals make poor societies even poorer and more dependent upon first-world nations. The dependency theorists want to see market systems replaced with government-based economic policies.

What are the consequences of the shift in production from the United States to other counties? The most immediate consequence is the loss of many skilled and semi-skilled jobs in the secondary sector of the economy. The loss of industrial jobs has led to downward mobility for many families. Many industrial workers who held down unionized jobs had a middle class standard of living. However, once laid-off most are having a difficult time finding employment in the secondary sector of the economy and are having to settle for jobs in the service economy, at vastly reduced wages. Some are unable to find jobs at all, which increases the poverty rate and reliance on public assistance.

Concentration of Wealth. The concentration of corporate wealth in the hands of a small number of corporations is increasing. It cannot be good for consumers that 80 percent of the food production industry is controlled by a mere 1 percent of agribusinesses. In the over all United States economy, the situation is similar: less than 1 percent of United States corporations control 80 percent of the economy! This situation exists in almost every sector of the economy.

The Ford Motor Company, for example, while ridding itself of thousands of workers and closing several plants in the United States has revenues greater than all but seven of the nations of the world. General Motors, Exxon-Mobil, and Wal-Mart have similar revenues. In fact, the top six multinational corporations have combined revenues greater than any nation save the United States. Yet in spite of their fabulous wealth, whenever spokespeople for these corporations are interviewed we are told that they are in dire economic straits and that downsizing, layoffs, plant closings, union givebacks, and the gutting of pension and benefits programs are necessary or they will go bankrupt.

Wealth is also highly concentrated in the hands of individuals and families. For example, 13,000 elite families in the United States earn more income than the entire bottom 20 million families. There are a growing number of billionaires in the United States.

343

Table 14.2   Household Wealth

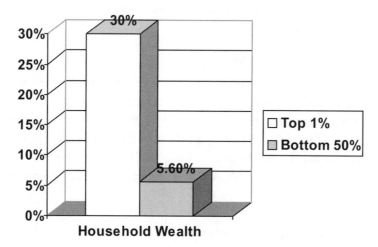

Topping the list is Bill Gates, Warren Buffet, and the heirs to the Wal-Mart retail chain. The top one percent of United States families control 30 percent of total household wealth, compared to a mere 5.6 percent for the bottom 50 percent! A similar but not as extreme picture emerges for household income: the top 20 percent of earners control 50.1 percent of the national income while the bottom 20 percent of earners manage to bring in only 3.5 percent of the national income.

Table 14.3   **Household Income**

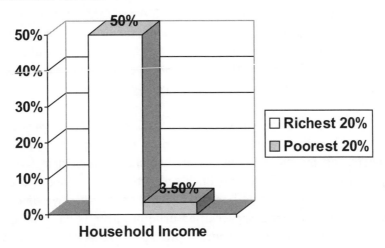

An interesting area of income inequality is that of CEO pay. In the 1980s, CEOs earned about 40 times as much as the average worker. In the 1990s, this increased to nearly 100 times as much as an average worker. By 2001, CEO pay had increased to over 400 times as much. The average CEO compensation package is about $37.5 million, compared to the average worker's salary of $38,000. Consider this—your salary has increased by 1.6 percent since 1980, adjusting for inflation, compared to the average CEO whose salary increase by over 400 percent during the same time span.

Since the 1980s, and the beginning of the Reagan-Bush era, helped along by many of the policies of President Clinton, the gap between the rich and everyone else has grown ever wider. To explain fully what lead to the income and wealth gap would take another entire volume. However, a brief review of a few of the facts will further our understanding. At the top of the list has to be the changes in the tax laws. The estate tax, the government's only tax on wealth, has been seriously eroded and is set to be repealed entirely in 2009. This tax raises about $30 billion a year and generally applied only to the top one percent of families. Also, taxation of stock dividends has declined dramatically. President Bush has suggested that this tax also be eliminated, which will cost the government about $800 billion over the next ten years. This tax affected mostly the top five percent of wealthiest Americans. Additionally, in 2001 and 2003, President Bush asked for, and the Congress approved, massive tax cuts that virtually eliminated the budget surplus. These tax rebates went mostly to the richest one percent of Americans. Millionaires, arguably the least in need of tax relief, received an average tax refund of $100,000 while the average American received a little more than $400. Taxes were also reduced on corporate profits and unearned income, such as capital gains. If you purchase a gallon of gasoline today, you paid more in tax than many United States corporations did last year. Ford received a tax rebate.

The other side of tax reform has been the conservative attack on social programs. In the past, conservative Republicans were particularly fond of reducing services and government aid to the poor, as demonstrated by the welfare reform legislation passed in the late 1990s. Today, almost everything is on the table. President Bush's plan to privatize social security seems dead as of this writing but the very fact that he backed such a plan is indicative of conservative plans and intentions. The Bush administration's prescription drug program is an unmitigated social disaster. Within weeks of implementation of the new prescription plan, 33 states have had to pass emergency legislation to ensure that elderly people on Social Security can get the prescription drugs they need. Social programs related to education, school lunch and breakfast programs, health care, prescription drugs, higher education, student loans, and a long list of related social spending is slated for budget cuts or outright elimination. It is not just the poor who depend on social spending. Many middle and working class families will not be able to afford to send their children to college, for example, if funding for student loans continues to be cut.

Work is one of the central ways in which our lives are structured. In a capitalist economy, almost every material reward, including income, standard of living, housing, and other social rewards, including self-esteem, status, happiness, and fulfillment flow from work. Of course, depending upon the type of work, some people are happier than others. The greatest social and material rewards accrue to those who are involved in creative, non-routine, work that requires mental ability where the individual employee has a large role in deciding how the work will be accomplished. The least rewarding work, in material and social rewards, is associated with repetitive, routine, highly supervised work.

The economic future is cloudy indeed, if you do not happen to be a member of the top 20 percent of earners. We have seen that wages for average Americans have remained stagnant. For example, median family income was $1,000 greater in 1989 than it was in 1996 in spite of the fact that families were working more than 200 hundred hours longer. The share of workers receiving employer-provided health care is declining and, even worse, major corporations are trying to find ways to abandon their health care and retirement packages entirely. Some of the corporations seeking to divest their pension and benefit programs are among the richest and most powerful in the world. Wages are falling for entry-level work and for workers who lack a college education. For the third year in a row, income for college-educated workers has declined.

Globalization and deindustrialization are having significant negative consequences for large numbers of Americans. We must bear in mind that the United States still has the largest economy, as measured by Gross Domestic Product (GDP), of any nation in the world. However, the economic success engendered by globalization has improved the economic wellbeing of only a handful of Americans and major corporations. Exxon-Mobil, General Motors, Ford, Wal-Mart, General Electric, IBM, Citi-Group, and other major United States corporations have done extremely well. Unfortunately, GDP is not an accurate measure of the health of a nation. The wealth measured by GDP is held by private corporations, not average citizens. These corporations have improved their profits by workforce reductions, replacing workers with computers and machines, replacing United States workers with foreign workers when possible, shutting down plants in the United States and opening plants in the Third World, busting unions, keeping wages and benefits low, fighting government safety standards, insisting on union give-backs, and a variety of other strategies. Large numbers of workers who previously earned a middle class living in the industrial sector have been shifted to the lower tier of the service economy, suffering serious losses of income and benefits. These people understand what it means to be poor in the richest nation in the world.

Economists and social scientists are increasingly alarmed at the trend toward a two-class system in the United States. Imagine what our society will look like if the estate tax, windfall profits tax, and taxes on unearned income are entirely eliminated. The idea of meritocracy, in which everyone receives social rewards according to the effort they put forth and the abilities and skills they bring to the job market, will be dead. The elite class will truly be above the rest of us at that point. There will be a "caste" of people, about 1 percent of families at the top of the stratification system, who inherit billions of tax-free dollars every generation. While the elite will still have to pay taxes on their earned income. Nevertheless, the basis of their affluence, inherited wealth, will remain undisturbed.

14 | The Sociology of Economic Life: How the "What" Gets Produced and Distributed.
by Frank O. Taylor, IV, Ph.D.

ക ര ഇ ര

DEFINITIONS

Alienation. A feeling that develops when workers have no control over the process of work or their labor and the work seems particularly meaningless. The feeling that you are not in control of your life. It is a feeling of powerlessness, normlessness, and of being cut off from the product of one's labor, from other people, and from oneself.

Authoritarian Socialism. Characterized by a socialist economy controlled by a political elite kept in power through control of the military.

Autonomy. Immunity from arbitrary exercise of authority. Personal independence.

Blue-Collar. Referring to occupations that primarily involve manual work.

Command Economy.   In a command economy, a rational assessment of social needs is undertaken and the economy is directed and organized in a manner best aimed at achieving those needs.

Communism. A socialist economy combined with an authoritarian political system.

Corporate Capitalism. Used to indicate that the economy is controlled by a political policy and political policy is set by a handful of giant corporations.

Deindustrialization. The shifting from industrial economic activities to service and information economies. Decline in the share of manufacturing industries in the country's economy. Typically, industrial plants are closed down and not replaced, and service industries increase. Refers to the movement of labor-intensive work to the Third World, where unions, pro-labor legislation, and environmental protection laws are non-existent and works are often paid mere pennies a day.

Democratic Socialism. Is achieved with the support of the people through democratic institutions. Representatives of the socialist state are answerable to the people they represent.

Discouraged Workers. Those who have given up looking for a job.

Division of Labor. The delegation and assignment of certain specified tasks, jobs, or work (or parts of them) to be completed by certain specified individuals, groups, categories, and classes of people. Sex, age, education type and level, and the occupation area of one's family are the most traditional bases for differentiating occupational activities.

348

Economic Institutions. Enduring arrangements of cultural ideas and social relationships through which goods and services are produced and distributed in societies.

Egalitarianism. The position that there should be structurally a degree of equality in reference to access to control, influence, and direction over events that affect one's life. There should also be a degree of similarity of rights, duties, responsibilities, treatment, protection, and rewards for all members of a group, category, and society. Equality does not mean sameness, however. Many disaffected individuals and groups that are working for a more egalitarian society in which to live do not see that such a development can come about by working within the existing system but that the system itself needs some basic value alterations.

Extrinsic Rewards. Refer to the tangible benefits, such as income, benefits, or job security.

Functional Requisites. Products and services needed for a society to survive.

Great Society. Was a set of domestic programs enacted in the United States on the initiative of President Lyndon B. Johnson (1963-1969). The Great Society was later partially overturned by President Ronald Reagan's first budget.

Indirect Interlocks. Refers to when a person to serves simultaneously on the boards of two corporations that are not in direct competition with each other.

Industrial Core (or the **primary labor market**). Characterized by large bureaucracies, relative job security, higher wages, benefits packages that include pensions and health care, and thousands of employees.

Internal Labor Market. Once hired one embarks on a "career" and moves up through a promotional ladder that is explicitly defined. Upper-level positions are filled from the lower ranks.

Intrinsic Rewards. Are related to the work itself—you obtain intrinsic rewards when you find the work satisfying and you feel pride in your creative abilities.

Invisible Hand. Metaphor created by Adam Smith to illustrate the principle of "enlightened self interest." Today, this principle is associated with psychological egoism. In *The Wealth of Nations*, Adam Smith makes the claim that, within the system of capitalism, an individual acting for his own good tends also to promote the good of his community.

Laissez-Faire. In economics and politics, doctrine that an economic system functions best when there is no interference by government. It is based on the belief that the natural economic order tends, when undisturbed by artificial stimulus or regulation, to secure the maximum wellbeing for the individual and therefore for the community as a whole.

McJobs. A new term sociologists have coined for jobs in the lower tier of the service economy. Referred to as dead-end jobs or jobs with low pay and limited advancement possibilities.

Means of Production. In Marxist theory, the ability to produce; including the physical, technological, political, economic, and social ability to do so. The means of production may be broken down into the forces of production and the relations of production. In capitalism the relations of production essentially refer to the institution of private property and to the class relations between those who are propertied and those who are not. The forces of production can be seen as referring to both material and social elements. They include natural resources (land, minerals, etc.) insofar as they are used as objects as labor, physical equipment (tools, machines, technology, etc.), science and engineering (the skills of people who invent or improve the physical equipment), those who actually work with these skills and tools, and their division of labor as it affects their productivity. - C. Wright Mills, *The Marxists* (New York: Dell Publishing Company, 1962), pp. 82-83.

Multinational Corporations. Large corporations that operate on a global basis and often wield more power and economic resources than the nations that host them.

Periphery (or the **secondary labor market**). Composed of competitive small businesses, most of which are family owned or operated by a small group of partners.

Pink-Collar. Referring to occupations that are primarily designated to the secondary labor market work, traditionally or most likely done by women; usually used in disparagement.

Primary Production. This type of production is based on extracting raw materials directly from nature and includes hunting, farming, herding, fishing, logging and mining.

Professions. Occupations that demand specialized skills, education, a high degree of personal involvement, creative freedom, work with the mind rather than the hands, and a sense of obligation to a professional community.

Reserve Pool of Labor. Unemployed workers who can be called into the job market during an economic expansion or laid-off during a recession.

Secondary Production. Characterized by large bureaucratically organized units of production, heavy reliance on modern energy, such as gasoline, electricity, or nuclear power, and the processing of raw materials.

Self-Direction. Refers to the degree to which an employee is given a set of abstract goals and granted the freedom to achieve them.

Service Economy. This type of economy can be divided into two tiers, an upper tier and a lower tier. The **upper tier** of the service economy is comprised of occupations in fields of medicine, health care, insurance, communications, education, accounting, law, and the mass media among others and are typically white-collar. The **lower tier** of the service economy is comprised of low-paid, low-skill, no benefits, and no advancement jobs. Working as a maid, janitor, cooks, hamburger-flipper, or waiter, and so on, in the service economy are common jobs in the lower tier.

Shared Monopolies. Also known as oligopolies, exist when four or fewer firms supply fifty percent or more of a given market.

Tertiary Production. The production of services rather than goods.

Trade Deficit. When a country buys more goods from foreign nations than they buy from their own, more money is removed from an economy.

Underemployment. A situation in which a worker is employed, but not in the desired capacity, whether in terms of compensation, hours, or level of skill and experience. While not technically unemployed, the underemployed are often competing for available jobs.

Underground Economy. This informal economy is characterized by lack of record keeping and the state, although aware of the underground economy, is largely unable to regulate it.

White-Collar. Referring to occupations that primarily involve mental work.

REFERENCES

The ideas expressed in my essay on the economy and the information presented are based on the following works:

Americans for Democratic Action. 2004. "Income and Inequality: Millions Left Behind. 3rd ed." Washington, DC: Americans for Democratic Action, Retrieved April 16, 2006 (http://www.adaction.org/Income2004.pdf).

Barlett, Donald L. and James B. Steele. 1994. *American: Who Really Pays the Taxes*. New York: Simon and Schuster.

Barlett, Donald L. and James B. Steele. 2001. "How the Little Guy Gets Crunched." *Time*, February 7, pp. 40-43.

Barlett, Donald L. and James B. Steele. 2004. "Has your Life Become a Game of Chance?" *Time*, February 2, pp. 42-44.

Barnet, Richard J. and Ronald E. Muller. 1974. *Global Research: The Power of Multinational Corporations*. New York: Simon and Schuster.

Baron, James N. and William T. Beilby. 1984. "The Organization of a Segmented Economy." *American Sociological Review* 49 (August):454-73.

14 | The Sociology of Economic Life: How the "What" Gets Produced and Distributed.
by Frank O. Taylor, IV, Ph.D.

Bechhofer, F. and B. Elliot. 1985. "The Petite Bourgeoisie in Late Capitalism." *Annual Review of Sociology* 11:181-207.

Berger, Peter. 1986. *The Capitalist Revolution*. New York: Basic Books.

Berle, Adolf. 1959. *Power without Property*. New York: Harcourt Brace.

Bonacich, Edna. 1976. "Advanced Capitalism and Black/White Relations in the United States: A Split Labor Market Interpretation." *American Sociological Review* 48:468-79.

Bottomore, T. B. (trans.). 1976. *Karl Marx: Selected Writings in Sociology and Social Philosophy*. New York: McGraw-Hill.

Branigan, William. 1997. "Sweatshops Are Back." *Washington Post National Weekly Edition,* February 24, pp. 6-7.

Caproni, Paula J. 2004. "Work/Life Balance: You Can't Get There from Here." *Journal of Applied Behavioral Science* 40(2) (June):208-218.

Carre, Francoise, and Chris Tilly. 1998. "Part-Time and Temporary Work." *Dollars and Sense* 215 (January/February):22-25.

Children's Defense Fund. 2004. "While Corporations and the Wealthy Benefit from Huge Tax Cuts, Poor Families Still Struggle." Press Release, April 14.

Clifford, Lee. 2001. "Fortune 500." *Fortune*, April 16, pp. 101-103.

Cohen, Albert K. and Harold M. Hodges, Jr. 1963. "Characteristics of the Lower-Blue-Collar Classes." *Social Problems* 10:303-34.

Davis, Gerald F. 2003. "American Cronyism: How Executive Networks Inflated the Corporate Bubble." *Contexts* 2-3 (Summer):34-40.

Della Fave, Richard. 1980. "The Meek Shall Not Inherit the Earth: Self-Evaluation and the Legitimacy of Stratification." *American Sociological Review* 45:955-71.

Domhoff, G. William. 1970. *The Higher Circles*. New York: Random House.

Domhoff, G. William. 1974. "State and Ruling Class in Corporate America: Reflections, Corrections, and New Directions." *Critical Sociology* 25(2-3) (July):260-265.

Domhoff, G. William. 1978. *The Powers That Be: Processes of Ruling Class Domination in America*. New York: Random House.

Domhoff, G. William. 1990. *The Power Elite and the State: How Policy Is Made in America*. Hawthorne, New York: Aldine De Gruyter.

Drucker, Peter F. 1993. *Post-Capitalist Society*. New York: Harper-Collins.

Edwards, Richard. 1979. *Contested Terrain: The Transformation of the Workplace in the Twentieth Century*. New York: Basic Books.

Eitzen Stanley D. and Maxine Baca Zinn. 2006. *Social Problems*. 10th ed. New York: Allyn and Bacon.

Forbes. 2003. "American's Top 500 Companies." *Forbes*, April 14, pp. 144-198.

Garten, Jeffrey E. 1999. 'Megamergers Are a Clear and Present Danger." *Business Week*, January 25, pp. 28.

Gray, Charles. 1999. "Corporate Goliaths: Sizing Up Corporations and Governments." *Multinational Monitor* 20 (June):26-27.

Greenstein, Robert and Issac Shapiro. 2003. "The New, Definitive CBO Data on Income and Tax." *Center on Budget and Policy Priorities*, September 23.

Greenwald, John. 1994. "The New Service Class." *Time*, 144(20), November 14, pp. 72-74.

Greider, William. 1993. *Who Will Tell the People: The Betrayal of American Democracy*. New York: Simon and Schuster.

Greider, William. 2001. "Pro Patria, Pro Mundus." *Nation*, 273(15), November 12, pp. 22-24.

Harrington, Michael. 1976. *The Twilight of Capitalism*. New York: Simon and Schuster.

Heclo, Hugh and Henrik Madson. 1987. *Policy and Politics in Sweden: Principled Pragmatism*. Philadelphia, PA: Temple University Press.

Hightower, Jim. 1987. "Where Greed, Unofficially Blessed by Reagan, Has Led." *New York Times*, June 21, pp. 25.

Hightower, Jim. 1997. "Class War." *Dollars and Sense* 214 (November/December):7.

Hightower, Jim. 2002. "Looting the Treasury under Cover of the Flag." *The Hightower Lowdown* 4 (February):1-4.

Hunnicut, Benjamin K. 1990. "Are We Working Too Hard? No Time for God of Family." *Wall Street Journal*, January 4.

Ivins, Molly. 2000. "Capitalism Gets a Really Bad Name." *Progressive Populist*, May 15, pp. 22-23.

Ivins, Molly. 2003. "Bush Tax-Cut Plan Wrong in Oh So Very Many Ways." *Rocky Mountain News*, January 9, 39A.

Jones, Del. 2003. "CEOs, Heirs to Stock Fortune Win Big with Cut." *USA Today*, January 9, 3B.

Kalleberg, Arne, Barbara F. Reskin, and Ken Hudson. 2000. "Bad Jobs in America: Standard and Nonstandard Employment Relations and Job Quality in the United States." *American Sociological Review* 65(2) (April):256-78.

Koblik, Steven. 1975. *Sweden's Development from Poverty to Affluence 1750-1970.* Minneapolis, MN: University of Minnesota Press.

Kohn, Melvin and Carmi Schooler, and Associates. 1983. *Work and Personality: An Inquiry into the Impact of Social Stratification.* Norwood, NJ: Ablex.

Marx, Karl. 1967. *Capital: A Critique of Political Economy.* Vol. 1. New York: International.

Michalowski, Raymond J. and Ronald C. Kramer. 1987. "The Space Between Laws: The Problem of Corporate Crime in a Transnational Context." *Social Problem* 34:34-53.

Miller, David. 1991. "A Vision of Market Socialism." *Dissent* 38 (Summer):406-414.

Miller-Loessi, Karen. 1992. "Toward Gender Integration in the Workplace: Issues at Multiple Levels." *Sociological Perspectives* 35(1):1-15.

Mintz, Beth A. and Michael Schwartz. 1985. *The Power Structure of American Business.* Chicago, IL: University of Chicago Press.

Murphy, Cait. 2000. "Are the Rich Cleaning Up?" *Fortune*, September 4, pp. 252-262.

Nelson, Joel I. 1994. "Work and Benefits: The Multiple Problems of Service Sector Employment." *Social Problems* 42(2) (May):240-55.

Reed, Madlen. 2004. "USA Sets Record for Billionaires." *USA Today*, September 24, 8B.

Ritzer, George. 1996. *The McDonaldization of Society: An Investigation into the Changing Character of Contemporary Social Life,* rev. ed. Thousand Oaks, CA: Pine Forge Press.

Sklar, Holly. 1992. "Reaffirmatve Action." *Z Magazine* 5 (May/June):9-15.

Sklar, Holly. 2003. "CEO Pay Still Outrageous." *Progressive Populist* June 15:1, 18.

Statistical Abstract of the United States. 2005. Washington DC: Bureau of the Census, Tables: 11, 186, 309, 1337.

Taub, Amy. 1998. "Oligopoly! Highly Concentrated Markets across the U.S. Economy." *Multinational Monitor* 20 (November):9-12.

United States Bureau of the Census. 1995. *Statistical Abstract of the United States.* Washington, DC: Government Printing Office.

United States Department of Labor Statistics. 1999. *Employment and Earnings* 46(1) (January).

United States Department of Labor Statistics. 1999. *Women's Bureau.* Women Business Owners: 1999. [Online] Available February 12, 2000, at http://www.dol.gov/dol/wb/public/wb-pubs.wbo.htm.

Useem, Michael. 1984. *The Inner Circle: Large Corporations and the Rise of Business Political Activity in the U.S. and U.K.* New York: Oxford University Press.

Werlin, Robert J. 1972. "Marxist Political Analysis." *Sociological Inquiry* 42(3-4):157-181.

15 | Stratification and Social Class: Where is Mine?
by Frank O. Taylor, Ph.D.

STRATIFICATION

All societies are stratified. **Stratification** refers to the distribution of social rewards. It is an institutionalized system of ranking based on social status and access to resources. When you think about stratification, think about ranks or groups of people who have similar **life chances**. Life chances refers to what share of social rewards you will have access to, such as income, health care, education, power, housing, and material wealth. Stratification is a system that limits and constrains us. Stratification is not a function of individual differences; it is built into the normal operation of society. For example, affluent parents are able to pass on estates, stocks and bonds, income, trust funds, and social networks to their children, whereas most parents are unable to do much, in terms of an inheritance, for their children beyond leaving their home. That is a systematic advantage children born in the upper class have over everyone else. Stratification persists across generations. There is some mobility, especially between the margins of one class and another. However, most people spend their lives in the social class into which they were born. Stratification exists because it is obscured by ideology. When you believe that people succeed or fail due to individual differences, you are much less likely to look for systematic explanations of inequality. The ideologies of meritocracy, individualism, and the Protestant ethic obscure institutionalized systems of inequality and focus our attention on the individual. We are taught to believe that anyone can succeed. While there is some truth to that belief, if it were true we would not see generation after generation of the same family in the same social class.

There are three important systems of ranking in American society. First, people are ranked by social class, which refers to groups of people who have similar life chances due to similar types of occupation, education, and status. For example, the neighborhood you live in is highly correlated with your social class due to zoning laws and property values. People with similar incomes tend to live in the same neighborhoods. Secondly, people are also ranked by gender. In the United States, gender inequality is still prevalent. A single parent family headed by a woman will be much worse off financially than the same family headed by a man, depending on her occupation and education she may be better or worse off compared to other women. The third system of stratification in the United States is based on race and ethnicity. Our long history of prejudice and discrimination, which persists today, has made it more difficult for people of color to reach the middle class. Although inequality based on gender and racial and ethnic characteristics has declined in modern times, it remains significant in our society.

Many people believe that what you get out of life is a function of how much effort you expend. The ideology of meritocracy focuses our attention on achievement. **Achieved statuses** are those that are acquired due to hard work, motivation, and success. Usually achievement is based on some performance related criteria. The grade you receive in this class, for example, will be based on how well you perform on the assessment measures compared to others. **Ascribed statuses** are given at birth. You are born male or female. Femininity and masculinity are achievements because you have to learn gender. Obviously, race, ethnicity, and gender, are major ascribed statuses that are related to our system of stratification. It is a myth that your success in life is based solely on achievement. Stratification is a system that ranks families. Families at the top have more resources than families at the bottom to begin with. As we will discover in the chapter on politics, affluent families are very active politically, largely because they are interested in legislation that will ensure their continued systematic advantages in future generations.

Inequality exists in every society. It is not that we oppose inequality, necessarily, but we must ask what it is based on. If inequality were based on competition and equal access to social resources, most of us would agree that is acceptable. In other words, if we had a social system that ensured that everyone had access to the same educational resources, then the grades people received would more likely be a matter of their individual efforts. On the other hand, if we divide this very class into three groups, an upper class, a middle class, and a lower class, and limit educational resources depending upon which class you happen to be in, we could never separate ascribed characteristics from achieved characteristics. This means that students in the upper class division of the course, who had all the advantages, could always point to their grade as proof that they did not receive any special benefits. Imagine being in a course where upper class students had educational extras, such as additional books, tutors, extra hours of instruction, field-trips, and internships, while the students in the middle class received a book and one hour of instruction a day and students in the lower class were only allowed to attend the class and did not even have a book. That situation would be one of institutionalized differences. It would still be true that a student from any of the three conditions could achieve an excellent grade. However, it is also true that students in the most favored condition would have the advantage. Most of the students in the upper class division of the course would have little difficulty earning high grades, while one or two goof offs would do poorly. A handful of students in the middle class would earn excellent grades but most would receive average grades. One or two students from the lower class may receive excellent marks in spite of their disadvantages.

We can think about two types of stratification systems at the ends of a continuum based on whether the system is open or closed. In an open stratification system people would, through achievement, be able to change their status quite easily. In a closed stratification system, people would remain in whatever class they were born into. The Hindu **caste system**, that was widely practiced in India during the nineteenth century, and still has some force today, is a good example of a closed system. In a caste system life chances are controlled by your status at birth. In India, members of the lower castes are considered inferior and are widely scorned. Members of the higher castes are more respected and have greater access to social resources. In a caste system people remain in the caste into which they were born. Three mechanisms help perpetuate a closed system. Traditions specify that 1) the members of different castes not have any social relationships with each other, 2) children step into the occupations of their parents, and 3) marriage can occur only within the same caste.

An open society allows for social mobility, either up or down in social ranking. The United States was founded on the principle of equal opportunity, which, interestingly enough, does not mean that everyone should have the same status or that inequality should not exist. Equal opportunity means that everyone should succeed or fail based on individual merit and equal access to the same opportunities. In a **class system**, the share of social rewards you receive is based on your achievements. A class system has institutionalized methods of allowing social mobility, whereas a caste system does not. **Social mobility** refers to the process of changing your social class position. In the United States, the pattern of upward social mobility is based on access to a good education. For many people getting a better education often leads to obtaining a better job and more income. Of course, downward social mobility is often experienced as well. There are many factors associated with downward mobility, including United States economic policies, factory closings, downsizing, layoffs, outsourcing, and even divorce, particularly for women. The point is that a class system has built-in patterns of social mobility. If your parents are working class and you, through education, wind up in the middle class, your family experienced **intergenerational**

mobility. You, on the other hand, experienced **Intragenerational mobility** because you changed your social class position within your own lifetime.

Structural mobility refers to society wide changes that lead to upward or downward social mobility for large segments of the population. Structural changes usually take place in the economic and political institutions of society. For example, following the Second World War the United States Congress passed several entitlement programs for veterans, such as the G.I. bill. Consequently, veterans of the armed forces were able to take advantage of funds set aside for them to go to college. Veterans who obtained college degrees, which they did by the thousands, were able to find white-collar employment. Additionally, many veterans were able to take advantage of low-interest loans from the Veterans Administration to finance first homes. Other people were able to put aside money from middle and working class tax breaks and refunds to help save for the down payment for a home. After WWII, the United States experienced an unprecedented rate of economic growth and prosperity. The rising economic tide tended to lift everyone's boat and many families experienced upward social mobility. This was the experience of your parents.

Unfortunately, beginning in the mid-1970s this period of economic prosperity began to decline. United States corporations began to face serious competition from foreign corporations, particularly in the steel and automobile industries. The situation was exacerbated by a series of conservative presidential administrations, starting with the election of Ronald Reagan. These administrations ushered in a series of economic and political changes that dramatically affected social mobility in the nation. Spending for the military grew to become the largest item in the federal budget, draining money away from investment in the nation's infrastructure. The United States became a debtor nation, requiring loans from foreign nations to fund the budget each year. This has lead to a national debt of titanic proportions, some trillions of dollars. Unions were busted and union membership began to decline. Each year the trade deficit became worse, with the United States importing more goods than exporting goods. Restrictions upon businesses were relaxed, which led to a frenzy of mergers. Perhaps the most devastating blow to the standard of living of ordinary citizens was the movement of United States heavy industry out of the country. When major corporations move their plants and factories to Mexico, China, Taiwan, and elsewhere in the Third World, high paying middle class jobs are removed from our economy. This was followed by corporate downsizing, layoffs, and outsourcing. The result of these economic changes has been stagnant wages for the middle and working classes.

Since about 1980, earnings for most American workers have stagnated. Between 2000 and 2005, after adjusting for inflation, most American workers actually lost ground. In order to make due, the number of Americans holding more than one job has risen, from 4.7 percent in 1975 to 6.0 percent by 1998. To make matters worse, the highly unionized good paying jobs in industry that have left the United States have been replaced, by and large, with dead-end jobs, which offer little income. The number or workers earning poverty wages increased to over 15 percent by 1998. Unfortunately, not everyone shared this dim economic picture. Affluent families saw their incomes rise by a whopping 44 percent between 1980 and 2000. The upward redistribution of wealth from the middle and working classes to the rich will probably continue for the near future. For example, 42.6 percent of President George Walker Bush's tax cut went to the top 1 percent of earners, who had annual incomes in excess of $300,000 per year. The tax rebate for the top 1 percent averaged $46,072. Only 5 percent of the $1.6 billion tax package was refunded to the lowest 60 percent of earners. The average middle class family received a tax rebate of a mere $453.

Clearly, a caste system does not exist in the United States. However, because inequality is still highly correlated with race, ethnicity, and gender, a pure class system does not exist either. What we have is something in between a caste and class system. Whether you are born male or female still matters. Men tend to earn more than women do. Whether you are male or female, White or Hispanic, Protestant or Jewish, continues to influence what opportunities you will be exposed to in life. In other words, your ascribed characteristics greatly influence your achieved characteristics. Ascribed characteristics interact with social class to limit and constrain your life chances. Ascribed characteristics will help determine the type of housing you will live in, where you will live, how much education you will have, how healthy you are, how much money in your savings account, and other important aspects of your life.

THE DIMENSIONS OF SOCIAL CLASS

There are three important dimensions of social class that; wealth and income, power, and prestige. Wealth is the primary dimension of social class. **Wealth** refers to property, home equity, and the value of machinery, cars, stocks, bonds, rents, royalties, and so on. The wealthiest 10 percent of United States citizens own 70 percent of the nation's wealth. However, if we look at the top one percent of American's we see that they own 33 percent of the nation's wealth. The total amount of wealth in the nation is equal to about 33 trillion dollars. When you consider that 70 percent of that wealth is owned by just ten percent of families, which amounts to a little over 23 trillion dollars, you realize just how concentrated wealth is at the top.

Wealth is not the same thing as income. **Income** refers to what is earned through wages and salaries. In terms of income, the top fifth of earners bring home about one-half of the nation's wages. The bottom fifth of earners manage to bring in a paltry 4.2 percent of the nation's income. In 1935, the top fifth of earners took in 52 percent of the total income. In the years between 1935 and 1970, the incomes of the top fifth of earners declined somewhat, while the income of the middle three-fifths of earners went up. During this time, as mentioned previously, structural changes were redistributing the income downward. A progressive tax system, which increases the rate of taxation as income increases, and other taxes such as the estate tax, the windfall profits tax, and other taxes on wealth, held the top fifth of earners to around 40 percent of the nation's total income, a sizable chunk of change. However, due to tax relief for the rich the top fifth of earners and other political and economic changes since the 1970s they have seen their incomes increase while the middle three fifths of earners have lost income. Between 1984 and 1991 the income of the richest fifth increased by almost nine percent while the income of the other four-fifths declined by over 10 percent.

The biggest winners in the United States in recent decades are the chief executive officers (CEOs) of the nation's largest corporations. The income of a CEO includes their salary, stock bonuses, and stock options. The median CEO salary is over three million dollars per year, or 83 times what the average United States worker earns in a year. However, CEOs with earnings near the median are poor compared to some CEOs, who can earn tens of millions of dollars per year and receive other benefits, such as dividends, limousines, free rent in luxury homes or apartments, and other perks. Imagine how dramatically different your life style is from people who earn this amount of money. Right about now you may be thinking that money does not buy happiness. However people with poverty level incomes are more likely to be the victims of violent crime and are more likely to take days off from work for illness. This is because poor people live in poor neighborhoods and cannot afford health care.

Power is another dimension of stratification. Power refers to the ability of some individuals and groups to force their will on others, who may even resist. Those who have economic, political, and cultural power have mastery over critical resources and can use those resources to make the economic and political system work for them. Some people and groups control the distribution of social rewards, the judicial system, and the media. They are able to force everyone else to play by their rules. Certainly, you have the right to vote and in a democracy, thankfully, politicians must still be elected, although recently there has been some debate about that. Just because you get to vote does not mean you have a voice in the big decisions of our time. Has anyone contacted you recently about your opinion on the environment? Was your opinion about nuclear energy valued? Before the invasion of Iraq, did anyone ask you if you thought it was a good idea? You get to vote for the decision makers but decisions that can affect the entire society are largely made outside of the view of the public. If you donated $100 to either the Republican or Democratic national party and later called the White House on some issue important to you, would the President take your call? What if you donated $100,000?

Sociologists have long theorized that the **power elite** does exist. Power is concentrated in the hands of the few, rather than the masses. The instrumental power elite theorists argue that the ruling class controls political officials through the influence of money, since being elected, particularly at the national level, is prohibitively expensive. The government is used as a tool of the ruling class through which they protect their interests, directly through the manipulation of state power and indirectly through pressure and influence. The structural elite theorists argue that political and economic policy must protect the capitalist economy. Indirectly, the state serves the needs of the elite because the interests of big business must be met to avoid a depression or recession. Both groups of theorists note that the elites are psychologically similar, due to similar origins and lifestyles. In other words, the values and psychology of the power elite is developed by the institutional positions they hold and similar socialization. Additionally, the power elite are socially similar as well. They are involved in an overlapping set of social groups, including private boarding schools, elite Ivy League Colleges, corporate boards, churches, neighborhoods, and even vacation at the same resorts.

The decisions made in the corporate, military, and governmental realms of power, while crucial to all citizens, tie leaders of each sector of power together because decisions made in one sector are likely to affect the other sectors. Thus, the members of the power elite have coinciding interests. Their primary interest is the maintenance of the capitalist system. They owe their wealth and power to the capitalist system and they are interested in not only preserving it but keeping themselves firmly in control. Many of these individuals are involved in the operation of multinational corporations with operations overseas. Therefore, they are interested in foreign policy decisions by the federal government that will continue to allow them to make profits. They are also interested in seeing that their overseas property is protected and support spending for defense. Increased defense spending by the government benefits both the military and the defense industry, which realizes immense profits from military spending on weapons systems.

Thus, in a capitalist economy, the government, according to power elite theorists, cannot remain neutral. Foreign policy is made to protect United States multinational corporations and export market based capitalism. Domestic social and economic policy protects business. Moreover, defense spending enriches the defense industry. Without the approval of the power elite the government can make no major decision. The power elite works behind the scenes with elected officials to determine the nation's foreign and domestic policies. The members of the executive branch of the government largely come from the power elite, and they control the major corporations, the mass media, foundations, universities, and important government councils for foreign and domestic policy, such as the Council on Foreign Relations, the Committee for Economic Development, The National Security Council, and the National Industrial Conference Board. Although the power elite does not control local or state politics, at the federal level they are the dominant group and they plan, initiate, and carry out United States foreign and domestic policies.

A third dimension of social class is that of **social status**. An example of status is related to occupational prestige. Some occupations have more social status than others do. Why is this? Because some occupations require more education, they pay more, they require mind power, rather than physical labor, and they offer greater autonomy. Social status and prestige involves respect and admiration. Prestige, although mostly something that is intangible, can be seen in conspicuous displays, leisure, and consumption, in titles, degrees, a seat of honor, a key to the city, and rituals of deference. When you refer to your course instructor as Professor So-and-so or Dr. So-and-so, you are engaging in a ritual of deference. Usually, the professor calls you by your first name and you acknowledge the professor by using the title "Doctor." When you engage in this behavior, you are paying respect to the professor for their years of experience and education.

When you finally reach graduation, you will be involved in an enjoyable ritual of deference. In your cap and gown, with your friends and relatives gathered together to celebrate your accomplishment, you will walk across the stage in a grand auditorium, to receive your diploma, while the professors in their regalia watch and applaud you. If you look carefully, you will notice some distinction in the regalia you and others wear. There will be minor differences between those receiving an Associate's degree and those receiving a Bachelor's degree. Generally, as you move up the ladder from Associate's degree to Doctor of Philosophy the regalia become fancier and more colorful. Among the faculty, those with Master's degrees and Ph.D.'s have a colorful hood, indicating in which discipline they achieved their degree in and what college or university they attended.

Social status is also reflected in the occupational prestige scale. Supreme court judges and college professors are always near the top, psychologists, teachers, nurses and pharmacists are generally also highly respected and in the top one third of occupations. Actors, coaches, social workers, and police officers are near the middle in terms of occupational respect. Barbers, waitresses, truck drivers, cab drivers, and factory workers are in the lower half in terms of occupational prestige. Janitors, shoe shiners, and street sweepers receive the least amount of social respect. There is a great deal of consistency in the ranking across nations. For example, college professors are always ranked higher than professional athletes are. People with less occupational prestige perform jobs that require less education, more physical labor where getting dirty is part of the job, and are more closely supervised. Blue-collar jobs tend to be given less social respect than white-collar jobs and are generally at the bottom of the list. However, the aristocracy of labor, electricians, carpenters, and plumbers are generally in the middle of the ranking in occupational prestige.

MEASURING SOCIAL CLASS

One way of measuring social class is simply to ask people. Self-identification is a subjective and direct way to measure social class. Most people have an idea of which social class they belong. Very few people have no opinion on this matter. One problem with the self-identification approach is that the vast majority of people in the United States feel that they are middle class. Obviously, that cannot be the case. Nevertheless, the fact that most people can identify which class they think they belong to indicates that awareness of social class is widespread.

Sociologists are interested in a more precise measure of social class than self-identification yields. **Socioeconomic-status**, therefore, is the most used measure of social class and it ranks people according to their income, education, and occupation. Knowing how many years of school people have completed, their occupation, or their family income allows sociologists to rank groups of people from higher to lower. This approach is much more accurate than self-identification. Occupation is probably the best indicator of a person's social class position. The occupational prestige scale is a list of occupations that are ranked from high to low depending on how important or prestigious the occupations listed are relative to each other. Occupational prestige has been measured all over the world and the results are quite consistent.

THE UNITED STATES CLASS STRUCTURE

Sociologists generally describe social class in terms of six classes, differentiated by occupation, level of education, income, and percentage of the population. This typology is referred to as **socioeconomic-status**. The six social classes, from highest to lowest are

1) the capitalist or elite class,

2) the upper class,

3) the middle class,

4) the working class,

5) the working poor, and

6) the lower or underclass.

As you move down the ladder of social class, there is less wealth and income, power, and status and prestige. It should not escape your attention that education is one of the primary determinates of social class position.

At the top of the social class structure, representing a mere 1 percent of the United States population is the elite class. The typical capitalist graduated from a prestigious university, is an investor, heir, or top executive, and has a yearly income of over $1,000,000. Those in the capitalist class own businesses, control corporations, own stocks and bonds, and other income producing assets, such as rents, royalties, and patents. There is a distinction between **rentiers**, who live off their capital, and **entrepreneurs**, who use their capital to start and run businesses. There is also a distinction between old money and new money in this social class. The **nouveau riche**, are those who have new money, attaining great wealth in business, sports, entertainment, or through invention or the stock market. However, they are at the bottom of the capitalist class. The nouveau riche did not attend the right schools and lack the long established social networks of the old rich. True blue bloods are listed in the *Social Register*, and comprise only one-tenth of one percent of the United States population.

Those with the highest incomes in the elite class derive a greater proportion of their wealth from capital. Generally, people who earn less than $100,000 per year derive all of their income from wages, and this constitutes the majority of the population. For those who earn over $1,000,000 a year, and they constitute only 2 percent of the population, nearly 70 percent of their wealth is produced from capital. This accumulation of capital provides a degree of economic security the average wage earner does not have. As you move up in the elite class wealth becomes highly concentrated. The richest 1 percent of families control nearly 40 percent of the nation's wealth. Including the next 10 percent yields control over 60 percent of the nation's wealth. The richest 1 percent own most of the assets that provide income, such as bonds, stocks, trust funds, real estate, and business assets.

Since the 1980s, continuing through the 1990s, and today, the trend is toward sharply increasing wealth inequality. Research suggests that during the 1980s the rich exerted great influence over public policy, supporting supply-side economics theory. In brief, supply-side economics, nicknamed "trickle-down" economics, argued that reducing taxes on the wealthiest citizens would spark investment spending in new businesses, which, in turn, would create more jobs and income for the middle and working classes. This logic was used to justify everything from the elimination of the estate tax to the creation of a flat tax. If you are reading this book, a flat tax would be highly detrimental to you. Imagine that you have one hamburger or veggie sandwich if you are so inclined. I have one hundred million hamburgers, because I am a member of the capitalist class. Now, I think a flat tax rate of 33 percent is fair. After all, it is only fair that everyone pay the same rate. I should not be punished for being successful should I? Forget the fact that I inherited my wealth. Of course taking 33 percent of your sandwich will ensure that you go hungry. On the other hand, I could lose 33 percent of my one hundred million sandwiches and still never be able to eat them all in my lifetime. Clearly, one of the main areas the wealthy are interested in exerting power over is tax law. This is why the wealthy try to cloak their policies in the language of justice and as beneficial to all, as in trickle-down ideas. One result is that corporate taxes, an indirect way of taxing the rich, have fallen from 33 percent of federal tax revenues in 1950 to only 15 percent today.

Members of the elite class are intensely private, preferring to stay out of the limelight, public debates, and controversies. If an elite woman desires an abortion she can simply fly out of the country. Elite families enjoy a measure of luxury most in the middle class would find completely alien. The spacious homes, the extended vacations in various parts of the world, the nannies, and the household staff grant the elite a standard of living far beyond what ordinary people can afford. Parents from the elite class can afford to send their children to private schools in the Northeast, such as Exeter Academy, Groton School, Deerfield Academy, or Woodberry Forest School, where they will be indoctrinated in upper class values and build social networks important for their business and marital future. Their completion of prep school gives the children of the elite an advantage over middle class children when applying for acceptance into the highly selective Ivy League Colleges and Universities.

We turn now to the second-highest social class. One tier down from the elite class is the **Upper Class**. The typical upper class individual has a College or University education, usually with an advanced degree, has a professional occupation or is an upper level manager, with yearly earnings of greater than $125,000 per year. About 15 percent of the United States population is upper class. This class is highly shaped by their education. Many upper class members have advanced degrees in business, law, or medicine. The upper class is often referred to as the **managerial class**, because they manage the businesses owned by the elites. The ranks of the upper class include successful salespersons, doctors, lawyers, managers, and businesspersons. Research indicates that very few of the upper class went from rags to riches. Most members of the upper class had parents from the middle class who were able to give them a good education at excellent schools. Bill Gates for example, the richest man in the world, dropped out of Harvard. His mother was on the University of Washington Board of Regents, and his father is a prominent attorney in Seattle. It certainly took a certain degree of smarts to found Microsoft and turn it into the largest software company in the world, but William Henry Gates III hardly came from a modest background.

The **middle class** is composed of people who have at least a high school degree, many have college degrees, some have advanced degrees usually a Master's Degree, and others have completed apprenticeships in vocational settings. Middle class individuals are semiprofessionals and low-level managers, craftspeople, or foremen, who earn between $30,000 and $125,000 per year in income. About 34 percent of the United States population resides in the middle class. Thus, the middle class includes a broad cross section of United States society.

We can think of the middle class as being subdivided into an upper middle class, middle class, and lower middle class. Those in the upper middle class have a lot in common with the upper class. They usually have a college degree and are upper level professionals and managers. Many hold advanced degrees. They have earnings between $60,000 and $125,000 per year. They are primarily white-collar professionals and semiprofessional. People in the middle of the middle class have earnings between $60,000 and $45,000 per year. Membership in a union can translate into a middle class lifestyle for those with high paying blue-collar jobs or vocational training. The lower middle class is composed of foremen and non-retail sales people earning between $30,000 and $45,000 per year. This group is most likely to have only a high school education. Those that have some college education usually have an Associate Degree. Many people in the lower middle and middle class follow orders given to them from their upper class managers.

Middle class occupations are primarily white collar and the worker usually sits at a desk and stays physically clean. Middle class workers often supervise others and can have relatively high incomes. People in the middle class do not work with their hands and they do not derive wealth from capital.

Many of the benefits of the middle class accrue to individuals on the basis of their job. Because people in the middle class do not have wealth, they must rely upon social security and private pensions after retirement. Blue-collar workers are much less likely to participate in pension plans, and therefore are even more reliant upon social security. In terms of social security, those with higher incomes generally receive more cash benefits upon retirement. Medical insurance for people in the middle class is also tied to employment. As long as they continue with an employer who offers medical benefits, people in the middle class generally have some level of health care. For example, only 10 percent of those who earn $50,000 to $75,000 per year are not covered. Sick leave is another benefit people in the middle class often enjoy. About 70 percent of those in the middle class can stay at home to recover from an illness or minor surgery and still be paid. Most blue-collar workers, on the other hand, must go to work or face loss of income if they stay at home sick. About 60 percent of white-collar workers have disability insurance to protect their income when they are incapacitated and unable to work. Only 26 percent of blue-collar workers enjoy this benefit. Many middle class workers have vacation and personal leave time as well, giving white-collar workers more time to attend parent-teacher conferences, vote, go to the doctor or dentist, or deal with a personal problem without worrying about loss of pay. Only about 15 percent of blue-collar workers enjoy this benefit. Lastly, top level middle class workers enjoy a wide range of fringe benefits, including company cars, expense accounts, access to dining rooms and meal plans, personal liability insurance, and even stock options in some cases.

Lifestyle separates the middle class from the working class. Middle class people usually have more leisure time, larger homes filled with nice furnishings, and the amenities of life, such as a television in every room, computers, and a washer and dryer. However, middle class means different things to different people. Consider the following three families: A male physician married to a female physician with family earnings of well over $200,000 per year. If asked, this couple, and others like them, often self-identify as middle class; a female nurse and a high school principal with a combined yearly income of over $80,000 per year making them solidly in the middle class; lastly, a female social worker and male police officer with a combined income of just under $60,000 per year. These three families would all self-identify as middle class, yet they would live in different neighborhoods, vacation in different places, shop in different stores, and send their children to different colleges.

The **working class** comprises about 30 percent of the United States population. Working class individuals normally have a high school education and tend to be employed as factory workers, clerical workers, and in low-paid retail sales or low-skill manual labor. Working class people earn between $20,000 to $30,000 dollars annually, work at unskilled blue and white-collar jobs, that are less secure, more routine, and under more supervision than middle class jobs. Working class families often lack pension plans, health care, sick days, personal leave, disability insurance, and other fringe benefits with which middle class workers are familiar. The working class has been hard hit by deindustrialization, globalization, outsourcing, and the introduction of computer and robot technology. As many factories in steel, auto manufacturing, rubber, and other heavy industries, formerly the mainstay of good paying working class employment, have moved to the Third World, more and more working class families are being laid off. With only a high school education people in the working class cannot find jobs that will replace the income they earned at the factory when they are laid off. They usually end up in the service sector of the economy in low paid, low-skill, dead-end jobs.

There are some major differences between the middle class and the working class. Blue-collar workers, as previously mentioned, have lower occupational prestige than do white-collar workers. Blue-collar workers generally identify with the working class, and see working with their hands as an honorable way to earn a living. The children of blue-collar parents often end up in the working class themselves. Since blue-collar workers perform manual labor, they often wear some form of protective clothing at work, and often have negative stereotypes about the "suits" in the middle class. In the working class, the threat of being laid off is ever present. Middle class workers often work in an office setting, which is relatively clean, somewhat peaceful, and more relaxed. Blue-collar work is frequently dangerous. Blue color workers are often exposed to high levels of noise, dangerous machines, inadequate lighting, poor ventilation when toxic and noxious vapors are present and extreme temperature variations. Some blue-collar workers must brave the elements, such as bricklayers, mail carriers, and electricians. The most common on the job accident leading to fatality involves operating a vehicle, exposing blue-collar workers involved in trucking, moving, hauling, handling, and construction to a greater threat of on-the-job injury than white-collar workers. Blue-collar workers labor under strict rules and supervision, often not being allowed to talk to each other or use the restrooms without permission. The intense pressure to work quickly often reduces the blue-collar worker to a human machine. Blue-collar workers have less job security, income, and higher rates of unemployment than white-collar workers do.

Next to last on the ladder of social class are **the working poor**. The working poor earn between $10,000 and $20,000 dollars per year, work at the lowest paid manual, retail, sales, and service work, most have not finished high school, many are functionally illiterate, and they comprise around 16 percent of the United States population. Many of the jobs performed by the working poor are seasonal and temporary. They are disaffected politically, do not usually vote, and largely ignored by both major political parties. The working poor are dependent upon help from the government, charity, and food banks to survive. During a recession, many of the working poor end up on the streets homeless. To see how this might happen imagine that you will earn $12,000 this year. Now, working with that sum come up with a monthly budget that includes, rent, utilities, food, insurance for your automobile, gasoline to drive back and forth to work, and basic clothing.

Research indicates that 1.4 million of the working poor who work at least fifty weeks out of the year cannot escape poverty. Another 2 million of the working poor remained poor holding down part-time employment. In spite of employment, nearly 3 percent of full-time employed workers are paid so little they remain in poverty even when they are bringing in a paycheck. A worker earning minimum wage and working full-time cannot earn enough in this country to get above the poverty line. When sociologists look at the poor it becomes clear that the poor are categories of people, not disparate individuals. For example, if we know that single parent families headed by women are more likely to be poor than intact families, the evidence points to society rather than to individuals as the locus of the problem. The working poor are poor, not so much because of personal characteristics, but because their jobs do not pay enough to live on.

This brings the discussion to the lowest rung on the social class ladder, the **underclass**, or lower class. Individuals in the underclass are unemployed or employed at part-time menial jobs and rely to a large degree on public assistance. They have incomes of less than $10,000 per year. Most are high school dropouts. The underclass represents about 4 percent of the population. Homeless men and women are part of the underclass. Life is harsh for this population, especially children and the elderly. Members of the underclass rely on food stamps and food banks for support. Lacking an education and technical skills, this group of disenfranchised citizens cannot pull themselves out of poverty.

More and more, the affluent of society wish the homeless and other members of the underclass would just go away. In many cities, the homeless are rounded up in police sweeps and incarcerated. There is no precise count of the homeless. Academic researchers put the figure at about 500,000 on any given night, and as many as 1.5 million people will be homeless at some point in the year. The old stereotypes about the homeless, which focused on male hobos and female bag ladies, no longer apply. The new homeless are people who lost their jobs due to plant closings and layoffs, or they were forced out of their apartments due to condominium conversions, or unable to pay their mortgage or rent payments due to job loss, bankruptcy, or unforeseen medical emergencies. Many affluent people prefer to blame the personal traits of the homeless themselves for their situation, rather than society. This psychological rationalization allows people to ignore their plight. However, many of the new homeless are entire families. Can we hold children responsible for being homeless? Many of the homeless suffer from mental illness and drug addiction. However, we must ask ourselves if drug addiction caused them to be homeless, or homelessness caused their mental illness and drug addiction. How long could you watch your child suffer from hunger and malnutrition before you felt like escaping reality, even if only for a few hours? Certainly, there are jobs. If you have an address, a place to wash up and clean clothes, you can get a McJob and bring in $450 a month, but can you live on that? Not without help from welfare and food stamps, programs that have faced deep cuts in recent years as conservatives "get tough" on the poor. Homelessness is created by structural changes in the economy, low-paid jobs, and out-of-reach property values.

SOCIAL CLASS AND EVERYDAY LIFE

Social class affects every aspect of our lives. Our family life, values, health, and political attitudes are all influenced by our position in the stratification system. For one thing, people who are healthier live longer. Is there a relationship between social class and access to health care? Absolutely. People in the upper class can afford the best health care, are able to travel to the most respected medical hospitals and clinics for health care, and are treated by the best doctors. The affluent can afford the best and most nutritious food. People in the lower classes often have no health care at all and rely upon public clinics and emergency room care. Consequently, people in the elite class tend to live an average of seven years longer. People in the lower classes are more likely to smoke and eat food of questionable health value. Additionally, affluent people have few mental health issues because they enjoy a higher standard of living that is less stressful. A lifetime of hard work, in stressful, dangerous, often toxic working environments, with inadequate health care, and an inadequate diet will take a few years off your life. In sum, at every age level, lower class people are more likely to die sooner than upper class people.

Social class influences our family life in a number of important ways. Researchers often find that middle class couples are more egalitarian than working class couples are. Middle class couples tend to divide household chores equally, share more activities, particularly leisure activities, and express greater intimacy. Working class families, on the other hand, tend to have a division of household labor that is more traditional and based on gender.

Lower class individuals rarely go to college; therefore, they are more likely to marry at an earlier age. Of course, since they get married earlier they tend to have larger families. Lower and working class parents are more likely to encourage their children to conform to traditional norms and show respect to authority figures. Middle class parents encourage their children to express individuality, imagination, and creativity. These attitudes toward the socialization of children are related to the types of jobs parents hold. There are social class differences regarding child development. Middle class parents tend to think their children need a lot of attention and guidance in order to develop good mental and social skills. Working class parents are more likely to view child development as a natural process. They feel that children will develop appropriately if they set limits and boundaries and provide for the basics of life. Middle class parents tend to be much more involved in their children's lives.

Researchers have long realized that economic hardship is highly correlated with divorce. In many affluent families, the male breadwinner earns enough money to enable the mother to stay home with the children. Low paid service work, part-time work, menial labor, and unemployment are stressful. Dead-end jobs pay low wages and have few benefits. Therefore, lower class families face a variety of stresses affluent families do not have to deal with, including insecure jobs, low wages, lack of health care during illness, and the struggle just to put food on the table. Economic stress and hardship often leads to marital stress and divorce.

Old money is passed down from generation to generation through inheritance. Therefore, families in this group have a great sense of ancestry and family history. Marriage and family are very important in the preservation of great wealth. These families encourage their children to marry within their class, which is the primary function of elite boarding schools. Old money families are intensely private and focus on manners and culture. Sending their children to private schools allows them to meet and interact with others of their social class background. Since this group accounts for less than 1 percent of United States families, there are not a great number of eligible people to meet and date. Parents in this social class use debutant balls, private boarding schools, and Ivy League Colleges to influence their children's choice of mate.

There are some interesting differences in values between the social classes. For instance, affluent and educated people are much more tolerant of a wide range of behaviors, such as homosexuality. People in the working class are raised in a much more supervised environment with strict discipline. Since they are less likely to attend college, they will experience less diversity and tend to be less tolerant.

A general rule of thumb is that people that are more affluent tend to support the Republican Party. Less affluent people usually support the Democratic Party. In economic terms, this makes sense. While both political parties accept donations from big business, the Democratic Party tends to favor legislation and social policies that remediate the worse effects of capitalism. The Republican Party, on the other hand, tends to oppose policies that help the poor. Many Republicans were stridently opposed to social programs such as Social Security, Medicare, and other programs that created the social safety net, including food stamps, welfare, school breakfast and lunch programs, and a range of other programs for the poor. Therefore, in strictly economic terms, lower class people, since they are more likely to be at risk of poverty, should support the Democratic Party. The working class has generally supported the Democratic Party due to the strong pro-union policies of the democrats. For example, democrats usually support increasing the minimum wage and universal health care—policies republicans and people in business strongly oppose. Thus, on strictly economic issues, lower and working class people tend to be liberals while affluent people tend to be conservative.

When it comes to social issues, however, highly educated, more affluent people tend to be more liberal. Less affluent people tend to be more conservative. Thus, on issues such as affirmative action, feminism, homosexuality, abortion, and related social issues, the affluent are generally more liberal than the less affluent. It is probable that education plays a major role in one's position on these issues. The more you learn about controversial issues, and the more familiar you become with the complexities of culture, the more tolerant you tend to become. Thus, it is not the case that liberal minded people conspired to create a liberal educational system, but rather that education itself is liberalizing. In recent years, the Republican Party has been extremely successful in using wedge issues to attract lower and working class people to their party, in spite of their economic interests, which generally lie with the Democratic Party. The issue of values is extremely complex. For example, it is likely that every individual, depending upon their social class, their religion, gender, age, race and ethnicity, and so on, will be conservative on some issues and liberal on others.

Education tends to increase the further we move up the socioeconomic ladder. As mentioned previously, children of the elite attend private boarding schools, such as Exeter Academy and Woodberry Forest School, which prepare upper class children for universities in the Ivy League. Working and lower class children attend pubic schools. Under-class children are most likely to attend one of the nation's inner city schools, many of which are crumbling, condemned, and failing. Middle class parents understand that education is the key to their success and will be the key to their children's success as well. Thus, middle class parents are likely to spend a great deal of time reading to their children and being involved in their instruction and teaching. Often, middle class children start school with the ability to recite the alphabet, count to ten, and read at the first grade level. Frequently they have memorized their telephone number and address.

We have noted that every culture is stratified, although the criteria for stratification can vary. Some societies are stratified based on a caste system. Other societies, such as the United States, are stratified based on social class, gender, race, and ethnicity. We will return to the discussion of gender, racial, and ethnic inequality in later chapters. Although the ideology of equal opportunity is prevalent in the United States it takes very little effort to find enough evidence that inequality in the United States is based largely on group membership, rather than personal characteristics. This discussion relied heavily on the criteria of education, occupation, and income, to identify several social classes. The elite class is at the top of the social class structure, and they control half of the nation's income and most of the wealth. The upper class, commonly thought of the managerial class because they administer and run the businesses owned by the elite class, follows the elite class in the social class hierarchy. Next down on the social class ladder is the middle class, followed by the working class, the working poor, and the underclass, which includes the homeless, respectively. As you move from the bottom of the social class hierarchy to the top, occupational prestige and income improves and the amount of education members of each social class achieve is greater.

Income inequality in the United States has not changed greatly in the two centuries prior to 1973, in spite of the War on Poverty, increases in educational attainment, greater numbers of women entering the workforce, and greater numbers of dual-earner families. In general, the gap between the rich and the poor in the United States is greater than in many other industrial nations. Since 1973, however, income inequality in the United States has increased. The structural transformation of the United States economy is largely the reason. Following 1973, the meager gains of labor began to be rolled back. Today, people work longer hours for less pay. Holiday and sick leave have contracted by over 15 percent. The nation has experienced corporate downsizing, union busting and labor concessions, the elimination of good paying jobs in industry and middle level management, workers have been laid off and outsourced without being replaced, many workers who remained on the job were turned into contingent workers or private contractors, consequently losing their benefits and experiencing a reduction in pay. States have changed their labor laws to protect the ability of business to layoff or fire workers under the guise of "right to work" laws. Employees have been forced into early retirement, or replaced by workers in foreign labor markets, fringe benefits have been reduced or eliminated, and the minimum wage has not been increased for decades. The degree to which you are vulnerable to the structural changes is highly correlated with your social class standing.

℘ ℭ ℘ ℭ

DEFINITIONS

Achieved Status. A status entered after birth and usually due at least in part to individual behavior.
Ascribed Status. A status assigned at birth.

Caste System. A social category in a stratification system in which membership depends on ascribed statuses and cannot be changed after birth. Marriage between members of different categories is prohibited.

Class System. A social system in which the economic factor is the most important and achieved statuses (gained by ability, available resources, and merit) are the principle means of determining a person's rank.

Entrepreneurs. A person who attempts to make a profit by starting their own company or by operating alone in the business world, especially when it involves taking risks.

Income. The amount of money received over a period of time either as payment for work, goods, or services, or as profit on capital.

Intergenerational Mobility. Differences in the social status of parents and their offspring.

Intragenerational Mobility. Changes in an individual's social ranking over the course of his or her lifetime.

Life Chances. Opportunities for securing such things as health, education, autonomy, leisure, and a long life.

Managerial Class. A supposed social class in modern industrial-bureaucratic societies, most appropriately conceptualized as a specific part of the middle or white collar class. It particularly refers to that stratum of people who are given the administrative and management chores and functions within big business (the corporate world) and big government.

Middle Class. Social class broadly defined occupationally as those working in white-collar and lower managerial occupations; sometimes defined by reference to income levels or subjective identification of the participants in the study.

Nouveau Riche. Those who have new money, attaining great wealth in business, sports, entertainment, or through invention or the stock market. However, they are at the bottom of the capitalist class. The nouveau riche did not attend the right schools and lack the long established social networks of the old rich.

Power Elite. A small group of top corporate, political, and military leaders who dominate American politics.

Rentiers. A person whose income is from investments and who therefore does not have to work.

Social Mobility. The processes through which people move from one position in a stratification system to another.

Social Status. A position in a social relationship, a characteristic that locates individuals in relation to other people and sets of role expectations.

Socioeconomic-Status. An overall rank based on characteristics such as education and occupation, used to describe people's positions in stratification systems.

Stratification. The hierarchical arrangement of social classes, social castes, and social strata in a society. In Marxian theory, social stratification is explained primarily in economic terms. The distribution of resources, wealth, power, prestige, and ideologies are regarded as "having their roots" in the relationship of the differing social classes to the means of production and distribution.

Structural Mobility. Refers to society wide changes that lead to upward or downward social mobility for large segments of the population. Structural changes usually take place in the economic and political institutions of society.

Underclass (lower class). Unemployed and unemployable persons who are so removed from the mainstream that their poverty is more or less a permanent condition.

Upper Class. A class of people having the highest social rank or standing based on wealth, family connections, and the like. The social group with the highest status, especially the aristocracy.

Wealth. Valued possessions not needed for immediate consumption.

Working Class. Relating to or belonging to the part of society made up of people who work for hourly wages, not salaries, especially manual or industrial laborers.

Working Poor. Workers earning inadequate income as judged by government-established standards of poverty.

REFERENCES

The ideas expressed in my essay on stratification and social class and the information presented are based on the following works:

Aldrich, Jr., Nelson W. 1989. *Old Money: The Mythology of America's Upper Class*. New York: Vintage Books.

Baltzell, E. Digby and Howard G. Schneiderman. 1988. "Social Class in the Oval Office." *Society* 25 (September/October):42-49.

Baltzell, E. Digby. 1979. *Puritan Boston and Quaker Philadelphia*. New York: Free Press.

Beegley, Leonard. 2000. *The Structure of Stratification in the United States*. Newton, MA: Allyn and Bacon.

Bertoli, Fernando and Associates. 1984. "Infant Mortality by Socioeconomic Status for Blacks, Indians, and Whites: A Longitudinal Analysis of North Carolina, 1868-1977." *Sociology and Social Research* 68:364-77.

Blau, Peter M. and Joseph E. Schwartz. 1984. *Cross-Cutting Social Circles.* Orlando, FL: Academic Press.

Blau, Peter M. and Otis Dudley Duncan. 1967. *The American Occupational Structure.* New York: John Wiley.

Bose, Christine E. and Peter H. Rossi. 1983. "Gender and Jobs: Prestige Standings of Occupations as Affected by Gender." *American Sociological Review* 48 (June): 316-330.

Burris, Val .2000. "The Myth of Old Money Liberalism: The Politics of the *Forbes* 400 Richest Americans." *Social Problems* 47(3) (August):360-378.

Chin, Nancy P., Alicia Monroe, and Kevin Fiscella. 2000. "Social Determinants of (Un)Healthy Behaviors." *Education for Health: Change in Learning and Practice* 13(3) (November):317-328.

Cohen, Patricia. 2004. "Forget Lonely, Life Is Healthy at the Top." *New York Times*, May 15.

Cookson, Jr., Peter W. and Caroline Hodges Persell. 2005. "Preparing for Power: Cultural Capital and Elite Boarding Schools." In *Life in Society: Readings to Accompany Sociology A Down-to-Earth Approach.* 7th ed., edited by James M. Henslin. Boston, MA: Allyn and Bacon.

Davis, James Allan and Tom W. Smith. 1986. *General Social Surveys, 1972-1986.* Chicago, IL: National Opinion Research Center.

Davis, Kingsley and Wilbert E. Moore. 1945. "Some Principles of Stratification." *American Sociological Review* 10 (April):242-249.

Davis, Mike. 1986. *Prisoners of the American Dream: Politics and Economy in the History of the U.S. Working Class.* London, UK: Verso Books.

Domhoff, G. William. 1979. *The Powers That Be.* New York: Random House.

Domhoff, G. William. 1990. *The Power Elite and the State: How Policy Is Made in America.* Hawthorne, NY: Aldine De Gruyter.

Domhoff, G. William. 1998. *Who Rules America? Power and Politics in the Year 2000.* 3rd ed. Mountain View, CA: Mayfield Publishing.

Duncan, Greg. 1984. *Years of Poverty, Years of Plenty.* Ann Arbor, MI: Institute for Social Research.

Duncan, Otis Dudley, David L. Featherman, and B. Duncan. 1972. *Socioeconomic Background and Achievement.* New York: Seminar Books.

Dye, Thomas R. 1983. *Who's Running America: The Reagan Years.* 3rd ed. Englewood Cliffs, NJ: Prentice-Hall.

Dye, Thomas R. 1986. *Who's Running America: The Conservative Years.* 4th ed. Englewood Cliffs, NJ: Prentice-Hall.

Fabrikant, Geraldine. 2005. "Old Nantucket Warily Meets the New." *New York Times*, June 5.

Faris, Robert E. L. and Warren Dunham. 1939. *Mental Disorders in Urban Areas.* Chicago, IL: University of Chicago Press.

Fletcher, June. 1997. "Address Envy: Fudging to Get the Best." *Wall Street Journal*, April 25, B10.

Gilbert, Dennis L. 2003. *The American Class Structure in an Age of Growing Inequality*, 6th ed. Belmont, CA: Wadsworth Publishing.

Gilbert, Dennis L. and Joseph A. Kahl. 1998. *The American Class Structure: A New Synthesis.* 4th ed. Belmont, CA: Wadsworth Publishing.

Gold, Ray. 1952. "Janitors Versus Tenants: A Status-Income Dilemma." *American Journal of Sociology* 56:486-493.

Halle, David. 1984. *America's Working Man: Work, Home, and Politics Among Blue-Collar Property Owners.* Chicago, IL: University of Chicago Press.

Hellinger, Daniel and Dennis R. Judd. 1991. *The Democratic Façade.* Pacific Grove, CA: Brooks/Cole.

Hochschild, Jennifer. 1981. *What's Fair? American Beliefs About Distributive Justice.* Cambridge, MA: Harvard University Press.

Hodge, Robert W., Donald J. Treiman, and Peter Rossi. 1966. "A Comparative Study of Occupational Prestige." In *Class, Status, and Power.* 2nd ed., edited by Reinhard Bendix and Seymour Martin Lipset. New York: Free Press.

Hodge, Robert W., Paul Siegel, and Peter Rossi. 1964. "Occupational Prestige in the United States, 1926-63." *American Journal of Sociology* 70 (November):286-302.

Hurst, Charles E. 1995. *Social Inequality: Forms, Causes, and Consequences.* 2nd ed. New York: Allyn and Bacon.

Kerbo, Harold R. 1991. *Social Stratification and Inequality: Class Conflict in Historical and Comparative Perspective.* 2nd ed. New York: McGraw-Hill.

Kohn, Melvin L. 1959. "Social Class and Parental Values." *American Journal of Sociology* 64:337-351.

Kohn, Melvin L. 1963. "Social Class and Parent-Child Relationships: An Interpretation." *American Journal of Sociology* 68:471-480.

Kohn, Melvin L. 1976. "Occupational Structure and Alienation." *American Journal of Sociology* 82:111-130.

Kohn, Melvin L. 1977. *Class and Conformity: A Study in Values.* 2nd ed. Homewood, IL: Dorsey Press.

Kohn, Melvin L. and Carmi Schooler. 1983. *Work and Personality: An Inquiry into the Impact of Social Stratification.* New York: Ablex Press.

Kohn, Melvin L., Kazimierz M. Slomczynski, and Carrie Schoenbach. 1986. "Social Stratification and the Transmission of Values in the Family: A Cross-National Assessment." *Sociological Forum* 1(1):73-102.

Krueger, Alan B. 2002. "The Apple Falls Close to the Tree, Even in the Land of Opportunity." *New York Times*, November 14.

Lareau, Annette. 2002. "Invisible Inequality: Social Class and Childrearing in Black Families and White Families." *American Sociological Review* 67:747-776.

Lenski, Gerhard. 1954. "Status Crystallization: A Nonvertical Dimension of social Status." *American Sociological Review* 19:404-413.

Lenski, Gerhard. 1966. *Power and Privilege: A theory of Social Stratification.* New York: McGraw-Hill.

Lipset, Seymour Martin. 1959. "Democracy and Working-Class Authoritarianism." *American Sociology Review* 24:482-502.

Mannheim, Karl. 1929. *Ideology and Utopia: An Introduction to the Sociology of Knowledge.* San Diego, CA: Harcourt Brace Jovanovich.

Mills, C. Wright. 1959. *The Power Elite.* New York: Oxford University Press.

Morris, Joan M. and Michael D. Grimes. 2005. "Moving Up from the Working Class." Pp. 365-376 in *Down to Earth Sociology: Introductory Readings.* 13th ed. edited by James M. Henslin. New York: The Free Press.

Navarro, Vicente, ed. 2002. *The Political Economy of Social Inequalities: Consequences for Health and Quality of Life.* Amityville, NY: Baywood Publishing.

O' Hare, William P. 1966. "A New Look at Poverty in America." *Population Bulletin* 51(2) (September):1-47.

Samuelson, Paul Anthony and William D. Nordhaus. 2005. *Economics.* 18th ed. New York: McGraw Hill.

Statistical Abstract of the United States. 2005. Washington DC: Bureau of the Census, Table: 621, 953, 670, 696.

Thomas, Evan and Bob Cohn. 1995 "Rethinking the Dream." *Newsweek*, June 26, pp. 18-21.

Thomas, Melvin E. 1993. "Race, Class, and Personal Income: An Empirical Test of the Declining Significant of Race Thesis, 1968-1988." *Social Problems* 40(3) (August):328-342.

Thomas, Paulette. 1994. "Widening Rich-Poor Gap is a Threat to the "Social Fabric," White House Says." *The Wall Street Journal*, February 15, A10, A18.

Weber, Max. 1970. "Class, Status, and Party." In H. H. Gerth and C. Wright Mills (trans.) From *Max Weber: Essays in Sociology.* New York: Oxford University Press.

by Frank O. Taylor, IV, Ph.D. with Alexander F. Rice

When I was a graduate student attending the University of Nebraska, I once took my son downtown for lunch. Since he was, and still is, a pizza lover, we decided to eat at a pizza buffet near the campus. The campus is a land-grant institution, which means that any citizen of the state has a right to be on the premises. This includes homeless citizens of the state, of which there were more than a few scattered around the campus. I saw one homeless man in particular almost everyday. He lived on one of the benches downtown, across the street from the campus. On most days, I would pass by him and observe him having a conversation with himself. I suspect that he had some form of mental illness and may at one time actually have been institutionalized, before President Reagan cut funding for mental illness, resulting in many residents of mental health institutions being thrown out onto the streets.

The bench he occupied was adjacent to the pizza parlor my son and I were walking to. We were about a half a block away when we saw two businessmen in expensive suits and three well-dressed women, probably their secretaries, since the women were each carrying several boxes of pizzas and the men carried nothing, emerge from the pizza establishment, and begin to make their way down the street. Their path took them right past the homeless man on his bench. We were walking toward all these folks and were quickly within hearing distance when the homeless man politely asked if they could spare a piece of pizza.

The two businessmen stopped, and with their secretaries standing behind them in a semicircle, they started calling the homeless man a variety of names (which cannot be repeated here). Their secretaries quickly joined in. The gist of their harangue was language to the effect that he was a lazy bum who should get a job and stop harassing honest working people on the street, or words to that effect. I fear my ten-year-old son had never heard language as foul as that coming out of the mouths of these obviously affluent people. I am sure that no one would hire a homeless man with obvious mental health issues. After a minute or two of abusing the poor man, they lost interest and continued on their way.

Taking my son by the hand, we followed this bunch down the street until we all had to stop at the crossing light. Maneuvering directly behind the two businessmen, I asked my son in a voice loud enough to be heard by the entire crowd of people what Jesus thought about the poor. This got everyone's attention and conversations stopped completely. In his tiny little boy voice, my son answered back that Jesus loved the poor and we were supposed to help the poor. At this point, I could see that the two mean-spirited businessmen were getting quite upset. However, when your accuser is a small ten-year old boy, what are you going to do? Then my son asked a very interesting question. Everyone at the light was paying attention. He asked if I thought the businessmen would "burn in hell" for not helping the homeless man. I did not get a chance to answer because the light turned green the businessmen and their secretaries ran as fast as they could across the street to get away from us. There are some problems, as a nation, we cannot run away from. Poverty is one of them.

Defining Poverty. When you think about poverty you may recall television advertisements asking you to contribute to one charity or another that helps children in the third world. This has the effect of drawing our attention away from the United States, creating the illusion that extreme poverty is a problem elsewhere in the world. Generally, when you see these advertisements you are shown video of children who are so hungry they are emaciated, and they live in shantytowns without electricity, running water, sewage, or any of life's amenities we take for granted. The poverty you see in these ads is **absolute poverty**. Absolute poverty is life threatening poverty. It is related to hunger, malnutrition, disease, squalor, unemployment, and high rates of mortality.

Although there are some pockets of absolute poverty in the United States, in our nation poverty is not usually life threatening in the short run. Poverty in the United States is more likely to be **relative poverty**. Relative poverty means that some people are poorer compared to others. For example, if you earn over thirty thousand dollars a year we can hardly say that you are suffering from absolute poverty. Nevertheless, if you are married and have six children you will have an income that "officially" makes you poor, according to the 2005 Federal Poverty Guidelines. Absolute poverty leads to hunger, malnutrition, and eventually death. Relative poverty means you cannot afford many of the things the affluent take for granted, such as new clothes, eating out, expensive food, a new car, good quality housing, and so on. Relative poverty is a major problem facing the nation.

Poverty Line. It seems clear that a **poverty line**, in which those below a certain income are considered poor and those above are not, my be difficult to establish. How are the poor separated from the non-poor?   The Social Security Administration developed the official formula for calculating who is and is not poor. First, they assumed that poor people spend about one-third of their income on food. Then they took the cost of an adequate diet (the minimum number of calories it takes to survive on a daily basis) and multiplied it by three. A fairly simply approach. The following table presents the official poverty line data.

Table 16.1   Official Poverty Line Data

Size of Family Unit	Income
1	$9,570
2	$12,830
3	$16,090
4	$19,350
5	$22,610
6	$25,870
7	$29,130
8	$32,390
Additional person, add	$3,260

Source: Federal Register, Vol. 70, No. 33, February 18, 2005, pp. 8373-8375.

Using the federal guidelines, the Bureau of the Census estimates that 12.5 percent of the United States population falls at or below the official poverty line, or just about 36 million people.

Is this an accurate accounting of the number of poor people? The accuracy of the Census data rests upon the assumption that poor people spend one-third of their income on food. If, for example, poor people spend a greater proportion of their income on food, as some critics suggest, the poverty line is skewed too low. In this case, the true extent of poverty in the United States is masked by the official poverty line. The poverty line is adjusted annually for inflation by using the Consumer Price Index. However, the government has not kept up with inflation. Other issues would lead us to believe that the bar for falling into poverty is set too low. For example, the cost of housing now takes up a larger percent of family budget than food. In addition, what about the costs of fuel, health care, insurance, clothing, and other things usually associated with our standard of living? The cost of all these things has continued to increase yearly. Some researchers suggest that a more realistic poverty line would be 50 percent greater than the existing measure, increasing the number of poor to over 50 million.

The Functions of Poverty. Why does poverty persist? Before taking a look at some of the explanations of poverty, we will consider the "functions" of poverty for society. From a functional perspective, if poverty continues to exist it may be serving some useful function for society. Our society is composed of different groups, with different standards of living and different levels of power.   It may be the case that what is functional for some individuals and subgroups is dysfunctional for others.

The sociologist Herbert Gans identified a number of ways in which poverty is useful for society, or at least for some people in our society. First, the poor do the "dirty work" of society. They work in the lowest paying jobs with the least amount of job security and other benefits. Since the poor typically have the least amount of education and training, and few job skills beyond the willingness to perform manual labor, they cannot afford to turn down low paying jobs at the bottom of the occupational structure.

The poor also subsidize many of the activities of the affluent, either directly or indirectly. Have you ever worked in the restaurant industry? I have. I worked as busboy for a major restaurant chain. I never received more than twenty hours a week, for which I received wages that kept me poor.   Many restaurants hire part-time workers deliberately, rather than full-time workers, in order to avoid paying overtime or healthcare benefits. Obviously, keeping overhead from wages low ensures greater profit for the owners. The less you earn as their employee, the more they take out of the business as profit for themselves. The affluent often hire domestic workers to take care of their children and homes, usually paying minimum wage. The less the affluent have to pay domestic labor, the more money they have to spend on themselves, or reinvest in their businesses, or simply put in a savings account.

The poor pay a greater proportion of their income in taxes than the affluent. A report by Citizens for Tax Justice found that 43 percent of President Bush's first tax cut ended up in the hands of the top 1 percent of earners, those least in need of tax relief, while only about 13 percent went to the bottom 60 percent of earners. The average middle class taxpayer received a paltry $435, while those with earnings of more than $300,000 per year received over $45,000. Taxes subsidize many state and local programs and services that serve the needs of the affluence, yet they are paying taxes at a lower and lower rate.

The present railing against taxes, especially property taxes, strikes me as downright weird. Where does the government's budget come from? Where else but from taxes? Taxes pay for schools, roads and highways, community centers, parks, hospitals, sports stadiums, colleges and universities, schools, in short, almost everything we require to have a community. It is extremely disturbing to listen to elderly people complain about tax increases for schools. If they no longer have children in the home, many older people will not vote to increase the budgets for public schools, even though they, and their children, had to be educated too. Some of the largest corporations in the world, such as Ford and GM, actually have received tax refunds in recent years. The loss of funds from corporations has caused many states to cut their budgets, decimating funds for programs designed to help the poor.

Where would the prison industry be without the poor? Privatization of the penal system is one of the fastest growing industries in the nation. The defendants are much more likely to end up in the penal system than the affluent, who can afford good attorneys. Many studies have discovered that poor people have higher crime rates. Poor people are more likely to commit the types of crimes handled by the police, as opposed to white-collar crimes, like fraud and insider trading. Conventional crime, such as rape, robbery, assault, and larceny, are more likely to be committed by the poor. The poor are also more likely to be the victims of conventional crime. There is a relationship between the economy and the crime rate. When income inequality and unemployment increases so does the crime rate. It has been estimated that a 1 percent increase in the unemployment rate is correlated with 4 percent increase in the homicide rate and a 6 percent increase in the rate of robberies. Other research suggests that crime seems to follow unemployment. The conventional crime rate increases when the unemployment rate increases. Still other research suggests that cities with the greatest income gap between the affluent and the poor also have the highest rates of conventional crime.

The poor buy the goods that no one else wants. You know you are poor when you have to shop at the day-old bread store. Many poor college students' are so poor that they shop at second hand clothing stores. When I was first married, and even as recently in my life as my first professorship, I was so poor that I had to buy furniture from thrift stores and second hand stores. When I graduated from college with my undergraduate degree, I was able to take advantage of a program from Ford Motor Company that provided car loans for students going to graduate school. They approved the loan but I had to pay a very large interest rate. Recently I spoke to a relative of mine who sells cars. He indicated that he would sell every car on his "buy here pay here" used car lot at least four times per year, because poor will default on their payments and he will repossess the car. The last year I was in college I was so poor I bought a car that had been sitting in a lake. My greatest fear in life was that it would break down on the highway, which it did with regularity. In the wintertime in North Dakota, a mechanical breakdown could be life threatening.

When I was a young man, people used to point out hobos: homeless men who moved around the country by railroad and panhandled wherever they went. They would point to these wretched souls and say some pretty absurd things: "there goes a free man," for instance. Usually, the poor are pointed out as having maladaptive values. There are a number of **myths about the poor**: they are lazy, they use the system, and they are dishonest, alcoholic, and promiscuous, they are stupid, and so on. When parents point out the poor and start mentioning these myths they are acting as agents of social control, attempting to get their children to buy into middle class values and beliefs. They say, "Look what will happen to you if you fail to have the right values." Work hard, study hard, plan for the future, save money, are the watchwords of the middle class. Of course, it helps not to be born poor in the first place. Did you ever try to save any money at a minimum wage job?

I cannot say how many times I have heard people comment, when seeing a homeless man holding the "I will work for food" sign, that the man probably is not poor at all and is just conning us. It is estimated that half a million people are homeless each evening in the nation with over one million experiencing homelessness some time during the year. Focusing on a handful of con artists, if there actually are any in the first place, tends to distract from the larger reality of homelessness. If you believe that every homeless person you see is potentially a con artist trying to con you out of your dollar, you are unlikely to care much about homelessness as a national problem. With over a million homeless people on the streets of the nation, what is the likelihood that the homeless person you see holding the sign is a con artist? I once did the math in class showing students that out of thirty-eight million poor people, there were about three-hundred thousand individuals who could potentially get a job because they were not elderly, less than eighteen, a student, a mother with a minor child in the household, or suffering from some type of disability. On the face of it, they did not meet the criteria for the **deserving poor**. Some students had argued that the nation should end welfare because some people were abusing the system. In order to punish several thousand free loaders, they seemed willing to punish millions of children who make up the majority of the poor. Are children to blame for their poverty?

Another function that the poor serve is making us feel good about ourselves when we do reach out to help them. Where would charities be without their poor clients? It makes us feel good to help the deserving poor. When we help people who are down on their luck, we derive a sense of emotional satisfaction. Thus, poor people serve the function of reinforcing some of our major values. To get children to internalize values related to honesty, hard work, planning for the future, and a whole range of other values related to the middle class, we point to the poor as proof of what happens to people without those values. On the other hand, helping the poor reinforces the values of compassion, pity, altruism, and charity. In many respects, poverty helps guarantee the status of those who are not poor.

Many people in the middle class believe that the poor are deviant. Poor people are thought to be drug addicted promiscuous alcoholics. Instead of seeing such behavior as the result of despair, when such behavior is present, which it is not for the vast majority of the poor, affluent people like to engage in fantasies about how they would behave if they were poor. Affluent people sometimes believe that if they were poorer they would enjoy life more! They could have more sex, consume alcohol and drugs more freely, and so on. Thus, one function of the poor is to provide affluent people with vicarious fantasies. In fact, most poor people are no different from anyone else. They go to work, to church, and try to raise their children with the same values as parents in the middle class. If you do not believe that the poor are exploited in this manner, you have never been to the movies! How many middle class patrons of movie theaters want to go to the movies and see poor people behaving well? No, they demand sex, drugs, and violence. As a young graduate student, I once was lost in Chicago and found myself in a poor neighborhood. I did not hear any gunfire; no one tried to sell me any drugs; nor did a prostitute approach me. It was all pretty normal. I was definitely not in fear for my life, as I would have been had it been a scene from a movie.

For example, the blues and jazz, which lead to the birth of rock and roll, were musical art forms that emerged from the despair of poverty. Rap is another form of entertainment that emerged out of the inner city as a response to the lack of social mobility and grinding poverty that prevails there.

There are a number of cultural functions served by the poor. The poor help keep the affluent busy through volunteer work. What would all those movie stars do without the poor? What would all those socialites do without their charity balls and benefits to help the homeless and other establishments who work with the indigent? Bono, a musician who for years has been involved in social movements related to poverty and peace, was recently on the cover of Time magazine for his efforts to get the World Trade Organization to forgive debts made to third world nations. Bill Gates set up a $28 million dollar fund to help the poor. Helping the poor is a major function of a variety of churches. A number of churches have established their own welfare programs to help their members. Such activities are laudable. However, volunteer work and charity will not end the structural, political, and economic causes of poverty.

Another function of poverty is that the poor serve as **symbolic constituencies** or opponents for several groups. Liberal politicians and leaders often try to impress their liberal constituencies by proposing legislation or policies to help the poor. They use the poor to serve political functions. Conservatives, on the other hand, also using the poor for political functions, often try to impress their constituencies by "getting tough" on the poor. Liberals try to paint their opponents as "waging war on the poor." Conservatives try to claim that liberals who complain about political legislation to help the affluent, such as tax cuts, are "waging class warfare." Recently for example, the governor of Michigan proposed that women on welfare be forced to work for forty hours a week doing civil service, such as sweeping streets in orange prison jumpsuits with a capital "W" on the back. In some states, women receiving public aid are forced to take birth control. Other conservatives have proposed sterilization and even lobotomies for the poor!

The last function of poverty mentioned by Gans that I want to review is that the poor are powerless and can serve the function of being made to absorb the costs of political and economic growth. Currently, Congress is attempting to find money to help rebuild after the hurricane Katrina. This money will be hard to come by considering the tax-cuts that have gone to the affluent in the recent past. Several proposals have been debated, all of which include severe cuts in funding for programs that help the poor. When state and local governments need to find space for expansion poor neighborhoods are often targeted, largely because people in those neighborhoods lack the political power to prevent such activity. Cities and states need to build or expand community colleges, four-year colleges and universities, expressways, urban renewal projects, and other forms of economic expansion that have to be located somewhere. When debating where to locate an expressway, for example, affluent citizens frequently take the "not in my backyard" attitude and have the resources to mobilize against the expansion. Poor people have no such resources. When toxic and medical waste has to be put somewhere, or incinerated, frequently it is put in lower class neighborhoods.

Poverty and Employment.   One prevalent myth concerning poverty is that poor people simply refuse to work. I have held a number of jobs in my lifetime that did not pay enough, no matter how hard I worked, to lift me out of poverty. I used to work for a roofing company. My job was to carry hot liquid tar up to the roof where the better-paid employees applied it. This was backbreaking, repetitive, dirty work. I earned minimum wage. There were no benefits of any kind and very little overtime. Other people working in the service industry are often unable to find anything but a **dead-end job**. These are minimum wage jobs, mostly part-time, without health care or retirement benefits. According to the United States Census Bureau, almost 90 percent of poor households have at least one employed person, blasting the myth that the poor do not want to work. The problem is not the bad values of poor people but the type of jobs poor people find in the service economy. Researchers find that most of the working poor would remain in poverty even if they worked full-time. Even if you worked full-time, at minimum wages you will still be far below the poverty line. Full-time minimum wage will only get you to 76 percent of the poverty line. Most poor people who do not work are generally considered deserving of our help, including disabled people, children, or the elderly.

Another myth related to poverty is that you can always find a better job. In other words, according to the myth, if your job pays poverty wages you simply need to find a better job or move to a location where there are higher-paying jobs. Can you imagine me traveling across country with my family in my 1971 Dodge Dart (remember that car on Married with Children?) that had been pulled out of a lake and was prone to breaking down? I would have been stranded on the highway in very short order. Not an appealing prospect if you have an infant in the family. I seriously doubt that people earning minimum wage at a part-time job, most of who do not own automobiles, would be able to pick up and move. Recall that many of the Katrina victims had no way to escape New Orleans for similar reasons. Additionally, poor people tend to be less educated. So moving from one dead-end job to another dead-end job will not solve any problems, assuming you can find a job. There have been significant reductions in the high paying unionized jobs in steel, auto, and rubber in recent decades. As factories close in the United States and are relocated to the Third World, workers are increasingly unlikely to find other factory jobs or regain their standard of living.

We live in a capitalist economy and unemployment is functional for the affluent because it is commonly believed to reduce inflation. Here is how it works. For the sake of argument, let us say you work at Joe's Pizza Palace earning minimum wage and working twenty hours a week. You are a good worker, very reliable, but tired of being poor. You ask Joe if you can either work more hours or get a raise. Joe tells you that if he gives you more hours he will have to grant you some benefits, which he says he cannot afford or he will go out of business. Joe also declines to give you more than minimum wage. Although you are a little disappointed, you cannot quit your job because the factory downtown just closed and you know there are hundreds, if not thousands, of unemployed people who would love to have your job. These unemployed workers are a **reserve pool of labor**, which can be called into the job market during an economic expansion or laid-off during a recession.

Unemployment clearly favors your employer in this case because you can be easily replaced, since flipping pizza requires no special training. When everyone has a job, there is tremendous consumer pressure to purchase a limited amount of goods, which leads to inflation. The government takes steps to limit inflation by raising interest rates and taxes, or in other words, encouraging unemployment. Has there ever been a time in your life in which you can recall that unemployment was zero? The answer, of course, is no. There is always some level of unemployment in a capitalist society. This implies that some people, no matter their motivation or how hard they look, will have to go without jobs. In a capitalist economy, the government tries to avoid inflation and capitalist want to depress wages. In order to accomplish this there are always fewer jobs than people who want jobs.

Some people have to go without jobs. Who are they? They are disproportionately people of color. African American men are twice as likely as White males to be unemployed. About one-fourth of Black males between the ages of 16 and 22 are unemployed and not attending school.

Latinos, Native Americans, teenagers, and residents of cities in the Northeast, are all disproportionately likely to be unemployed.

Causes of Poverty. The "cause" of poverty is a topic that has generated a considerable amount of debate. People generally fall into one of two categories when thinking about the causes of poverty. I will call these two typologies 1) system-blamers and 2) victim-blamers. System blamers generally argue that people are poor because the system has failed them. System-blamers point to failing educational systems and neighborhoods with high rates of crime and unemployment as the causes of crime. From this point of view, people are poor because society has failed to provide opportunities for social mobility. Victim-blamers, on the other hand, focus on the attributes of the individual. From this point of view, people are poor because they are intellectually or culturally inferior, have low motivation, are lazy, or have some other character flaw that prevents them from achieving upward mobility.

Let us consider the victim-blamers first. There is a very old idea operating here called **Social Darwinism**. The sociologist Herbert Spencer held that people were poor because they were unfit. Furthermore, he stressed that helping the poor would interfere with the natural process of nature. Here he is probably borrowing from another theorist Thomas Malthus, who held that famine and starvation were nature's way of bringing populations back in line with natural resources. Thus, Social Darwinism proposes that poor people are poor due to personal characteristics that insure that they will not be successful. These characteristics are transmitted genetically from one generation to the next. And lastly, social programs aimed at helping the poor will only perpetuate the problem because, first, the poor will not be able to take advantage of such programs to achieve social mobility, and second, providing aid will only guarantee that the poor will have children who will grow up to be poor. Presumably, these theorists see starvation and death as nature's way of getting rid of the socially "unfit."

Modern Social Darwinists have focused on intelligence. Some psychologists have noted that Whites score significantly higher on IQ tests than Blacks. They attribute the difference to genetics. They argue that intelligence is inherited. According to this school of thought, society is composed of hereditary castes based on intelligence. In other words, the elite class is the most intelligent and they have the best paying jobs. The lower class is the least intelligent, and they have the worst paying jobs. Social mobility, in turn, depends upon one's job. Higher paying occupations require higher levels of intelligence. Some have even suggested that there is an "unemployment gene." Thus, they claim that cognitive ability creates social stratification. Of course, these claims rest entirely on an assumption – that IQ test scores are an adequate measure of intelligence. Research into this issue has suggested that IQ tests are culturally biased to favor the children of the elite. Another important assumption made by the Social Darwinists is that IQ is relatively stable across the lifespan. However, researchers have discovered plenty of evidence that IQ can be significantly increased with good quality day care and by Head Start. Children with stimulating social environment in day care achieved much higher IQ scores than children without those experiences, suggesting that IQ is responsive to the environment and not simply a matter of genetic inheritance.

The Social Darwinist explanation of poverty rests on two basic arguments. First, there is a biological basis to human social stratification. The underclass is made up of genetically inferior people, from this point of view. Further, helping people in the underclass is a waste of time and resources because genetic deficiencies cannot be remediated. Second, racial differences on the IQ tests are genetic. Additionally, for these claims to be true it must also be true that intelligence can be depicted by a single number, which is genetically based and cannot be changed or improved. Research into the mutability of IQ has already suggested that IQ can be changed. It seems, on the face of it, rather ludicrous to claim that a single number is an accurate measure of the sum total of an individual's intelligences and I doubt that a pen and pencil test is the best way to measure IQ in the first place. In any case, these theorists are talking in absolutes and IQ test results clearly indicate that many Whites score below the Black average on the tests while many Blacks score above the White average. This is hardly proof that people of color are intellectually inferior to Whites.

Another victim-blamer school of thought can be in the **Culture of Poverty Thesis**. According to this theory, the poor have a maladaptive subculture that stresses a different set of values than those of the middle class. It is pointed out that the lifestyle of the poor is different from that of the middle class. There are more female-headed families and extended families among the poor. There are more out-of-wedlock births among the poor, and the poor seem more fatalistic, less interested in formal-education, more prone to divorce, and more present-oriented. Culture of Poverty theorists claim that children raised in poor families internalize the values of poverty and they grow up with the same values as their parents. The argument, from this point of view, is that if the poor subscribed to middle class values they could pull themselves out of poverty.

There is much to criticize regarding the Culture of Poverty Thesis. There is very little evidence that suggests that poor people actually have a deviant value system. Poor people tend to have the same hopes and dreams for themselves and their children as anyone else. Living in an extended family is less a matter of values than it is a matter of economic survival. Many aspects of poverty that Culture of Poverty theorists claim are matters of deviant values are in actuality logical adaptations to the social environment. Families live together because they cannot afford to live in single-family arrangements. Divorce is more prevalent among the poor because economic strain is highly correlated with marital problems. A present-orientation may not mean that poor people are unconcerned about saving money or their future, but may be a result of a meager existence where it is a struggle just surviving from one day to the next. It turns out that poor people are much more willing to share what they have and help each other out than are middle class people, which suggests that poor people have some good values. If they seem to be less interested in education it may be because they cannot afford to go to college. It seems to me that some people are too quick to condemn poor children. In what respect are poor children to blame for their poverty. After all, who can pick their parents?

We have reviewed two theories that focus on individuals, rather than social structure, when explaining poverty. We can accept that it is possible to make bad decisions in life and wind up living in poverty. But simply focusing on the individual and ignoring economic conditions related to poverty, such as downsizing, factory closings, low-wages, and dead-end jobs, is too simplistic. Why are genetic arguments so attractive in spite of the fact that almost no evidence suggests any type of "unemployment" gene or "intelligence" gene? First, they are single-cause explanations of complex behaviors, which make it simple to understand. Whenever human behavior can be reduced to simple causes or preferable a single cause, complexity and the required mental effort it takes to understand complexity can be avoided, at least for lay people. Second, such explanations appeal to people who want to believe that some races and ethnic groups are inferior to others. Third, affluent people can be relieved of feeling responsible for the failure of others. If you can simply say to yourself that poor people are poor because they made bad decisions you can avoid thinking about the ways in which your advantages may have been a factor in their poverty. Fourth, if poverty is a matter of personal failure, as in the case of the Culture of Poverty Thesis, or birth, as in the case of Social Darwinism, it seems not only natural but also just. Lastly, if you do not want to pay taxes, the victim-blame theories provide a rationalization for you to argue that poverty programs are a waste of money.

Now we will consider how the organization of society is related to poverty. We want to examine two conceptual explanations of poverty: opportunity structures and institutional discrimination. **Opportunity structures** refer to the opportunities for upward social mobility that are provided by society. In our culture, for example, people in the middle and working classes largely rely upon education in order to attain their desired standard of living. In addition to education, we also rely upon an occupational structure to help us achieve a good standard of living. Thus, society provides a range of opportunities from which people take advantage. No matter what your level of intelligence or how driven you are to succeed, without an opportunity structure you cannot be successful. Imagine living in the South during my childhood and being Black, you would have been denied the opportunity for an education beyond the eight-grade, until the passage of the Civil Rights Act. Certainly, you may have obtained an education by using the public library. However, would you have been able to obtain employment if a college degree was necessary? One powerful explanation for poverty, therefore, is that the opportunity structure in the United States is in a state of decline.

Is living in a middle class neighborhood with little to no crime a benefit? Is it an advantage to have educated parents? What about a good nutrition? How important is it to feel secure in your home, neighborhood, school, and church? Is there a relationship between cultural capital, such as computers, literature, encyclopedias, etc., in the household and educational success? How important is to have access to high quality libraries and schools or stimulating teachers with advanced degrees in their field? Is education more than reading, writing, and arithmetic? Are physical facilities, such as gymnasiums, computers, and classrooms with smart technology, art and music resources, and Olympic swimming pools important for educational success or is it just a matter of values? Why is it that poor students have none of these things but affluent students have all of these opportunities? If there is an intelligence gene that affluent children are born with why do they need all of these advantages?

Imagine two mothers. One mother lives in publicly subsidized housing. The other mother lives in a middle class neighborhood in a single-family dwelling. The mother who lives in public housing is a single parent. She lives on the top floor of a high-rise apartment building. Everyday her children must walk by liquor stores, an army surplus store, a pawnshop, and other businesses usually located in lower class neighborhoods on their way to school. There is a basketball court in between her high-rise building and the neighboring building, where unemployed men pass the time. The middle class mother has a fence around her yard. In the yard, there is a swing set, swimming pool, trampoline, and other objects for the children's entertainment. In order to monitor her children all she has to do is look out her picture window. There is a **social structure of mothering** that gives middle class mothers a clear advantage over mothers in the inner city. The structure of their living arrangements allows the middle class mother to practice more effective mothering.

One explanation for poverty is that the opportunity structure functions more effectively for the middle class than it does for the lower class. If you have taken college preparation courses in high school, you may do better in college than students who have not had that exposure. The classes offered in your neighborhood school are beyond the ability of the individual to control. These are matters of property taxes, school boards, curriculum committees, and other decision makers. A middle class parent who desires such classes for their children has more resources to change schools than does a parent from the lower class. Education is the key that opens up the occupational structure. However, educational opportunities are limited for children in the lower class. Shall we claim that children attending failing schools around the nation are responsible for the failure of schools to educate them, as the victim blamers would have us believe?

In recent decades, **structural transformations** in the United States economy have dealt a major blow to the standard of living of the poor. When we refer to structural transformations, we mean major changes in the economy that affect almost every citizen. Not too many years ago it was possible for working class children to graduate from high school and obtain employment in a factory producing steel, automobiles, or other industrial products, and attain a middle class standard of living. This was largely possible because of the strong unionization movement in the nation. When Ronald Reagan declared war on the unions in the early 1980s, it marked the beginning of the end of an era. Union busting by and large decimated the standard of living of the working class and reduced many opportunities for poor people to lift themselves out of poverty through secure jobs paying a high wage. Many states have passed right to work laws, virtually ending the power of unions. The decline of unions has been a major structural transformation in the United States that is limiting the opportunities for the poor and working class.

Another major structural economic change affecting the lives of not just the poor but also every citizen is **globalization**. Globalization refers to the political, economic, and cultural interconnections between everyone, regardless of national origin. Products are now produced under a global capitalist economy. If you shop at Wal-Mart, for example, you will be able to purchase products produced all over the world. Automobiles sold in the United States are made with components assembled in a variety of nations before they end up in your automobile. Advances in communications technology, such as satellite communication and the Internet have spurred globalization. Managers can now be in continuous contact with their plants and factories in any corner of the world. Of course as factories are exported to the Third World, United States jobs are also exported.

Globalization has occurred hand in hand with **deindustrialization** in the United States. Deindustrialization refers to the loss of industrial jobs and industrial capacity in the nation and the switch to an economy based on service and information. The search for cheap labor, less restrictive labor laws, lack of unions, and an absence of environmental laws have led businesses to the Third World. The North American Free Trade Agreement (NAFTA) and the General Agreement on Trade and Tariffs (GATT) have accelerated the process, eliminating many trade barriers. It is important to realize that deindustrialization has been the result of political decisions made by our leaders.

When plants are moved out of the United States to a variety of developing nations, money is drawn out of our economy. This phenomenon is referred to as **capital flight**. It takes money to build new factories and purchase machinery, tools, software, and the like, in order to keep products flowing off assembly lines. When investment of this sort takes place in the United States, new jobs are created. However, when factories in the United States are closed and new factories are built overseas, the money that would have been invested at home is instead invested in a foreign economy. In the early phase of deindustrialization those hardest hit by capital flight were members of the working and lower classes. Due to advances in communication technology now white color jobs in software development, engineering, design, accounting, customer services, and a wide range of other occupations are being **outsourced** to nations with English speaking populations where employees work for a fraction of the wages normally paid to United States workers.

The highest concentrations of poor are found in the nation's largest metropolitan areas. Since the 1950s, several major trends have occurred which have negatively affected United States cities, and consequently the poor who live in inner cities. One major trend has been the process of Suburbanization. **Suburbanization** refers to the out migration of people from the city to the suburbs. The suburbs are outlying parts of a city or town within commuting distance of the larger metropolitan area. Many people report that they want to live in neighborhoods with better school systems, less crime, and less noise and traffic. Most of those who moved to the suburbs were affluent Whites. Some researchers suggest that the process of suburbanization was driven by the desire of affluent Whites to move away from minority populations.

When affluent families move out of the city the result often has a negative impact on the city's tax base. Affluent people tend to own homes that are more expensive and pay more money to state and local governments in the form of property taxes. This applies whether the family is White or a minority. After the passage of the civil rights legislation in the 1960s, which outlawed **hidden covenants**, the language in mortgage contracts that forbade owners from selling their property to people of color, the social barriers that maintained segregation began to crumble. Affluent minority families began to move out of the inner cities. They began to move into predominantly White neighborhoods. This is probably to origin of White flight. However, imagine the negative impact on communities when affluent people of every stripe begin to leave. What goes with them besides their ability to pay property taxes? They take their skills, businesses, savings, their volunteer activities, and their ability to be outstanding role models. The impact on cities was devastating. Taxes pay for schools, infrastructure, and essential services for children, the elderly, and the infirm. In many inner cities across the nation, the poorest of the poor were left behind.

Where money goes, business follows. When affluent people began to migrate out of the city, business and industry followed. Soon, strip malls, industrial centers, and commercial zones began to appear in the suburbs. People who lived in the suburbs could find employment in the suburbs and shop in the suburbs. Moreover, many employers discovered they could open new offices and plants in the suburbs and avoid many problems they associated with inner city minorities, such as unions, affirmative action, and equal employment opportunity laws. By the end of the 1980s, the inequality between the suburbs and the cities had vastly increased, as had the level of **de facto segregation** in the nation.

Deindustrialization, the shift from an industrial economy to a service and information economy, also had a negative impact on cities and the poor, especially in the Northeast and Midwest. As manufacturing began to move out of the country, new jobs in the service economy were being created. Real estate, communications, insurance, financial services, and the health care sectors of the economy, to name a few, experienced rapid growth. Developers began converting the old factories in the central cities into office spaces for businesses in the service economy. Today you can go to the downtown of nearly any major city and find a host of office buildings with tenants in the service economy. In Addition, there are lots of jobs and occupations related to the service economy. This has set the stage for a **jobs/skills mismatch**. Poor people, who often live close to downtown, lack the skills and education required to work in the upper tier of the service economy. Often there are no jobs at all for inner city poor. For those who do find employment in the lower tier of the service economy the wages are not enough to lift the family out of poverty.

Thus, we see that **disinvestment** in urban inner cites has severely diminished the opportunity structure for the poor. What this means is that corporations often find it more profitable to relocate plants out of the country rather than modernize existing plants or build new facilities in the United States. Banks and insurance companies are reluctant to do business downtown. In fact, many financial institutions practice redlining, in which they literally draw a red circle on the map and their agents and loan offices are not to conduct any business with clients from within the circle, who live in neighborhoods considered to have rates of crime and other risks too high. The lending policies of the FHA (Federal Housing Authority) and the VA (Veterans Administration) tend to favor new housing in the suburbs. Consequently, poor people living in the nation's inner cities have been victimized by a variety of social trends that have combined to limit their social mobility.

In addition to a diminished opportunity structure, another social structural explanation of poverty is **institution discrimination**. Unlike overt acts of discrimination, institutional discrimination is very hard to see. Institutional discrimination refers to the ways in which the normal operation of institutions is systematically biased to favor the affluent and disadvantage the poor. One example of institutional discrimination is the college SAT examination. On the face of it, the SAT is supposed to be an objective assessment of how successful a prospective college student will be. It seems fair that individuals who score high on the test, and therefore are presumably better candidates for college, be allowed to continue on to higher education, while people who score lower are less likely be allowed to continue their education. All anyone has to do is study hard to do well on the tests, right?

Research suggests that the SAT test is biased to favor students who have been exposed to a curriculum of college preparation courses in high school. We have discussed a number of important social trends that negatively affected lower class neighborhoods and school districts. Educational resources are largely based on local property taxes. When your neighborhood experiences a severe reduction in property values, revenue from property taxes also is reduced. Since educational budgets are derived in part from property taxes, when tax revenues decline so do the funds to support education. In practical terms, this usually means cuts in art, music, literature, and other programs and courses related to success in college. Reductions in funding force inner city schools to focus on the basics. Advanced courses in chemistry, physics, biology, and other courses in the natural and social sciences are severely cut back or eliminated entirely. The results on SAT performance, depending on social class, are predictable. Children of the affluent do better on the tests because they have had a lot of educational preparation. Poor children, who are lucky to get a basic education, are less likely to do well on the SAT tests.

This is why we stated that institutional discrimination is hard to see. It is easy for a child who does well on the SAT test to feel that their performance is entirely a matter of their personal motivation and ability. Since affluent children are more likely to have an educational background that prepares them for college, and since they do have to study and work hard to pass those courses, it is little wonder that they view their performance as simply a matter of their individual effort. Since we tend to take our social surroundings for granted, few people are willing to grant a role to superior resources ad family background when explaining their successes in life. Still, it is hard to see how we can expect children who are forced to attend failing schools, through no fault other than being born to poor parents, to perform very well on the SAT. Moreover, because of such educational disadvantages poor children, as a group, are less likely to attend college. If every child were exposed to an identical high school curriculum and attended schools with identical resources, the SAT would be a more objective measure. However, that is sadly not the case. Poor children rarely have the opportunity to enroll in college preparation courses.

A college education is the key to social mobility for children in the middle and lower classes. Not having a degree is highly correlated with other disadvantages in life. Thus, poverty leads to multiple forms of disadvantage. Poverty is highly correlated with inadequate nutrition. Nutrition, in turn, is important for educational success. An inadequate education places poor people at a severe disadvantage in the job market, where jobs in defense, finance, computer software and hardware development, real estate, the media, health care, insurance, and other professional services require a college degree. Other good jobs, which serve local populations, including firefighters, police officers, schoolteachers, municipal employees, doctors, and lawyers also require extensive training or college degrees. Poverty wages keeps poor people in poor neighborhoods and their children in failing schools, which perpetuates the cycle. Therefore, a poor education is correlated with poverty wages, poor housing, poor health care, poor food, lack of savings, inability to qualify for loans, poor transportation, and lack of other resources necessary to lift yourself out of poverty.

Being poor probably means that your children will receive an inferior education. This means that your children will face difficulties finding good employment. Without a good job, your children are unlikely to own property. Additionally, your children will probably not have health care. The low educational attainment of poor children will keep them in unstable, low-paid, dead-end jobs. The institutions of society, and primarily the institution of education, sift and sort individuals according to criteria such as gender, race, and social class background. Affluent individuals often have difficulty accepting this because they did have to work hard in school to achieve good grades. However, they also had the advantage of being exposed to better schools and teachers and greater educational resources. Research consistently finds that educational attainment is more strongly correlated to parent's social class background than to the student's grades. What does that mean? It boils down to this: if, as a researcher, you could only have access to one set of data, you will make more accurate predications about student success if you base your predications on parent's social class rather than student's grades! This is a systematic process that goes far beyond the efforts of a single individual to change or defeat.

Feminization of Poverty. Although women, especially women of color, have always been more poor than have men, as a group, women increasingly make up a larger proportion of the poor. At all class levels, the number of households headed by women is growing. In the 1960s, only 25 percent of poor households were headed by women. By the 1980s the percent of poor households headed by women had increased to over 50 percent. Households headed by women are more likely to be poor than households with both a husband and a wife. On average, women earn about 70 percent of the income earned by a man.

Myths of Poverty.   Perhaps the most popular myth is that poor people are lazy. They are poor because they do not want to work, so the saying goes. A large percentage of the poor are considered to be deserving of help because they are either too old or too young to be expected to work. About 40 percent of the poor are less than 18 years old and 10 percent are 65 years of age or older. Almost 90 percent of poor households have at least one earner. The problem is not that people do not want to work. The problem is that many jobs pay minimum wage or less. The greatest increase in the ranks of the poor in recent decades has been among the working poor: those people who have full time jobs but whose wages do not lift them out of poverty.

The myth that the poor rely primarily on welfare is widespread. First we must note that in 1996 Congress passed the Personal Responsibility and Work Opportunity Conciliation Act, which ended welfare as a federal entitlement program. Welfare no longer exists. Funds are now allocated to the States and recipients must find work within two years and cannot collect assistance for longer than five years in a lifetime.   The conservative Congress also slashed supplemental assistance, such as food stamps and child nutrition programs. Conservatives have long believed, in spite of research to the contrary, that welfare is a disincentive to work. In other words, some people believe that the poor prefer welfare to work and that in order to force people to be responsible welfare would have to be eliminated. We have gone to great pains in this essay to point out that most of the poor are deserving poor, they are too young or too old to work, are disabled, or have children under the age of five in the home.

Let us consider whether or not the assumptions about welfare as a disincentive to work were ever true in the first place. First, welfare never accounted for more than about one-fourth of the income of poor adults. Most of the income of poor adults came from work. In addition, the poor have always been more likely to receive non-cash benefits such as Medicaid, food stamps, or housing assistance, than they were to receive cash benefits. The majority of poor people who received cash benefits were off welfare in two years. If welfare is a disincentive to work, then people on welfare should have a higher standard of living than could be obtained with full time work. However, researchers indicated that even when poor families did not work and only received cash welfare benefits they had an annual income far below the poverty line, which is hardly a disincentive to work. They would have been better off to be in the labor force than on welfare.

The assumption was that by ending the welfare entitlement program people would be forced to enter the labor market and their standard of living would improve. Has research born out that assumption? Research indicates that three-fourths of women formerly on welfare who had found jobs had incomes below the federal poverty line. Additionally, they were only able to meet their basic needs by relying on food stamps. Welfare had provided healthcare for their children, which they no longer had because the dead-end jobs they found, had few, if any, benefits. Those who face the most hardships had the least amount of education and the youngest children. Many suspect the real goal of the welfare reform legislation was simply to push people off the roles. Six million people have left the welfare roles for the work force, but the vast majority of them remain poor.

Another myth is that poor people cannot escape the cycle of poverty. Most families experience poverty for less than a year. The majority of children born in poverty do not grow up to be poor adults. There is a cycle of poverty in which people move in and out of poverty. Only about 12 percent of people live in poverty for longer than a period of five years. The highest concentrations of poverty are to be found in the nation's inner cities and some rural areas.

Many people believe that the majority of poor are persons of color. This is a myth. The vast majority of the poor are white. The rate of poverty, as a percentage of their group, is higher for African Americans and Latinos. However, over one-half of the 34 million poor in the United States are white. Another 20 percent of the poor are African American and 20 percent Hispanic. Native Americans make up about 2 percent of the poor. Asian Americans account for 3 percent of the poor. If we look at percentage of group, we see that only 8.2 percent of white people are poor, compared to 24.4 percent of African Americans and 22.5 percent of Latinos. We conclude that minorities have higher rates of poverty, but in terms of numbers the majority of poor people are White.

Another popular myth is that most poor people are single mothers and their children. It is true that female-headed mother only households make up 38 percent of the poor. However, 34 percent of the poor are married householders. An additional 22 percent of the poor live alone or with non-relatives.

by Frank O. Taylor, IV, Ph.D. with Alexander F. Rice

Many people belief that most poor people live in the inner city. This is a myth. However, poverty in inner cities is pernicious and largely the focus of this essay. About 42 percent of the poor live in the inner city. Nevertheless, it is true that 36 percent of the poor live in the suburbs and 22 percent of the poor in rural settings.

Public Assistance and Poverty. Recently I was standing in line at a large grocery store waiting to pay for my purchases. As I patiently waited my turn, the woman in front of me in the line attempted to pay for a pack of cigarettes with her food stamp card. When she was informed that she could not use the access card for cigarettes she took out her wallet and paid cash for the cigarettes. The cashier and some others in the line took offense to her having cash. I listened to several people complain that if she had cash she should not be on welfare. I asked the cashier, when it was my turn to pay, if she knew what else could not be purchased with an access card. As she stared blankly at me, I listed off several items: gasoline for your car, clothes for yourself and your children, birthday presents for your children, rent, and utility bills came quickly to my mind. She admitted that she had never thought about it that way before. I thanked her and went on my way.

When thinking about the value of public assistance programs, it is a good idea to keep in mind where the money is going. In whose hands does this money ultimately end up? The media and conservative politicians only want you to follow the money from the tax base to the poor, and no further. If you follow the money as far as the poor, then welfare will seem like a handout to you. However, if you scratch surface appearances you will soon discover that public assistance amounts to an upward redistribution of wealth.

Let us assume that you become impoverished due to a layoff at work, downsizing, outsourcing, a plant closure, bankruptcy, or a divorce. In other words, you are not some lazy bum who is refusing to work. Due to marital dissolution or job loss, you and your children have become temporarily poor. You have no one else to turn to so you apply for whatever forms of public assistance for which you qualify. For the sake of example, let us agree that you qualify for food stamps, some cash, health care benefits, and a housing allotment.

When you shop for food at the store, you use money that came from the tax base. Nevertheless, as soon as you spend it you no longer hold it. The grocery store receives the money.

That money, in part, pays for the wages of those who work in the grocery store, profits for the owners, and even profits for those who supply the groceries, such as farmers. In fact, this spending amounts to an indirect subsidy for a number of other agents. When you pay your rent, the money comes from the tax base but ends up in the hands of property owners. To some degree, it is beneficial to those who rent homes and apartments that welfare programs exist because poor people will always have to pay for housing. When your children get sick you visit the clinic. Here again, the money that pays for the visit comes from the tax base but ends up helping to pay the wages of nurses, nurses aids, janitors, and others who work in the clinic. Doctors, of course, receive some portion of it as profit.

The poor receive public assistance to pay for food, shelter, medical treatment, and other needs. When the poor spend the money on the necessities of life, they return the money to the non-poor, where it is received in the form of wages and profits. Thus, the claim that welfare is a drag on the economy is completely false. The only way welfare could have a negative effect on the economy would be if the poor managed to save money. In that case, welfare would be a downward redistribution of wealth. However, we know that the poor are not saving any money. The money comes from the working and middle classes and is given to the poor. The poor spend the money and it is transferred back to the working and middle classes in the form of wages. Some of the money is transferred to the business class because they make profits on the products sold to the poor. This is an upward redistribution of wealth, in which the poor only hold the money for a short time. The system of public aid accomplishes two main goals: first, it supports the status quo because it does not lift the poor out of poverty, and second, it alleviates, to some degree, human suffering and deprivation.

In this essay, we discussed two types of poverty, absolute and relative. Absolute poverty is life-threatening poverty. Relative poverty means that some people are poorer compared to others.

We have also discussed the poverty line, in which those below a certain income are considered poor and those above are not. From a functional perspective, if poverty continues to exist it may be serving some useful function for society.

Herbert Gans identified a number of ways in which poverty is useful for society, or at least for some people in our society. First, the poor do the "dirty work" of society. They also subsidize many of the activities of the affluent, either directly or indirectly. The poor also pay a greater proportion of their income in taxes than the affluent. They also buy the goods that no one else wants.

There are a number of cultural functions served by the poor. The poor help keep the affluent busy through volunteer work. Another function of poverty is that the poor serve as symbolic constituencies or opponents for several groups. The last function of poverty mentioned by Gans is that the poor are powerless and can serve the function of being made to absorb the costs of political and economic growth.

There are a number of myths about the poor: they are lazy, they use the system, and they are dishonest, alcoholic, and promiscuous, they are stupid, and so on. When parents point out the poor and start mentioning the myths they are acting as agents of social control, attempting to get their children to buy into middle class values and beliefs.

One prevalent myth concerning poverty is that poor people simply refuse to work. The problem is not the bad values of poor people but the type of jobs poor people find in the service economy. Many of these are considered dead-end jobs. Workers cannot quit these jobs because there is a high reserve pool of labor, or in other words, unemployed workers that can easily fill these positions. Another myth related to poverty is that you can always find a better job. In other words, according to the myth, if your job pays poverty wages you simply need to find a better job or move to a location where there are higher-paying jobs. The myth that the poor rely primarily on welfare is widely believed. Another myth is that poor people cannot escape the cycle of poverty. Those families that do experience poverty are poor for less than a year. Many people believe that the majority of poor are persons of color. Actually, the vast majority of the poor are white.

The "cause" of poverty is a topic that has generated a considerable amount of debate. People generally fall into one of two categories when thinking about the causes of poverty. These two typologies are 1) system-blamers and 2) victim-blamers. System blamers generally argue that people are poor because the system has failed them. From this point of view, people are poor because society has failed to provide opportunities for social mobility. Victim-blamers (Social Darwinists), on the other hand, focus on the attributes of the individual. From this point of view, people are poor because they are intellectually or culturally inferior, have low motivation, are lazy, or have some other character flaw that prevents them from achieving upward mobility.

According to Culture of Poverty Theory, the poor have a maladaptive subculture that stresses a different set of values than those of the middle class. There is very little evidence that suggests that poor people actually have a deviant value system.

Since we have reviewed theories that focus on individuals, rather than social structure, when explaining poverty, we can accept that it is possible to make bad decisions in life and wind up living in poverty. But simply focusing on the individual and ignoring economic conditions related to poverty, such as downsizing, factory closings, low-wages, and dead-end jobs, is too simplistic.

We also must consider how the organization of society is related to poverty. We examined two conceptual explanations of poverty: opportunity structures and institutional discrimination. When plants are moved out of the United States to a variety of developing nations, money is drawn out of our economy and outsourced to nations, where employees work for a fraction of what Americans make. In addition, disinvestment in urban inner cites has severely diminished the opportunity structure for the poor.

The Feminization of Poverty shows that although women have always been poorer than men have, as a group, women, especially women of color, increasingly make up a larger proportion of the poor. At all class levels, the number of households headed by women is growing.

The poor also receive public assistance to pay for food, shelter, medical treatment, and other needs. When the poor spend the money on the necessities of life, they return the money to the non-poor, where it is received in the form of wages and profits. Thus, the claim that welfare is a drag on the economy is false. When thinking about the value of public assistance programs, it is a good idea to keep in mind where the money is going. In whose hands does this money ultimately end up? The media and conservative politicians only want you to follow the money from the tax base to the poor, and no further. If you follow the money as far as the poor, then welfare will seem like a handout to you. However, if you scratch surface appearances you will soon discover that public assistance amounts to an upward redistribution of wealth.

୧୦ ଓଃ ୧୦ ଓଃ

DEFINITIONS

Absolute Poverty. An extremely low standard of living—for example, lacking adequate water, food, clothing, shelter, or basic health care, due to sheer lack of income or assets.

Capital Flight. This occurs when money is drawn out of our economy because factories and manufacturing plants, among other businesses, are moved out of the United States to a variety of developing nations.

Culture of Poverty Thesis. A theory that states that the poor have a maladaptive subculture that stresses a different set of values than those of the middle class.

De Facto Segregation. Segregation that is an unintended consequence of social or ecological arrangements.

Dead-End Jobs. Minimum wage jobs, mostly part-time, without health care or retirement benefits. Occupations with low pay and limited advancement possibilities.

Deindustrialization. The shifting from industrial economic activities to service and information economies. Decline in the share of manufacturing industries in the country's economy. Typically, industrial plants are closed down and not replaced, and service industries increase. Refers to the movement of labor-intensive work to the Third World, where unions, pro-labor legislation, and environmental protection laws are non-existent and works are often paid mere pennies a day.

Deserving Poor. Those considered are the very old, the sick, or the severely disabled.

Disinvestment. A reduction in capital investment, especially in urban inner-city areas. Corporations often find it more profitable to relocate plants out of the country rather than to modernize existing plants or build new facilities in the United States.

Globalization. Refers to the worldwide phenomenon of technological, economic, political, and cultural exchanges, brought about by modern communication, transportation, and legal infrastructures as well as the political choice to consciously open cross-border links in international trade and finance. It is a term used to describe how human beings are becoming more intertwined with each other around the world economically, politically, and culturally. Although these links are not new, they are more pervasive than ever before.

Hidden Covenants. The language in mortgage contracts that forbade owners from selling their property to people of color.

Institutional Discrimination. Refers to the ways in which the normal operation of institutions is systematically biased to favor the affluent and disadvantage the poor.

Jobs/Skills Mismatch. The labor pool that lives close to a specific type of occupation, such as the service industry, often lack the skills and education required to work in the upper tier of the service economy. Often there are no jobs at all for inner city poor. For those who do find employment in the lower tier of the service economy the wages are not enough to lift the family out of poverty.

Myths about the Poor. Various false terms used to describe poverty-stricken people such as, they are lazy, stupid, dishonest, alcoholic, promiscuous, and they use the system to their advantage.

Opportunity Structures. Refers to the opportunities for upward social mobility that are provided by society, such as education.

Outsourced. To seek resources outside of an organizational structure, usually to save money and/or exploit the skills of another entity.

Poverty-Line. Represents the minimum income needed to feed, house, and clothe household members.

Relative Poverty. The inability of a citizen to participate fully in economic terms in the society in which he or she lives. This means below the American standard of poverty or classifies entities as "poor" not by comparing them to a fixed cutoff point, but by comparing them to others in the population under study.

Reserve Pool of Labor. Unemployed workers who can be called into the job market during an economic expansion or laid-off during a recession.

Social Darwinism. A late nineteenth century theory (used to explain and justify social inequality) that held that the most capable people will and should gain more in the struggle for survival than the less capable.

Social Structure of Mothering. Gives middle class mothers a clear advantage over mothers in the inner city. The structure of their living arrangements allows the middle class mother to practice more effective mothering.

Structural Transformations. Major changes in the economy that affect almost every citizen.

Suburbanization. Refers to the out migration of people from the city to the outlying parts of a city or town within commuting distance of the larger metropolitan area.

Symbolic Constituencies. The poor used as a political function for several political groups. The revolutionary Left "could not live without the poor" and the political Right need "the welfare scrounger" (from Herbert Gans "The Positive Functions of Poverty").

REFERENCES

The ideas expressed in my essay on poverty and the information presented is based on the following works:

Allegretto, Sylvia. 2004. "Economic Snapshots." *Economic Policy Institute* (July).

Armour, Stephanie and Michelle Kessler. 2003. "USA's New Money-Saving Export – White Collar Jobs." *USA Today,* August 18, 1B-2B.

Beeghley, Leonard. 2000. *The Structure of Social Stratification in the United States.* New York: Allyn and Bacon.

Blau, Judith R. and Peter M. Blau. 1982. "The Cost of Inequality: Metropolitan Structure and Violent Crime." *American Sociological Review* 47(1):114-29.

Braithwaite, John. 1979. *Inequality, Crime, and Public Policy.* Boston, MA: Routledge and Kegan Paul.

Braithwaite, John. 1981. "The Myth of Social Class and Criminality Reconsidered." *American Sociological Review* 46(1):36-57.

Broder, David. 1996. "Mass Movement to Suburbs Continues." *Liberal Opinion Week* July 8:26.

Brogan, Pamela. 1994. "Gender Pay Gap Runs Deep in Congress, Study Finds." *Denver Post*, February 26, 17A.

Bureau of Labor Statistics. 2004. "Employment Situation Summary: May 2004."
    (http://bls.gov/news.release/pdf/empsit.pdf).

Campbell, F. A., C. T. Ramey, E. P. Pungello, J. Sparling, and S. Miller-Johnson. 2002. "Early Childhood Education: Young Adult Outcomes from the Abecedarian Project." *Applied Developmental Science* (6):42-57.

Campbell, Frances A. and Craig T. Ramey. 1994. "Effects of Early Intervention on Intellectual and Academic Achievement: A Follow-Up Study of Children from Low-Income Families." *Child Development* 65 (April):684-698.

Chafel, Judith A. 1997. "Societal Images of Poverty." *Youth and Society* 28 (June):432-463.

Children's Defense Fund. 2001. *The State of America's Children 2001.* Washington, DC: Children's Defense Fund.

Children's Defense Fund. 2003. "Child Poverty Tops 50 Percent in 14 US Counties." June 4.
    (http://www.childrensdefense.org/familyincome/childpoverty/default.asp).

Children's Defense Fund. 2004. "While Corporations and the Wealthy Benefit from Huge Tax Cuts, Poor Families Still Struggle." Press Release, April 14.

Conlin, Michelle and Aaron Bernstein. 2004. "Working and Poor." *Business Week,* May 31, pp. 57-68.

Cook, Philip J. and Gary A. Zarkin. 1985. "Crime and the Business Cycle." *Journal of Legal Studies* 14(1):115-28.

DeFronzo, James. 1983. "Economic Assistance to Impoverished Americans." *Criminology* 21(1):119-36.

Dreier, Peter and John Atlas. 1995. "Housing Policy's Moment of Truth." *American Prospect* 22 (Summer):68-77.

Dreier, Peter. 1992. "Bush to Cities: Drop Dead." *The Progressive* 56 (July):20-23.

Edelman, Peter. 2001. "The Question Now Isn't Just Poverty. For Many, It Is Survival." *Washington Spectator* 21 (August 1):1-3.

Eitzen, D. Stanley. 1996. "Dismantling the Welfare State." *Vital Speeches of the Day* 62 (June 15):532-536.

Eitzen, Stanley D. and Maxine Baca Zinn. 2006. *Social Problems*, 10th ed. New York: Allyn and Bacon.

Gans, Herbert J. 1992 [1971]. "The Uses of Poverty: The Poor Pay All." Pp. 327-333 in *Down To Earth Sociology*. 6th ed., edited by James M. Henslin. New York: Free Press.

Ganz, Alexander. 1985. "Where Has the Urban Crisis Gone? How Boston and Other Large Cities Have Stemmed Economic Decline." *Urban Affairs Quarterly* 20 (June):449-68.

Gould, Stephen Jay. 1994. "Curveball." *New Yorker*, November 28, pp. 139-149.

Harrington, Michael. 1984. *The New American Poverty*. New York: Holt, Rinehart and Winston.

Herrnstein, Richard J. 1971. "I.Q." *Atlantic* 228 (September):43-64.

Herrnstein, Richard J. 1973. *I.Q. in the Meritocracy*. Boston, MA: Little, Brown.

Herrnstein, Richard J. and Charles Murray. 1994. *The Bell Curve: Intelligence and Class Structure in American Life*. New York: Free Press.

Hockstader, Lee. 2002. "Dreams among the Poorest of the Poor." *Washington Post National Weekly Edition*, September 2-8, pp. 29.

Kemper, Vicki. 1991. "Operation Urban Storm." *Common Cause Magazine*, July/August, pp. 10, 12-16, 39-40.

Kim, Marlene. 1998. "Are the Working Poor Lazy?" *Challenge* 41(May/June):85-99.

Lichter, Daniel T. and Martha L. Crowley. 2002. "Poverty in America: Beyond Welfare Reform." *Population Bulletin* 57(2) (June):1-36.

Magdoff, Fred and Harry Magdoff. 2004. "Disposable Workers: Today's Reserve Army of Labor." *Monthly Review* 55 (April):18-35.

Maschinot, Beth. 1995. "Behind the Curve." *In These Times*, February 6, pp. 31-34.

O'Hare, William P. 1996. "A New Look at Poverty in America." *Population Bulletin* 51(2) (September):1-47.

O'Hare, William P. 1996. "U.S. Poverty Myths Explored: Many Poor Work Year-round, Few Still Poor After Five Years." *Population Today: News, Numbers, and Analysis* 21(10) (October):1-2.

O'Hare, William P. and Margaret L. Usdansky. 1992. "What the 1990 Census Tells Us about Segregation in 25 Large Metros." *Population Today* 20 (September):6-7, 10.

Piven, Frances Fox and Richard A. Cloward. 1971. *Regulating the Poor: The Functions of Public Welfare*. New York: Random House.

Reed, Jr., Adolph. 1990. "The Underclass as Myth and Symbol: The Poverty of Discourse about Poverty." *Radical America* 24 (January/March):21-40.

Reed, Jr., Adolph. 1994. "Looking Backward." *Nation*, November 28, pp. 654-62.

Reed, Jr., Adolph. 2004. "Majoring in Debt." *The Progressive* 68 (January):25-27.

Reich, Robert B. 2000. "The Great Divide." *American Prospect*, May 8, pp. 56.

Reiman, Jeffery H. 2001. *The Rich Get Richer and the Poor Get Prison: Ideology, Class, and Criminal Justice*. 6th ed. Boston, MA: Allyn and Bacon.

Richmond, Julius B. 1994. "Give Children an Earlier Head Start." *USA Today*, April 12, 13A.

Ryan, Joanna. 1972. "IQ – The Illusion of Objectivity." In *Race and Intelligence*, edited by Ken Richardson and David Spears. Baltimore, MD: Penguin.

Stack, Steven and Mary Jeanne Kanavy. 1983. "The Effect of Religion on Forcible Rape: A Structural Analysis." *Journal for the Scientific Study of Religion* 22(1):67-74.

Statistical Abstracts of the United States. Washington DC: Bureau of the Census, published annually.

Stecklow, Steve. 1995. "SAT Scores Rise Strongly after Test Is Overhauled." *Wall Street Journal*, August 24, B1, B12.

Steinberg, Jacques. 1994. "W.S. Social Well-Being Is Rated Lowest Since Study Began in 1970." *New York Times*, "Themes of the Times" Fall:4.

Thornberry, Terence and Margaret Farnworth. 1982. "Social Correlates of Criminal Involvement: Further Evidence on the Relationship between Social Status and Criminal Behavior." *American Sociological Review* 47(4):505-14.

Thornberry, Terence and R. L. Christenson. 1984. "Unemployment and Criminal Involvement: An Investigation of Reciprocal Causal Structures." *American Sociological Review* 49(3):398-411.

Wilson, William J. 1987. *The Truly Disadvantaged: The Inner City, the Underclass, and Public Policy*. Chicago, IL: University of Chicago Press.

Wilson, William J. 1996. *When Work Disappears: The World of the New Urban Poor*. New York: Knopf.

Wilson, William J. and Andrew J. Cherlin. 2001. "The Real Test of Welfare Reform Still Lies Ahead." *New York Times*, July 13. (http://www.nytimes.com/2001/07/13/opinion/13WILS.html).

17 | Inequality, Race, and Ethnicity: Some Ways of Splitting Up the "What."
by Frank O. Taylor, IV, Ph.D.

When I was a graduate student I shared an office with a Black Ph.D. candidate. We became friends and would often go to lunch together. One day, we were walking along and discussing some topic from one of our seminars on our way to lunch. When we came to the street corner, since no traffic was coming, I started across. I was chattering away when I realized my friend was not beside me. Still in the street, I turned to see what was keeping him. He had stopped at the light and was waiting for it to turn green. I motioned for him to hurry up and cross the street; after all, it was lunchtime. He shook his head no and discreetly motioned for me to look down the street. Looking in the direction he indicated I noticed a bicycle patrolman.

Now, I will never know whether or not my friend would have been ticketed for jaywalking had he stepped into the street with the police officer watching him. I was in the street and did not receive a ticket. That is not the point. The point is that my friend altered his behavior because the police office was present. I asked him later why he had not followed me into the street and he referred to previous negative encounters with the police. This indicates that the two of us had different perceptions of the police entirely. From my point of view, I failed to notice the officer, and even if I had, I would not have felt fear. One the other hand, my Black office-mate perceived the police officer as a threat to his safety, and clearly took pains to avoid any contact with him. The police officer was White. I am White. My friend is Black. We lived in the same neighborhood, went to the same school, and walked on the same streets, but his *experience* of that reality was not the same as mine. For instance, when I was a small child my mother always told me to find a police officer if I was in any kind of trouble. His mother told him that if he wanted to stay out of trouble he should avoid the police.

In the discussion so far, we have used the terms White and Black. What do they mean? They imply race. Conceptually, **race** refers to physical characteristics to which social importance is attached, often illogically. These characteristics include hair texture, width of the nose, color of the skin, thickness of the lips, and so on. Skin color is probably the most noticeable physical characteristic. What constitutes a race is determined by society. In the United States, we tend to lump people together into racial categories based on the skin color.

by Frank O. Taylor, IV, Ph.D.

Ethnicity refers to your cultural heritage and ancestry. Ethnicity can be based on language, traditions and customs, national origin, religion, certain types of food, clothing, and family name. The Amish, for example, can be considered an ethnic group because they are bound together by religious beliefs and a distinctive set of customs. Jews are often mistaken for a racial group but they are really an ethnic group. Because of intermarriage, Jews exhibit all manner or physical characteristics. Asian Jews, for example have mongoloid features. Jews from Northern Europe, on the other hand, may have white skin and blue eyes. What is distinctive about the Jews, therefore, is their religion.

A **racial group** would be a group that is distinguished by their physical characteristics. An **ethnic group** is distinguished by their cultural distinctiveness. We should bear in mind that race is closely related to ethnicity. White people tend to take race for granted. Said another way, when a White person looks in the mirror, they tend not to see their race as much as their physical attributes. However, anyone who is not Native American is a descendant of people who migrated here from elsewhere. Thus, Americans who descended from German, Irish, French, Swiss, Dutch, and other Northern European stock, are generally considered White, although they may attempt to preserve some of their ethnic heritage. In general, African Americas, Mexican Americans, Latinos, Native Americans, and Asian Americans, are usually considered racial groups, because they can be distinguished by physical traits. Bear in mind that to a large degree these distinctions are social constructions. Amish, Mennonite, and Jewish people constitute ethnic groups because they are distinguished from the dominant group by their culture. It is probably more appropriate to refer to groups of people who are distinguished be skin color and a common social, cultural, and economic background as **racial-ethnic groups**.

This brings the discussion to two more important concepts: dominant group and minority group. The **dominant group** dominates less powerful groups through control of the economic, political, and cultural institutions of society. A **minority group** is a group that is dominated by another group and lacks economic, political, and cultural power to improve its situation. Defining a minority group is a matter of history and politics. Blacks are considered a minority group because of the legacy of slavery. Mexican-American and Native Americans are considered minority groups due to the legacy of conquest.

17 | Inequality, Race, and Ethnicity: Some Ways of Splitting Up the "What."
by Frank O. Taylor, IV, Ph.D.

Our society has a long history of **racial stratification**, with White Europeans on the top of the social ladder, and people of color on the bottom. Racial stratification means that White people have more access to education and better occupations, which translates into more income and a higher standard of living, than people of color do. Racial stratification produces opportunities for some and oppression for others.

Researchers have discovered that genetic differences between groups of people previously thought of as racially different do not exist. The DNA evidence strongly suggests that all humans are members of one race, which evolved over the last 100,000 years, and originated in Africa. The "out of Africa" hypothesis states that, genetically, we are all Africans. Therefore, the idea of biological races is misplaced. However, race as a social idea is very real and has consequences in the real world. Race exists because we *think* it exists and we *act* as if it exists and we *treat* people as if it exists. Race is a social construct.

The idea of race may be a myth but it has lead to horrific consequences. One dimension of racial stratification is the idea that one race, or another, is superior to all other races. In the first wave of immigration to the United States, immigrants came largely from Northern Europe, and if they did not speak the exact same languages, they were culturally related. In other words, the original settlers had a lot in common in terms of values, beliefs, and a Protestant religious background.

The early settlers were further bound together by their struggles against the Native Americans and Great Britain. The Anglos saw Native Americans as inferior for a number of reasons. First, the natives lived on the land and had no real sense of property. Anglo tradition viewed land as a resource to be used. Secondly, Native Americans had developed only a stone-age technology. Technologically, the Anglos were vastly superior to the natives. The Anglo stance toward the natives was extremely **ethnocentric**. The Anglos viewed their own culture as superior to the culture of Native Americans. The clash of values and cultures that emerged led to warfare and **genocide**. Genocide refers to the attempts of the dominant group to exterminate the minority group.

In the late 1800s and early 1900s, and particularly from 1900 to about 1920, people began to immigrate to the United States from the nations of Southern and Eastern Europe. While the

United States had experienced industrialization, advances in literacy, and urbanization, the new immigrants came mostly from agrarian backgrounds. They did not speak English, ate different foods, were illiterate, had different customs and traditions, and were largely Catholic. They were different, and being from rural and Catholic backgrounds, tended to have large families. (One of the consequences of literacy, industrialization, and urbanization is that families begin to voluntarily restrict the number of children they produce. In a farming environment, children can be put to work, and are therefore an economic asset. However, in an urban environment, children are an economic liability.)

Anglos soon began to fear of the reproductive power of the new immigrants. This fear soon led to the birth of the Eugenics movement. **Eugenics** refers to the attempt to achieve racial purification through control of genetic factors. The eugenicists argued that non-Anglos were genetically and therefore racially, inferior. During the early 1900s IQ testing was used to "prove" that non-Anglo immigrants were intellectually inferior, due to their poor test scores. Of course, the fact that the vast majority of immigrants had no formal education and could not speak English was largely overlooked. Nevertheless, the eugenicists managed to convince the United States Congress to pass a number of immigration laws, restricting immigration from non-Northern European nations, and China in particular. These immigration laws are an example of **passive eugenics**, which is the attempt of the dominant group to restrict the numbers and power of the minority group by limiting their reproductive capabilities. A number of states also passed legislation making it legal to sterilize individuals who scored low on IQ tests, thereby preventing such people from giving birth.

The practice of passive eugenics exists to this very day. Many states require that women on public assistance submit for the forced use of contraceptive devices, such as Norplant. These laws are based on the myth that women on welfare have more children to increase their benefits. However, no state has public assistance benefits generous enough to lift a family out of poverty and no state ever did. Most states grant no assistance beyond the second child in any case. The rate of childbirth for women on public assistance is less than the national average for women in general.

The "get tough on crime" policies enacted by most states in recent decades are also based on passive eugenics. Politicians knew full well which racial-ethnic groups the laws they enacted would ensnare. The differential punishment for crack cocaine verses powder cocaine is a prime example of how the law can be used to support program of passive eugenics. Cocaine is widely used by all ethnic groups and social classes. However, since powder cocaine is prohibitively expensive crack cocaine is used primarily by the poor and the Black underclass. Mandatory sentences for possession of crack run into the decades. There is research that suggests that our prisons are being filled with non-violent drug offenders serving long sentences. Nearly 50 percent of African Americans between the ages of 15 and 35 are ensnared at one time or another in the criminal justice system, virtually guaranteeing that the families in the Black underclass will be fractured. High rates of incarceration and unemployment can only have negative effects on the Black family.

Active eugenics refers to the actual attempts by the dominant group to exterminate the minority group by force. Perhaps the most recognized example of active eugenics is that of the holocaust. Adolph Hitler's belief in the racial superiority of the Aryan race led him to pursue genocide against homosexuals, Jews, Gypsies, Slavs, and people with mental and physical disabilities. Hitler was greatly impressed with the American eugenics movement and the writings of the American eugenicists were widely read in Nazi Germany. More recently, genocides have erupted in Rwanda and Bosnia. In Rwanda, hundreds of thousands of Tutsis were slaughtered by Hutus. In Bosnia Serbs massacred thousands of Muslims.

Racism and discrimination are two separate concepts. **Racism** refers to the illogical belief that one race is superior to all others. Racism is a negative attitude toward certain races. **Discrimination** requires an action. It is possible to be a racist but not discriminate. Such people are referred to as timid bigots. A bigot is someone who has racist attitudes and does discriminate. Additionally, it is possible not to be a racist and to discriminate. Such people are referred to as fair-weather liberals. For example, it is possible to follow discriminatory hiring guidelines and not have negative attitudes toward women and minorities.

Differences among Ethnic Groups.   There are some important differences between the major ethnic groups in our society in terms of education, income, unemployment, and poverty. Prior to the 1950s, **De jure segregation** existed in the South. De jure segregation refers to the legal barriers that kept the Black population largely separate from the White population. In 1954 as a result of the landmark *Brown v. Board of Education* ruling of the Supreme Court, legal segregation ended. However, fifty years after the historic ruling **De facto segregation** not only remains, but there is evidence that segregation is growing.

414

Figure 17.1   High School Graduation Rates

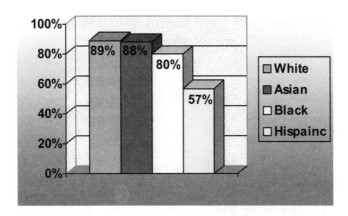

One area in which segregation is apparent is education, in spite of Brown v. Board of Education. Schools in minority neighborhoods have limited resources, largely due to tax cuts and diminishing levels of funding for public education. Very few minority parents can afford to send their children to private schools. Hispanic students often face language barriers. Consequently, minority students lag behind Whites in educational achievement. Hispanics have the lowest high school graduation rates. White and Asian students have the highest graduation rates. Having a high school diploma, while positive overall, masks some dramatic disparities. While the children of middle class Black parents generally attend quality high schools, children in the inner city attend schools that are vastly inferior. Thus, many minority students receive an education that is not marketable, which is reflected in the number of minority students who do finish a college degree. Educational segregation is largely an artifact of neighborhoods segregated by social class, which is indirectly related to race and ethnicity since minority families tend to be in the lower classes. Researchers have often discovered that when minority students are bused to affluent neighborhoods they are segregated internally through tracking.

Native Americans and Hispanics have the lowest rates of college graduation. Only 11 percent of Native Americans and Hispanics receive a Bachelor's Degree. Asian Americans achieve the highest rate of college graduation. Fully one-half of Asian Americans receive a Bachelor's Degree. Whites have a college graduation rate of nearly 30 percent. Only 17 percent of African Americans attain a Bachelor's degree. A college degree is highly correlated with annual income, another area of disparity between ethnic groups. Students of color have generally low retention rates after they enroll in college. Discrimination on and off the campus remains a problem and minority students typically have higher levels of alienation than White students do.

Figure 17.2   **Four Year College Education (2003)**

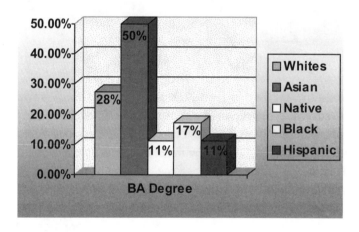

Of course, education and income are closely related. More educational attainment usually translates into higher earnings. Asian Americans report the highest level of annual income, with a median of slightly over $50,000 per year. Whites are close behind earning a median income of about $48,000 per year. It is interesting to note that the annual income of White families nearly equals that of Asian families in spite of the fact that Asians have higher rates of college attainment. Other minority families, however, lag behind in annual income. Black families have an annual median income of slightly less than $30,000 per year, while Native Americans and Hispanics fare only slightly better with median income of $31,000 and $33,000 per year respectively.

Income refers to money earned through salary and wages. We see that there is a large gap between the earnings of Whites and Blacks, Hispanics, and Native Americans. However, the picture is worse when wealth is considered. Wealth refers to financial resources such as stocks, bonds, royalties, land, home equity, investments, savings accounts, and the like. Wealth is anything other than salary and wages that yields a financial advantage. Wealth tends to be passed from generation to generation through inheritance. White families tend to have greater amounts of wealth. This translates into advantages for White children that minority children lack.

Figure 17.3   Median Household Income (2003)

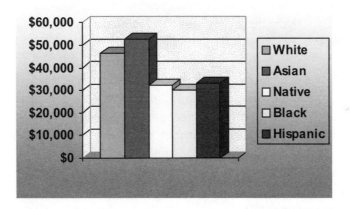

Employment is another measure of the well-being of any group. We note that Blacks and Hispanics have much higher rates of unemployment than do Asians and Whites. Whites have the lowest rates of unemployment. The official unemployment rate is woefully inadequate. Economists point out that the unemployment rate is probably three times higher than the government estimates. There are a number of reasons for this. For one thing, the government only tracks people looking for work in the last few weeks. Anyone who has not looked for work recently or have stopped looking altogether because they cannot find a job are not counted at all. Other groups of people are not counted either. This includes the underemployed, people who are not employed in their field or who have more education than their job requires, and people who work part-time.

Therefore, it is quite likely that rates of unemployment are higher for all ethnic groups, but especially for minorities. A final problem with the unemployment rate is that it is a national average. This means that the unemployment rates in local areas are obscured because they are mixed in with national data. In many of the nation's inner city neighborhoods, unemployment rates can be as high as 50 percent.

Another problem for minority workers, in addition to high rates of unemployment, is that they tend to be employed in different types of jobs than Whites. There is a great deal of research that indicates that minorities face discrimination in hiring and promotions. Blacks and Hispanics are more likely to work in low paid, low skill occupations with few benefits and chances for promotion. Even when Blacks and Hispanics find employment in higher status occupations they often face a situation similar to what women face, a job ceiling that prevents them from reaching the top rungs of the executive promotion ladder. There is some positive news, however. In spite of the barriers that people of color face, there have been slight increases in recent years in the number of minorities hired in managerial positions.

Another area of concern for minority workers is the restructuring that has occurred in the United States economy in the last decades. Unskilled and poorly educated minority workers were able to find jobs in the smokestack industries of the Northeast, in steel, auto, and rubber. Globalization and the movement of United States plants and factories out of the country are removing an important source of employment for blue-collar workers, many of whom are minorities. Additionally, government downsizing is also eliminating many jobs minority workers were often successful in obtaining.

Figure 17.4   **Unemployment Rate (2004)**

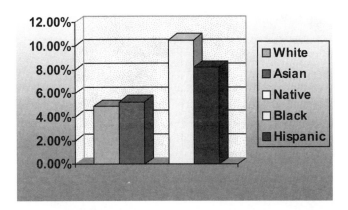

There are serious differences in poverty rates between the ethnic groups. Since Whites and Asians have higher levels of educational achievement, higher incomes, and lower levels of unemployment, it is not surprising that they have lower rates of poverty. Native Americans have the highest rates of poverty, at 26 percent. Blacks have a poverty rate of 24 percent. Hispanics have a poverty rate of 22 percent. If we break the poverty rates down by age, however, the numbers become even worse. Examining the poverty rate for children under the age of eighteen, we find that 32 percent of Native Americans, 32 percent of African Americans, and 28 percent of Latinos are impoverished. As in unemployment figures, national statistics obscure local conditions. Rates of poverty are higher for those living in the inner cities and rural areas than for those living in the suburbs. Female-headed households, for all ethnic groups, have the highest rates of poverty.

Figure 17.5   Poverty Rate (2003)

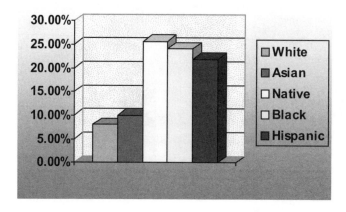

CONTINUING PROBLEMS

Although territory in what was to become the United States was claimed by several European powers, such as Great Britain, France, and Spain, the British eventually became the dominant power. The Protestant English settlers brought with them their language, legal system, religious beliefs and traditions, and established their values and beliefs as the dominant culture. This group of White Anglo Saxon Protestants, WASPs for short, established the nation's economic, political, and religious institutions. This group was also extremely ethnocentric, and demanded that that other immigrants **assimilate**. Assimilation refers to becoming a member of the dominant culture, or at least adopting the language, values, and beliefs of the dominant group.

African Americans. African Americans are the second largest racial minority in the United States after Hispanics, currently about 12 percent of the nation's population. Similar to Native Americans, African Americans were not voluntary immigrants to the United States. Almost all of the African Americans living in the nation today are decedents of slaves. Prior to the Civil War, 90 percent of Blacks lived in the South in relatively stable two-parent families. For the most part, Blacks worked as laborers but a few managed to attain a trade skill. Due to fears about a slave uprising, education for Blacks was banned in the South. After the Civil War Blacks fared poorly, since they lacked education and skills, although they were free. About 4 million illiterate Blacks lived in poverty in the rural South.

The fortunes of African Americans began to change after World War II. Many Blacks served in the nation's Armed Forces. After fighting for freedom and democracy elsewhere in the world they expected to be granted the full rights of citizenship upon their return. The Civil Rights Movement began to get into full swing with the return of the Black veterans. Rapid social change soon followed. Segregation was banned in the Armed Forces in 1948. School segregation was banned in 1954. The Civil Rights Act passed in 1964 and the Affirmative Action laws followed in 1968. There can be no doubt that African Americans have come a long way since beginning of the nineteenth century. Between 1940 and 1970 African Americans realized major gains in civil rights, income, and education. However, social advances for Blacks stalled in the 1980s and continued concerns remain regarding political, educational, and economic inequality.

African Americans are now participating at every level of politics, from local and state office to national office. African Americans have been elected as mayors of major cities, state Governors, and to the Congress of the United States. Recently African Americans have served at the highest level of federal power, including the President's Cabinet and as Secretary of State. Although their participation in the political process has increased over 500 percent since 1970, African Americans are still dramatically underrepresented in politis. Bear in mind that prior to the 1970s, African Americans were almost entirely absent from the political scene.

On the education issue, African Americans have also realized major progress. As we have discussed, Blacks have narrowed the gap in high school diplomas compared to White students. Today only 9 percentage points separate the two groups, whereas in 1940 White students were three times more likely to graduate from high school than black students were. However, in terms of higher education African Americans are only half as likely to attain a college degree as Whites are.

As discussed previously, African American income is significantly less than White income. One explanation of why Blacks earn less than Whites is their higher unemployment rate. Recall that Blacks are more than twice as likely to be unemployed than Whites, with an official rate of unemployment around 11 percent. In all probability, the real unemployment rate is likely closer to 30 percent. Additionally, Blacks have not been able to attain a college education in the same numbers as Whites, which has a negative impact on family income. Furthermore, many Blacks live in the South where wages are low. Economic stress is highly correlated with the divorce rate. The lack of good paying jobs for Black males and a high divorce rate have led to high rates of single-parent households headed by Black women—46 percent compared to 13 percent for White families. Intact families with two earners or a male breadwinner tend to have much higher levels of income than single parent families headed by women. The fact the women typically earn less than men puts even more strain on these families.

Some people believe that anyone can succeed if just try hard enough. To these people, it seems like poor decision-making on the part of Black people is the primary cause of their economic problems. This is known as **blaming the victim**. Black people are victimized by economic trends, the legacy of slavery, negative stereotypes, racism, and discrimination. There is plenty of empirical evidence that Black job seekers still face discrimination in hiring. In one study Black and White job applicants were paired on the basis of similar education, job experience, and job history. Several teams were matched and sent out to apply for the same job. Bear in mind that the only difference between the two applicants was that one was Black and the other White. White applicants were significantly more likely to advance in the interviewing and hiring process than were Black applicants.

In another study, college students were assigned to one of three experimental groups: White speakers of middle class English, African Americans who spoke with a thick "Black" accent, and African Americans who spoke middle class English but with a distinguishable black accent. This research was designed to measure to what extent a caller could be identified racially by their speech. Thus, there were two groups of students who spoke with a middle class accent, but the Black students could still be recognized because of their manner of speaking. The third group of students was instructed to use black slang when speaking. The students, following the identical script, then made telephone calls to local realtors answering advertisements for apartment rentals. White students speaking in a middle class accent were most likely to be told an apartment was available. Black students speaking in a middle class accent were second most likely to be told an apartment was available. However, Black students speaking with the thick "black" accent were least likely to succeed, being told an apartment was available less than a third of the time. These and other studies suggest that African Americans are still widely discriminated against.

Asian Americans.   Asian American is a catchall concept. Clearly, the Chinese culture and the Vietnamese culture are vastly different and both groups are considered Asian Americans not because for social reasons, rather than some underlying racial factor. Some 12 million individuals are lumped together under the category Asian American. The largest group are the Chinese, representing about 24 percent of the Asian American population. Looking at the country of origin of Asian Americans, China is followed by the Philippines, India, Vietnam, Korea, and Japan. About 12 percent of Asian Americans are from other Asian nations, such as Samoa, Pakistan, and Laos for example.

Figure 17.6   Asian American Groups

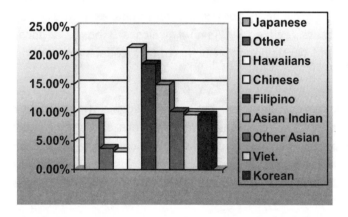

It is important to remember the history of discrimination directed toward Asian Americans in the United States. Many Chinese immigrants, especially during the mid to late 1800s, were drawn to the United States by work for the railroads or the promise of striking it rich during the gold rush. Many Asians were seen as shifty, lazy, and untrustworthy. On several occasions, legislation was passed at State and Federal levels aimed at limiting ability of Asians to find employment or immigrate to the United States. In 1850 the Foreign Miner's Act required the Chinese to pay a

$20 per month fee in order to work, about what they would earn working for the month. Chinese were restricted from testifying against Whites by the California Supreme Court. The Chinese Exclusion act, passed in 1882, suspended all immigration from China for ten years. Needless to say, Japanese Americans faced a great deal of discrimination during the Second World War, after Japan attacked Pearl Harbor. The Japanese were rounded up and confined in internment camps without trials or being charged with a crime and the government confiscated their businesses and property.

When examining the data on education, employment, income, and poverty, Asian Americans fare very well compared to other minorities and Whites. There are some explanations for their success story. However, it is important to remember that not all Asian Americans are financially successful. Asian Americans of Chinese and Japanese descent tend to be the most financially secure. For one thing, these two minority groups are highly assimilated. Large number of Chinese and Japanese Americans graduate from college, the key to economic success. Additionally, Chinese and Japanese Americans often marry outside of their ethnic group. In addition, Asian Americans, in general, are more likely to grow up in close-knit intact families that stress self-discipline and hard work. The economic success realized by Asian Americans is based, in large part, on a low divorce rate, political activism and participation, a high rate of college graduation, and socialization that stresses hard work and, self-discipline.

Hispanic Americans.   Like Asian American, Hispanic American is also a catchall concept. Mexican Americans, Cubans, Puerto Ricans, and Americans of Central and South American decent are lumped together under the Hispanic label. Hispanics are, therefore, distinct populations identified with ethnic ancestry and national origins. The vast majority of Hispanic Americans are of Mexican descent, not surprisingly since the United States defeated Mexico and annexed a vast amount of their territory. A distant second are the Cubans, amounting to slightly more than 10 percent of Hispanic Americans. Puerto Ricans and Cubans make up approximately 5 percent and less than 10 percent, respectively, of the Hispanic American population. The great majority of Hispanics live in the Southwest United States. Los Angeles, for example, is nearly 50 percent Hispanic.

Figure 17.7   Major Hispanic Groups

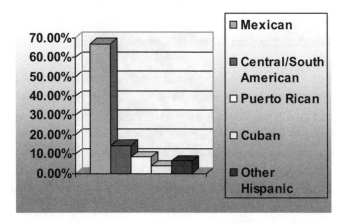

Mexican Americans are the largest Hispanic group. Many Mexican American families have lived in the United States since the Mexican American War (1846-48).   Nevertheless, most Mexican Americans are recent immigrants and more people immigrate to the United States from Mexico than from any other nation. Many Mexican Americans work as low-wage migrant workers in the agricultural industry.   Mexican Americans generally attain less schooling and have a higher dropout rate than the average United States adult. The median income for Mexican Americans is a little over $31,000, or about two-thirds of the national standard. About 25 percent of Mexican Americans are poor, a poverty rate much higher than the national average.

Just like the territories wrested from Mexico, Spain relinquished Puerto Rico when they were defeated by the United States during the Spanish-American War in 1898. About one million Puerto Rican Americans live in New York City, with about 40 percent living in poverty. The vast majority of Puerto Ricans speak Spanish at home, which helps them maintain a strong ethnic identity. On the other hand, inability to speak English may hamper economic success. Many recent immigrants from Puerto Rico have difficulty finding employment. With a median income of slightly over $30,000, Puerto Ricans are the most disadvantaged Hispanic minority.

Following the Marxist revolution in Cuba, nearly a half million Cubans immigrated to the United States. Many of those who came to the United States were highly educated professionals who found employment in the professions or founded successful businesses shortly after their arrival. Cubans have balanced economic success with maintenance of their ethnic identity and are the most likely of all the Hispanic groups to speak Spanish at home.

Native Americans.   When Columbus arrived in the Western hemisphere in 1492, 12 to 15 million Native Americans lived in the territory that became the United States. By 1850 their numbers had been reduced to just 250,000. Diseases such as smallpox and measles, introduced by Europeans, for which they had no biological defense, decimated Native Americans. In roughly 350 years following first contact with Europeans Native Americans experienced catastrophic population decline, and the loss of their lands and livelihoods. The United States government went to great lengths in their efforts to wipe out Native American culture. The first known use of biological warfare occurred when the United States Army deliberately gave disease-infected blankets to Native Americans. Native American children were kidnapped from their families, for example, and sent to boarding schools in the East and forced to renounce their traditional customs, learn English, and practice Christianity. The 1830 Indian Removal Act forced all of the Eastern tribes to relocate to the west of the Mississippi River. Fifteen thousand Cherokees were forced to march on foot from the Carolinas and Georgia to Oklahoma in the dead of winter. Over 4000 died on the Trail of Tears. Following the Indian wars, and the massacre of 350 men, women, and children at Wounded Knee, Native Americans were forced onto reservations, primarily in the Southwest. Native Americans were not granted United States citizenship until 1924.

Today, in spite of the United States government's official policy of genocide, over 200 tribes survive, representing a wide variety of languages and cultures. However, Native Americans are the most destitute of all the minorities in the United States. They have an average family income similar to Blacks, but compared to all the minority groups, they have the highest rates of infant mortality, the highest rates of alcoholism, the lowest educational attainment, and the highest rates of poverty. There have been some positive economic signs in the last two decades. The Navajo's, for example, are developing the mineral reserves on their reservation lands and other tribes are experimenting with casino gambling, with mixed results. Native Americans, although the smallest of all the minorities with just 0.8 percent of the United States population, can be found in all of the professions and occupations of modern society.

by Frank O. Taylor, IV, Ph.D.

The government's attempts to force Native Americans to assimilate eventually failed. The reason for this failure is that Native American culture and the dominant Anglo culture have always been at odds. The Europeans, for instance, viewed the land as a resource to be used. Native Americans valued the land for its beauty and had no concept of individual ownership of the land. The Black Hills, in what is today South Dakota, was valued for spiritual reasons and several Native American tribes, such as the Sioux and Cheyenne, fought hard to retain it. Native Americans culture did not value clocks and schedules and is more concerned with traditions than an orientation toward the future, as was the case of European culture. Many Native Americans have a non-competitive view of life, which coupled with low educational attainment virtually ensures that the corporate world so familiar to most Americans will be alien to them. Additionally, many Native Americans have dark skin and still experience prejudice and discrimination.

Recently, Native Americans have rediscovered their pride in their languages, traditions, and cultures. Beginning in the 1960s, however, several tribes won a series of legal victories that restored to them some of their former land. Additionally, since many tribes never willingly became part of the United States they retained the right to their autonomy and remain theoretically independent from the United States government. The **Pan Indian** social movement has sought to emphasize a Native American identity that incorporates elements common to most tribes. The result of these developments has been a surge in tribal membership.

INSTITUTIONAL DISCRIMINATION

In years past, discrimination was overt, public, and in most cases legal. A prime example of overt discrimination was the many civic ordinances that segregated Blacks in the South. These laws dictated where Blacks could sit on a public bus, where they could eat, watch a movie, shop, work, where they could live, and in extreme cases what times of the day they could be in certain parts of the city. All of these restrictions on the civil liberties of Blacks were legal in the **Jim Crow** South. Other forms of discrimination that were not necessarily legal, such as lynching Blacks for presumed crimes, often went unpunished even though the perpetrators where known in many cases. Recently, there have been several high profile trials of Whites accused of murdering Blacks decades ago.

Additionally, many Southern states had restrictions on the ability of Blacks to participate in the political system. These restrictions included poll taxes, the grandfather clause, or some type of civics test and were effective in keeping Blacks away from the voting booth. Poll taxes required voters to pay a tax prior to casting their ballot. Of course, such taxes prevented poor people from voting, who were mostly Black. Quite a few poor White people were also unable to pay the tax. States that had a grandfather clause making it illegal for Blacks to vote if one of their grandfathers had been a slave. This law virtually eliminated the possibility of any Black person voting, since they were all descendants of slaves. In spite of the Fourteenth Amendment, in the South, political participation for Blacks had been effectively prevented and this type of discrimination did not end until the passage of the Civil Rights legislation in the 1960s.

Did discrimination against people of color end because the federal government passed legislation against it? Many people believe that discrimination is a thing of the past and that Black people should "just get over it." Regrettably, there is ample evidence from research that discrimination against people of color has become covert and hidden. Perhaps the most damaging form of hidden discrimination is institutional discrimination. **Institutional discrimination** refers to patterns of discrimination that are built into the normal operation of society.

Institutional racism can be related to laws, customs, social power, social stratification, and even religious beliefs. For example, only a few religious denominations allow women to be ordained. If women are prevented by custom and religious doctrine to be ordained, then we can agree that sexism, in that case, is institutionalized.

How is racism institutionalized? If you are Black and you attend a school in East Saint Louis, your school will have very few educational resources. Setting aside whatever level of intellectual ability you actually have, your educational background will be less conducive to success in college, if you manage to be accepted. Educational success is not just a matter of motivation and intellectual ability; you will need educational opportunities as well. Educational opportunities may include up-to-date computer technology, advanced courses, honors programs, college preparation courses in mathematics, science, literature, art, history, and a broad range of other subjects, teachers with advanced degrees, and a social environment conducive to learning in addition to other resources. Because educational opportunities tend to be funded by local property taxes, they are indirectly tied to social class and neighborhood.

You might respond to this by saying that nothing is stopping the person from moving to a different neighborhood.   However, what does it take to move your family?   You will need transportation, a new job in the city or neighborhood you are moving to, savings, and so on. Poor people can not just up and move. People who are living on minimum wage below the poverty level are not very mobile. They tend to be locked into the neighborhoods in which they live and must make do with the educational resources they have.

Institutions have the power to reward and punish.   Children who live in middle class neighborhoods have the opportunity to take advantage of educational resources not available to children in the nation's inner cities. Disadvantage in one institution often leads to disadvantages in other institutions. If you receive an inferior education, you may not be able to find a very good job, which in turn leads to a poor income. A poor income is related to a host of other social problems, such as lack of health care, poverty, and even divorce. If you are poor, it is highly likely your children will be poor, and consequently they will also receive an inferior education. The institutions of society are interrelated; therefore a disadvantage in one institution often leads to a disadvantage in every institution.

It is not necessary to be a bigot to discriminate. There are a number of institutionalized mechanisms that contribute of inequality, including IQ tests, educational tracking, seniority systems, and educational requirements for hiring. College entrance examinations, for example, seem to be fair and neutral, on the face of it. However, these tests are frequently biased against minorities. For example, Blacks have never had the same access to quality education as Whites, particularly in the South. You may not be prejudiced against people of color at all. However, if you work in a college admissions office and participate in the exclusion of anyone, White or Black, because of low SAT scores, you are, in fact discriminating.   Research links SAT scores to educational resources, as much as to motivation. In other words, you may have all the desire in the world to learn, but someone has to teach you.

The low educational attainment and lack of job skills tends to keep minorities in dead-end jobs. The institutions of society are programmed to sift and sort people based on gender, age, race, and social class. A consistent finding in the research on education is that when controlling for social class, merit is not significantly related to grades in school. In other words, the social class of your parents is a better predictor of your grades than how hard you study! This is a systemic process that goes far beyond the efforts of a single individual to change, no matter how hard one studies.

Consider this: when a White child stands before a White teacher, the color of the child's skin is not an issue. To be sure, other social categories, such as gender or social class, may become issues that hinder a child's interaction with a teacher, but not race. Not all teachers and employers are prejudiced, of course, but one does not necessarily have to be prejudiced for discrimination to take place. Our minds are full of ideological stereotypes and schemas which we use to think. The effects of color on the interaction between a child and a teacher are something very few White children have to deal with.

Institutional discrimination also shows up in the political economy. Neighborhoods are directly related to social class due to zoning laws. **Zoning** is a tool used by the elite class to protect their land and property values by specifying what type of housing can be built in any given neighborhood. Zoning laws are political decisions made by city councils and county commissions. The members of such boards are largely drawn from the local business and white-collar occupations, people who can afford to run for local office. Zoning ordinances often specify the cost of a home in certain neighborhoods and what types of materials go into the construction of new homes. This is why people of similar social class background live in the same neighborhoods. The homes for several city blocks around you are of similar property value, because it is usually specified by law. Zoning ordinances are often biased toward the middle class and upper class, forbidding multifamily dwelling or inexpensive housing.

Redlining is another form of institutional discrimination related to race. In order to purchase a home you must be able to qualify for a home loan and obtain home insurance. Before you can purchase a home, or even remodel a home, you must be insured. Research indicates that in certain parts of the city, populated largely by minorities and low-income families, insurance and mortgage home loans are more difficult to obtain. Insurance companies practice certain forms of discrimination, such as termination of policies in redlined areas, not writing policies in redlined areas, or overcharging residents of inner cities. Frequently, the insurance rates residents of inner cities are charged are much higher than the risk of fire or vandalism warrant.

A similar situation exists for home loans. Although the Federal Housing Authority and the Veteran's Administration underwrite nearly 50 percent of all mortgage loans in the nation, minorities and the poor still face major obstacles to home ownership. Preference for home lending is usually given to new construction, rather than renovation of run-down housing. Additionally, suburban development is encouraged over development in the central city. These trends in home lending, combined with redlining, have contributed to the decline of inner cities and to urban decay. It is important to remember that urban decay is the result of political and economic decisions made by local, state, and federal decision and policy makers. When we see a run-down home, we often wonder why the owner does not fix the property up. However, most people rely upon home equity loans or second mortgages to fund major renovations. When a poor neighborhood is redlined, the residents will be unable to obtain funding to maintain their homes. Consequently, a cycle of urban decay results—property values fall and the condition of housing deteriorates even further.

Every city encourages economic development. When businesses open, or locate stores, outlets, and headquarters in a city, new jobs are created. A city that enjoys economic expansion and development sees property values generally increase. When property values increase, homeowners pay higher taxes and city budgets may also increase. Thus, many people have a vested interest in growth. The issue is *where* the growth will take place. Cities need shopping malls, housing development, highways, bridges and other infrastructure, parks, hospitals, clinics, schools, business parks, and all of the other types of economic development necessary to thrive. However, members of city councils and city government, who generally come from the elite class, do not want this economic development in their neighborhoods. When neighborhoods must be destroyed to accommodate economic development, they tend to be lower class neighborhoods that lack the political power to prevent the development. This **"not in my backyard" syndrome** of economic development has resulted in urban sprawl.

Several trends have conspired to create a **jobs/skills mismatch** for inner city minorities and poor. Large numbers of minorities live in working class neighborhoods in central cities. These neighborhoods used to be adjacent to working class industrial jobs. Many of these jobs have disappeared as the nation's economy shifted from an industrial base to a service and information base. During the same period of time the process of urbanization resulted in new economic development away from city centers and on the periphery, moving jobs further away from downtown. Recently, many old factories and industrial buildings in downtown areas have been renovated and turned into offices for the service and information economy. Insurance companies, law offices, real estate companies, medical offices and clinics, and other entrepreneurial enterprises, for example, have occupied these renovated buildings. These employers are generally looking for employees with college degrees.   Thus, minorities and poor people often live in neighborhoods situated near economic expansion but lack the job skills, experience, and education to take advantage of those jobs. Additionally, the jobs in the service economy they are qualified for tend to be located further and further away from the central city.

Many cities must make decisions about where to locate new development. As cities grow, highways, universities, colleges, medical centers, housing, parks, malls, and other infrastructure must be built. City planners must find the space to accommodate such expansion. Often, due to the lack of political power to resist, this development is located in lower class neighborhoods. During the 1960s and 1970s, under the guise of urban renewal, many lower class neighborhoods inhabited by minorities and the poor were torn down so that highways could be widened, universities and medical facilities could expand, or new economic development could take place. Displaced families from the "renewed" urban areas were then housed in new high-rise apartment complexes, such as the Robert Taylor in Chicago.   As well intentioned as such development may have been, in retrospect, it probably was not a good idea to warehouse large numbers of people suffering from every manner of social problems, from unemployment and divorce to poverty, right on top of one another.

Gentrification is another process that limits opportunities for minorities and the poor. As cities renovate downtown areas for business in insurance, medicine, communications, finance, and other white-collar jobs, homeowners who work in those occupations often look for housing near their place of employment. Generally, the older neighborhoods that surround downtown are full of historically interesting homes. Middle class, white-collar employees are drawn to the Queen Anne, Victorian, and Colonial period homes that are found in the city's older neighborhoods. These two and three story homes have often been converted from single-family dwellings to apartment buildings, housing two or three families. When upwardly mobile middle class families purchase the home, they usually convert it back to a single family dwelling, thereby reducing the available housing for the poor even further.

17 | Inequality, Race, and Ethnicity: Some Ways of Splitting Up the "What."
by Frank O. Taylor, IV, Ph.D.

The structural problems facing minorities and the poor are daunting and far beyond the ability of a single individual to change. First, many minorities attend inferior schools and receive an inferior education. Educational deficiencies limit both opportunities for higher education and employment prospects. Additionally, deindustrialization has removed many of the jobs that minorities depended upon for their livelihood. The new jobs the economy created were largely in the service and information economy. White-collar jobs in the new economy are difficult to obtain without a college degree, even though many are physically located near minority populations. Blue-collar jobs in the service and information economy are often located away from the central city and require a commute. If you do not own a car or public transportation is too expensive or non-existent, it may be difficult to find a job in the suburbs.

In this chapter, we learned that race and ethnicity are different. Race refers to physical characteristics to which social importance is attached, often illogically. These characteristics include hair texture, width of the nose, color of the skin, thickness of the lips, and so on. Skin color is probably the most noticeable physical characteristic. What constitutes a race is determined by society. In the United States, we tend to lump people together into racial categories based on the skin color. Conversely, ethnicity refers to your cultural heritage and ancestry. Ethnicity can be based on language, traditions and customs, national origin, religion, certain types of food, clothing, and family name.

We also discussed two other important concepts: dominant group and minority group. The dominant group dominates less powerful groups through control of the economic, political, and cultural institutions of society. A minority group is a group that is dominated by another group and lacks economic, political, and cultural power to improve their situation.

Also covered was racial stratification, with White Europeans on the top of the social ladder, and people of color on the bottom. Racial stratification means that White people have more access to education and better occupations, which translates into more income and a higher standard of living, than people of color do. Racial stratification produces opportunities for some and oppression for others. Although this trend has been changing, it still occurs today.

Many believe also that some races are inferior to others. Researchers have discovered that genetic differences between groups of people previously thought of as racially different do not exist. Thinking one's own culture as superior to other cultures is known as ethnocentrism. For example, the Anglos saw Native Americans as inferior for a number of reasons. First, the natives lived on the land and had no real sense of property. Anglo tradition viewed land as a resource to be used. Secondly, Native Americans had developed only a stone-age technology. Technologically, the Anglos were vastly superior to the natives. The clash of values and cultures that emerged led to warfare and genocide. Genocide refers to the attempts of the dominant group to exterminate the minority group.

Anglos feared the reproductive power of new immigrants. This fear led to the birth of the Eugenics movement. Eugenics refers to the attempt to achieve racial purification through control of genetic factors. The eugenicists argued that non-Anglos were genetically and therefore racially, inferior. There were two types of eugenics used. During the early 1900s, IQ testing was used to "prove" that non-Anglo immigrants were intellectually inferior, due to their poor test scores. Of course, these tests were biased. This type of testing gave rise to what is known as passive eugenics, which is the attempt of the dominant group to restrict the numbers and power of the minority group by limiting their reproductive capabilities. A number of states also passed legislation making it legal to sterilize individuals who scored low on IQ tests, thereby preventing such people from giving birth. Active eugenics refers to the actual attempts by the dominant group to exterminate the minority group by force. Perhaps the most recognized example of active eugenics is that of the holocaust.

Also discussed was racism and discrimination, which are two separate concepts. Racism is a negative attitude toward certain races. It is the illogical belief that one race is superior to all others. Discrimination requires a negative action.

Prior to the 1950s, De jure segregation existed in the South. De jure segregation refers to the legal barriers that kept the Black population largely separate from the White population. In 1954, as a result of the landmark *Brown v. Board of Education* ruling of the Supreme Court, legal segregation ended. However, fifty years after the historic ruling, De facto segregation, which is segregation that is an unintended consequence of social or ecological arrangements, not only remains, but there is evidence that it is growing.

We also discussed the importance of education and employment as the well being of a group. Schools in minority neighborhoods have limited resources, largely due to tax cuts and diminishing levels of funding for public education. Very few minority parents can afford to send their children to private schools, so many do not receive the education that is available to those higher up on the stratification ladder.

Employment is also an issue for minorities. Blacks and Hispanics are more likely to work in low-paid, low-skill occupations with few benefits and chances for promotion. Even when Blacks and Hispanics find employment in higher status occupations they often face a situation similar to what women face, a job ceiling that prevents them from reaching the top rungs of the executive promotion ladder. One of the main concerns for minority workers is the restructuring that has occurred in the United States economy in the last decades. Unskilled and poorly educated minority workers were able to find jobs in the smokestack industries of the Northeast, in steel, auto, and rubber. Globalization and the movement of United States plants and factories out of the country are removing an important source of employment for blue-collar workers, many of whom are minorities. Additionally, government downsizing is also eliminating many jobs minority workers were often successful in obtaining.

We discussed the concept of institutional discrimination. Zoning and redlining are key factors in institutional discrimination. Zoning is a tool used by the elite class to protect their land and property values by specifying what type of housing can be built in any given neighborhood. Redlining is a type of discrimination that many financial institutions practice, in which they literally draw a red circle on the map and their agents and loan offices are not to conduct any business with clients from within the circle, who live in neighborhoods considered to have rates of crime and other risks that are too high.

Several trends have conspired to create a jobs/skills mismatch for inner city minorities and poor. Large numbers of minorities live in working class neighborhoods in central cities. These neighborhoods used to be adjacent to working class industrial jobs. Many of these jobs have disappeared as the nation's economy shifted from an industrial base to a service and information base.

Gentrification is another process that limits opportunities for minorities and the poor. Gentrification is a process of community change through which housing in old neighborhoods is restored, often resulting in higher rents and the displacement of previous tenants who can no longer afford to live there. Since many of the new occupations are service oriented, the blue-collar workers jobs are located away from these areas and require a commute. If you do not own a car or public transportation is too expensive or non-existent, it may be difficult to find a job in the suburbs.

Inequality is something that is inescapable. Although many advances toward equality have been made, much more is still needed. Throughout this chapter, you have learned the concept of inequality. Using the information contained here will help you better understand the barriers that different racial and ethnic backgrounds face in the United States.

ജ ഇ ജ ഇ

DEFINITIONS

Active Eugenics. Refers to the actual attempts by the dominant group to exterminate the minority group by force.

Assimilate. Assimilation refers to becoming a member of the dominant culture, or at least adopting the language, values, and beliefs of the dominant group.

Blaming the Victim. Focuses on the attributes of the individual as the cause for their economic or other problems.

De Facto Segregation. Segregation that is an unintended consequence of social or ecological arrangements.

De Jure Segregation. Refers to the legal barriers that kept the Black population largely separate from the White population in the south.

Discrimination. Positive or negative behavior based on stereotyped beliefs about the occupants of a status.

Dominant Group. Dominates less powerful groups through control of the economic, political, and cultural institutions of society.

Ethnic Group. Distinguished by their cultural distinctiveness.

Ethnicity. Refers to your cultural heritage and ancestry. Ethnicity can be based on language, traditions and customs, national origin, religion, certain types of food, clothing, and family name.

Ethnocentric. An attitude that one's own culture, society, or group is inherently superior to all others. Judging other cultures by your own cultural standards and since, of course, other cultures are different, they are therefore inferior.

Eugenics. Refers to the attempt to achieve racial purification through control of genetic factors.

Genocide. The systematic attempt to kill all occupants of a particular status, especially ethnic, religious, racial, or national.

Gentrification. A process of community change through which housing in old neighborhoods is restored, often resulting in higher rents and the displacement of previous tenants who can no longer afford to live there.

Institutional Discrimination. Refers to the ways in which the normal operation of institutions is systematically biased to favor the affluent and disadvantage the poor.

Jim Crow. Racist laws and actions that deprived African Americans of their civil rights by defining Blacks as inferior to Whites, and as members of a caste of subordinate people.

Jobs/Skills Mismatch. The labor pool that lives close to a specific type of occupation, such as the service industry, often lack the skills and education required to work in the upper tier of the service economy. Often there are no jobs at all for inner city poor. For those who do find employment in the lower tier of the service economy the wages are not enough to lift the family out of poverty.

Minority Group. A group that is dominated by another group and lacks economic, political, and cultural power to improve their situation.

"Not In My Backyard" Syndrome. Grass roots efforts of like-minded residents of an area who seek to maintain the status quo (e.g., a healthy environment in which to live and raise children) by opposing the development of nearby land (especially for a polluting industry).

Pan Indian. A social movement that sought to emphasize a Native American identity that incorporates elements common to most tribes. These developments resulted in a surge in tribal membership.

Passive Eugenics.   The attempt of a dominant group to restrict the numbers and power of the minority group by limiting their reproductive capabilities.

Race. Biologically, a collection of people with distinct physical characteristics that are passed on through reproduction. Socially, a social status defined in terms of cultural beliefs about biological race.

Racial Group. A group that is distinguished by their physical characteristics.

Racial Stratification. The ranking of people to have more access to education and better occupations, which translates into more income and a higher standard of living because of race. Racial stratification produces opportunities for some and oppression for others.

Racial-Ethnic Groups. Groups of people who are distinguished by skin color and a common social, cultural, and economic background.

Racism. Refers to the illogical belief that one race is superior to all others. Racism is a negative attitude toward certain races.

Redlining. A type of discrimination that many financial institutions practice, in which they literally draw a red circle on the map and their agents and loan offices are not to conduct any business with clients from within the circle, who live in neighborhoods considered to have rates of crime and other risks too high.

Zoning. A tool used by the elite class to protect their land and property values by specifying what type of housing can be built in any given neighborhood.

REFERENCES

The ideas expressed in my essay on racial and ethnic inequality and the information presented are based on the following works:

Adorno, T. W., et al. 1950. *The Authoritarian Personality*. New York: Harper and Brothers.

Allport, Floyd. 1954. *Social Psychology*. Boston, MA: Houghton Mifflin.

Angier, Natalie. 2000. "Do Races Differ? Not Really, DNA Shows." *New York Times*, August 22.

Angier, Natalie. 2000. Scientists: DNA Shows Humans Are All One Race." *Denver Post*, August 22, 2A, 5A.

Aponte, Robert. 1991. "Urban Hispanic Poverty: Desegregations and Explanations." *Social Problems* 38(4):516-528.

Armas, Genaro. 2003. "White Male With Degree Still Earns the Most," *The Denver Post*, May 21, 221A.

Baca Zinn, Maxine and Bonnie Thornton Dill. 1994. "Difference and Domination." Pp. 3-12 *Women of Color in U.S. Society*, edited by Maxine Baca Zinn and Bonnie Thornton Dill. Philadelphia, PA: Temple University Press.

Bamshad, Michael J. and Steve E. Olson. 2003. "Does Race Exist?" *Scientific American* (December):78-85.

Benokraitis, Nijole and Joe R. Feagin. 1974. "Institutional Racism: A Review and Critical Assessment of the Literature." Paper presented at the American Sociological Association, Montreal, Canada, August.

Blauner, Robert. 2002. *Still the Big News: Racial Oppression in America*. Philadelphia, PA: Temple University Press.

Blee, Kathleen M. 2005. "Inside Organized Racism." Pp. 45-57 in *Life in Society: Readings to Accompany Sociology: A Down-to-Earth Approach, 7th ed.*, edited by James M. Henslin. Boston, MA: Allyn and Bacon.

Bogardus, Emory S. 1968. "Comparing Racial Distance in Ethiopia, South Africa, and the United States." *Sociology and Social Research* 52(2) (January):149-56.

Bohland, James R. 1982. "Indian Residential Segregation in the Urban Southwest: 1970 and 1980." *Social Science Quarterly* 63 (December):749-761.

Bonacich, Edna. 1992. "Inequality in America: The Failure of the American System for People of Color." Pp. 96-109 in *Race, Class and Gender*, edited by Margaret L Andersen and Patricia Hill Collins. Belmont, CA: Wadsworth.

Bonilla-Silva, Eduardo. 1996. "Rethinking Racism: Toward a Structural Interpretation." *American Sociological Review* 62 (June):465-480.

Bonilla-Silva, Eduardo. 2003. *Racism without Racists*. Lanham, MA: Rowman and Littlefield.

Carmichael, Stokely and Charles V. Hamilton. 1967. *Black Power: The Politics of Liberation in America*. New York: Random House.

Churchill, Ward. 1997. *A Little Matter of Genocide: Holocaust and Denial in the Americas, 1492 to the Present*. San Francisco, CA: City Lights Books.

Crowley, Sheila. 2002. "The National Low Income Housing Coalition." *Poverty and Race* 11 (January/February):24-26.

Cummings, Scott and Thomas Lambert. 1997. "Anti-Hispanic and Anti-Asian Sentiments among African Americans." *Social Science Quarterly* 78(2) (June):338-53.

Del, Pinal Jorge and Audrey Singer. 1997. "Generations of Diversity: Latinos in the United States." *Population Bulletin* 52 (October).

Dobyns, Henry F. 1983. *Their Numbers Became Thinned: Native American Population Dynamics in Easter North America*. Knoxville, TN: University of Tennessee Press.

Dollard, John, et al. 1939. *Frustration and Aggression*. New Haven, CT: Yale University Press.

Du Bois, W. E. B. 1903. *The Souls of Black Folks: Essays and Sketches*. Chicago, IL: McClurg.

Du Bois, W. E. B. 1967. *The Philadelphia Negro: A Social Study*. New York: Schocken Books. First published in 1899.

Du Bois, W. E. B. 1992. *Black Reconstruction in America: An Essay Toward a History of the Part Which Black Folk Played in the Attempt to Reconstruct Democracy in America, 1860-1880*. New York: Atheneum.

Feagin, Joe and Melvin P. Sikes. 1994. *Living with Racism: The Black Middle-Class Experience*. Boston, MA: Beacon Press.

Feagin, Joe R. 1997. "Death by Discrimination?" *Society for the Study of Social Problems Newsletter* 28 (Winter):15-16.

Fost, Dan. 1991. "American Indians in the 1990s." *American Demographics* 13(12) (December):1-4.

Gotham, Kevin Fox. 1998. "Race, Mortgage Lending, and Loan Rejections in a U.S. City." *Sociological Focus* 31(4) (October):391-36.

Gourevitch, Philip. 1995. "After the Genocide." *New Yorker*, December 18, pp. 78-94.

Gross, Jan T. 2001. *Neighbors*. New Haven, CT: Yale University Press.

Harris, Roderick J. and Claudette Bennett. 1995. "Racial and Ethnic Diversity." Pp. 141-210 in *The State of the Union: America in the 1990s*, Vol. 2., edited by Reynolds Farley. New York: Russell Sage.

Hartley, Eugene. 1946. *Problems in Prejudice*. New York: King's Crown Press.

Higginbotham, Elizabeth. 1994. "Black Professional Women: Job Ceilings and Employment Sectors." Pp. 113-131 in *Women of Color in U.S. Society*, edited by Maxine Baca Zinn and Bonnie Thornton Dill. Philadelphia, PA: Temple University Press.

Hill, Mark E. 2002. "Skin Color and the Perception of Attractiveness Among African Americans: Does Gender Make a Difference?" *Social Psychology Quarterly* 65(1):77-91.

Huttenback, Henry R. "The Roman *Porjmos*: The Nazi Genocide of Europe's Gypsies." *Nationalities Papers* 19(3) (Winter):373-394.

Johnson, Dirk. 1991. "Census Finds Many Claiming New Identity: Indian." *New York Times*, March 5, A1, A16.

Johnson, Dirk. 1994. "Economies Come to Life on Indian Reservations." *The New York Times*, July 3, 1Y, 10Y-11Y.

Johnson, Paul. 1998. *A History of the American People*. New York: Harper Collins.

Lind, Michael. 1995. *The Next American Nation: The New Nationalism and the Fourth American Revolution*. New York: Free Press.

Lucal, Betsy. 1996. "Oppression and Privilege: Toward a Relational Conceptualization of Race." *Teaching Sociology* 24 (July):245-255.

Massy, Douglas and Nancy Denton. 1993. *American Apartheid: Segregation and the Making of the Underclass*. Cambridge, MA: Harvard University Press.

Massy, Douglas. 1996. "Latino Poverty Research: An Agenda for the 1990s." *Items*, The Social Science Research Council 47 (March):7-11.

Matthiessen, Peter. 1984. *Indian Country*. New York: Viking Press.

McIntosh, Pegg. 1992. "White Privilege and Male Privilege." Pp. 70-81 in *Race, Class, and Gender*, edited by Margaret L. Andersen and Patricia Hill Collins. Belmont, CA: Wadsworth.

McLemore, S. Dale. 1994. *Racial and Ethnic Relations in America*. Boston, MA: Allyn and Bacon.

Merton, Robert K. 1976. "Discrimination and the American Creed." Pp. 189-216 in *Sociological Ambivalence and Other Essays*. New York: Free Press.

Miles, Robert. 1989. *Racism*. New York: Tavistock.

Montagu, M. F. Ashley. 1964. *The Concept of Race*. New York: Free Press.

Montagu, M. F. Ashley. 1999. *Race and IQ: Expanded Edition*. New York: Oxford University Press.

Moore, Joan W. and Raquel Pinderhughes (eds.). 1994. *In the Barrios: Latinos and the Underclass Debate*. New York: Russell Sage Foundation.

Mwwakkil, Salim. 1998. "Real Minority, Media Majority: TV News Needs to Root Out Stereotypes about Blacks and Crime." *In These Times* (June 28):18-19.

Nagel, Joane. 1994. "Constructing Ethnicity: Creating and Recreating Ethnic Identity and Culture." *Social Problems* 41(1) (February):152-76.

Nagel, Joane. 1996. *American Indian Ethnic Renewal: Red Power and the Resurgence of Identity and Culture*. New York: Oxford University Press.

Newman, William M. 1973. *American Pluralism: A Study of Minority Groups and Social Theory*. New York: Harper and Row.

O' Hare, William P. 1993. "Diversity Trend: More Minorities Looking Less Alike." *Population Today* 21 (April):1-2.

Oliver, Melvin L. and Thomas M. Shapiro. 1995. *Black Wealth/White Wealth: A New Perspective on Racial Equality*. New York: Routledge.

Omi, Michael and Howard Winant. 1994. *Racial Formation in the United States*, 2nd ed. New York: Routledge and Kegan Paul.

Parenti, Michael. 1978. *Power and the Powerless*, 2nd ed. New York: St. Martin's Press.

Passel, Jeffery S. 2005. "Unauthorized Migrants: Numbers and Characteristics." *Pew Hispanic Center*. June 14.

Peters, Jeremy W. and Danny Hakim. 2005. "Ford's Lending Practices Challenged in a Lawsuit." *New York Times*, March 1.

Pollard, Kelvin M. and William P. O'Hare. 1999. "America's Racial and Ethnic Minorities." *Population Bulletin* 54(3) (September). Washington, DC: Population Reference Bureau.

Reskin, Barbara F. 1998. The Realities of Affirmative Action in Employment. Washington, DC: *American Sociological Association*.

Sale, Kirkpatrick. 1990. *The Conquest of Paradise: Christopher Columbus and the Columbian Legacy.* New York: Alfred A Knopf.

Schaefer, Richard T. 2004. *Racial and Ethnic Groups.* 9th ed. Upper Saddle River, NJ: Prentice Hall.

Skinner, Jonathan, James N. Weinstein, Scott M. Sporer, and John E. Wennberg. 2003. "Racial, Ethnic, and Geographic Disparities in Rages of Knee Arthroplasty." *New England Journal of Medicine* 349(14) (October 2):1350-1359.

Smith, Tom W. 1997. Research results reported in "Anti-Semitism Decreases but Persists." *Society* 33(3) (March/April):321-31.

Spencer, Martin E. 1994. "Multiculturalism, Political Correctness, and the Politics of Identity." *Sociological Forum* 9(4) (December):547-567.

Spickard, P. R. S. 1989. *Mixed Blood: Intermarriage and Ethnic Identity in Twentieth Century America.* Madison, WI: University of Wisconsin Press.

Stolberg, Sheryl Gay. 2001. "Blacks Found on Short End of Heart Attack Procedure." *New York Times*, May 10.

Takaki, Ronald. 1993. *A Different Mirror: A History of Multicultural America.* Boston, MA: Little, Brown.

Thomas, Paulette. 1992. "Boston Fed Finds Racial Discrimination in Mortgage Lend is Still Widespread." *Wall Street Journal*, October 9, A3.

Thornton, Russell. 1987. *American Indian Holocaust and Survival: A Population History Since 1492.* Norman, OK: University of Oklahoma Press.

Tienda, Marta and Susan Simonelli. 2001. "Hispanic Students Are Missing from Diversity Debates." *Chronicle of Higher Education* June 1, A16.

Tyler, S. Lyman. 1973. *A History of Indian Policy.* Washington DC: United States Department of the Interior, Bureau of Indian Affairs.

United States Bureau of the Census. 1998. "Race of Wife by Race of Husband: 1960, 1970, 1980, 1991, and 1992." Online. Available: http://www.census.gov/population/socdemo/race/interractab1.txt.

United States Bureau of the Census. 2000a. "The Asian and Pacific Islander Population in the United States, 1999." *Current Population Reports.* Series P20-529. Washington, DC: United States Government Printing Office.

United States Bureau of the Census. 2000b. "The Black Population in the United States." *Current Population Reports.* Series P20-541. Washington, DC: United States Government Printing Office.

United States Bureau of the Census. 2001a. "Overview of Race and Hispanic Origin: Census 2000 Brief." *Current Population Reports* (March). Washington DC: United States Government Printing Office.

United States Bureau of the Census. 2001b. "The Hispanic Population in the U.S.: March 2000." *Current Population Reports.* Series P20-535. Washington DC: United States Government Printing Office.

United States Bureau of the Census. 2003. "Income in the U.S.: 2002." *Current Population Reports* (September) P60-221.

United States Bureau of the Census. 2004. "Hispanic and Asian Americans Increasing Faster than Overall Population." (June) Online. Available: http://www.census.gov/hhes/hlthins/hlthino2/hi02t3.pdf.

Wagley, Charles and Marvin Harris. 1958. *Minorities in the New World.* New York: Columbia University Press.

Wirth, Louis. 1945. "The Problem of Minority Groups." In *The Science of Man in the World Crisis*, edited by Ralph Linton. New York: Columbia University Press.

18 | Gender Inequality: Another Way of Splitting Up the "What."
by Frank O. Taylor, IV, Ph.D.

Social Structure and the Individual.   What is inequality? Sociologically, we can define inequality as differential amounts of social rewards. Almost anything can be construed as a social reward. For example, access to a good education could be thought of as a social reward as well as health care, income, housing, nutrition, savings, and material goods.   Even marriage can be considered a social reward. You probably think that marriage and family are all matters of individual interest. You meet someone you are interested in, find attractive, and begin dating. Dating leads to going steady and eventually to becoming engaged. Finally, you get married. It seems to be entirely a matter of individuals getting together and making choices. Simple?

Not really. People certainly make choices, and suffer the consequences of bad decisions or the benefits of good decisions. However, the choices we make in life are highly structured. Long before you can find someone attractive, you have to have the opportunity to meet and interact with that person. This is the **principle of propinquity**. You can only meet and date people who are in close proximity to you. Sure you can always admire someone from a distance, but this is hardly going to lead to marriage. It is possible, under certain conditions, such as shopping at the mall or having fun at a theme park, that the people who are physically close to you are so based on pure random chance. Most of the time, on the other hand, there is a structural reason people are near you. Let us consider the structural underpinnings of three settings where people are near each other for non-random reasons, including the neighborhood, school, and employment.

You probably grew up in a certain neighborhood. While you were busy making friends and occupying yourself with children's games, did you ever stop to think about why you lived in that particular neighborhood and not another? You probably did not think about it very often, but the reason you lived where you did as a child had a lot to do with what type of housing your parents could afford. Usually, this is a function of your parent's education and income. Neighborhoods are composed of areas of similar property values. The homes on your block, and for several blocks around you, were of similar value. The education and income of your parents, and everyone else's parents in your neighborhood, was the underlying factor in why you lived where you did. In other words, the children you played with, made friends with, and went to school with, were similar to you in many ways.   This is the **principle of similarity** at work.   The people around you in your neighborhood are not there by random chance alone. Similarity and propinquity conspire to limit your choices, and not just in terms of whom you may interact.

The school you attended was probably near your home and neighborhood, unless you were bused to school. Schools are funded by local property taxes. Some schools, located where property values are higher, have excess resources. These schools can afford teachers with advanced degrees, the latest computer technology, indoor Olympic sized swimming pools, and track, field, basketball and football facilities. These schools often have a curriculum that includes art, industrial arts, foreign language, and music. Children who attend the best schools often take for granted the resources their school derives from property taxes, if they are aware of it at all. Generally, students tend to view their school in individualistic terms based on their grades. Schools located in poorer districts often lack the extra activities and classes that make going to school fun in the first place. Your childhood friends lived in your neighborhood and attended the same school as you did. Random chance has nothing to do with it. If you were lucky enough to have upper or middle class parents, you had more educational opportunities than children born in the working or lower class did. Of course, you have to take advantage of opportunities. It is possible to have opportunities and not take advantage of them. This is the intersection of individualism, propinquity, and similarity.

If you are reading this book, you are a college student. Why are you going to this university instead of Harvard or Yale? Ostensibly, you could have enrolled in Penn State or the University of Pittsburgh but you did not? There are a number of possible reasons. Perhaps your SAT scores were not high enough to allow you to be accepted to a more prestigious college or university. Sociologists know that what high school you attended and your performance on the SAT is highly correlated. Some high schools have honors programs where students take courses aimed at college preparation. If you attended one of these schools and managed, through hard work and study, to get into the honors program, you are likely to perform better on the SAT than students from poorer schools or students from your school not in the honors courses.

Regardless of your SAT score, you still have to pay for college. Here we see that your performance on the SAT is partly a function of individual effort but also a function of what you have been taught, which, in turn, is a function of the high school you attended and the courses offered. Publicly funded state universities and colleges generally serve the children of the middle class who cannot afford either a private institution of higher learning or a flagship state institution. The point is you are where you are educationally due to economics and social class as much as individual effort.

If you do not like your job you can always quit and get a different job, right? Wrong! Maybe you never paid attention to political and economic issues very much but you should. Can you remember a time in your life when there was an unemployment rate of zero? In other words, everyone who looked for a job found a job. In a capitalist economy, this never happens because it would lead to rampant inflation. The government tries to balance economic growth against inflation. Generally, if the economy slows down the government tries to revive it by cutting taxes, lowering the prime leading rate, and spending money. However, when the economy grows too fast inflation may rise. In this case, the government increases taxes, raises the prime lending rate, and spends less money. During an economic expansion, the unemployment rate goes down. One the other hand, during an economic recession, the unemployment rate goes up. Never is there full employment in a capitalist economy.   There is always some level of unemployment—higher during an economic contraction, lower during an economic expansion.

In addition, you cannot just get any job either. Except for menial labor and service sector work, upper tier jobs generally require certification and education. If you are a teenager and you work at McDonald's but do not like your work, your options are extremely limited. You can quit McDonald's but the next job you find will have similar pay and may still be in fast food. If you want to get a corporate job, you will have to go to college and get a degree. The unemployment rate is not uniform; it is different—higher or lower, depending on where you live. If you are unfortunate enough to live in one of the nation's inner cities, where economic investment and growth is stagnant, you probably do not want to quit your job at all because you are lucky to have one. And too, the income you can earn at any job depends on where it is in the nation, what sector of the economy it is in, what type of education is required, and so on. Many factors apply beyond your personal choice or ability. For example, thousands and thousands of highly skilled workers in auto manufacturing, steel, and rubber, lost their jobs in the last decade due to corporations moving their plants and factories out of the United States, in search of cheaper labor. Most of these workers were never reemployed in their respective industries, even though they would have preferred to be. You see, you just cannot create opportunities out of thin air or take advantage of opportunities that no longer exist. Success in life depends on a lot more than just desire, willpower, talent, and ability. More than anything else, success depends upon social structure.

Effort, talent, skill, knowledge, and motivation are important characteristics that distinguish one individual from another. These differences can go a long way toward explaining why some people have more and others have less. However, when explaining inequality we also must consider social structure. One way of thinking about social structure is to view it as an opportunity structure, composed of different types of jobs and occupations and the types of training, knowledge, and certification required to obtain them. If you live in a neighborhood where unemployment is over 50 percent and economic activity is almost nonexistent, property values will be very low. The tax base of your neighborhood will be small and local government will be unable to provide many opportunities. Your school may be unable to afford much in the way of advanced technology, stimulating extra-curricular activities, or honors curriculum.

If success in life were just a matter of discipline and motivation we would see a constant reshuffling of individuals throughout the social class structure, as people who work hard, strive to succeed, and get educated, claw their way up the stratification ladder displacing others higher up. However, when we examine social mobility, a mixed picture emerges. About one third of children born to the poorest Americans remain poor as adults. Conversely, about one third of children born to the richest 10 percent of parents remain rich. Therefore, about two-thirds of the poorest children eventually experience upward social mobility, while two-thirds of the richest children experience downward social mobility. Just how far are people who experience social mobility moving? People who manage to move up only move a short distance and most do not cross class boundaries. Thus, the one-third of people who were born poor and experienced upward social mobility only managed to be less poor than their parents; they did not make it into the middle class. Likewise, for the children of the rich, they ended up slightly less rich than their parents. The range of opportunities an individual will be able to squander or take advantage of in their lifetime is limited by social structure.

GENDER INEQUALITY

Today, one-half of the work force is comprised of female workers and 60 percent of all women work at least part-time. In the past few decades gender roles for women have changed to the extent that it is considered normal for women to work, whether they have children or not. About 40 percent of women work in retail sales and administrative support occupations, but women can be found in almost any occupation. Since the beginning of deindustrialization and the growth of the service and information economy in the 1980s, the labor force participation rate for men has declined slightly and women have taken 80 percent of new jobs created in the economy. Has this increase in work force participation for women led to equality with men? The rising rates of employment for women will undoubtedly bring many economic benefits. Nevertheless, women hold a mere 15 percent of jobs and occupations usually defined as men's work. Conversely, men hold only 8 percent of jobs usually defined as women's work, such as nurses, teachers, and waitresses. Thus, work is highly gender segregated. The following tables report the jobs most likely and least likely to be held by women.

Table 18.1   Jobs Most Likely and Least Likely to be Held by Women

Occupation	Percent Female
Preschool and Kindergarten Teachers	98.3
Secretaries and Administrative Assistants	96.3
Receptionists and Information Clerks	93.2
Bookkeeping, Accounting, and Auditing Clerks	91.4
Teacher Assistants	90.9
Elementary and Middle School Teachers	80.6
Registered Nurses	90.2
Nursing, Psychiatric, and Home Health Aides	89.0
Office Clerks, General	83.8
Cashiers	75.5

Occupation	Percent Female
Small Engine Mechanics	0.0
Structural Iron and Steel Workers	0.0
Heating, Air Condition, and Refrigeration Mechanics and Installers	0.6
Electrical Power-Line Installers and Repairers	0.9
Brick Masons, Block Masons, and Stone Masons	0.9
Bus and Truck Mechanics and Diesel Engine Specialists	0.9
Heavy Vehicle and Mobile Equipment Service Technicians and Mechanics	1.0
Pipe Layers, Plumbers, Pipe Fitters, and Steamfitters	1.0
Dredge, Excavating, and Loading Machine Operators	1.1
Roofers	1.3

There is clear evidence that jobs are gendered in our culture. In other words, electricians, mechanics, welders, tool and die makers, machine operators, engineers, and construction workers, among other occupations, are jobs society usually defines as men's work. On the other hand, nursing, teaching, clerical work, housekeeping, secretarial and administrative work, and teaching assistants are jobs our society generally defines as women's work. Men tend to be employed in higher paying jobs that are highly unionized and have health, retirement, and other fringe benefits. Although many of the benefits associated with unions are disappearing. Women tend to be employed in occupations with low pay and few benefits.

Starting around 1970 and continuing into the 1990s women made significant inroads in the occupations of law, medicine, business, higher education, and journalism. Even though women have worked their way into higher status occupations, they still have not achieved parity with men.

About 29 percent of lawyers are women, a little over 40 percent of university and college professors are women, and about 30 percent of doctors are women. Even though women have made gains in the business world, women head only 8 of the Fortune 500 corporations. Women of color have not fared as well as white women. Affirmative action programs, which mandated that firms doing business with the government comply with hiring guidelines, widely adopted throughout the corporate and academic environment, allowed white women to move into occupations dominated by men, such as business, medicine, and law. Women of color moved into jobs previously dominated by white women, such as social work and teaching.

Perhaps the most important area of gender inequality in the work force is the **pay gap**. Consider this fact: the average male college graduate will earn over a million dollars more than the average female worker will over the course of his career. During the 1990s women closed the gap between their earnings and the earnings of men. At one point, women had narrowed the gap to 73 percent of what men earned. Today women earn about 68 percent of what men earn, and the gap is only set to widen as the **backlash** against women's equality continues to gather momentum. Women earn an average of $7,700 for every $10,000 men earn, losing $2,300 per year. Overall, the average male income equals $52,435 compared to an average female income of $35,863. Women earn less then men regardless of working in similar occupations, years of experience, or years of education. Hotel managers, flight attendants, police, and firefighters, are occupations pursued by both men and women. Nevertheless, men earn substantially more than women do in these fields.

The pay gap between women's earnings and men's earnings exists for all levels of education. Male high school dropouts, for example, earn just about $30,000 compared to about $20,000 for female dropouts. Men who graduate from high school have average earnings of $37,680 compared to $27,184 for women graduates. Men who have completed some college realize an average income of over $46,000 compared to similar women who earn just over $31,000. Men with an associate's degree have average earnings of over $48,000 compared to about $34,000 for women with an associate's degree. Moreover, for college graduates men earn over $80,000 while women lag behind at $51,000. In fact, a male high school dropout earning $30,000 a year does better than a female high school graduate and about as well as women with some college or an associate's degree.

Figure 18.1   Female and Male Earnings

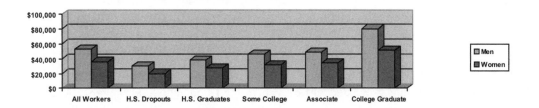

There seems to be a glass ceiling that prevents women from reaching the top positions in their respective fields. The **glass ceiling** is a structural barrier that tends to keep women in the lower rungs of the corporate ladder. Discrimination is illegal but the glass ceiling is constructed of covert forms of discrimination, such as different promotional ladders based on job titles. Women are steered into secretarial tracks while men are steered into administrative tracks with promotional ladders into upper level management, and old-boys networks. Men who work in careers normally held by women, such as nursing or elementary school teaching, frequently report finding themselves on a **glass escalator**, in which they experience rapid promotions into administrative positions with higher pay. Some women have cracked the glass ceiling by adopting masculine strategies and becoming very competitive. These successful women usually have supportive husbands who are willing to contribute to household and childrearing duties and are supportive of their wives careers.

In addition to gendered work and the gender pay gap, sexual harassment must also be considered as a form of gender inequality. **Sexual harassment** refers to unwanted sexual attention in the workplace or school. Sexual harassment comes in the form of looks, sexual comments, touching, and pressure to have sex in return for favors. This problem is more than an issue of men pressuring women to whom they are attracted. When men abuse their position of authority and force unwanted sexual activity upon women a structural problem exists.

There are two main forms of sexual harassment. Quid pro quo harassment occurs when someone is asked to exchange favors for sex. Generally, since men occupy most of the positions of authority in the workplace, men tend to be the harassers, offering women exchanges such as a promotion, a transfer, or other forms of compensation. A variant of quid pro quo occurs when the harasser threatens to discipline an employee unless they grant sexual favors. A second form of sexual harassment is the hostile environment, which develops when the harasser interferes with another employee's ability to perform their job due to sexual intimidation, sexual jokes, use of pornography, and so on.

It is interesting to note that women are not a unified group. Women of color face **double jeopardy**, discrimination based on gender and race or ethnicity when it comes to earnings. In 2003, White women earned almost 80 percent of White men's earnings. However, the situation was worse for Black and Hispanic women, who earned 68 percent and 57 percent of White men's earnings, respectively. Black women earned only 88 percent of Black men's earnings. Similarly for Hispanic women, who earned 88 percent of Hispanic men's earnings.

Figure 18.2   Percent of White Male Earnings

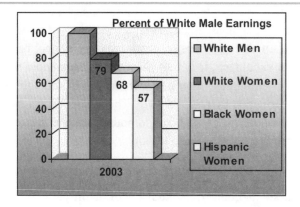

Women of color make up about 10 percent of the workforce and they are the most likely to be concentrated in the bottom rungs of the occupational structure. The jobs at the bottom are referred as **dead-end jobs** because they are low paying, have high rates of turnover, few benefits, little status, poor working conditions, and few promotional ladders. For example, 38 percent of White women hold managerial and professional jobs, compared to 30 percent of Black women and 21 percent of Hispanic women. Women of color tend to be concentrated in jobs as cashiers, nurses aids, secretaries, household cleaners, janitors, and textile machine operators.

What explains gender inequality? There is no known society in which women and men are equals. Women have made important gains all over the world and in the United States but they continue to be discriminated against. Why are women so often in the inferior position? There are competing explanations for gender inequality.   The **biological perspective** stresses innate chromosomal, hormonal, and reproductive differences between women and men. Androgens make males taller and more muscular than women. Estrogens are related to menstruation, the development of breasts, and lactation. However, both hormones are present in women and men. We are talking about average differences, not absolute differences. Some women are taller than some men are. Likewise, some women are stronger than some men are. There is greater variability among women and men, in terms of height and strength, than there is between women and men.

It is unlikely that biological differences can completely explain women's inequality. For one thing, we cannot forget that culture plays a large role in physical development as well. For example, body size is influenced by exercise, diet, and nutrition. These are cultural factors. What is considered feminine or masculine varies from culture to culture, which would not be expected if biology were the basis of differences between the sexes. Additionally, what is considered feminine or masculine within a culture changes over time, as definitions of appropriate behavior, for the sexes, change. Gender roles for women in the United States have changed dramatically in the past fifty years, for instance. Race, class, ethnicity, and sexuality all have the ability to shape feminine and masculine behavior.

To study the social basis of gender inequality sociologists differentiate between sex and gender. **Sex** refers to the biological differences between women and men. **Gender** refers to the social construction of femininity and masculinity. Differences in body mass, strength, and height are biological matters. Differences of character, behavior, and attitudes, however, are social matters. You may be born female or male but you have to learn femininity and masculinity. Gender socialization is a basic experience shared by all human beings. Every society has certain definitions about women and men, in terms of basic character and potential. In other words, every society has a **gender system** that is designed to produce, through the process of socialization, women and men who have the desired social traits. Gender systems include language and symbols, power, names, clothes, religion, education, and nearly every aspect of life. Moreover, societies are not uniform in their expectations about feminine and masculine behaviors, which tend to suggest that culture is more powerful in shaping gender than biology.

From a sociological point of view there are two main explanations for women's inequality, the **gender roles approach** and the social structural approach. The gender roles approach emphasizes the socialization process, through which individuals come to internalize a set of traits associated with femininity and masculinity. The **gender structure approach** emphasizes the role of social structure in creating differentials of power and opportunities for women and men.

Gender role socialization begins at the moment of your birth and continues throughout your lifetime. In fact, the influence of the gender system is present even before you are born. Most parents, upon finding out that they are expecting a child, begin to think about what to name their child. We associate certain names with girls or boys. A few years ago there was a very popular song called "a boy named Sue." If was funny precisely because Sue is considered a girl's name. In the song, the boy grows up to be tough because of being picked on due to having a girl's name. Of course, tough is considered a masculine attribute. Researchers have discovered that mothers and fathers use different words to describe the movements of female and male children while still in the mother's womb. Boys are described as athletic, strong, and big. Girls, on the other hand are more likely to be described as small, tender, and weak. This indicates that parents are predisposed to apply cultural definitions of femininity and masculinity to their children before they have even been born. Parents who accept these cultural stereotypes about their children are likely to continue to employ them after their children are born.

Parents play a very influential role in the process of gender role socialization. Girls and boys are given different names. Although some names in our culture, such as Francis, are gender neutral, most are not and imply one sex or the other. Girls and boys are dressed differently too. Blue is for boys and pink is for girls. Parents also give children different toys to play with. Care giving and housekeeping traits are associated with femininity. Thus, girls are more likely to receive dolls, toys associated with care giving, like stuffed animals and life-like babies that cry and require diaper changing, and a multitude of toys associated with homemaking, including miniature baking ovens, tea sets, and other house wares. In fact, if you go to the toy section of any major department store you will come upon the "pink" isle, eventually. The imitation washer and dryers, ironing boards, and dolls are all packaged in pink boxes. In the boy's section you will find, knives, pistols, rifles, machines guns, hand grenades, army helmets, and imitation weapons of mass destruction of every type, along with balls, cars, and construction materials. These toys, of course, emphasize competition, being tough, risk taking, leadership, and building things. Toys for little girls tend to emphasize cooperation and communication.

Parents typically treat daughters and sons differently. Daughters tend to be given household chores, such as doing the laundry, babysitting younger siblings, or washing the dishes. Boys tend to be given chores outside, like mowing the lawn, taking out the garbage, and so on. Fathers tend to be more interested in monitoring gender behavior than mothers, particularly for sons. Daughters tend to be monitored more closely and frequently sons are allowed to date earlier, drive sooner, and stay out later. Daughters are often encouraged to engage in cross-gender behavior or neutral behavior, which suggests a loosening of the power of traditional gender norms over girls. The same pattern has not been observed for boys, who continue to be encouraged to follow traditional masculine gender roles. Traditional fathers are most likely to transmit their attitudes regarding gender to sons, rather than daughters. Liberal mothers are no more likely to transfer their gender attitudes to daughter or sons.

Androgyny refers to the combination of feminine and masculine gender traits within one individual. Adolescent girls are more likely to support egalitarian gender roles than their parents are. On the other hand, adolescent boys tend to oppose changes in traditional gender roles, as do their fathers. Research indicates that androgynous children have high self-esteem and are more effective in handling stress. Also, androgynous children have better relationships with their parents.

Peer groups are also influential in reinforcing society's gender norms, especially same-sex peers. Researchers have discovered that boys and girls stress different social skills and abilities in their peer groups. Boys are more likely than girls to play outside, to play in larger groups, and are more likely to play competitive games. Boys are less interested in playing games dominated by girls as well. When boys and girls do interact, boys use more space, treat girls as if they have "cooties," and interfere with the girls' play. Girls tend to be more accepting of boys during play than the other way around. When girls and boys interact they socially construct gender in an active and ongoing process. Sometimes the boys compete against the girls, and in so doing construct gender divisions and gendered groups. Other times, girls and boys cooperate, during play or on projects for school, and thus modify gender identities and gender meanings.

Gender socialization continues during informal and formal education. Children's books often stress gender stereotypes, portraying boys as courageous, employed, outgoing, problem-solving, breadwinning leaders, and girls as timid, passive, unemployed, associated with the home and care giving, and nearly invisible. The number of female characters in elementary reading texts is nearly equal to male characters but the characters are still based on stereotypes. Women are depicted as affectionate and emotionally supportive. Men on the other hand, are portrayed as competitive and aggressive. In high school, boys tend to take more upper level science, computer, and math courses than girls. Boys tend to score higher on standardized tests while girls tend to earn better grades in their courses. In the classroom boys receive preferential treatment and often believe that innate differences exist between girls and boys. There continue to be inequalities in the budgets of women and men's athletic teams, favoring the boys.

We turn now to the gender structure approach and examine the influence of social structure on gender inequality. The following discussion highlights various forms of **institutional discrimination**. One explanation of why women earn less than men is **workplace segregation**. Men and women are generally employed in different jobs. As noted earlier, women tend to be concentrated in clerical sales. Men, on the other hand, tend to dominate blue-collar jobs. Blue-collar jobs tend to be highly unionized and collective bargaining has yielded fairly high wages and health care and retirement benefits. Conversely, about 50 percent of women are employed in poorly paid jobs with few benefits and few promotional opportunities. There tend to be almost equal numbers of women and men in managerial, professional, and executive positions. However, men still tend to earn more than women in those occupations do. In the professions, doctors still tend to be men and nurses women. There has been only slight improvement in the last thirty years.

What explains workplace segregation? Women and men are segregated largely due to the idea of women's work and men's work. **Gendered jobs** helps explain why women and men are congregated in different types of work. For example, construction work and other work involving manual labor has traditionally been considered men's work. Nursing, care giving, and childrearing have been considered women's work. Women who work in male dominated occupations often feel discriminated against and excluded from the informal decision-making network. These women often report experiencing sexual harassment and hostility from male co-workers. Increasingly women are moving into jobs traditionally held by men, such as bus driver, police officer, and insurance adjuster, as wages and working conditions deteriorate.

Different qualifications are a major explanation for gender inequality in income. When people decide upon a major in college they tend to major in fields they have some experience in, gained either in high school or during the process of socialization. Women tend to pick majors that have poor earnings to begin with, such as social work, education, English, social studies, or journalism. The most popular professional major is probably nursing. However, nurses earn significantly less than doctors do. Even when women pursue medicine, they tend to major in the less paid specialties such as general practitioner, gynecology, or pediatrics. On the other hand, college majors like business administration, finance, economics, law, engineering, science, and medicine tend to be dominated by men, jobs that pay significantly higher wages than female oriented majors do.

Additionally, women continue to be hampered by family obligations. A large proportion of women work part-time because they have minor children in the household to care for. Researchers have discovered that women often perform a **second-shift** of paid labor in the workforce and 20 to 30 hours of unpaid labor in the home. Women are much more likely than men to have a disjointed work experience. Women take time off after childbirth, are more likely to move for their husband's job, and often work to put their husband's through college. Consequently, women are more likely than men to go into and out of the workforce for a variety of reasons, which tends to place them at a disadvantage in terms of experience and on-the-job training. Professional women often lament the fact that they do not have a wife at home performing the necessary unpaid household labor that would support their labor force participation. Work place segregation, gendered jobs, different qualifications, and the double-shift are all types of institutional discrimination that conspire to prevent women from enjoying the same economic benefits men do.

At this point, you may be inclined to argue that no one is forcing women to choose college majors and occupations that pay less. On some level these appear to be voluntary choices. For one thing, this argument neglects the power of socialization. No one seems to question men's desire to obtain masculine jobs. When society establishes gender norms and emphasizes different realities for girls and boys we should not be surprised when young women tend to enroll in college majors that duplicate in the work place roles women play in the household. Secondly, this argument also neglects the force of discrimination. How many times do you have to be told that boys are naturally better at math, for example, by your teachers, before you decide to be interested in other subjects, regardless of your actual abilities? Many women do wish to pursue employment in occupations traditionally dominated by men but they face discrimination, sexual harassment, and hostility from their male supervisors, co-workers, and employers.

Many male employers and supervisors have been found to subscribe to a number of negative stereotypes about women, which provides the basis for discrimination. One popular stereotype holds that women will place their family obligations before their careers. However, evidence suggests that men take more time off for sickness and family related problems than women do. Women are often stereotyped as overly emotional scatterbrains who gossip, prefer shopping to work, and spread rumors. Perhaps the most popular, and damaging, stereotype, is the notion that women will just get pregnant and leave, making them less dependable than men. Men are less likely to hire women for positions that require commitment to long career tracks or geographical moves because they feel women's family obligations will hamper them. Married women with dependent children face greater levels of discrimination than do single women with no family ties.

Men often believe that women are the **weaker sex**, making them unfit for certain occupations, such as police officers, fire fighters, or combat soldiers. In spite of that stereotype, history abounds with examples of the strength and courage of women. You just have to look harder for it. During the labor movement, for example, the Women's Auxiliary Brigade physically fought and won pitched battles with the police and company men on a regular basis, often protecting male sit-down strikers locked inside of the factory from physical harm. Female Israeli soldiers are widely feared and respected in the Middle East, having participated in combat for decades, dealing death with Uzi machine guns. During World War II, Russian women piloted obsolete wood and canvas bi-planes to their deaths by the hundreds in dogfights against the vastly superior and modern German air force. They fought and died with such valor, and were so feared by the German pilots because they could only attack by cover of night, that they earned the nickname "Night Witches." Women marched with George Washington during the Revolutionary war and with the Army of the Potomac during the Civil War.

During the 1970s my combat instructor, while this author was in the Armed Forces, was a woman who barely weighed 100 pounds, but not a man in our platoon, regardless of size or strength, could out-fight her. She was lethal. Her nickname was "30 seconds," because in less than that amount of time you would be on your back. Sexist men often believe that a woman could not carry them out of a fire or to safety if they were wounded during combat. They tend not to notice that more than half of their male classmates would be unable to carry them either. One thing is true: "his" story tends to neglect the role of women in history and perpetuate the myth of feminine weakness.

Institutional discrimination is also manifest when women and men have the exact same job but different earnings. Women are often hired as executive assistants while men are hired as assistant executives. Although the job is nearly identical, assistant executives are paid at a higher rate. When it comes to management, for example, men tend to be employed in larger firms, which pay more and have better benefits than the smaller firms women tend to be employed in. Additionally, women tend to choose employment close to home in order to meet their family obligations.

The segmented labor market is another form of institutional discrimination that benefits men in general, and capitalists in particular.   The **segmented labor market** is a two-tiered occupational structure that is highly gendered. The lower tier is composed of low paying dead-end jobs in the service economy. The upper tier of high paying jobs is reserved for men. How does this benefit the capitalist? The reserve pool of labor of which the vast majority are women, are used to absorb the flux in the capitalist business cycle. When the economy expands, women are drawn into the workforce in the lower tier. However, when the economy contracts, woman can be laid off quickly. This benefits the capitalist class by having a supply of labor to cushion economic cycles. Some female social theorists have claimed that the home and housework is the location of women's inequality and have argued that household kitchens should be illegal. Imagine what the economic consequences would be if every man had to pay for the household labor their wives provide, free.

Sexism is the belief that women and men have different capacities and potentials as the result of innate biological differences. Sexism is part and parcel of the stratification system. Men, as a group, have more access to status, income, power, and have systematically attempted to limit the access of women to social rewards. People who have economic resources are less dependent and can be more assertive in their relationships with others. When men can exclude women categorically, as a group, the need to compete with women on an individual basis is eliminated. Sexism limits opportunities for women and diminishes their talents and ambitions. We live in a culture where one-half of the population must live with diminished expectations. Women are so concentrated in lowest rungs of the occupational structure, for example, that our economy is dependent upon **institutional sexism**.

Men are not exempt from sexism either. Men are encouraged to be risk takers, which can result in injury and death. The leading cause of death for teenage boys is automobile wrecks. The ideology of machismo often drives young men into the armed forces, often with deadly results. The ideology of machismo creates men who are stoic, bottling up their emotions until high levels of stress lead to strokes and heart attacks. Men who never learn to share their feelings and emotions lead lonely lives and often find themselves isolated in their elder years. Often teenage boys who feel that they have no one to talk to and share their problems with become suicidal. Research indicates that men die seven years sooner, on average, than women, due to higher levels of stress. Monitoring family relationships is generally considered women's work and men who do not find a woman to share their lives with often die alone. Not a pleasant thought, is it?

Patriarchy is a social system in which men are the dominant group and occupy the positions of power. Undoubtedly, our culture has come a long way since the days of the "rule of thumb," in which beating your wife with a stick larger than the circumference of your thumb was considered unmanly. Nevertheless, there can be little doubt that the United States remains a patriarchal society. Wherever you find the ability to use force legitimately, you find men. Men predominate in the legal system, politics and government, the armed forces, the police, and anywhere else an official has the authority to force us to comply over our objections. Indeed, men also dominate the traditional positions of authority. Most people believe that fathers should have the right to discipline their children and control their wives. The vast majority of religious leaders are male, and people generally believe that pastors and priests have a right to lead their congregations in spiritual matters.

Patriarchy and sexism create social systems that oppress women. Violence against women is a prime example. Violence in the home includes spousal battering, marital rape, and incest. With the possible exception of the military, the home may be the most violent setting where men and women interact. Some social scientists have referred to the marriage license as a "hitting" license.

Government estimates indicate that upward of 2 million women are assaulted each year in a variety of settings.

One of the most severe forms of violence against women is the **clitoridectomy**, or female circumcision. In patriarchal societies across Africa and the Middle East wives are expected to be virgins. Men and women in these societies feel that young women who have had their clitoris surgically removed, often without anesthesia, are less likely to violate sexual norms. They believe that women who can experience sexual pleasure are less likely to be faithful. In extreme cases, the entire external genital area is mutilated and sewn together, leaving only enough space for urination. Worldwide, millions of women have undergone female circumcision, including young women in the United States. Many immigrant women in the United States insist that their daughters have the procedure, due to the lax sexual mores here, often relying on relatives to perform it.   The consequences of genital mutilation include loss of sexual sensation, persistent pain, infection, infertility, and even death.

Rape is another form of violence that many women fear. According to the FBI, 7 out of every 10,000 women aged 12 and older are raped annually. Self-report data, however, indicates that only about one third of rapes are reported by victims, leading to a more realistic rate of 21 women out of every 10,000. That may seem like a fairly low rate, but it adds up to 430,000 sexual assaults and 316,000 rapes per year. Added to the number of physical assaults suffered by women each year, these numbers are pretty grim. Most women who are assaulted or raped know their assailant, as is the case in date or **acquaintance rape**. Researchers have concluded that most female students, and even some male students, have experienced forced or coerced sex. Date rapes go largely unreported because the victims often feel that they are partially to blame because they know the person and went on the date voluntarily.

Men are more likely to murder women, all over the world, than the other way around. Women make up 51 percent of the United States population but men make up 89 percent of the nation's murders. Note also that men are more likely to be the victims of murder than women are, another disadvantage of gender for men. However, when women are murdered nine times out of ten the killer is a man.

Figure 18.3   Murders and Their Victims

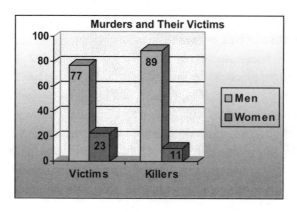

The abuse of women may be built into our culture. Most rapes involve men often trusted by the victim. The forms of violence against women constitute a culture of rape, from the attempts to control female sexuality through patriarchy, rape, and pornography, through wolf whistles directed at women on the city streets. Even language is used to control the sexuality of women. When men are referred to as dogs or studs, they are rarely offended. However, referring to women as dogs, bitches, or foxes equates women with animals, who are controlled by reproductive instincts. In addition, animals are considered a property. Men often use the female pronoun to refer to property, such as their cars or boats, referring to them as "beauties." There are a number of sexual norms related to patriarchy. For example, it is generally accepted that men should be older than their spouse and more sexually experienced. Men often initiate sex, decide what position to engage in, and how long it lasts. Clearly, such norms help men control the sexuality of women.

When we examine power, both in social institutions and in personal relationships, we find that women are systematically disadvantaged. Power is an important source of prestige. Regardless of the social institution, be it the family, church, or work place, most women occupy positions subordinate to men. Norms govern the way individuals interact with each other. There are some clear differences in the systematic ways men and women interact that indicate women's lower prestige and power in our society. For example, women smile more. Smiling is a way to demonstrate deference to the person with whom you are interacting. Additionally, research indicates that men regularly dominate women in conversations, taking up more time speaking and interrupting women often. Women are more likely to state their opinions as questions during conversation, indicating that they are less assertive than men are. Research also indicates that patients are more likely to interrupt a female doctor than a male doctor. Regardless of occupational status, women simply get less respect in our society.

We have discussed a number of explanations of gender inequality, focusing on two areas primarily, socialization and social structure. Every society has a **gender system** that is designed to produce women and men who have the desired social traits. Gender systems include language and symbols, power, names, clothes, religion, education, and nearly every aspect of life. Individuals come to internalize a set of traits associated with femininity and masculinity. Gender role socialization begins at the moment of your birth and continues throughout your lifetime, occurring in the family, at school, in peer groups, in the workplace, and in every interaction you have. Gender roles and norms are reinforced by interactions in our family, with friends and peers, and by society.

When examining the role of social structure in producing gender inequality we identified several types of institutional discrimination. About one-half of the pay-gap between women's earnings and men's is likely attributable to sexism and discrimination. Employers pay women less because they believe in a number of irrational stereotypes. The most prevalent stereotype is that women are unreliable workers because they will put their families before work. Another prevalent stereotype regarding women is that they are the weaker sex. Several aspects of the work place help explain women's inequality, including workplace segregation and gendered jobs, which restrict women to occupations largely in the lower rungs of the segmented labor force, with low pay and few benefits. Additionally, we identified differential qualifications as an explanation of why women pursue careers in occupations associated with "women's work," explaining that it is not at all unusual to expect women to pursue careers they have been socialized all their lives to desire. We also indicated that women continue to be responsible for raising children and caring for a household, responsibilities that tend to interfere with work experience and on-the-job training. Women remain in inferior positions relative to men in the family, education, work, religion, and interpersonal relationships.

Are women a minority? A **minority** is any category of people who are economically, culturally, and politically disadvantaged. Clearly, women face serious economic disadvantages. However, most White women do not think of themselves as a minority but the evidence suggests that women, as a category, meet the criteria for minority status. White women are represented at every class level, unlike women of color. However, at every class level women have less power, income, and wealth then the men in their respective class. White women appear to be suffering from a form of **false consciousness**.

Cultural power refers to the ability to use culture to protect or enhance your status. A group that has **cultural power** has the ability to control their symbolic representations in the broader culture. Therefore, the cultural representations of women in the mass media can give us a good idea of how much cultural power women actually have. Researchers have analyzed the mass media and found that media promotes gender stereotypes and helps perpetuate gender inequalities. Children's television programming tends to revolve around active male characters with strong leadership and problem solving abilities. Female lead actors are often depicted as manipulative and vindictive.   Although women make up the majority of majors in journalism and communication classes, they represent only 37 percent of newsroom staff, and 25 percent of news directors, and their number is declining. Women's magazines continue to portray women's lives in terms of husbands and lovers. Music videos almost universally portray women in sexualized terms, with strippers, prostitutes, and sluts as common roles for women. Much of the content of music videos is actually violent toward women.

Commercials are highly gender stereotypical. Women are less represented then men and more likely to appear in the household. If the commercial is about travel, finance, driving, or vacationing, male actors predominate. If there is a voice-over, usually you hear the voice of an authoritative male. If the commercial is about cleaning, washing, cooking, using baby products, female actors predominate. The advertising aimed at career women suggests that they should strive to be a super-woman, someone who can cook, clean, change diapers, keep a man sexually satisfied, and bring home a paycheck, simultaneously and happily. How often do you see a television commercial where a man cheerfully strides in from a hard day at the office and starts cooking dinner with a smile on his face? Never. Commercials aimed at working women perpetuate male advantage because they emphasize that even though she has a job certain consumer products will help her fulfill her other roles, housewife and caregiver. There has certainly been progress for women in the media, but overall the mass media reinforces negative stereotypes about women.

Until the passage of the Nineteenth Amendment to the Constitution in 1920, women were not legally allowed to vote in national elections. Think about that. For most of us, our grandmothers were the first women in our families to vote. Today, thousands of women are involved in the political process, which has to be seen as a positive improvement. Nevertheless, at the highest levels of political power women are underrepresented. In the 200-year history of the United States, there has never been a female president or vice president. Only a handful of women have served in the Congress or as state Governors. In 2003, women held 45 percent of the seats in Sweden's parliament. Costa Rica, Canada, Spain, Denmark, and many of our other democratic peers have higher political participation by women than the United States.

ຄ ຕ ຄ ຕ

DEFINITIONS

Acquaintance Rape. Any non-consensual sexual activity between two or more people who know each other.

Androgyny. The combining of masculine and feminine personality traits in a single individual.

Backlash. Have an unexpected and undesired effect.

Biological Perspective. Explanation for gender inequality that stresses innate chromosomal, hormonal, and reproductive differences between women and men.

Clitoridectomy (female circumcision). Refers to a number of procedures performed for cultural, rather than medical, reasons on the female genitalia. It is the partial or total removal of the external part of the clitoris.

Cultural Power. Refers to the ability to use culture to protect or enhance your status.

Dead-End Jobs. Minimum wage jobs, mostly part-time, without health care or retirement benefits. Occupations with low pay and limited advancement possibilities.

Double Jeopardy. Discrimination based on gender and race or ethnicity when it comes to earnings.

False Consciousness.   Any belief, idea, ideology, etc., that interferes with an exploited and oppressed person or group being able to perceive the objective nature and source of their oppression.

Gender Roles Approach. Emphasizes the socialization process, through which individuals come to internalize a set of traits associated with femininity and masculinity.

Gender Segregated. Segregation based on gender.

Gender Structure Approach. Emphasizes the role of social structure in creating differentials of power and opportunities for women and men.

Gender System. System that is designed to produce, through the process of socialization, women and men who have the desired social traits.

Gender. Refers to the social construction of femininity and masculinity.

Gendered Jobs. The idea of women's work and men's work.

Glass Ceiling.   A barrier that tends to keep women in the bottom rungs of the corporate ladder.

Glass Escalator. Males in a female-dominated profession that experience a push upwards in the profession because of their gender.

Institutional Discrimination. Refers to the ways in which the normal operation of institutions is systematically biased to favor the affluent and disadvantage the poor.

Institutional Sexism. The collective failure of an organization to provide an appropriate and professional service to people because of their gender. It can be seen or detected in processes, attitudes and behavior which amount to discrimination through unwitting prejudice, ignorance, thoughtlessness and sexist stereotyping, which disadvantage and discriminate against women.

Minority.   Any category of people who are economically, culturally, and politically disadvantaged.

Patriarchy. A social system in which men are the dominant group and occupy positions of power over women. The subordination of women to men. Male dominance in society and the family.

Pay Gap.   Refers to the discrepancy between average earnings of women and men.

Principle of Propinquity (nearness of time and place). We tend to care most for those with whom we spend the most time.

Principle of Similarity. The tendency to be around those with whom we share common characteristics.

Second-Shift. The "other" job gainfully employed wives and mothers have in the home, doing the bulk of household tasks.

Segmented Labor Market. A two-tiered occupational structure that is highly gendered. The lower tier is composed of low paying dead-end jobs in the service economy. The upper tier of high paying jobs is reserved for men.

Sex. Refers to the biological differences between women and men.

Sexism. The belief that women and men have different capacities and potentials as the result of innate biological differences.

Sexual Harassment. Refers to unwanted sexual attention in the workplace or school.

Social Rewards. Benefits, such as status, esteem, and prestige, resulting from some action construed by societal norms as acceptable. This can include health care, income, housing, nutrition, savings, and material goods.

Weaker Sex. The belief that women are naturally weaker than men and unable to perform work requiring muscular or intellectual development. In most preindustrial societies, for example, domestic chores were relegated to women, leaving "heavier" labor such as hunting and plowing to men. This ignored the fact that caring for children and doing such tasks as milking cows and washing clothes also required heavy, sustained labor. However, physiological tests now suggest that women have a greater tolerance for pain, and statistics reveal that women live longer and are more resistant to many diseases. *(Excerpted from Compton's Interactive Encyclopedia, Copyright (c) 1994, 1995 Compton's NewMedia, Inc.)*

Workplace Segregation. Occurs when there is a concentration of specific types of jobs stereotyped as "male" and "female" occupations.

REFERENCES

Academe. 2001. *Bulletin of the American Association of University Professors* 87 (March/April).

Acker, Joan. 1992. "Gendered Institutions: From Sex Roles to Gendered Institutions." *Contemporary Sociology* 21 (September):565-568.

American Association of University Women. 1992. "How Schools Shortchange Girls." Executive Summary. *AAUW Report.* Washington, DC: American Association of University Women Educational Foundation.

American Council on Education. 2000. "ACE Study Shows Gains in Number of Women College Presidents, Smaller Gains for Minority CEOs." Available online: http://www.acent.edu/news/press-release.

Amott, Teresa. 1993. *Caught in the Crisis: Women and the U.S. Economy Today.* New York: Monthly Review Press.

Andersen, Margaret L. and Patricia Hill Collins (eds.) 2001. *Race, Class, and Gender: An Anthology.* 4th ed. Belmont, CA: Wadsworth.

Anderson, Margaret L. 2003. *Thinking about Women.* 5th ed. Boston, MA: Allyn and Bacon.

Ando, Faith H. 1990. "Women in Business." Pp. 222-230 in *The American Woman: A status Report 1990-91*, edited by Sara E. Rix. New York: Norton.

Baca Zinn, Maxine and Bonnie Thornton Dill. 1994. "Difference and Domination." Pp. 3-12 in *Women of Color in U.S. Society*, edited by Maxine Baca Zinn and Bonnie Thornton Dill. Philadelphia, PA: Temple University Press.

Baca Zinn, Maxine, Pierrette Hondagnew-Sotelo, and Michael A. Messner. 2000. *Gender through the Prism of Difference*. Boston, MA: Allyn and Bacon.

Baca Zinn, Maxine. 1990. "Family, Feminism and Race in America." *Gender and Society* 14 (March):62-68.

Balswick, Jack and Charles Peck. 1971. "The Inexpressive Male: A Tragedy of American Society." *Family Coordinator* 20:363-368.

Balswick, Jack, with James Lincoln Collier. 1976. "Why Husbands Can't Say 'I Love You.'" Pp. 58-59 in *The Forty-Nine Percent Majory*, edited by Deborah S. David and Robert Brannon. Reading, MA: Addison-Wesley.

Bannon, Lisa. 2000. "Gender-Specific Toy Marketing Irks Some." *Wall Street Journal*, February 17, 7D.

Basow, Susan. 1996. "Gender Stereotypes and Roles." Pp. 81-96 in *The Meaning of Difference*, edited by Karen E. Rosenblum and Toni-Michelle Travis. New York: McGraw-Hill.

Beeghley, Leonard. 2005. *The Structure of Stratification in the United Sates*. 4th ed. Boston, MA: Allyn and Bacon.

Bellas, Marcia L. 1994. "Comparable Worth In Academia: The Effects on Faculty Salaries of the Sex Composition and Labor-Market Conditions of Academic Disciplines. *American Sociological Review* 59(6) (December):807-821.

Benokraitis, Nijole and Joe R. Feagin. 1995. *Modern Sexism*. 2nd ed. Upper Saddle River, NJ: Prentice-Hall.

Berk, Laura. 1989. *Child Development*. Newton, MA: Allyn and Bacon.

Bernard, Jessie. 1981. *The Female World*. New York: Free Press.

Bernard, Larry Craig. "Multivariate Analysis of new Sex Role Formulations and Personality." *Journal of Personality and Social Psychology* 38(2) (February):323-336.

Bernstein, Aaron. 2004. "Women's Pay: Why the Gap Remains a Chasm." *Business Week*, June 14, pp. 58-59.

Bianchi, Suzanne M. and Daphne Spain. 1996. "Women, Work, and Family in America." *Population Bulletin* 52(3) (December).

Bianchi, Suzanne M., L. Bubaiya, and J. R. Kahn. 1999. "The Gender Gap in the Economic Well-Being of Nonresident Fathers and Custodial Mothers." *Demography* 36:195-203.

Boyle, D. Ellen, Nancy L. Marshall, and Wendy W. Robeson. 2003. "Gender at Play: Forth-Grade Girls and boys on the Playground." *The American Behavioral Scientist* 46(10):1326-1345.

Bureau of Labor Statistics. 2004. "Employment Situation Summary: May 2004." Online. Available: http://bls.gov/news.release/pdf/empsit.pdf.

Burt, Keith B. and Jacqueline Scott. 2002. "Parents and Adolescent Gender role Attitudes in 1990s Great Britain," *Sex Roles* 46(7/8):239-245.

Cahill, Spencer E. 1983. "Reexamining the Acquisition of Sex Roles: A Social Interactionist Perspective." *Sex Roles* 9 (January):1-15.

Campenni, C. Estelle. 1999. "Gender Stereotyping of Children's Toys: A Comparison of Parents and Nonparents." *Sex Roles* 40(1/2):121-138.

Chaftez, Janet Saltzman. 1997. "Feminist Theory and Sociology: Underutilized Contributions for Mainstream Theory." *Annual Review of Sociology* 23:97-120.

Charles, Maria. 1992. "Cross-National Variation in Occupation segregation." *American Sociological Review* 57(4) (August):483-502.

Cohen, Lloyd R. 1991. "Sexual Harassment and the Law." *Society* 28(4) (May/June):8-13.

Courtney, Alice E. and Thomas W. Whipple. 1983. *Sex Stereotyping in Advertising*. Lexington, MA: DC Heath.

Cowan, Carolyn Pope. 2002. *When Partners Become Parents*. New York: Basic Books.

Crabb, Peter and Dawn Bielawski. 1994. "The Social Representation of Material Culture and Gender in Children's Books," *Sex Roles* 30(1/2):69-79.

David, Deborah S. and Robert Brannon. 1980. "The Male Sex Role." In *Family in Transition*. 3rd ed., edited by Arlene S. Skolnick and Jerome H. Skolnick. Boston, MA: Little, Brown.

Davis, Donald M. 1993. Cited in "T.V. Is a Blond, Blonde World." *American Demographics*, special issue: Women Change Places. Ithaca, NY.

Dubeck, Paula J. and Dana Dunn (eds.). 2002. *Workplace/Women's Place: An Anthology*. Los Angles, CA: Roxbury.

Dunayer, Joan. 1995. "Sexist Words, Speciest Roots." In Carol J. Adams and Josephine Donovan (eds.), *Animals and Women: Feminist Theoretical Exploration*. Durham, NC: Duke University Press.

Dunn, Dana. 1996. "Gender and Earnings." Pp. 61-63 in *Women and Work: A Handbook*, edited by Paula J. Dubeck and Kathryn Borman. New York: Garland.

Dwyer, Jeffery W. and Karen Seccombe. 1991. "Elder Care AS Family Labor: The Influence of Gender and Family Position." *Journal of Family Issues* 12(2) (June):229-247.

Edwards, Renee and Mark A. Hamilton. 2004. "You Need to Understand My Gender Role: An Empirical Test of Tannen's Model of Gender and Communication." *Sex Roles* 50(7/8):491-504.

Ehrenreich, Barbara. 1983. *The Hearts of Men: American Dreams and the Flight from Commitment*. Garden City, NY: Anchor Books.

Eisenstein, Zillah. 1979. "Developing a Theory of Capitalist Patriarchy and Socialist Feminism." Pp. 5-40 in *Capitalist Patriarchy and the Case for Socialist Feminism*, edited by Zillah Eisenstein. New York: Monthly Review Press.

England, Paula. 1992. *Comparable Worth: Theories and Evidence*. Hawthorne, NY: Aldine.

Evans, Lorraine and Kimberly Davies. 2000. "No Sissy Boys Here: A Content Analysis of the Representation of Masculinity in Elementary School Reading Textbooks." *Sex Roles* 42(3-4):255-270.

Faust-Sterling, Anne. 1992. *Myths of Gender: Biological Theories about Women and Men*. New York: Basic Books.

Folbre, Nancy. 1985. "The Pauperization of Motherhood: Patriarchy and Social Policy in the U.S." *Review of Radical Political Economics* 16(4).

French, Marilyn. 1985. *Beyond Power: On Women, Men, and Morals*. New York: Summit Books.

Fuchs, Victor R. 1986. "Sex Differences in Economic Well-Being." *Science* 232 (April 25):459-464.

Garrahy, Deborah A. 2001. "Three Third-Grade Teachers' Gender-Related Beliefs and Behavior." *The Elementary School Journal* 102(1):81-94.

Giele, Janet Z. 1988. "Gender and Sex Roles." Pp. 291-323in *Handbook of Sociology*, edited by Neil J. Smelser. Newbury Park, CA: Sage.

Gilligan, Carol. 1982. *In a Different Voice: Psychological Theory and Women's Development*. Cambridge, MA: Harvard University Press.

Goffman, Erving 1974. *Gender Advertisements*. New York: Harper and Row.

Hacker, Helen Mayer. 1951. "Women as a Minority Group." *Social Forces* 30 (October):60-69.

Hanna, Annett and Tamar Murchaver. 1999. "Gender and Conversational Style as Predictors of Conversational Behavior." *Journal of Language and Social Psychology* 18(2):153-174.

Heath, Julia A. and W. David Bourne. 1995. "Husbands and Housework: Parity or Parody?" *Social Science Quarterly* 76(1) (March):195-202.

Hedges, Larry V. and Amy Nowell. 1995. "Sex Differences in Mental Test Scores, Variability, and Numbers of High-scoring Individuals" *Science* 269(5220) (July 7):41-46.

Henle, Robert J. 1994. "The Role of Women in Catholic Parish Life." *American* 171 (September):6-7.

Hurst, Charles E. 1995. *Social Inequality: Forms, Causes, and Consequences*. New York: Allyn and Bacon.

Hyde, Janet S., Elizabeth Fennema, and Susan Lamon. 1990. "Gender Differences in Mathematics Performance: A Meta-analysis." *Psychological Bulletin* 106:139-155.

Idle, Tracey, Eileen Wood, and Serge Desmarias. 1993. "Gender Role Socialization in Toy Play Situations: Mothers and Fathers with Their Sons and Daughters." *Sex Roles* 28(11/12):679-691.

Kanter, Rosabeth Moss. 1977. *Men and Women of the Corporation*. New York: Basic Books.

Kessler, Ronald C. and Jane McLeod. 1984. "Sex Differences in Vulnerability to Undesirable Life Events." *American Sociological Review* 49 (October):620-631.

Kimmel, Michael S. and Michael A. Messner (eds.) 2004. *Men's Lives*, 6th ed., Boston, MA: Allyn and Bacon.

Kimmel, Michael. 1992. "Reading Men, Masculinity, and Publishing." *Contemporary Sociology* 21 (March):162-171.

Kimmel, Michael. 2004. *The Gendered Society*. 2nd ed. New York: Oxford University Press.

Krueger, Alan B. 2002. "The Apple Falls Close to the Tree, Even in the Land of Opportunity." *New York Times*, November 14.

Landers, Rene M. 1990. "Gender, Race, and the State Courts." *Radcliffe Quarterly* 76(4) (December):6-9.

Lauer, Nancy Cook. 2002. "Studies Show Women's Role in Media Shrinking." Online: Available: http://www.equality2020.org/media.htm.

Lengermann, Patricia Madoo, and Ruth A. Wallace. 1985. *Gender in America: Social Control and Social Change*. Englewood Cliffs, NJ: Prentice Hall.

Lever, Janet. 1976. "Sex Differences in the Games Children Play." *Social Problems* 23 (April):478-487.

Lorber, Judith. 1994. *Paradoxes of Gender*. New Haven, CT: Yale University Press.

Love, Alice Ann. 1998. "Gender Wage Gap Shrinks Slightly." *USA Today*, June 10, 1A.

Loy, Pamela Hewitt and Lea P. Stewart. 1984. "The Extent and Effects of Sexual Harassment of Working Women." *Sociological Focus* 17(1) (January):31-43.

Marini, Margaret. 1989. "Sex Differences in Earnings in the United States." *Annual Review of Sociology* 15:343-380.

McAdoo, John. 1988. "Changing Perspectives on the Role of the Black Father." Pp.79-92 in *Fatherhood Today, Men's Changing Role in the Family*, edited by P. Bronstein and C. P. Cowan. New York: Wiley.

McGeorge, Erina L., Angela R. Graves, Bo Feng, Seth J. Gillihan, and Brant R. Burleson. 2004. "The Myth of Gender Cultures: Similarities Outweigh Differences in men's and Women's Provision of and Responses to Supportive Communication." *Sex Roles* 50(3/4):143-175.

Messner, Michael A. 1992. *Power at Play: Sports and the Problem of Masculinity*. Boston, MA: Beacon.

Messner, Michael A. 1996. "Studying Up on Sex." *Sociology of Sport Journal* 12:221-237.

Nardi, Peter. 1992. *Men's Friendships: Research on Men and Masculinities*. Newbury Park, CA: Sage.

National Organization for Women. 2002. Watch Out, Listen Up! *Feminist Primetime Report*. Washington, DC: National Organization for Women.

Nilges, Lynda M. and Albert F. Spencer. 2002. "The Pictorial Representation in Notable Children's Books: 1995-1999." *Sex Roles* 45(1/2):89-101.

O'Hare, William P. and Jan Larson. 1991. "Women in Business: Where, What, and Why." *American Demographics* 13(7) (July):34-38.

O'Kelly, Charlotte. 1980. *Women and Men in Society*. New York: Van Nostrand.

Orenstein, Peggy. 1994. *School Girls: Young Women, Self-Esteem, and the Confidence Gap*. New York: Doubleday.

Ortner, Sherry B. 1974. "Is Female to Male as Nature Is to Culture?" pp. 66-68 in *Woman, Culture, and Society*, edited by Michelle Zimbalist Rosaldo and Louise Lamphere. Stanford, CA: Stanford University Press.

Oskamp, Stuart, Karen Kaufman, and Lianna Atchison Wolterbeek. 1996. "Gender Role Portrayal in Preschool Books," *Journal of Social Behavior and Personality* 11(5):27-39.

Paul, Eileen Frankel. 1991. "Bared Buttocks and Federal Cases." *Society* 28(4) (May-June):4-7.

Pearce, Diana. 1978. "The Feminization of Poverty: Women, Work, and Welfare." *Urban Change Review* 2 (February):24-36.

Pleck, Joseph H. 1981. "Prisoners of Manliness. " *Psychology Today* 15 (September):68-83.

Reskin, Barbara F. and Patricia A. Roos. 1990. "Jobs Queues, Gender Queues: Explaining Women's Inroad into Male Occupations." Philadelphia, PA: Temple University Press.

Richmond-Abbott, Marie. 1992. *Masculine and Feminine: Sex roles Over the Life Cycle*, 2nd ed. New York: McGraw-Hill.

Ridgeway, Cecilia L. and Lynn Smith-Lovin. 1999. "The Gender System and Interaction." *Annual Review of Sociology* 25:191-216.

Risman, Barbara J. 1998. *Gender Vertigo: American Families in Transition*. New Haven, CT: Yale University Press.

Robinson, J. Gregg and Judith McIlwee. 1989. "Women in Engineering: A Promise Unfulfilled." *Social Problems* 36:455-472.

Rogers, Susan Carol. 1978. "Woman's Place: A Critical Review of Anthropological Theory." *Comparative Studies in Society and History* 20(1):123-162.

Romaine, Suzanne. 1999. *Communicating Gender*. Mahwah, NJ: Erlbaum.

Rosaldo, Michelle Zimbalist. 1974. "Women, Culture, and Society: A Theoretical Overview." Pp 389-417 in *Woman, Culture, and Society*, edited by Michelle Zimbalist Rosaldo and L. Lamphere. Stanford, CA: Stanford University Press.

Sacks, Karen. 1974. "Engels Revisited: Women, the Organization of Production, and Private Property." Pp. 207-222 in *Woman, Culture, and Society*, edited by Michelle Zimbalist Rosaldo and Louise Lamphere. Stanford, CA: Stanford University Press.

Schapiro, Mark. 1994. "The Fine Art of Sexual Harassment." *Harper's Magazine*, July, pp. 62-63.

Shapiro, Judith. 1981. "Anthropology and the Study of Gender." Pp. 110-129 in *A Feminist Perspective in the Academy*, edited by Elizabeth Langland and Walter Gove. Chicago, IL: University of Chicago Press.

Shelton, Beth Anne. 1992. *Women, Men and Time*. New York: Greenwood Press.

Sklar, Holly. 2004. "Break That Glass Ceiling." *Progressive Populist* (June 15): 16.

Spencer, Porche and E. Toleman. 2003. "We've Come a Long Way – Maybe: New Challenges for Gender Equity in Education." *Teachers College Record* 105(9):1774-1807.

Stack, Carol B. 1990. "Different Voices, Different Visions: Gender, Culture, and Moral Reasoning." Pp. 19-27 in *Uncertain Terms: Negotiation Gender in American Culture*, edited by Faye Ginsburg and Anna Lowenhapt Tsing. Boston, MA: Beacon Press.

Tanner, Deborah. 1994. *Talking from 9 to 5: How Women's and Men's Conversational Styles Affect Who Gets Heard, Who Gets Credit, and What Gets Done At Work*. New York: William Morrow and Co., Inc.

Thompson, Linda and Alexis Walker. 1989. "Gender in Families." *Journal of Marriage and Family* 51:845-871.

Thorne, Barrie. 1993. *Gender, Play: Girls and Boys in School*. New Brunswick, NJ: Rutgers University Press.

United States Department of Labor, Bureau of Labor Statistics. 2004. *Women in the Labor Force: A Databook*. Washington, DC: Division of Labor Statistics.

United States Department of Labor, Women's Bureau, 1997a. *Nontraditional Occupations for Employed Women in 1997*. Washington, DC: United States Government Printing Office.

United States Department of Labor, Women's Bureau, 1997b. *20 Leading Occupations of Employed Women*. Washington, DC: United States Government Printing Office.

Valian, Virginia. 1998. "Running in Place." *Sciences* 38 (January/February):18-23.

Wagner, David G., Rebecca S. Ford, and Thomas W. Ford. 1986. "Can Gender Inequalities Be Reduced." *American Sociological*

Review 51 (February):47-61.

Waldfogel, Jane. "The Effects of Children on Women's Wages." *American Sociological Review* 62(2) (April):209-217.

West, Candace and Don Zimmerman. 1987. "Doing Gender." *Gender and Society* 1:1125-151.

Witt, Susan. 1997. "Parental Influence on Children's Socialization to Gender Roles." *Adolescence* 32(126):253-259.

19 | Social Change and Social Order: Is Any Sense to be Made in a [Too] Rapidly Changing World?
by Lawrence J. Mencotti, Ph.D.

Sociologists, as a whole, are bipartisan in their view of the world. On their personal side they lean toward political liberalism. However, on their professional side they have an abiding interest in traditional conservative concerns: social order and how it is maintained in the face of social change.

Let us begin with social change and then return to the problem of social order. Social change is an amorphous topic. To many ancient eastern and western sages it could mean that all is flux. It could also mean to more earthy folksy philosophers such as Yogi Berra that "the past ain't what it used to be."

Attempts at humor aside the types and numbers of explanations of social change are many in number and varied in type. Let us just state that the pace, direction, and breadth of change increasingly encompasses the globe. In the last 125 years or so: we have seen the invention, introduction, refinement, and widespread adoption of the telephone, automobile, airplane, radio, antibiotics, immunizations, television, computer, and cell phone to name some of the more important ones. Let us take just one of them and look at it briefly. In the early 1990s the worldwide web was a novelty to most people if they thought of it at all. Today, a great many people do not just use it but rely upon it for both their professional and personal lives. Further, think how quickly it has been adopted and how pervasive its effects have been and all in a span of about 15 years. Think about living your life without it. Now go back to the others listed earlier in this paragraph and think about living your life without all of those.

In a more general fashion, our evolution undoubtedly wired us for life in small face-to-face groups with in-group/out-group as the basic principle of social organization. In this evolutionary setting all of our senses came into play. Seen from this perspective technology undercuts our biological heritage while it serves as a graphic reminder that technology is one of our most distinctive inventions as humans. However, with our technologies threatening to overwhelm our biological heritage one human reaction has been to try and use technology to reestablish connection with our evolutionary heritage. The pseudo intimacy of TV and internet chatrooms are examples of this.

More importantly, there is the rapidly expanding strategy of manipulating "human nature." Joel Garreau argues in **Radical Evolution** that we are at an "inflection point" where current and near future advances in genetics, robotics, information and nanotechnologies are altering ourselves, how we think of our selves, and thus eventually our societies. If in spite of our tremendous reliance on psychotherapy, religion, and shopping which all have promised but failed to provide so many of us with a satisfaction let alone an authenticity so many of us crave then perhaps bio-intervention into our very beings might lead us to the long awaited utopia. Alternatively, such intervention might deliver us to a hell which would make contemporary society seem like the good old days.

Globalization as the Integration of Societies. If money is what makes the world go round then global financial markets make the idea of an autonomous society a chimera. If oil is the lifeblood of modern society then dependence upon foreign oil reserves also puts to rest the idea of an autonomous society. Further, the outsourcing of jobs illustrates the interconnectedness of societies and thus the transnational inputs of achieving domestic social order. Put another way, the problem of social order for a particular society is no longer strictly internal to that particular society. Not only are the events of 9/11 sufficient to bring home the globalization of terror so is the more mundane but no less noteworthy outsourcing of jobs.

In **The World is Flat**, Thomas Friedman explores the wide-ranging reach of the world-transforming process which we call globalization. Actually, globalization is something of a misnomer since it is not so much a single process as a series of developments acting simultaneously and not always in the same manner or same direction. Globalization is the ongoing net result of these developments. Friedman illustrates the flattening of the globe by citing former face-to-face encounters that now take place hundreds or thousands of miles away but have the same qualitative effect on our lives. For example, "chances are good that Bhavya in Bangalore will read your next x-ray," or as Thomas Friedman learned first hand, "Grandma Betty in her bathrobe will make your Jet Blue plane reservation from her Salt Lake City home." Friedman argues new technologies [especially the 'Net] enable people from literally all over the globe to participate in an integrated cyber-economy that is literally transforming how we live our lives. The more important "flatteners" include the rise of supply chaining, offshoring, outsourcing, and insourcing. The rise of a world connected by fiber optic cable [and increasingly becoming wireless] along with the emergence of three hugely populous countries: Russia, India, and China in a 'Net integrated world have converged to connect us all, quite thoroughly, whether we want to be connected or not. Though Friedman has his critics he is on to something and we have the good fortune that he has acutely analyzed this phenomenon while it is transforming our lives.

With globalization comes a reluctant acknowledgment that in a rapidly shrinking world the effects of one's actions are increasingly felt beyond the doers' space and time. No better symbol of the downside of globalization can be found than global warming. In turn, global warming is not just symbolic of how normal climate changes can be intensified by human inputs. It is also symptomatic of a world in which for the foreseeable future population growth will continue apace and consumer expectations of formerly Third World societies [e.g., China and India—each with a population of at least one billion!] will rise even faster. These trends do not bode well for Mother Earth. Choices must be made and even if the choices are the correct ones a painful future for many if not most of the world's inhabitants seems guaranteed.

Of course, from a sociological point of view the worst-case scenario is when an entire society passes into oblivion—however it may die. What Jared Diamond does in **Collapse: How Societies Choose to Fail or Succeed** is to examine a variety of case studies in which some societies "go under" [e.g., Easter Island, Anasazi, the Lowland Maya, Angkor Wat] while others [New Guinea Highlands, Tokugawa Japan, Tikopia] do not. Especially when read in conjunction with Friedman's work one thought jumps out: no one [no individual nor society] can go it alone. Like it or not, we are in this global society together. The irony of this, of course, is that the world's remaining superpower running massive deficits while hocking its future to pay for its profligate spending habits still is saddled with an ideology of being "first and foremost." Not daring to face up to the implications of our own domestic policies our leaders prefer to posture and pose. While their base constituencies become more shrill the rest of the citizens of the country [and of the world] wait for some responsible leadership. Whether it is even possible to make the correct choices for a flourishing future is anyone's guess. If it is possible, whether we will make the correct choices is also problematic.

Social Order and *THE* Social Order. Please think of this question: with the pace, breadth, and depth of profound social change sweeping the global how, in the midst of all of this social swirl

473

and flux, is society possible? This is another way of addressing the fundamental problem of sociology: how is social order maintained?

Now there are at least two meanings to social order that concern us. The first emphasizes order in social settings. Order in the classroom is the major prerequisite if any learning is to be accomplished. If chaos in the classroom is the rule of the day not much that passes for knowledge will be acquired. So, social order refers to group encounters in which deviance and social control are prime concerns. However, *THE* social order is a problem of macro sociology.   If society is to exist then the most basic prerequisite is to maintain order among its constituent units as whole; or, at least among a sufficient number that the overall functioning of a society is made possible. In turn, this means strong viable institutions that will accomplish all of the tasks necessary for social life. The alternatives to social order: anarchy, civil war, and so on are terrifying enough when experienced in books and movies; in real life they are truly horrific as the recent examples of Darfur and Iraq testify.

Traditionally, the problem of social order has been seen primarily as an endogenous problem—that is, a problem internal to a particular society and even when its proximate cause is a foreign invasion as with Iraq it is still a problem **in** Iraq.

Maintaining the social order is imperative under any circumstance and one problem any society faces is: what to do with deviants who are perceived as threats. This has already been addressed in the essay on deviance and social control so we will only touch on it briefly here.

From a Durkheimian perspective the labeling and isolation of serious deviants "sends a message" to all deviants as well as to all of the righteous citizens who now realize the terrible consequences that befall those who screw up and are caught. Mead would agree with Durkheim that deviance functions by reinforcing solidarity among straight citizens and taking his perspective we would also emphasize that by successfully internalizing society's standards people, in a sense, are inoculated against the temptations of deviance. From a deterrence theory perspective those who are most deterred from committing a crime are those who are already righteous.   Those whom society thinks are most in "need" of deterrence are those folks already committed to deviance or crime and thus are exactly the ones who are least likely to be deterred. Ironically then deterrence works best on those who need it the least and vice-versa.

Virtue may be its own reward but very often the righteous need affirmation that their foregoing of the pleasures of deviance has been worthwhile. What better way than to tsk-tsk at the heinous violations of the offenders. In other words, the righteous need their righteousness to be reaffirmed by the public display of criminals being caught and punished. However, in a society such as ours with 300 million citizens everyone going down to the town square and hurling insults, if not objects, at the malefactors is simply not feasible.

As befitting a mass society the mass media ride in for the rescue. The criminal justice drama—detecting, investigating, pursuing, capturing, and ultimately punishing the criminal—is far more effective [and exciting] on television, in the movies, or with detective novels than in real life. Perhaps the righteous need the reassurance from mass entertainment of an effective criminal justice system since the real life counterpart is usually at once removed from everyday life and also seen to be no where near 100 percent effective.

The above developed example leads us to an important consideration. What kinds of social mechanisms and policies are to be pursued in a quest for a reasonable and just social order. As Thomas Sowell so brilliantly demonstrates in **A Conflict of Visions**: there is a "constrained" vision which sees human nature as selfish and unchanging and there is an "unconstrained" vision which emphasizes change and perfectibility. While these competing visions are currently [and have been for centuries] animating humans' hopes [and fears] and have thus impacted how private lives and public policies have been managed it is beyond the goals of this text to directly analyze moral ideologies for their truth or falsity. However, we can look at how social mechanisms do function within a social system especially in relation to how social order is maintained.

Now, we know that America is a land of tremendous diversity and individuality so a likely starting point is to ask: with all of these differences what are the commonalities? Well, we mostly speak varieties of English but then the same can be said for Canadians, the Irish, and the English. We reside within the boundaries of the United States but Iraqis reside within the boundaries of Iraq and so merely residing within common borders does not mean that a social order is guaranteed. We do participate in political processes but many fewer than two-thirds ($^2/_3$) of us bother to vote in national elections.

475

So what else? Well, as a nation we like sports but perhaps not any more than other peoples. As a whole we see ourselves as a religious people but even within the major religious orientation there is such diversity and differences in theology and practice that it is difficult to maintain that there is a religious tradition that binds us together. Though in the piece of religion we did discuss Bellah's "civil religion" that does give us something in common but it is not traditional religion which, in any case, is decreasingly civil the more it enters the political arena.

What else? We do like to shop. So, can we say that we have in common sports, salvation, and shopping? Well, that might strike you as hyperbole but all three do occupy the time and energy of a great plentitude of Americans and all are examples of what sociologists call tension-management: ways of dealing with stress, conflict, and frustrations of life that are especially important to America at the beginning of the twenty-first century. In addition, all three provide acceptable outlets for social regression [i.e., denying the implications of massive social change and seeking instead palatable diversions].

Let us look at this a bit more closely. **Tension-Management** refers to those mechanisms that socially sublimate frustrations into acceptable channels. Tension-management is prevention through distraction. Think of the old phrase: "idle hands are the devil's workshop." Tension-management are the ways we take people's time, energy, and attention and put them to uses that benefit the system [and coincidentally those who benefit from the system]. This is not about just allowing citizens to blow off steam a few times a year [e.g., Mardi Gras, Carnival, Fasching, New Year's Eve, Homecoming, etc.]. The need for tension-management is ongoing and from a system standpoint the more pervasive and effective the tension-management the better.

We have already analyzed one major tension-manager: religion and that need not detain us for long except to say that the repentant sinner maintaining his/her firm belief that all are equal in the sight of God knows that though this life is a constant struggle the next life will bring peace and contentment.   However, if that was all that was necessary to channel [and explain away] frustrations then there would be no need in our society for mass consumerism and its handmaiden: mass entertainment.

Now it is time for a sweeping generalization: there is so much need for continuing tension-management because the system itself continually creates the conditions for the most corrosive of the seven deadly sins: **envy**. To review, to be jealous is to fear of losing what we already possess while envy is the ill-feeling of wanting what we do not have. As Scheler has pointed out pure envy combines covetousness with impotence: you desperately want something you cannot possess. Envy is also closely related to some other distasteful phenomena. For example, envy is often found with contempt: you may envy your 'betters' and what they have or what they are but you hold in contempt those whom you consider to be your inferiors.   Envy is also to be found with *schadenfreude* [the malicious joy one feels when something bad happens to others]. As fascinating as these variables are [and for a full exposition see Helmut Schoeck] we will not spend much time with them.

As Lyman points out envy arises from an asocial solidarity where people are bound together by asymmetrical scarcity. In plain English this means that you and I are bound together when you possess what I do not and I want it. When this occurs typical responses on my part include to attack/belittle/deprive/steal the object of my envy.

All in all, we can say that envy does not seem to be much of a way to run a social system but, in fact, what our consumer capitalist society does is to harness envy for a greater "good." It institutionalizes envy and then sublimates it into acceptable channels. It does so we will argue by arousing envy and then at least pretending to resolve it via consumerism. Now how does consumer capitalism do this?

Envy is an ugly state and one we are loathe to admit to experiencing. So in a consumer society to keep the system running as smoothly [and as profitably] as possible direct appeals to envy are rare. Rather resentment at relative deprivation is more subtly pitched [the entire field of marketing and advertising] by arousing envy without calling it such. What the media pitchmen [and women] do is to call out a supposed need [something you lack entirely or else have a much inferior example of] and then tell you that by purchasing such-and-such you will become better, healthier, sexier, whatever needs to be said to get you to buy.

Well, consumer capitalism depends on advertising to create and sustain an endless stream of "needs" to be met [temporarily] by endless purchases of goods, services, experiences, etc. In so doing **consumer capitalism unbinds envy from scarcity and harnesses it with plentitude**. That is, it moves away from a you-win and I-lose situation to a we-all-can-win situation. This can only be accomplished however by ensuring an endless supply of goodies to be purchased and an endless number of purchases of goodies.

The other side of this is that we are forever rendered to a situation where the old is seen as inferior to the new. This is a perpetual state of consumer dissatisfaction and to the extent that our self-concept derives from what we buy—purchases as status markers—then **anomie**, in the sense of shifting norms and standards, becomes endemic to the social system.

The New Tribalism. Why do people pay for clothes [other consumer goods qualify as well] that have manufacturers' ID emblazoned on the item? In many instances, the identifying trademark is accompanied by a markup in price. The consumer, in effect pays a premium to become a walking ad for the corporation. Just what is in it for the consumer? One possibility is that the corporate logo becomes an emblem which allows the bearer to be a transitory member of some arbitrary clan [populated by mostly strangers] which, at least in one area, shares an affiliation with you. As befitting a mass consuming, mass mediated, mass society group membership is no longer just among people that you know face-to-face; rather this "brand membership" illustrates a membership among [mostly] strangers in a kind of one-dimensional affiliation.

A prominent [and fairly expensive] example of this would be those who sport the jackets of their favorite high school, college, or professional athletic team. Wearing it, especially after a victory, is a validation of one's worthiness for identifying with a winner. Wearing the garb and rooting for the team it represents illustrates that one is a member in good standing of this particular kind of tribe.

Note that in the case of professional sports teams [other fan-based groups include those that might organize around rock groups, motorcycles, and automobiles] and certainly with particular kinds of consumable goods one is pledging allegiance to an organization whose primary reason for being is to make money. In effect, you give them money plus whatever time and energy it takes to be a fan and they give you the opportunity to be, along with countless others, a fan. While the identification with a particular team can bring a great [though fleeting] satisfaction what is especially important to note is the significance of this kind of affiliation. Unlike family membership one can unilaterally withdraw from this new tribe with a lot less psychic cost than disowning your family and with a lot less monetary disruption than divorcing your spouse. What we have is designer

478

group membership in addition to disposable group membership. What we also have is evidence that traditional [gemeinschaaft] modes of grounding one's identity are either obsolete or at the very least insufficient to the task.

To consume for its own sake; that is to buy for the sake of buying is a manifestation of a compulsion. But to enter the race of consuming to keep up with reference groups has as its logical conclusion just such compulsive behavior. Many people who have the means to consume at more rarified levels do so not needing to keep up but rather to distance themselves from their inferiors. As such they are not followers but pacesetters. They practice what the great iconoclast Veblen once called **conspicuous consumption**. They "overbuy" in wasteful examples of competitive display. The bling of many pro athletes and their $60,000 Rolex watches would be one such blatant example. The purchase of McMansions by empty nest couples [each evidently needing their own separate suite of rooms] would be another.

The New Tribalism [and its mass consumer roots] reaches its most developed form with commercial television perhaps the most pervasive form of entertainment extant in modern society [though surfing the 'Net seems to be catching up].

As with capitalism as a whole television works on the principle of arousing envy which is to be satisfied [temporarily] by some purchase of a consumable good or service. Commercial television programs [be they, news, sports, weather, sitcoms, reality programs, whatever] function as audience-collectors by broadcasting programs in the hope of attracting huge audiences. These audiences are exposed to a variety of ads in the hopes that an unknown but hopefully very large number will buy what is advertised. From this view the programs are the means and exposure to ads are the goals of television. As Mander so succinctly put it: advertising is the delivery system of capitalism and television is the delivery system of advertising.

From a system standpoint endless shopping and endless television viewing are perfect ways for citizens to continue to behave. You may agree with this writer that perhaps dysfunction is a more apt term but still the system does chug along and most people do not want out of it. Rather, they want to increase their share. If this be slavery then it is voluntary servitude.

In any case, the system operates by linking envy with greed and consumption thus making people continually anxious about their place and identity in a constantly changing world. These are distractions to help assuage a citizenry that can best be described as Durkheim did long ago: chronically anomic.

A Note on Force and Fraud. From a system's standpoint well-behaved, productive, [and more importantly] hyper-consuming citizens are the ideal. However, if the standard measures of maintaining social order are seen as insufficient by the powers that be then more direct measures can be enacted. Drawing upon the above discussion there is a mutual accommodation between television news and politics. Each is made for each other as each makes each other. Television uses its news programs—heavily laced with politics—to collect audiences [each news program comes with the standard advertising fare of pain relievers] while the political system attempts to use the news exposure to put the best possible spin [propaganda] on their particular issue. The elements of fraud should be obvious to all. In fact, the neglected sociologist Gustav Ichheiser once posited that the two major ways in which those in power keep themselves in power [and thus maintain the social order] are by force and fraud. He termed the subjects of these techniques as being fearful of gangsters and fearful of swindlers. The mere idea of governments and corporations separately or colluding to perpetrate such crimes against their citizens was unfortunately well represented by such totalitarian states as Hitler's Germany, Stalin's Russia, and Mao's China. It goes without saying that in a free, open, and responsible democracy such as that of the contemporary United States such crimes are unthinkable and thus do not exist and cannot exist.

ಬಿ ಛ ಬಿ ಛ

DEFINITIONS

Anomie.   A condition characterized by the absence or confusion of social norms or values in a society or group. According to Martindale, anomie is the "strict counterpart of the idea of social solidarity. Just as social solidarity is a state of collective ideological integration, anomie is a state of confusion, insecurity, 'normlessness'. The collective representations are in a state of decay." - From Don Martindale, *The Nature and Types of Sociological Theory* (Boston, MA: Houghton Mifflin Co., 1960).

Conspicuous Consumption. The open display of wastefulness. The purchasing of products intended to affirm or enhance an individual's prestige, and designed to impress others.

Envy. What you feel toward another when you want but do not have what they do.

Force. Coercion.

Globalization. Refers to the worldwide phenomenon of technological, economic, political, and cultural exchanges, brought about by modern communication, transportation, and legal infrastructure as well as the political choice to consciously open cross-border links in international trade and finance. It is a term used to describe how human beings are becoming more intertwined with each other around the world economically, politically, and culturally. Although these links are not new, they are more pervasive than ever before.

New Tribalism. Strong in-group loyalty and consciousness of belonging to a group.

Social Change. The ways in which the characteristics of social systems modify.

Social Order. Refers to social mechanisms that regulate individual and group behavior, in terms of greater sanctions and rewards. It may also designate the processes of informal social control such as custom and formal social control such as law of deviant behavior which falls beyond the bounds set by social norms.

Social Regression. Denying the implications of massive social change and seeking instead palatable diversions.

Tension-Management. Refers to those mechanisms that socially sublimate frustrations into acceptable channels.

REFERENCES

Arendt, Hannah. 1968. *The Origins of Totalitarianism*. San Diego, CA: Harcourt.

Diamond, Jared. 2005. *Collapse: How Societies Choose to Fail or Succeed*. New York: Viking Press.

Durkheim, Emile. 1950. *The Rules of Sociological Method*. New York: The Free Press.

Friedman, Thomas L. 2005. *The World is Flat: A Brief History of the Twenty-first Century*. New York: Farrar, Strauss, and Giroux.

Ichheiser, Gustav. 1970. *Appearances and Realities*. New York: Jossey-Bass.

Lyman, Stanford. 1989. *The Seven Deadly Sins: Societies and Evil*. New York: St. Martin's Press, Inc.

Mander, Jerry. 1978. *Four Arguments for the Elimination of Television*. New York: Harper Collins.

Mead, G. H. 1918. "The Psychology of Punitive Justice." *The American Journal of Sociology*,

Mencotti, Lawrence. 1983. "Television and Politics: A Case of Ascendant Mutualism." In *The Sociological Galaxy,* edited by Charles Babbitt. Harrisburg, PA: Beacons Publishing Co.

Pitts, Jesse R. 1961. *Theories of Society*. Vol. II. Glencoe, IL: The Free Press.

Scheler, Max. 1961. *Ressentiment*. New York: The Free Press.

Schoeck, Helmut. 1966. *Envy A Theory of Social Behavior*. New York: Harcourt, Brace World.

Sowell, Thomas. 2002. *A Conflict of Visions: Ideological Origins of Political Struggles*. New York, Basic Books.

Veblen, Thornstein. 1948. *The Portable Veblen*. New York: The Viking Press.

Subject Index